Human Cognition
Learning, Understanding and Remembering

John D. Bransford
Vanderbilt University

Wadsworth Publishing Company
Belmont, California
A Division of Wadsworth, Inc.

Psychology Editor: Kenneth King
Production Editor: Connie Martin
Designer: Detta Penna
Copy Editor: John Feneron
Illustrators: Florence Fujimoto and Lori Gilbo

Printed in the United States of America
      6 7 8 9 — 85 84

Library of Congress Cataloging in Publication Data

Bransford, John D.
   Human cognition.

   Bibliography: p.
   Includes index.
   1. Cognition.   2. Learning, Psychology of.
3. Comprehension.   4. Memory.   I. Title.
BF311.B7155   153.4   78-31698

ISBN 0-534-00699-X

To Todd and Jason
and to the memory of my father, their grandfather,
Paul W. Bransford, M.D., Ph.D.

Contents

Preface

There is little doubt that current research on human cognition has become more exciting and productive than in any previous time in history. The progress even within the past decade has been remarkable, and we now see cognitive scientists tackling problems like processes of comprehension, the nature of knowledge, relationships between text structures and learning, analyses of teaching styles and learning problems, and so forth. We have a long way to go, of course, but the beginnings of a coherent framework for studying cognition are becoming visible, and an increasing number of exceptionally qualified individuals are accepting the challenge of exploring cognitive processes in more detail.

In this book, I try to capture some of the excitement characteristic of researchers in the field of cognitive science, to communicate it in a way that is understandable to undergraduate students, and to help students appreciate the relationships between basic research and applications of that research. The goal is to help students understand *how* research is conducted and *why* it is relevant; for example, cognitive research has relevance for our everyday beliefs about the nature of intelligence, our evaluations of people (including ourselves) in terms of "learning abilities," and our assumptions about desirable versus undesirable educational practices. I also attempt to help students develop an organizational framework that will allow them to go beyond the information in this book and explore particular subareas of cognition in more detail. The purpose of the framework is to help students ask themselves relevant questions about areas that they want to understand.

The organization and content of this book reflect a personal perspective on problems of cognition, and I try to make this clear to students in the introductory chapter. This is not a survey text. I have selected experiments because they exemplify particular points in a clear manner, and I tend to discuss one or two prototypical experiments in an area rather than provide an exhaustive review of the research relevant to a particular domain. It is for this reason that the book is relatively short and is published as a paperback. Individual instructors will want to expand the treatment of various topics: to explore recent theories of attention, for example, or to treat work in artificial intelligence, imagery, linguistics, memory modeling and so forth in more detail. The structure of this book allows considerable flexibility with regard to the possibilities for expanded treatment, and should provide students with a basis for understanding the reasons for more detailed analysis of particular topics by showing them the relationship between these topics and the overall problem to be addressed.

The themes I have chosen to emphasize are those that I think have the best chance of surviving in the rapidly developing area of cognitive science. The major emphasis of this book is on the active nature of learning, understanding, and remembering; that is, on the importance of utilizing what we already know to interpret new information and to detect gaps in our current level of comprehension and mastery. From this perspective, effective learning is more related to the ability to ask relevant questions (of ourselves and others) than to the ability to state factual content, and I try to illustrate the potential importance of this point of view. The problem of helping people learn to learn is therefore presented as a challenge to cognitive science, and I think that this problem will receive more and more attention during the next decade of cognitive research.

It is my hope that, in some small way, this book will enable students to understand the value of basic research, to explore and evaluate advanced issues in cognition more productively, and maybe even to learn something about how they themselves learn.

This book could not have been written without the help of many individuals. First and foremost, I am grateful to the hundreds of researchers whose work fills the pages of this book. I am also extremely grateful for the opportunity to have worked with some outstanding people who have influenced my thinking greatly. These include J. R. Barclay, Jeffery Franks, James Jenkins, Robert Shaw, and Walter Weimer (beginning in my graduate school years); Marcia Johnson and Nancy McCarrell (beginning in my early post-graduate years); and Keith Clayton and Roy Albridge (beginning more recently). Jeff Franks and Jim Jenkins deserve special notes of thanks. They have been not only exceptionally valuable teachers and colleagues, but longtime friends as well.

I am also grateful to many people who began as students at Vanderbilt and quickly became valuable colleagues. These include Pam Auble, William Bailey, Jon Doner, Mary Hannigan, Carol Kronseder, Tommie Shelton, and Sal Soraci. Don Morris, Kathy Nitsch, and Barry Stein deserve a special expression of gratitude; their contributions are evident throughout this book. Of course, it should not be assumed that any of the people I have acknowledged will agree with everything I have written. What is certain, however, is that their contributions have made this a much better book than it would have been without their help.

I am also grateful for three of the most careful and helpful reviews I have ever received, reviews from David Hakes, Richard Mayer, and Peter Polson. They too should be absolved of responsibility for the final product, but their comments were of immeasurable value and have helped me improve virtually every chapter in this book.

The people at Wadsworth Publishing Company have also provided outstanding assistance and guidance. Ken King, the Psychology Editor, and Connie Martin, the Production Editor, deserve special notes of thanks. I am also indebted to staff members of the Vanderbilt Psychology Department, who so patiently and expertly transformed my scribbled handwriting into typed pages that were legible to the people at Wadsworth. Without the help of Pat Burns, Dorothy Timberlake, and especially Regina Kendrick (who has the dubious distinction of being able to read my handwriting and hence did most of the typing), publication of this book would have been an impossible task.

Last, but certainly not least, I am indebted to my wife, Bunny, who worked with me from the beginning of this project to the end. She not only typed and retyped, but provided constructive criticism, edited, and encouraged me during times of discouragement. I may have been able to write a book without Bunny's help, but it would have been vastly inferior to the present one and probably would have taken about ten more years to complete.

Much of the research reported in this book was supported by grants NE-6-00-3-0026 and BNS 77-07248 awarded to Jeffery Franks and me. Both of us are extremely grateful for this support. However, any opinions, findings, conclusions, or recommendations expressed herein are those of the author and do not necessarily reflect the views of the National Science Foundation or the National Institute of Education.

J. D. B.
January 16, 1979
Nashville, Tennessee

Note to the Student

In this book, I try to focus on the problem of understanding individual learners, which includes understanding ourselves as learners. For example, why might one person do well in a particular situation and another do poorly, and how can the learning abilities of the latter be improved? We will discuss attention, short-term memory, and so forth, but always from the perspective of understanding the over-all process of learning. This allows us to *analyze* the problem of learning and to *synthesize* information as well. The first chapter includes an organizational frame-work designed to facilitate these analytic and synthetic processes. This framework is developed systematically throughout the entire book.

One of the unique aspects of studying learning is that you will be attempting to do the type of thing you are reading about; you will be attempting to learn the information in the book or course. You can learn a great deal by paying attention to your own learning processes. Hopefully, the discussion of learning in the book will help you notice certain aspects of your own learning processes that you didn't explicitly realize before. Much of this discussion does not appear until later in the book, however, so it may be helpful to present a few simple suggestions that you can "try on for size."

The first suggestion stems from an analysis of my own learning processes when I was studying for exams in college. I was frequently inefficient because I did not focus my attention on the material I wanted to learn. I often found myself reading without having comprehended anything (I was just going through the motions of studying). I also tended to become impatient; for example, I would focus on how much of the chapter remained to be read rather than on the information in front of my eyes.

This book is structured in a way that can help alleviate some of these problems. Besides the introduction and the conclusion (which are short chapters), there are six major chapters. Each is divided into four sections with a summary at the end of each section. Instead of attempting to tackle an entire chapter at a single sitting, determine realistic goals and work on only one section at a time. Decide to work efficiently for relatively short amounts of time.

It may also be beneficial to note that the ability to comprehend or understand the points in a section does not necessarily mean that you have *mastered* the material. Everything you encounter can seem to make perfect sense as you read it.

If you ask yourself whether you can summarize the points in your own words, however, you will frequently find that you cannot. Try to get to the point where you can summarize the information in one section before proceeding to the next one. This will be especially helpful because each section refers to information in previous sections. If you master the prior sections, each new section will become easier. Failure to do this will mean that each new section will become harder to master.

If you are reading this book as part of a course, you face the challenge of passing examinations. One of the major points we will discuss is that there are many different ways to learn something, and that the way you learn it affects the kinds of test questions you can answer later on. As a simple example, you may be able to recognize the name of the author who wrote *Catch 22* if I present you with four possible names and ask you to choose the correct one. If asked just to produce the name, however, you may be less likely to succeed.

Since the way you learn information has a strong effect on the types of test questions you can answer, it is extremely important to get a sense of the kinds of information your instructor feels are important. Should you be able to answer questions like "What did researcher X do in her 1974 study?" Should you know *why* certain studies were conducted, *how* they were conducted, what possible *implications* they might have? Will test questions ask you to *define* specific concepts (e.g., "levels of processing") or will they tend to involve hypothetical learning situations where you must *apply* appropriate concepts? People are frequently able to define concepts, yet they experience great difficulty when asked to decide which concepts apply in a particular situation. These difficulties can be overcome if the information is learned in an appropriate way.

The most important thing you can do is to ask yourself questions about the information you are studying. For example, how does a particular study relate to the general problem of understanding how people learn? If you can't answer these questions yourself, ask your instructor or a classmate. It is only by thinking about the potential relevance of theories or experiments that you can decide whether you understand them and whether certain details are or are not relevant. In a memory experiment, for example, it probably makes little difference whether a participant was 5'6" or 6'5". When evaluating people's potential for playing basketball, however, this may well be a variable that counts.

It may be useful to discuss this last point somewhat further, but from a slightly different perspective. Students frequently complain that many exams test for "mere factual content" rather than "general understanding." I agree with these criticisms, but it is a mistake to assume that general understanding has nothing to do with factual content. Effective understanding requires knowledge of *significant details*. To understand many experiments, for example, we must attend to certain details that distinguish them from other experiments. Thus, different experimenters (or instructors) may use different tests to assess learning, and knowledge of these differences can be extremely important for understanding the results. Don't be misled into believing that all details are irrelevant and trivial. If you think about the purposes of experiments or concepts, you can decide which details are significant because they become meaningful in that context. Significant details involve differences that make a difference.

I hope that these suggestions for learning will prove helpful as you study the material in this book.

Human Cognition

Learning, Understanding
and Remembering

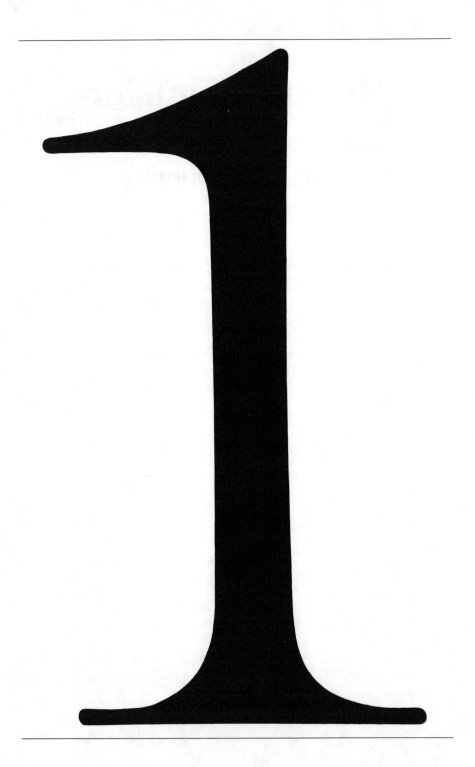

Chapter 1
Introduction

The purpose of this book is to explore some of the questions being asked by researchers in the rapidly developing area of cognitive science. We shall discuss what kinds of questions are being studied, why such questions are important, and how researchers are attempting to find answers to those questions. In general, we shall ask how people learn, understand, and remember information, and why some people seem to do these things better than others. We shall also ask whether people's abilities to learn and remember can be modified: Can people learn to learn, or is there some fixed capacity for learning that determines people's performance throughout their lives?

Note that these questions are broad in scope. There is a long history of thought regarding questions like these. For example, the Greek philosophers Plato and Aristotle formulated sophisticated theories about processes underlying the acquisition of knowledge (e.g., see translations by Lamb, 1967; Hett, 1964), and many of their ideas are still relevant today (e.g., see Anderson and Bower, 1973; Weimer, 1973). Hundreds of additional philosophers and psychologists have contributed to the ideas we shall be discussing (e.g., see Boring, 1950; Blumenthal, 1970; Brewer, 1974). We shall not explore the historical lineages in detail, however, because a book of this size must be selective. Our primary concern will be with recent rather than historical work. Nevertheless, knowledge of the historical evolution of ideas is extremely important (e.g., see Toulmin, 1972; Weimer, in press), and the interested reader will find it valuable to study the history of psychology and to see that many of the "modern" concepts we shall explore were discussed by earlier thinkers.

It is also important to note something else about this book's discussion of issues in cognitive science. As stated earlier, the goal is to discuss what kinds of questions are being studied, why the questions are important, and how researchers study the questions. The statement needs to be qualified, however. There are many people working in the area of cognitive science, and each of them has different ideas about the kinds of questions that are most important, the kinds of theories and studies that are most useful, and so on. Note, for example, that the topic to be explored is *cognitive science* rather than *cognitive psychology*. There is an important reason for this choice of terms.

Processes of cognition are being explored by researchers in many disciplines besides psychology, disciplines like computer science and linguistics, for example. Although we shall discuss many of the important contributions from the latter areas, our major focus will be on the psychological literature. A computer scientist or linguist might therefore emphasize different questions from those we shall be discussing. Furthermore, many psychologists hold views different from those expressed here. The reason for mentioning these differences is to help you avoid the mistake of assuming that this book is the final word on the current state of cognitive science. Be aware that this book illustrates one way of approaching certain questions about cognition. Read the book as a source of ideas to be scrutinized and criticized, keeping in mind that there are alternative perspectives. The perspective we shall adopt is discussed below.

An Overview of the Present Perspective

The purpose of the remainder of this chapter is to familiarize you with the general perspective that will guide our inquiry into processes of cognition. The first step is to gain a better understanding of the general questions to be considered—questions about learning, understanding, and remembering—and the importance of these questions for our everyday activities and beliefs. We shall therefore focus on the types of learning activities that you the reader are presently engaged in. For example, whether reading for your own interest or for a class assignment, you would presumably like to learn the present material. This involves being able to *understand* what you are reading, but other factors are involved, too. For example, if you simply understood each sentence but forgot it as soon as you read the next one, there would be little point in proceeding; you also have to *remember* the information, so that you can use it later.

As discussion proceeds, we shall have to define more precisely terms like *learning, understanding,* and *remembering,* but for present purposes it is sufficient to grasp these concepts at an intuitive level. You have had enough experience with situations involving learning, understanding, and remembering to have a general idea of what we will be studying. What may be unclear, however, is why it is important to study such processes. People have been learning, understanding, and remembering for centuries without needing a theorist to tell them what they were doing. Why do we need a science of cognition that attempts to build and tests theories about cognitive processes? This question is discussed below.

Why Develop a Cognitive Science?

A major goal of cognitive science is to formulate and test theories of the processes that underlie people's abilities to learn, understand, and remember information. Our present question involves the value of such an endeavor. Suppose we had an adequate theory of learning (which would include a theory of understanding and remembering). What difference would it make?

One way to approach the question is to consider the following: We all have theories about factors responsible for learning, understanding, and remembering. Our theories may not be explicitly articulated, but they nevertheless affect the way we think about ourselves and others. As an illustration, ask yourself how you feel about people who work hard, yet do poorly, in elementary school, high school, or college. How do you feel about yourself when you do better in a course than others or do worse than others? Notice the degree to which our society values people's "learning abilities," and the degree to which we evaluate people according to these "abilities." Notice how we also tend to make assumptions about factors responsible for differences in learning. When we assume, for example, that people are more or less intelligent, fast learners or slow learners, bright or dull, and so on, our use of such terms frequently reflects simplistic and usually untested assumptions about factors responsible for effective learning. When we say that someone "lacks intelligence," we are frequently assuming that he or she lacks some basic capacity for learning. We are therefore endorsing some sort of "fixed capacity" theory of learning without considering possible alternatives, and without really evaluating the adequacy of our assumptions. A major goal of cognitive science is to formulate explicit theories of learning and to test them as rigorously as possible. As an illustration, it is useful to consider some potential theoretical perspectives that one might adopt in order to explain differences in learning abilities. Several possible perspectives are discussed below.

Some Possible Reasons
for Differences in Learning

We have noted that most people make assumptions about factors that underlie the ability to learn, understand, and remember, that many of the words that we use to describe people reflect untested ideas about factors responsible for learning, and that we frequently assume that people have different capacities for learning without really questioning our assumptions. It is therefore useful to consider some potential alternatives to this fixed-capacity point of view.

Benjamin Bloom (1976) provides a perceptive account of different theoretical perspectives toward learning. Bloom is a Distinguished Service Professor of Education at the University of Chicago and has made important contributions to the fields of education and psychology. The preface to his 1976 book provides an excellent illustration of different theoretical orientations, as well as of the importance of the theoretical orientation that one holds. In the preface to his book, Bloom (1976) notes that when he first entered the field of educational research and measurement, there was a prevailing assumption that "there are good learners and there are poor learners" (p. ix). This is similar to the idea that people have fixed capacities for learning. For example, Bloom notes that "it was believed that good learners could learn the more complex and abstract ideas, while poor learners could learn only the simplest and most concrete ideas" (p. ix). He also suggests that those assumptions had important effects on educational systems. If one really believes that people have fixed capacities, the best thing to do is create an educational system that *selects* the most talented. This is different from a system designed to help people *develop* talents that they did not already have.

Bloom continues his preface by discussing an alternative theoretical perspective that was stressed by another important educational researcher, John Carroll (e.g., 1963). This perspective assumes that "there are faster learners and there are slower learners" (Bloom, 1976, p. ix). This is different from the preceding assumption. For example, the first assumption regarding "good" and "poor" learners included the belief that "good" learners could master complex and abstract materials whereas "poor" learners could master only simple and concrete materials. In contrast, Carroll's (1963) emphasis on "fast" versus "slow" learners assumes that nearly all people can master complex and abstract materials. Slow learners simply need more time to achieve their goal. Note once again that the latter assumption has important implications for education. As Bloom (1976) notes, many educators varied the amount of time that people were allowed to spend on certain types of materials. When this was done, it became clear that "slow" learners were capable of mastering materials that were abstract and complex.

Bloom also proposes a third orientation toward questions about individual differences in learning abilities. He suggests that "most students become very similar with regard to learning ability, rate of learning, and motivation for further learning—when provided with favorable learning conditions" (1976, p. x). Note that this third perspective differs from the second because even the rate or speed of learning is not assumed to be a fixed characteristic of the individual. Instead, a person's ability to learn (including the speed of learning) is assumed to depend on the quality of the instruction that he or she receives. The argument here is that we should not simply evaluate learners on the basis of their abilities to adapt to pre-set systems of instruction; we must also evaluate systems of instruction in terms of the degree to which they help people learn. Bloom therefore emphasizes the importance of learning environments, arguing that slower learners can become faster learners when the instructional environment is appropriate. This is a very important idea, and one that will be pursued later. For present purposes, it should be stressed that the more we understand about learning processes, the greater the probability of designing effective learning environments. Similarly, a better understanding of effective learning environments can provide important clues about processes of learning. We shall be concerned with both sets of considerations, although the major emphasis will be on cognitive processes that affect learning. The framework that will guide our inquiry is discussed below.

A Framework for
Exploring Learning Processes

The purpose of the previous discussion was to explain why it is important to explore processes underlying our abilities to learn, understand, and remember. We all make assumptions about factors responsible for learning, and these assumptions frequently affect our evaluations of people, ideas about optimal versus nonoptimal educational practices, and so on. Clearly, then, we owe it to ourselves to make our assumptions explicit and to evaluate them as carefully as possible; and researchers in the general area of cognitive science, whose work this book explores, have much to teach us.

Before we consider the work of some of these researchers, it is important to realize that there are thousands of theories, hypotheses, and experimental studies relevant to questions about learning. We could not possibly cover all of them, but even the number we shall cover is quite large. It is therefore important to have some kind of organizational framework that keeps us from getting lost in a maze of seemingly unconnected theories, experiments, and experimental results. An adequate framework must be simple enough to understand and remember, but not so simple that it leaves out crucial variables that affect people's abilities to learn, understand, and remember. We also need a framework that reminds us of the many possible reasons why an individual learner may or may not do well in a particular type of educational environment or experimental task.

The organizational framework we shall adopt is congruent with the ideas of many theorists (e.g., Ausubel, 1963; Bartlett, 1932; Bloom, 1976; Bransford, Franks, Morris, and Stein, 1978; Clayton, 1978; Jenkins, 1978). Jenkins (1978) has represented this framework in the form of a visual diagram. A slight modification of his diagram is reproduced in Figure 1.1. We shall refer to this diagram quite frequently, so it is important to learn it and to understand what it means.

Note first that the diagram in Figure 1.1 illustrates four basic factors that we must consider when evaluating questions about learning, understanding, and remembering. These include

1. The nature of the materials to be learned.

2. The characteristics of the learner—his or her current knowledge, skills, attitudes.

3. The learning activities, or the kinds of things that learners do when presented with material—do they, for example, attend to the information, rehearse the information?

4. The criterial tasks, or the kinds of test tasks used to evaluate the degree of learning—for example, we may ask people to remember a previously defined concept, to demonstrate that they can use that concept to solve a new problem, and so forth.

The four basic factors illustrated in Figure 1.1 occur in a wide variety of situations. For example, any course in school involves (1) certain types of materials to be learned, (2) students with varying degrees of previously acquired skills and knowledge, (3) an assumption that students will do something when presented with the material (attend to it, study it, and so forth), and (4) some type of test used to evaluate students' degree of learning. Note that any learning experiment performed in a laboratory also includes these four basic variables. One advantage of laboratory experiments is that some of these factors can be held relatively constant while others are varied. For example, an experimenter could hold (1), (2), and (4) relatively constant and vary the types of learning, or processing, activities that people are asked to perform while being presented with the materials. Studies like this will be discussed in Chapter 2.

Note that the four basic factors illustrated in Figure 1.1 are quite general and straightforward—so straightforward, in fact, that they probably seem intuitively obvious.

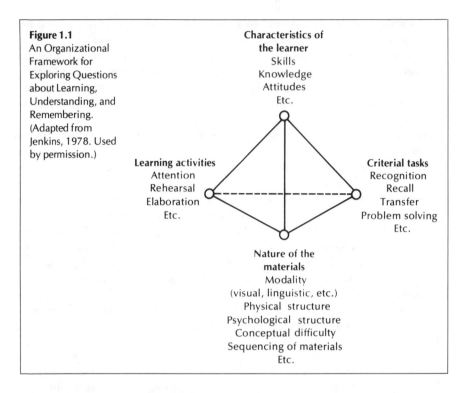

Figure 1.1 An Organizational Framework for Exploring Questions about Learning, Understanding, and Remembering. (Adapted from Jenkins, 1978. Used by permission.)

Characteristics of the learner
Skills
Knowledge
Attitudes
Etc.

Learning activities
Attention
Rehearsal
Elaboration
Etc.

Criterial tasks
Recognition
Recall
Transfer
Problem solving
Etc.

Nature of the materials
Modality
(visual, linguistic, etc.)
Physical structure
Psychological structure
Conceptual difficulty
Sequencing of materials
Etc.

The framework illustrated in Figure 1.1 becomes more important when it is realized that any question about learning involves the simultaneous consideration of all four basic variables. In any particular situation, it is easy to forget about one or two of these variables and hence arrive at erroneous conclusions. Consider, for instance, the question of "good" and "poor" learners. In most classroom situations some people do better than others. As noted earlier, a common assumption is that this occurs because some people simply have a greater capacity for learning than others. The framework illustrated in Figure 1.1 makes it clear that there may be alternative explanations why people do or do not learn.

As an illustration of the foregoing argument, consider just two of the four variables represented in our diagram; in particular, the variables indicating that learning is a function of the relationship between the materials to be learned and the characteristics of the learner. A student could experience difficulty in a course because he or she lacked certain concepts that the teacher assumed everyone knew and so didn't teach directly. Students who already knew these concepts would therefore find the course material much easier to understand and learn. Many educational researchers (e.g., Ausubel, 1963; Bloom, 1976; Novak, 1977) argue that students' classroom performance is strongly affected by the degree to which they have acquired necessary concepts and skills prior to taking a course. In fact, many educational studies suggest that if care is taken to ensure that students acquire the necessary concepts, "poor" or "slow" learners become equipped to learn the materials quite well (e.g., see Bloom, 1976).

The preceding illustration involved only two of the four major variables outlined in our framework in Figure 1.1. Performance in any situation is also determined by the activities carried out while learning and by the testing criterion that is used. For example, many people do not know how to approach learning tasks in an efficient manner. They may simply rehearse material rather than carry out more elaborate activities that can facilitate learning and retention (these will be discussed in Chapter 2). As we shall see, however, the value of certain types of learning activities will depend on the criterion used for testing. For example, most college students study differently for multiple-choice tests than for essay tests. The notion that overall performance is a result of learning activities in relation to particular testing criteria is another type of relationship illustrated in the framework in Figure 1.1.

It is also instructive to note that the choice of particular testing criteria reflects assumptions about what we mean by *learning*. Imagine that you memorize the definition of a concept but don't really understand it. Would you have learned or not? It seems clear that you would have learned something, but perhaps not as much as you would like. Whether or not this affects your grade in a course (or your performance in an experiment) will depend on the testing criteria. If you are simply asked to give the concept definition, you will appear to have learned the material. If asked to explain the concept in your own words or identify novel examples of the concept, however, you may have difficulty on the test. The framework in Figure 1.1 should therefore help remind us that there are many different ways to measure learning, and that these measures reflect different assumptions about what the term *learning* means.

To summarize our discussion, the framework in Figure 1.1 is simple, but it illustrates a complex set of relationships among factors that must always be kept in mind when exploring questions about learning, understanding, and remembering. As noted earlier, in any particular situation it is easy to forget about several potentially important factors and subfactors. When this happens, we are likely to draw erroneous conclusions regarding the particular situation we want to understand.

The possibility of drawing erroneous conclusions becomes especially strong when we evaluate theories and experiments that explore the nature of learning. Note that no single experiment can include all possible ranges of learners' skills and knowledge, all ranges of learning materials, all types of possible learning activities, and all possible types of testing situations. In fact, as we have noted, one advantage of experimentation is that some factors can be held relatively constant so that others may be more fully explored. We shall therefore use the framework in Figure 1.1 as a mechanism for reminding ourselves of the factors explored in a particular experiment and the factors left unmentioned. The framework is also useful for understanding how the rest of this book is organized.

The Organization of This Book

In general, the goal of this book is to explore systematically the factors illustrated in Figure 1.1 and to show how they influence one another. Different chapters emphasize the four different aspects of the diagram: Chapter 2 discusses types of learning activities;

Chapter 3, types of testing or retrieval environments; Chapter 4, the nature of the materials to be learned; and Chapter 5, the role of previously acquired skills and knowledge. Throughout our discussion we shall explore how these factors influence one another. Chapters 6–7 introduce variations in the basic framework illustrated in Figure 1.1. The final chapter, Chapter 8, synthesizes previously discussed ideas and suggests implications for evaluating both theories of learning and individual learners. Suggestions for further research are discussed as well.

Summary

The purpose of this chapter has been to provide a general overview of (1) the kinds of questions we shall explore, (2) why it is important to explore these questions, and (3) how we will organize our exploration. It was noted that our primary question involves processes of learning, understanding, and remembering. There are a number of reasons why it is important to understand these processes in more detail. One is that our society places great value on "learning abilities" and evaluates people according to such "abilities." We also tend to make assumptions about reasons why some people seem to learn better than others. This is equivalent to endorsing certain theories of learning without evaluating them and without subjecting them to experimental test.

One of the most important consequences of particular assumptions about learning is the effect they have on individual people. If you ever get the chance, talk with elementary-school children who are doing poorly in school. Try to get a sense of how they feel about themselves. As you would expect, many children are reluctant to discuss this topic, and others will claim that they don't care about their poor performance in school. From my own experience, however, I think you'll eventually find that their poor school performance does affect them. Many of these children have also devised an "explanation" for their performance; namely, that they are stupid and can't learn. These children seem to have some sort of capacity theory of learning, and this can have powerful effects on their self-image (e.g., see Holt, 1964). They seem not to realize that alternative explanations for learning difficulties exist.

Assumptions about learning also have other effects; for example, they influence ideas about education and instruction (e.g., see Bloom, 1976). It is possible to view the educational system as a set of hurdles or filters designed to select the fittest and discard the others. Alternatively, one can accept the challenge of creating learning environments that *develop* talent rather than merely select it (e.g., see Ausubel, 1963; Bloom, 1976; Carroll, 1963; Novak, 1977). The latter orientation is much more difficult, because one needs a much better understanding of individual learners as well as the processes underlying learning. Our goal is to better understand those cognitive processes that underlie our abilities to learn.

The diagram in Figure 1.1 illustrates the organizational framework that will be used to guide our inquiry into learning processes. Keep in mind that this framework illustrates only one of many possible orientations toward questions about learning, and that alternative orientations exist. The value of the framework illustrated in Figure 1.1 resides in its emphasis on a system of relationships that affect performance in any given situation; performance in a particular course, for example, or in a particular experiment is always a result of the total set of factors illustrated in the diagram, and each of these factors can influence the others. Note that although the next four chapters will emphasize individual factors, we must nevertheless keep reminding ourselves that all four factors are operating in every experiment. The importance of this point should become clearer as we proceed with our discussion. For present purposes, the most important point is that you learn the diagram, because we shall use it as an organizational base.

Chapter 2
The Active Nature of Learning

The purpose of this chapter is to discuss theories and experiments that explore learning activities, one of the four factors in our scheme in Figure 1.1. Of course, all the other factors will be operating in the experiments, too, and this must be kept in mind. The chapter is divided into four sections, which are briefly described below.

Overview

Section 1 discusses *some estimates of learning efficiency*. The purpose is, first, to show that under some conditions at least, a great deal of information can be acquired in a relatively short amount of time; and secondly, to use this fact to suggest a major reason why some people seem so much more capable than others, namely, that they have simply been exposed to much more information than others.

Section 2 examines *the role of attention*. The act of attending to information has important effects on learning. We shall see that although unattended information also has effects on the system, these effects are frequently fleeting. People's abilities to control their attention can therefore affect their ability to learn.

Section 3 discusses processes of *short-term retention,* like those involved in remembering a phone number long enough to dial it. The act of initially attending to a phone number may not be sufficient to remember it even for a brief time. We shall therefore discuss the importance of rehearsal activities for short-term retention tasks.

Section 4 will introduce the concept of levels of processing and discuss its importance for *long-term retention*. Many types of rehearsal activities are sufficient for short-term but not long-term retention. Memory is affected, then, by what one does during the learning task.

Section 1: Some Estimates of Learning Efficiency

In this section we shall first discuss some experiments illustrating people's remarkable potentials for learning. The experiments show that it is possible to learn large amounts of material in a relatively short time. Because this is so, even small differences in the amount of time during which people are exposed to information can result in large differences in the amount of information acquired. This suggests a basic and very important reason why some people seem so much "smarter" or "brighter" than others; they have simply been exposed to more information.

Memory for 600 Pictures

Imagine that you enter an experimental room equipped with a slide projector and a screen. You are informed that you will view slides of approximately 600 different pictures and will then be given a recognition test. The pictures will be of distinct events and scenes like those that might be depicted in magazine advertisements. You will be allowed to look at each picture for as long as you want before pressing the button to activate the next slide (this is called a self-paced procedure). Later, during the recognition test, you will be presented with one slide that you previously saw and one that you did not see. Your task will be to indicate which test picture is "old," that is, a picture viewed during the acquisition process, and which is "new" (this is called a forced-choice procedure). How sensitive do you think you would be to such exposures? What percentage of items do you think you would recognize in the forced-choice recognition test?

In contemplating your answer, consider the length of time you would spend simply viewing the 600 acquisition pictures. Suppose you spend an average of five seconds viewing each slide, and one second between presentations of slides; you would then spend a total of six seconds times 600 slides viewing the acquisition pictures, which would amount to sixty minutes of acquisition. This is a large amount of time to spend on a particular task, but a short time to spend on 600 disparate, separate inputs. How well do you think you would perform on the recognition test? Shepard's (1967) data indicate that college students perform at the level of approximately 98 percent accuracy. This suggests an incredible degree of learning efficiency. If you are unimpressed by these data, however, consider the following experiments.

Memory for Thousands of Pictures

Standing, Conezio, and Haber (1970) presented people with a sequence of 2,560 pictures, and they then gave them a forced-choice recognition test. Even here, the recognition scores were approximately 90 percent correct. These results were obtained even though most people received the memory test one and one-half days after they had viewed the acquisition list.

In a subsequent set of studies, Standing (1973) varied the number of pictures to be learned and included lists of 20, 100, 200, 400, 1,000, 4,000, and 10,000 distinct pictures. Clearly, Standing had to give people rest periods when presenting large numbers of pictures, so that the acquisition process sometimes spanned a number of days (five days for those viewing 10,000 pictures). Once again, he could find no limit on the possibility of storing experiences. To be sure, the absolute number of errors increased as the size of the acquisition set increased. However, greater list length still resulted in an increase in the number of pictures that were retained. Standing extrapolated the following estimate from graphs plotting list size against the absolute number of pictures recognized: For vivid pictures, if one million could be presented and recognition could be tested immediately, 986,300 would be retained. In short, people's potential for learning and retention seems almost magically unlimited.

A Brief Return to Our Organizational Framework

The studies cited above suggest that people have the potential to acquire large amounts of information in relatively short periods of time. The ability to learn almost 10,000 pictures in only five days is a remarkable feat. Of course, this particular potential for learning occurs only under certain circumstances. For example, imagine that people were presented with scrambled, nonmeaningful pictures or with English definitions of 10,000 unfamiliar words (for example, "*duduk* means 'to sit down' "). Following Shepard's procedure, we could give these people a forced-choice recognition test (for example, we could ask them whether they had read "*duduk* means 'to sit down' " or "*duduk* means 'thank you' "). Given 10,000 new words to learn in only five days, it seems clear that performance would be quite poor.

Note how this discussion relates to our theoretical framework illustrated in Figure 1.1. The picture-memory experiments by Shepard and by Standing involved materials that were meaningful because they were congruent with the current knowledge and skills of the learners (Chapter 5 discusses this issue in more detail). In contrast, materials that include jumbled pictorial arrangements or unfamiliar words (such as *duduk*) are not congruent with most students' previously acquired knowledge. The Shepard and Standing experiments therefore provide us with an estimate of learning potential, rather than an accurate statement of absolute learning abilities. Nevertheless, these estimates of learning potential (which may even be underestimates) are important for understanding some of the differences between people; for example, differences between experts and nonexperts. This point is discussed below.

Why Are Experts Experts?

It was suggested that the experiments by Shepard and Standing provide an estimate of certain learning *potentials*. It is useful to keep these estimates in mind, because one of the differences between experts and nonexperts is that experts have usually spent more time learning about a certain area than nonexperts; in fact, inasmuch as it is possible to learn a great deal in a relatively short time, even small differences in time spent learning about an area can result in large differences in the amount of information acquired.

As an illustration of this argument, assume that—even under the most ideal conditions—people could learn and retain no more than 10 pictures in an hour. Now assume that Person A has spent 10 hours viewing various pictures and person B has spent only 1 hour. Under ideal conditions Person A will therefore have retained 100 pictures, and Person B only 10. Assume, however, that people have the potential to acquire 100 pictures in an hour rather than only 10 (note that Shepard presented approximately 600 pictures in an hour). Under ideal conditions Person A would learn 1,000 pictures in 10 hours, while Person B would learn 100 in his 1 hour of exposure. In other words, if we consider the amount of information acquired, the difference between Person A and Person B becomes larger as our estimates of potential learning-efficiency increase (a difference of 90 in the first case and 900 in the second).

With the preceding discussion in mind, we now explore some further differences between experts and nonexperts. Consider the question why chess experts like Bobby Fischer are indeed experts. Do they possess some special aptitude or special form of intelligence? Perhaps, but we should consider more basic possibilities first. A number of psychologists (e.g., Chase and Simon, 1973; deGroot, 1965) have studied chess experts and compared their performance with that of skilled but less accomplished players. The sheer amount of time that chess experts have spent playing chess is a striking finding.

Chase and Simon (1973) estimate that the chess expert they studied had spent from 10,000 to 50,000 hours playing chess. Assume that a thirty-five-year-old person had spent 1 hour every day of his life playing chess, beginning at age five; that person would have accumulated approximately 10,950 hours of experience. To accumulate somewhere in the range of 44,000 hours of practice would require 4 hours of chess per day for a period of thirty years. These estimates do not include the amount of time spent simply *thinking about* chess games and positions; for example, many chess experts see life situations in terms of chess, viewing social interactions among people in terms of "attack" or "defense," analyzing them in terms of potential chess moves.

The estimate of 10,000 to 50,000 hours of experience for chess masters takes on increased significance when contrasted with the experiences of two less accomplished players, a Class A player (someone quite good but not a master) and a novice. Chase and Simon (1973) estimate that the Class A player they studied had spent from 1,000 to 5,000 hours playing chess; their novice had spent less than 100 hours (still a relatively long period of time). Chase and Simon note that the probability of a novice beating a Class A player, and of the latter beating a master, is extremely low. This is hardly surprising in view of the large variations in previous experience.

What is it that chess masters gain from their many hours of experience? One answer is that they acquire a "vocabulary" of recognizable chess configurations, much as an avid reader increases his vocabulary of words. Simon and Gilmartin (1973) estimate that a chess master has acquired a vocabulary of recognizable configurations numbering between 10,000 and 100,000 patterns, roughly equivalent to estimates of a good reader's recognition vocabulary of words.

Further Examples of the
Importance of Exposure

Clearly, differences in the amount of exposure are important for areas other than chess mastery. Indeed, many educational programs are designed to increase one's exposure to situations, preferably at an early age. Programs like "Head Start," and educational television programs (like "Sesame Street"), fall within this category. Similarly, instructional programs like "Reading Is Fundamental" attempt to give children access to books so that they will gain practice in reading; and other programs attempt to train parents so that they can provide richer educational experiences for their children during preschool years.

In 1977 a Tennessee newspaper reported an educational problem being studied in California. The writing skills of high-school graduates seemed to be decreasing, and more and more college freshmen were forced to take remedial writing courses instead of beginning in the regular freshman English courses taught throughout the state schools. An analysis of the situation suggested a possible reason: High-school students were receiving fewer and fewer opportunities to practice writing. During their last few years of high school the majority of the classes included multiple-choice tests, so that there was little need to produce sentences, only a need to distinguish a correct answer from others that were incorrect. Effective writing is a skill that requires a great deal of practice, and decreased practice may have contributed to the overall decline on college freshman English exams.

Some Implications of the
Role of Exposure and Practice

Experience and practice are so obviously important that one might question the value of even discussing the issue. Isn't this something everyone already knows? Yes, but there is a difference between knowing a fact and realizing its potential significance or implications. A sensitivity to the profound importance of differential degrees of experience can affect how one thinks about other kinds of events.

In his book *Uprooted Children,* Robert Coles (1970) discusses the plight of the children of migrant farm workers. Their ability to perform school-related tasks is usually quite limited. How easy it is to assume that they have below average intelligence, can't think properly, lack aptitude and potential, and so on. Coles, who worked closely with groups of migrant families over a period of years, presents data that help put the academic plight of the children into a more realistic perspective: "I had occasion, in the case of ten families, to check on the children's school attendance and found that each child put in, on the average, about a week and a half of school, that is, eight days, during the month" (p. 31). How could one expect children to do well with such relatively limited experience, especially when they also change schools frequently in order to follow the crops? A sensitivity to these simple data on experience can have important effects on one's assumptions. In this context hypotheses about inferior aptitude and intelligence seem tenuous and premature.

Summary of Section 1

Several points were emphasized in our discussion. First we noted people's remarkable potential for acquiring information as suggested by the experiments by Shepard and by Standing. We stressed that these studies illustrate learning potentials insofar as the materials to be learned were congruent with the students' previously acquired knowledge and skills (see Figure 1.1); in other words, they afford an estimate of learning potential, not a statement of absolute learning ability. Next we emphasized that an appreciation of learning potentials is nevertheless important, because small differences in the time spent studying some area can result in large differences in acquired content. One reason why some people do so well in specialized areas like chess may therefore be the large amounts of time they have spent learning about these areas. Finally we noted that this simple idea is valuable because it helps us avoid premature conclusions about differences in intellectual capacities; for example, in the case of Coles's children of migrant farm workers, who spent very little time in school.

Of course it would seem overly simplistic to argue that all differences among people are due to differences in exposure to information. The point of Section 1 was simply to argue that this is one factor that it is important to keep in mind. To better understand learning, we must more carefully analyze what people must do in order to benefit from exposure to sources of information. Aspects of this question are discussed in Section 2.

Section 2: The Role of Attention

The purpose of this section is to discuss a general type of activity that is important for learning: the act of attending to information. The importance of attention has long been recognized by psychologists. The famous psychologist William James (1890) emphasized that attention is *selective*: "It is the taking possession by the mind, in clear and vivid form, of one out of what seem several simultaneously possible objects or trains of thought" (p. 403). James also suggested that there are *limits* on the amount of information to which we can effectively attend, that attention "implies withdrawal from some things in order to deal effectively with others" (p. 404).

The importance of active attention is perhaps nowhere more apparent than in attempts to study. You have probably had the experience of going through the motions of reading a text and suddenly realizing that nothing had registered; attention had been directed somewhere other than toward the material to be learned. Similar problems arise when listening to lectures. We frequently begin to think about something else and only later realize that we missed what was said. How many things can we attend to simultaneously? Can we pay close attention to music, read a book, and think about the upcoming football game at the same time? Would it be possible to tape-record different class lectures and play one to each ear over earphones, thereby doubling our learning? Evidence suggests that there are limits to the number of areas to which we can simultaneously attend.

Experimental
Investigations
of Attention

Imagine that you enter an experimental room equipped with tape recorders and earphones. You are told that two different messages will be played over your earphones. Your task is to attend to one of the messages although other information is occurring at the same time. The task is similar to situations like those at cocktail parties where a listener frequently attempts to recognize what one person is saying while others are speaking at the same time.

Cherry (1953) performed many of the initial experiments on attention (see also Broadbent, 1958; Treisman, 1964). These were conducted with tape-recorded messages played over earphones, as in the procedure described above. Some of Cherry's experiments involved hearing two different messages simultaneously in both ears while attempting to attend fully to one of the messages. This task was extremely difficult, especially when the messages and voices of the speakers increased in similarity. With some sets of materials it was virtually impossible to separate Message 1 from Message 2 (see Cherry, 1953).

In other experiments Cherry played one message into the earphone on the listener's left ear and a different message into the earphone on the right ear. Under these conditions it was much easier to separate Message 1 from Message 2. Listeners were readily able to switch their attention from one ear to the other, depending on the message they were asked to attend to at a particular point in time.

Suppose that you participate in Cherry's latter experiment and are asked to attend to the message in your right ear. To ensure your attention, you may be asked to *shadow* the message; that is, to report each word you hear as soon as you can. Most people are able to do this quite easily. However, what happens to the information in the *left* ear? Is this information picked up, even though your attention is directed somewhere else?

A number of experiments have been conducted to investigate the fate of unattended information. In one experiment, Cherry (1953) changed the information in the unattended ear from English to German while the listener was shadowing the message in his right ear. When later asked to state the language of the message in the left ear, the listener reported that he had no idea but assumed it was English. Even this very general characteristic of the message (that it was not English) was not noticed when played into the unattended ear. Cherry found that some aspects of the unattended message *are* noticed; for example, a change from a male to female voice or a change from human speech to a pure tone of 400 cycles per second. However, listeners were unable to identify any particular word that occurred in the unattended ear.

An experiment by Moray (1959) explored the fate of unattended information still further. While listeners shadowed one message, he repeated English words in the unattended ear up to thirty-five times. It seems highly likely that thirty-five repetitions of the same word should be remembered even if exposed to the unattended ear; but Moray's results suggested that there was no retention of the material from the non-shadowed ear.

Does Unattended
Information Have Any Effects?

What happens to unattended information? Is most of it somehow filtered out so that it never makes contact with our knowledge system? Does the information have any effect on the system at all?

Everyone has probably had an experience similar to the following: You are reading or thinking about something and a friend makes a statement. You look up and ask, "What did you say?" No sooner have you asked the question than you suddenly "hear" your friend's previous statement; the information has somehow been preserved, and if you attend to it quickly enough, you can recapture what was said. Many psychologists (e.g., Neisser, 1967) postulate an immediate "echoic memory," a memory that is very accurate but fades very quickly. Perhaps this immediate echoic memory operates despite the fact that attention is directed somewhere else.

One way to test the preceding idea is to return to the experimental paradigm used by Cherry. Suppose a listener is shadowing the message in the right ear. Suddenly the tapes are stopped and the listener is asked to report what he or she has just heard in the left ear. Can the listener do this? Experiments by Norman (1969) and Glucksberg and Cohen (1970) suggest that the answer is yes. There appears to be a temporary echoic memory for these items. Unless quickly attended to, however, the information seems to become lost. Is there a visual analog to temporary echoic memory, which seems to fade unless it becomes the focus of active attention? The studies below suggest that there is.

Attention and Visual Information

Assume that an array of characters like those illustrated in Figure 2.1 is flashed on a screen for one tenth of a second. The characters are spaced closely together so that you will be able to see all of them. Given immediate testing, how many do you think you will be able to report accurately? Experimental investigations indicate that you will be able to report correctly only four or five of the visually presented characters. This could mean that you can perceive only four or five characters within the short exposure period. An alternative explanation is that you can perceive all the characters but your memory for them fades rapidly; perhaps the act of reporting a few of the characters you saw focuses your active attention on these particular characters, allowing the remainder of the visual information to fade away. The latter explanation is supported by the investigations of Sperling.

Sperling (1960) investigated the limits of visual perception (or apprehension). People who saw twelve characters for only one tenth of a second made two types of comments. First, they claimed that they could perceive all twelve visually presented characters. Secondly, they stated that although the physical presentation of the array lasted only one tenth of a second, they were able to "see" this information for a much longer time (about one second). Despite these statements, people were able to correctly report only four or five visually presented items. What should one believe? Are people's subjective reports more believable, or their actual performances?

Figure 2.1
An Array of
Characters Used
to Study Visual
Apprehension. (After
Sperling, 1960.)

P	4	N	7
B	F	2	K
9	D	L	6

Sperling devised an ingenious approach to the question. Assume that you *can* see all twelve characters but they quickly fade before they can all be reported. If you were asked to report only a subset of the characters, you should therefore be able to do so. However, if you don't know which subset you will be asked to report until *after* the array is presented, you have to retain the whole array in order to be accurate in your partial report.

To support this hypothesis Sperling utilized the following partial-report procedure. Immediately after seeing a visual array, people heard a high, medium, or low tone. They knew that the tone signaled which row of the array they should report: A high tone indicated the top row, a medium tone the middle row, and a low tone the bottom row. When there were four characters in a row, participants in the experiment averaged three items correct when tested by the partial-report procedure. Because they never knew in advance which row they would be asked to report, they must have retained an average of nine characters (three characters per row times three different rows). This indicates that we do indeed have the ability to retain large amounts of visual information. But the information quickly fades unless actively attended to; it seems likely, for example, that while one subset of the array is attended to, the unattended visual information quickly fades away. Neisser (1967) refers to the temporary persistence of this type of information as *iconic memory* in order to emphasize its visual characteristics. Remember that in our previous discussion *echoic memory* referred to the persistence of information that was in an auditory form.

Additional Effects of Unattended Information

Our discussion of echoic and iconic memory suggests that information persists for brief time periods. For example, the physical presentation of a visual array may last for only one tenth of a second but the information may appear to "be there" for approximately one second. One advantage of this brief echoic or iconic memory is that it may enable us to recapture information that was outside our primary focus of attention when first presented. For example, when a friend says something and we ask, "What did you say?" we are frequently able to recapture what was said before our friend responds. This suggests that even unattended information may have some effects, but these may be fleeting unless we actively attend.

Investigations by McKay (1973) provide further support for the notion that even unattended information has some effect on the listener. As an illustration, imagine that you are shadowing sentences presented to your right ear and you hear "They threw stones toward the bank yesterday." This sentence is ambiguous; it can refer to the bank of a river or to a place where money is kept. McKay asked whether unattended information presented to the left ear could influence listeners' interpretations of such ambiguous sentences. If the word *river* was presented to the left ear while listeners were shadowing the sentence "They threw stones . . ." in the right ear, the sentence might be interpreted in one manner; presenting the word *money* to the left ear might clarify the sentence in a different way.

After the shadowing task, McKay asked listeners to perform a recognition task on the shadowed sentences. Had they heard (A) "They threw stones toward the side of the river yesterday" or (B) "They threw stones toward the savings and loan association yesterday"? Results indicated that listeners who had received the word *money* in the left ear tended to choose Sentence B, and those who received the word *river* tended to choose A. Despite this, the listeners were unable to remember the unattended words presented to the left ear; the unattended information therefore appeared to have some effect, but not sufficient to allow listeners to remember the information after some period of time.

McKay's results suggest that unattended information can affect the system yet be quickly forgotten. Note, however, that it would be erroneous to conclude that unattended information therefore has no long-term effects. McKay's results suggest that unattended information affects people's interpretation of the material to which they are attending. Therefore if we assume that people remember their interpretations of information, then it is clear that unattended information *can* have long-term effects. The particular unattended information may be forgotten, but if it influences our interpretation of the material to which we are attending, its effects last as long as our memory for our interpretation remains. Tests of the ability to remember unattended information are therefore only one possible index of the influence of this information (note the emphasis on different testing criteria in Figure 1.1). This argument will reappear in our discussion of the possibility of learning while asleep.

Attention and Sleep Learning

Occasionally one finds magazine advertisements lauding the virtues of "sleep learning": For a modest sum of money (perhaps as much as fifty dollars), readers will easily be able to learn foreign languages, multiplication tables, school assignments, and so on. How? Simply by placing a miniature receiver under their pillow and allowing it to quietly broadcast the information while they sleep. Given the research on attention, how likely do you think it is that you can learn new information while sleeping? If you actively attend to the information, would you really be sleeping? If you are sleeping, are you actively attending to information in your surrounding environment?

In order to assess adequately the possibility of sleep learning, one needs an independent assessment of sleeping. If someone is lying in bed half-awake, he or she may indeed be able to learn the information played over the receiver, but this would hardly count as sleep learning; indeed, if being half-awake is necessary for learning in this situation, one would have to learn at the expense of sacrificing one's sleep. How, then, can one assess whether someone is really sleeping? One method is to record the electrical activity of the brain by placing electrodes on a person's skull and recording the electrical activity on an electroencephalogram (EEG). The EEG reveals different patterns of electrical activity of the brain as a person moves through such states as the following: awake but relaxed, drowsy, in a transition from drowsiness to light sleep, light sleep, deep sleep, very deep sleep.

Simon and Emmons (1956) made use of EEG recordings in order to investigate the possibility of learning new information while sleeping. They presented sleeping people with a different question and answer every five minutes, while at the same time monitoring their EEG patterns. Because people move from one level of sleep to another throughout the course of the night, it was important to record the EEG patterns at the time the information to be learned was presented. The following is an example of the kinds of questions and answers presented: "In what kind of store did Ulysses S. Grant work before the war?" "Before the war, Ulysses S. Grant worked in a hardware store." After awaking, participants were asked the questions previously presented, and their answers were recorded. Results indicated that the percentage of correct answers depended strongly on the level of sleep at the time the information was presented. Participants could answer 80 percent of the questions when the EEG indicated a state of being awake but relaxed, 50 percent when the EEG indicated a drowsy state, and only 5 percent when the EEG suggested a transition state between drowsiness and light sleep. For the actual states of sleep, light, deep, and very deep, there was essentially no evidence that learning had occurred.

In a similar experiment Bruce, Evans, Fenwick, and Spencer (1970) explored the nature of sleep learning still more closely. They presented new information to people who were actually sleeping and awakened them *immediately after* the stimulus presentation. Even under these conditions, they found that people could not remember the information presented during actual sleep.

The two experiments we have reviewed suggest that many claims about the magic of sleep learning should be viewed with suspicion. People may seem to learn while sleeping because they are actually awake and attending to the information they hear. Nevertheless, it would be a mistake to assume that the studies we discussed prove the impossibility of learning while sleeping. It may well be, for example, that activities like dreaming sometimes help us review and better understand previously experienced information. It is also possible that the content of dreams can be influenced by information presented while a person is sleeping; hence people might be prompted to review material they want to learn. A sleeping person might not remember the content of the information presented while he or she was sleeping, but this information might nevertheless influence dream activities, which might in turn affect learning. Remember that McKay's experiments suggested that although unattended information is quickly lost, this information can nevertheless have long-lasting effects by influencing people's interpretation of attended information. It is possible that people could learn in similar ways while sleeping.

It is important to note that our discussion of the possibility of learning while sleeping is pure speculation. It is mentioned because it illustrates how a problem or question might be approached from different perspectives, and how one's approach to a problem or question affects the types of criteria used for evaluation. For example, one criterion for evaluating sleep learning involves people's abilities to remember the information presented while they were sleeping. A different criterion might be the extent to which unattended information influenced something else (dreaming, for example) that people were doing at the time; this criterion would be more difficult to evaluate, but not necessarily impossible. As shown in Chapter 1, different testing criteria reflect different assumptions about what we mean by *learning*. The term *sleep learning*, too, can be understood in many different ways. Figure 1.1 should serve as a reminder that the choice of testing criteria is important, and that any particular experiment employs only some of these criteria. With this in mind, let us return to our discussion of attention and evaluate its importance in situations where one needs to learn and *retain* the information being presented. The concept of attention is important for gaining a clearer understanding of why some people may appear to have less capacity to learn.

Attention and Learning Abilities

We have noted that even unattended information may have long-lasting effects when it influences our interpretation of the information to which we are currently attending (a sentence we are shadowing, perhaps even the contents of our dreams). Nevertheless, there are many situations where we need to learn the information being presented. School is one such situation, and we should expect attention to play an important role.

In his classic book *How Children Fail,* John Holt (1964) explores some of the reasons why elementary-school children fail to achieve adequately. Once again, it is easy simply to dismiss such children as "unintelligent" or "slow learners." Holt's careful observations of students' behaviors provide alternative insights that go beyond such labeling or pigeonholing of students and reveal the importance of active attention.

> *During many of the recitation classes, when the class supposedly is working as a unit, most of the children paid very little attention to what was going on*. Those who most needed to pay attention, usually paid the least. *The kids who knew the answer to whatever question you were asking wanted to make sure that you knew they knew, so their hands were always waving. . . . But most of the time, when explaining, questioning, or discussing was going on, the majority of children paid very little attention or none at all. (Pp. 42–43; italics mine)*

Holt's observations suggest that differences in attention have important effects on the degree to which people learn.

Holt also suggests that most of us have imperfect control of our attention.

> *Watching older kids study, or try to study, I saw after a while that they were not sufficiently self-aware to know when their minds had wandered off the subject. . . . Most of us have very imperfect control over our attention. Our minds slip away from duty before we realize that they are gone. (Pp. 27 –28)*

Problems of focusing our attention seem especially apparent when we're trying to learn while we are concerned with personal problems, anticipating a party, feeling afraid that we may not learn, and so on. These thoughts direct our attention away from the information to be learned and can therefore hurt learning performance. Note, however, that this aspect of learning problems is very different from lack of learning capacity.

There is another aspect of attention that is important for understanding differences in learning abilities. As noted earlier, there are limits to the amount of information to which we can attend effectively (e.g., see James, 1890). If you are attempting to multiply a series of complex numbers, it is difficult to understand a lecture at the same time. Perhaps we can efficiently perform only one type of activity at a time.

Note, however, that you can probably tie your shoes and still attend to a lecture. Similarly, if you are a skilled driver you can drive a car and carry on a conversation at the same time. However, try to remember what it was like when you were first *learning* to drive a car. During the initial learning phase, most people have to attend carefully to individual components of driving, like pushing the gas pedal, disengaging the clutch while shifting (unless you learned on an automatic transmission), turning the wheel, finding the brake pedal, using the turn signals. During this phase of learning, it is extremely difficult to drive and carry on a conversation at the same time, and any extra information becomes very distracting and hurts performance on the driving task. Once you become proficient at driving, however, noises, conversations, become much less distracting under normal driving conditions. If you suddenly confront heavy traffic on a freeway, however, it may again become difficult to carry on a conversation, because you have to attend to complex traffic patterns in order to avert an accident.

The driving example illustrates that we may or may not be able to deal with several different tasks depending on the current level of our skills and knowledge. Analogous situations arise when we are trying to understand a lecture or read. For example, if we are reading material that is relatively unfamiliar and difficult, additional noises and brief statements by friends can be very distracting. If the material is familiar and easy, much less disruption occurs. In other words, we seem capable of coordinating several tasks at once when dealing with familiar material. For example, a parent might be able to read a novel while keeping an "ear out" for the children playing in the back yard, a student may be able to understand a lecture about familiar material while looking out the window and observing certain events.

Experiments by Johnston and Heinz (1974) suggest that our abilities to coordinate several tasks are indeed influenced by the familiarity of the material (see also Norman, 1976). They asked participants in an experiment to shadow messages presented over earphones. Two messages were presented, and each was recorded in the same voice and played to each ear. The participants therefore had to separate the two messages on the basis of their topics, and one message was designated as the target for the shadowing task. They were also told that a light would sometimes flash while they were shadowing. Their task was to continue shadowing and push a button as soon as they saw the light. When the information to be shadowed was unfamiliar, even this simple light-detection task was extremely disruptive. People could see the light and push the button, but when they did this, their ability to shadow the message was greatly impaired. Contrast this with situations where the material to be shadowed had been made highly familiar by the participants' prior exposure to one of the two messages. Under these conditions, they could respond to the light while maintaining their performance in the shadowing task.

It is instructive to note how this discussion of attention relates to problems of learning in classroom situations. There are many sources of information that compete for students' attention. Activities seen from the window, whispers from fellow students, the antics of a would-be prankster, personal thoughts, frequently seem more compelling than the information being presented by the teacher or a text. Students are therefore in a situation where they must coordinate several activities, and our discussion suggests that this becomes harder to do as the difficulty and unfamiliarity of the materials to be learned increase. If we further assume that difficulty is in part determined by unfamiliarity, we can see that people who know more about the material have an advantage; they are less disturbed by additional attention-demanding events.

Our discussion of attention also relates to the organizational framework illustrated in Figure 1.1. Although the present chapter focuses on learning activities, all the other factors in the framework are operating, too. For example, we have noted that people's abilities to coordinate several activities (such as response to a flash of light while shadowing a message) depend on the *nature of the materials* in relation to the current level of the *learners' skills and knowledge*. If experimenters had always presented people with difficult and unfamiliar materials, we might erroneously conclude that people could never coordinate several activities. Similarly, if we compared two people on a task and found that one could coordinate several activities but the other could not, we might wrongly conclude that one of these people has a greater capacity for attention rather than ask about the degree to which he or she was familiar with the particular materials used in the experiment. An adequate theory of attention that avoids such errors must therefore acknowledge the types of factors illustrated in Figure 1.1.

Norman and Bobrow (1975) propose a theory of attention that nicely captures the essence of our discussion. Only some aspects of their theory will be presented here. They note that various tasks require certain processing, or learning, resources. If people's resources are overtaxed, they will have difficulty coordinating several tasks. For present purposes the most important aspect of the theory is that the number of resources that must be devoted to a particular task depends on the previous degree of learning. If tasks are familiar and hence can be performed relatively automatically, fewer resources are needed and hence more are available for doing other things (such as carrying on a conversation while driving).

The importance of making certain activities automatic is also stressed by other theorists. For example, LaBerge and Samuels (1974) note that a task like reading involves a number of subtasks that compete for the reader's attention. One aspect of reading is the identification of written words on a page. However, we must also combine words into phrases and sentences and think about the meaning of what is being read. LaBerge and Samuels argue that if people's abilities to identify written words are not automatized, they must devote excessive resources to the task of word identification, leaving fewer resources available for doing other things like thinking about the meaning of the materials being read. An important implication of this position is that teachers must be sensitive to different criteria for assessing whether students have learned something (remember the test criteria of Figure 1.1). Students could be *accurate* at reading words presented on flash cards. However, accuracy does not necessarily imply *automaticity*, and unless processes of word identification become relatively automatic, students may have to devote too many resources to the task of identifying individual words.

Summary of Section 2

We began this section with some quotations from William James's (1890) discussion of attention. He suggested that attention is both *selective* and *limited* in capacity. The shadowing experiments performed by Cherry (1953) illustrate the selectivity of attention. For example, people could switch their attention to messages in either the right or left ear. The ability to focus our attention on some things and ignore others is extremely important because without it we should be overwhelmed by many extraneous events.

We also explored the fate of unattended information. In general, people cannot remember the content of information presented to the unattended ear. Nevertheless, even unattended information sometimes seems to persist for a brief time. Following Neisser (1967), we used the terms *echoic memory* and *iconic memory* to refer to the temporary persistence of auditory and visual information. This persistence may permit us to recapture information that was not the primary focus of our attention when it occurred.

Our discussion of McKay's (1973) experiment explored the fate of unattended information in more detail. He found that unattended information presented to one ear could influence people's interpretation of attended information in the other ear. Unattended information can therefore have long-term effects by influencing our interpretation of the information to which we are attending. This idea reappeared in our discussion of sleep learning. Several studies suggest that people could not remember the content of information presented while they were sleeping. However, this doesn't necessarily mean that sleep learning cannot occur. The term *sleep learning* is highly ambiguous. For example, it is possible that activities like dreaming can help us better organize and understand previously experienced information. It is also possible that information presented while people are sleeping could influence the content of their dreams and hence prompt them to review information that is important to learn and understand. It was stressed that these ideas on sleep learning are speculative, however. The purpose of the discussion was to illustrate how a problem can be approached in different ways and how one's approach can also affect the testing criteria that are employed.

The concept of attention was also discussed in the context of learning in school-related settings. As Holt (1964) observes, most of us have imperfect control over our attention. This seems especially apparent when we are concerned with personal problems and thoughts that keep competing with our attempts to learn information presented in school. It was also noted that students frequently have to coordinate a number of attention-demanding activities. Listening to a lecture while taking notes is a case in point. Our ability to coordinate several activities depends on the nature of the material in relation to our previously acquired skills and knowledge. Adequate theories of attention must therefore acknowledge the types of factors illustrated in our framework in Figure 1.1. Norman and Bobrow's (1975) discussion of attention explicitly acknowledges such factors. They note that certain abilities can become automatized, hence requiring fewer resources on the part of the learner. LaBerge and Samuels (1974) propose similar arguments regarding processes of reading and also stress that accuracy does not guarantee automaticity. If processes of word identification are not automatized, too many resources must be devoted to this subcomponent of reading tasks.

The overall goal of this section was to illustrate how theory and research on attention can contribute to our understanding of differences in learning abilities. Notice how personal problems and fears of being thought stupid can compete for our attention and hence impede learning. Note how previously acquired skills and knowledge can give some people an advantage because they need not devote as many resources to a particular task. It seems clear that questions about attention are extremely important for understanding learning. Nevertheless, there are additional factors to be considered. Section 3 discusses other types of activities that influence our abilities to learn.

Section 3: Short-Term Retention

Our goal in this section is to discuss additional types of activities that influence learning and remembering. We shall focus on short-term retention, on the types of activities necessary to remember things for brief time intervals of, say, fifteen or twenty seconds. Questions regarding long-term retention are addressed in Section 4. There are a number of reasons why it is important to study short-term retention. One is that even the ability to remember information for fifteen or twenty seconds depends on activities performed by the learner. Another reason is that there are limits on our capacities for short-term retention. If incoming information exceeds our capacity limitation, we will experience a breakdown in our abilities to understand and learn. Note further that some people perform better than others on tests of short-term retention. It is possible that some people have a greater capacity for short-term retention than others and that this is the reason why some "slow" learners experience learning difficulties. This possibility will be discussed later.

As an illustration of the type of question we shall discuss in this section, imagine looking up an unfamiliar number in a phone book. We shall assume that nothing else is competing for your attention, so that all your resources can be devoted to the act of initially attending to the number (see Section 2). Suppose you read the number once (we'll refer to this as "initially attending to" the number) and then think about something else as you walk across the room to dial the telephone. Or suppose you initially attend to the number and then a friend asks some question, which you answer. Will you be able to remember the number when you go to dial the phone? Chances are that you will forget the number, because you did not actively rehearse it. A number of experiments have investigated the rate of forgetting when rehearsal is prevented. Some of these are discussed below.

Short-Term Retention and Forgetting

Peterson and Peterson (1959) investigated the rate of forgetting in tasks of short-term retention. On any particular trial, students would be presented with strings composed of three consonants; for example, *CHJ* on Trial 1, *KBR* on Trial 2. In order to prevent rehearsal, students were required to count backwards by threes from a number they were given. For example, if given the number 98, the students would say 95, 92, 89, 86, and so on, until told to stop. They were then asked to recall the letter string they had just heard.

The experimental procedure allowed Peterson and Peterson to manipulate the amount of time students spent counting backwards. The intervals between presentation of a particular letter string and the request for recall included three, six, nine, twelve, fifteen, and eighteen seconds. Each student was given a number of trials, and students never knew in advance how long they would have to count backwards. Results indicated that the probability of correct recall fell sharply as the retention interval increased from three to eighteen seconds. By eighteen seconds, the probability of correct recall for a letter string was only about 10 percent. These data are illustrated in Figure 2.2.

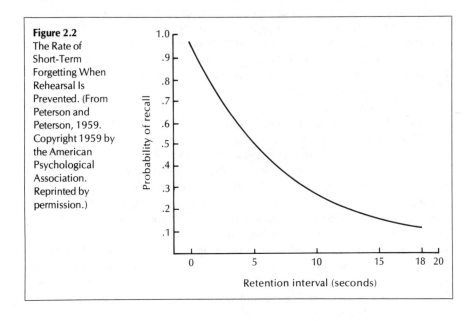

Figure 2.2
The Rate of Short-Term Forgetting When Rehearsal Is Prevented. (From Peterson and Peterson, 1959. Copyright 1959 by the American Psychological Association. Reprinted by permission.)

Reasons for Forgetting

The study by Peterson and Peterson suggests that without rehearsal, forgetting can be very rapid. However, it is one thing to know *that* people forget, a quite different matter to understand the reasons for forgetting. For example, one might assume that memory traces decay unless they are rehearsed actively. An alternative assumption might be that additional activities (saying numbers while counting backwards, in the foregoing experiment) interfere with the information one was trying to maintain.

In actuality, decay and interference theories of forgetting are not as different as one might suppose. For example, food decays, but this is not simply a matter of the time it is left standing. Food decays because certain bacteria interact with it—a process that can be delayed by refrigeration. Similarly, time per se cannot be the cause of the decay of memory traces. Time simply permits certain factors to operate. For example, additional information, thoughts, and ideas may affect the decay rate of memory traces. This analysis of decay begins to look like the interference theory of forgetting. Differences between decay and interference theories are therefore one of degree rather than kind. Nevertheless, they emphasize different types of factors. The studies below suggest that an emphasis on interference may be more important than an emphasis on decay. For example, interference theory would predict that certain kinds of information should be more interfering than others. This possibility is discussed below.

The Systematicity of Errors

On intuitive grounds one might expect that forgetting frequently involves confusions among similar items. This possibility is more strongly emphasized by theories of interference than by theories of simple decay. For example, imagine seeing lists of letters like BNSMCF and then attempting to recall them in the order in which they were presented. Frequently, people will mix up the order, perhaps recalling something like BNFMCS or BNSMVF. Is there any systematicity in the kinds of errors they make?

Conrad (1964) examined the similarity of various letters in terms of their sound patterns. For example, B sounds more similar to C than to X or N; F sounds more similar to S than to B; M sounds more similar to N than to X. Do these similarities in sounds affect people's performance in short-term retention tasks? Conrad found that recall confusions were much more likely when letters had similar sound patterns (see also Wickelgren, 1966). This was true even when the letter strings were presented visually (note than an F doesn't look like an S). These results illustrate that the similarity of materials has important effects on short-term retention. The results also suggest that even visually presented letters tend to be encoded according to these sound structures. If presented with a letter string like PSTVFB, wouldn't you tend to rehearse it auditorily rather than simply image (or perhaps in addition to imaging) the string of letters you have seen? It is also important to note the following: Evidence illustrating that errors are systematic suggests that interference influences forgetting insofar as some types of materials are more interfering than others. The experiments cited below provide further information about the role of interference in short-term retention tasks.

The Waugh and Norman Experiments

Waugh and Norman (1965) investigated short-term retention in a somewhat different manner from the previously cited studies. Their studies involved a "probe technique." They presented students with lists of sixteen digits like 391746521873652<u>8</u>. At the end of each list, students heard a high frequency tone. Students knew that the last digit in each list was the *probe digit*. Upon hearing the tone, their task was to recall the digit that *immediately followed the first occurrence of the probe digit*. For the list above, the probe digit is <u>8</u>, and the correct answer would therefore be 7.

Waugh and Norman's method allowed them to vary some important factors. First, they could vary the number of digits that intervened between the probe digit and the first occurrence of this digit. A list like 39174652187365<u>28</u> has fewer intervening items than a list like 391746582173652<u>8</u>. If memory is poorer for the second list, this could be due to the greater number of intervening items (which might be expected to produce more interference). On the other hand, one's memory might prove poorer in the case of the second list simply because of the time difference between the occurrences of the digits.

In order to differentiate time from interference, Waugh and Norman also varied the *speed* with which each list of digits was presented. Some lists were presented at a speed of four digits per second; others at a speed of one digit per second. This enabled the experimenters to examine the relative importance of number of intervening items versus time. Note, for example, that twelve items could intervene between initial presentation of a digit and the probe for this digit. Given the fast presentation rate (four digits per second), only three seconds separate the probe and the digit; at the slow presentation rate (one digit per second), twelve seconds will have elapsed. If time is the more important variable, fast presentation should be superior to slow presentation; if the number of intervening items is more important, the rate of presentation should have little effect.

Figure 2.3 illustrates the results of Waugh and Norman's study. Forgetting is strongly affected by the number of intervening items between the probe and its initial occurrence. These results are very similar to those of the previously cited study by Peterson and Peterson. (Note that whereas Peterson and Peterson prevented rehearsal with a task that required counting backwards, Waugh and Norman prevented rehearsal by presenting people with additional items and telling them not to rehearse.) The results in Figure 2.3 also illustrate that presentation rate had very little effect on retention. When rehearsal is prevented, forgetting is much more strongly influenced by the number of intervening items than by the passage of time.

Proactive Interference and Forgetting

The preceding experiment emphasizes the importance of interference. The task of processing additional information results in decrements in recall. Technically, this is called "retroactive" interference: Information processed *after* receiving the items to be remembered can hurt recall. Experiments by Keppel and Underwood (1962) point toward an additional source of interference in tasks of short-term retention. These

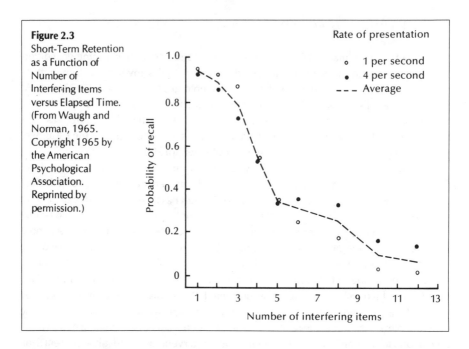

Figure 2.3
Short-Term Retention as a Function of Number of Interfering Items versus Elapsed Time. (From Waugh and Norman, 1965. Copyright 1965 by the American Psychological Association. Reprinted by permission.)

Rate of presentation

   o   1 per second
   •   4 per second
  – – – Average

y-axis: Probability of recall

x-axis: Number of interfering items

researchers found that information processed *prior* to the items to be remembered can also increase forgetting. The importance of this "proactive" interference is illustrated in the study below.

Keppel and Underwood utilized a modified version of the Peterson and Peterson experiment described earlier. Recall that Peterson and Peterson found forgetting occurred very rapidly when rehearsal was prevented by the task of counting backwards. Note, however, that each person in the experiment received a large number of individual test trials (fifty, including practice trials). Peterson and Peterson's data therefore reflect the average amount of forgetting across a large number of test trials.

Suppose that one source of interference comes from *previous* experiences with the task of remembering items (letter strings, for example). A larger number of previous trials might therefore increase the amount of proactive interference that occurs. To test this possibility, Keppel and Underwood measured the amount of forgetting that occurred during the first, second, and third trial in a study of short-term forgetting. They also measured forgetting as a function of the length of the retention interval (the amount of time spent counting backwards). For example, some students had a three-second retention interval on their first trial, whereas others had either a nine- or an eighteen-second retention interval. The results of the study are illustrated in Figure 2.4.

These data show that on the first trial, recall is essentially perfect at all three retention intervals. As the number of previous trials increases, recall declines as a function of the retention interval imposed. These data provide strong support for the concept of proactive interference. Previously processed information, then, can be a source of interference in short-term retention tasks.

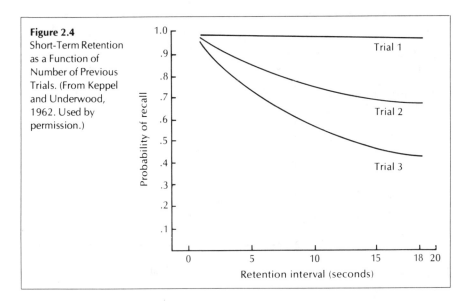

Figure 2.4
Short-Term Retention as a Function of Number of Previous Trials. (From Keppel and Underwood, 1962. Used by permission.)

Release from Proactive Interference

The concept of proactive interference can be clarified still further. Earlier we noted that the similarity of materials affects short-term forgetting; for example, people may confuse an *F* with an *S*. In the study just discussed, Keppel and Underwood used highly similar materials, namely, sets of letter strings. Previous experiences with letter strings produced proactive interference with subsequent retention of letter strings. Suppose, however, that someone receives a set of trials with letter strings and then is asked to remember different types of materials: for example, three-digit numbers. From our previously acquired knowledge, we know that numbers are different from letters; letters and numbers belong to different conceptual categories. Perhaps proactive interference can be reduced if the material we are now trying to remember (numbers) belongs to a different conceptual category from that of the material presented during earlier test trials (letters). This possibility of a release from proactive interference is explored in the studies below.

Experiments by Wickens, Born, and Allen (1963; see also Wickens, 1970, 1972) illustrate a release from proactive interference. In one experiment students received a number of short-term retention trials involving letters; they might receive *XLB*, count backwards and then recall, receive *OZQ*, count backwards and then recall, and so on. (This is like Peterson and Peterson's technique.) Because of proactive interference, their performance decreased over the first three trials (see the proactive interference studies by Keppel and Underwood). On the fourth trial some of the students were asked to remember a *number* string rather than a letter string. Their performance dramatically improved, whereas the performance of students presented with an additional letter string continued to decline. These results illustrate a release from proactive interference. The data are illustrated in Figure 2.5.

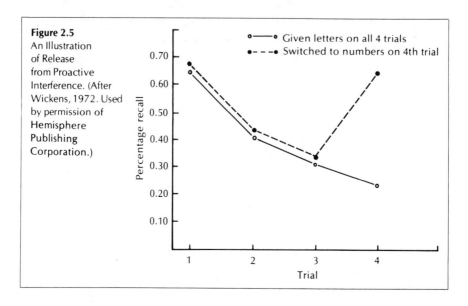

Figure 2.5
An Illustration of Release from Proactive Interference. (After Wickens, 1972. Used by permission of Hemisphere Publishing Corporation.)

These data show that even short-term retention is affected by the relationship of the materials to previously acquired knowledge (see framework in Figure 1.1). If the information to be retained can be related to a conceptual category that differentiates it from previously experienced information (if the material involves numbers rather than letters, as in the foregoing example), proactive sources of interference can be overcome. This is only one illustration of the importance of previously acquired knowledge for short-term retention. The use of previous knowledge can also help us overcome some capacity limitations on short-term retention. We will first discuss these capacity limitations and then show how previously acquired knowledge plays a role in helping us remember despite these capacity constraints.

Limitations on Short-Term Retention

The preceding discussion suggests that forgetting can be extremely rapid. Without active rehearsal both proactive and retroactive sources of interference can come into play. Suppose, however, that your rehearsal activities are not interrupted. Are there additional constraints on what you can retain?

Consider the following two numbers: 36 and 20. Without looking at them again, multiply them in your head. Now consider the following two numbers: 34 and 23. Again without looking back at them, attempt to multiply them in your head. For most people the second task is quite difficult. It is not difficult given a paper and pencil. When you attempt to do the problem in your head, however, it is hard to keep all the necessary information in mind.*

---

*I am indebted to Marlene Scardamalia for this example.

Similar problems arise when one attempts to remember strings of digits, letters, words, and so on. For example, we can maintain information about a phone number like 322-0516, but it is extremely difficult to maintain a series of numbers like 753186495760239 or 010011010110100; somewhere between six or seven and fifteen items our capacity for short-term retention becomes overtaxed.

Ebbinghaus (1885, 1902) was one of the first people to study memory processes experimentally. His investigations suggested a limitation on the span of short-term retention. For example, Ebbinghaus investigated the number of rehearsal trials that it took him to learn lists of different lengths (and to recall them in order). Lists composed of six items or less could be learned with only one rehearsal trial. When only a few more items were added to a list, however, the number of trials necessary for perfect performance increased considerably. For example, a list of ten items might require four or five rehearsal trials; a list of fifteen, twelve rehearsal trials or more. There is a sharp discontinuity between lists of six items or less and lists of ten or more.

In addition to Ebbinghaus, other investigators have emphasized the importance of constraints on short-term retention (e.g., Miller, 1956; Simon, 1969; Wundt, 1905). They stress an additional point as well: Our capacity for short-term retention depends on the degree to which we can use previous knowledge to encode materials into meaningful units. Read the following string of letters once and then try to recall them in order: GDOTCAUBNTSI. Now consider the following list to be remembered: DOG CAT BUN SIT. Both lists contain the same letters. Nevertheless, the second list is much easier to retain.

In a classic paper, Miller (1956) argues that the capacity for short-term retention is limited by "the magic number seven plus or minus two." However, the limitation is not on the number of items (for example, number of letters) that can be retained; instead, Miller proposes, the limitation should be expressed in terms of meaningful *chunks*. We may be able to retain approximately seven unrelated letters, but if letters form meaningful words, we may be able to retain seven words (and hence a larger number of letters). Familiar words are one example of meaningful chunks of information. Pauses can also help us chunk information. This is why most phone numbers are broken into two units.

The importance of prior knowledge to forming meaningful chunks can be further illustrated by considering the following short-term retention task. Imagine that you are exposed to a chess board illustrating the chess positions of two people playing one another. After you have viewed this configuration for only five seconds, the board is covered and you are asked to reproduce the previously seen configuration by placing chess pieces on a new chess board. How accurate do you think you would be?

Studies by deGroot (1965), and also by Chase and Simon (1973), show that accuracy is a function of previous chess experience. If you are a chess novice, you will be able to place accurately only a few pieces on their original board locations. If you are a chess expert, however, you can almost perfectly reconstruct the previously seen chess board, even after only five seconds of exposure (Chase and Simon, 1973; deGroot, 1965). But perhaps chess experts simply have better short-term memories than other people. Indeed, their short-term memory may be responsible for helping them become chess experts. It is therefore important to find ways to test this idea.

Experiments conducted by deGroot (1965) provide one test of the hypothesis that chess masters have greater capacities for short-term retention. Suppose chess experts are given a five-second exposure to a chess game that is not congruent with their previous chess knowledge. For example, all the chess pieces are randomly placed on the board and hence fail to illustrate a meaningful game of chess. If chess experts simply have better short-term memories than other people, they should still perform well in the reconstruction task. If their superior memory depends on their ability to relate information to their prior knowledge, however, they should perform quite poorly on this task. The results of deGroot's (1965) studies suggest that, given randomized chess positions, chess experts are no better than novices in short-term memory tests (see also Chase and Simon, 1973).

DeGroot's (1965) results emphasize some important considerations regarding the nature of short-term retention. As shown earlier, there is a limit on the amount of information we can actively maintain in short-term memory; somewhere between seven and fifteen items, our capacity for short-term retention becomes overtaxed. Note, however, that deGroot's chess masters remembered more than seven (plus or minus two) chess pieces when presented with meaningful chess configurations. From their knowledge of chess, masters were able to encode the information into meaningful chunks (see Chase and Simon, 1973). When they were exposed to randomized pieces, however, no meaningful chunks were apparent, and their short-term retention suffered. In sum, even short-term retention depends on relationships between particular inputs and the previous knowledge one has acquired. This has important implications for understanding why some people do better than others in tests of short-term retention. In the following discussion we shall first review the importance of short-term retention abilities and then consider the question of why some people do better than others in short-term retention tasks.

Some Implications of Research on Short-Term Retention

At the beginning of this section it was noted that research on short-term retention is important for a number of reasons. One is that we must be able to keep information in mind in order to perform additional activities. Without some capacity for short-term retention we could not remember unfamiliar phone numbers long enough to dial them, and we could not add and multiply numbers in our head. Similarly, we need to retain information for certain time intervals in order to solve problems, understand sentences, and so on. For example, consider a sentence like "Jim, the boy with red hair who lives next door and loves basketball, signed a college contract yesterday." Eventually, we need to realize that it was Jim who signed the contract, so we must keep *Jim* in mind until we receive the major verb of the sentence (*signed*). Because our capacity for short-term retention is limited, complex information that exceeds our momentary capacity can cause a breakdown in our abilities to comprehend and learn.

Note that people might differ in their short-term memory capacities. If so, some people might experience learning difficulties when the material to be learned exceeds their more limited capacities. Differences in short-term memory capacity could therefore be a major reason why "slow" learners learn slowly. In order to evaluate this possibility, we need a better understanding of what we mean by *short-term memory* and how it differs from other types of memories. This issue is discussed below.

An Information-Processing Model of Learning and Memory

The idea that our capacity for short-term retention is limited has led many theorists (e.g., Atkinson and Shiffrin, 1968; Waugh and Norman, 1965) to postulate the existence of a hypothetical short-term memory that has certain properties. One property is that information must be actively rehearsed or it will be forgotten. Another is that there is a limit to the amount of information that can be held in short-term store. Figure 2.6 illustrates an information-processing model that postulates a "short-term memory" and distinguishes it from "sensory registers" as well as from "long-term memory." Incoming information is first assumed to enter the sensory registers, next go to short-term memory and eventually to long-term memory. Let us consider this information-processing model in more detail.

Note first that examples of sensory registers were discussed in Section 2 of this chapter. We noted that incoming information can persist in echoic memory (as auditory information) and in iconic memory (as visual information) for brief time intervals. These brief stores are called sensory registers because they are assumed to capture information in its original sensory form. For example, if letters like F and S are presented visually, they are assumed to persist in iconic memory for brief time periods (see the studies by Sperling discussed in Section 2). Unless actively attended to, however, this information quickly fades. The model in Figure 2.6 assumes that after entering the sensory registers, information can enter short-term memory. Though its retention in the sensory registers is limited, information can remain in short-term memory indefinitely, *provided that it is actively rehearsed*. Note further that this active rehearsal may involve a "translation step"; for example, visually presented letters may be preserved visually in iconic memory yet be translated to an auditory code when rehearsed in short-term memory. As an illustration,

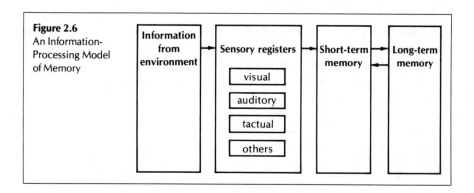

Figure 2.6
An Information-Processing Model of Memory

Information from environment → Sensory registers → Short-term memory → Long-term memory

visual

auditory

tactual

others

recall Conrad's experiments showing that even visually presented letters seem to be confused with letters that sound similar rather than with those that look similar. This suggests that people translated the letters from a visual to an auditory code in order to rehearse the information and hence maintain it in short-term memory.

In addition to the requirement for active rehearsal the other important property of short-term memory is its limited capacity. Miller's (1956) "magic number seven plus or minus two" provides an estimate of the amount of information that can be held in short-term store. Note that long-term memory is not assumed to have any limitations on the amount of storage. We shall discuss long-term memory in Section 4. At present, the most important issue involves the possibility that people may differ in terms of their short-term memory capacities.

Individual Differences and Short-Term Memory

In order to evaluate questions about differences in short-term memory capacities, we must relate the information-processing model illustrated in Figure 2.6 to our organizational framework in Figure 1.1. Our framework emphasizes that performance in any particular situation will depend on all four factors illustrated in the diagram. If two people differ on tests of short-term memory, the difference could be due to any of the factors noted there.

As an illustration of differences in short-term retention, imagine the following situation: You are presented with seven pictures of common objects (for example, one is a dog, one a chair). An experimenter points to three or four of the pictures; your task is to wait fifteen seconds and then point to the pictures in the same order as the experimenter. During the fifteen seconds you can no longer see the pictures, so that the task is analogous to looking up a phone number and then walking to the phone to dial it. What must you do in order to perform correctly on the task? The answer to this question seems obvious. You would probably rehearse the names of the pictures in their correct serial order (for example, "dog, chair, lamp . . . dog, chair, lamp"). The importance of rehearsing probably seems obvious to you now as an adult, but was it always so obvious? Existing data suggest that the answer is no.

Experiments by Keeney, Cannizzo, and Flavell (1967) provide an interesting illustration of the aforementioned argument. They used a picture memory-task like the one described above, but the experiment was conducted with first-graders. One of the experimenters was trained in lipreading, and he watched for any subtle lip movements that might accompany children's attempts to rehearse the information. Only some of the first-graders showed signs of rehearsal. The performance of these children was better than that of the ones who did not seem to rehearse.

Why might some children fail to rehearse the information? Were they unable to carry out rehearsal activities, or were they simply unaware of the importance of such activities? The latter seems to be the case. During one set of trials, the experimenters told the nonrehearsers to rehearse, and their performance improved to the level of the spontaneous rehearsers; they were therefore capable of rehearsing when told to do so. In subsequent trials, these children were given the option of rehearsing or not rehearsing. Over half of them did not rehearse; instead they reverted to their original strategy (they simply paid attention when the pictures were presented). These children seemed to want to remember, but they failed to utilize a rehearsal strategy. Their performance suffered as a result. Note, then, that the nonrehearsers in the study did not perform as well as the rehearsers. However, it would be erroneous to conclude that the nonrehearsers have an inferior short-term memory *capacity*. They simply failed to perform certain activities necessary to maintain information in short-term store.

Additional factors that can influence short-term retention include the nature of the materials to be remembered and the current level of the learner's skills and knowledge. For example, the research on chess masters discussed earlier suggests that prior knowledge can have powerful effects on short-term retention; chess masters don't have a greater short-term capacity than nonmasters do, but they seem to when presented with chess configurations that can be chunked into meaningful patterns. Similarly, a person who knew English letters but no English words would look as though he had an inferior short-term memory capacity when presented with twelve letters like *DOG CAT BUN SIT*. Note that the information-processing model illustrated in Figure 2.6 also acknowledges that one's knowledge (called "long-term memory" in the model) affects short-term memory. This is indicated by the arrow leading from long-term memory to the short-term memory store.

It is noteworthy that previously acquired knowledge can affect short-term retention even when the information to be remembered does not exceed our capacity. As an illustration, consider once again the studies by Peterson and Peterson (1959). They presented people with letter strings like *XQB* and asked them to count backwards, thereby preventing rehearsal. After eighteen seconds, the probability of correctly recalling a letter string was approximately 10 percent. Contrast this situation with one in which people are asked to remember three letters that form meaningful words (for example, *CAT*) and then asked to count backwards after each presentation. Experiments by Murdock (1961) show that people's ability to retain one three-letter word after counting backwards is much greater than their ability to retain three unrelated letters. Similarly, people can retain three three-letter words (a total of nine letters) as well as they can retain three unrelated letters. These results are illustrated in Figure 2.7. Note that a group of three unrelated letters does not exceed people's capacities for short-term retention. Nevertheless, people exhibited much less forgetting (after counting backwards) when given a meaningful three-letter word than when given three unrelated letters. Because words are meaningful only by virtue of previously acquired knowledge, these results provide further evidence for the role of prior knowledge in short-term retention tasks.

One possible explanation for Murdock's results is afforded by concepts we mentioned in our discussion of attention (Section 2). There we noted that there is a limitation on the number of resources that can be utilized in any particular situation (Norman and Bobrow, 1975). Materials and tasks that are highly familiar require fewer resources, so that more are available to devote to other kinds of activities. For example, as we become

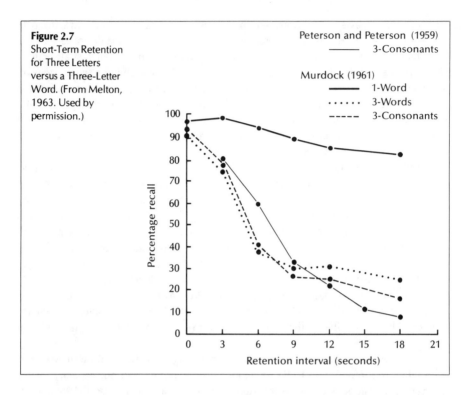

Figure 2.7
Short-Term Retention
for Three Letters
versus a Three-Letter
Word. (From Melton,
1963. Used by
permission.)

Peterson and Peterson (1959)
——— 3-Consonants

Murdock (1961)
——— 1-Word
⋯⋯ 3-Words
- - - - 3-Consonants

skilled at driving, we are able to perform additional activities, like carrying on a conversation while we drive. Note that many short-term retention tasks also involve the coordination of several activities. A person may be counting backwards yet trying to rehearse the information to be remembered at the same time. If the information is simple and familiar (a three-letter word, for example), fewer resources may be necessary to rehearse this information. A rehearsal-prevention task, like counting backwards, should therefore be less disruptive when people are trying to remember three-letter words rather than three individual letters. This possibility is congruent with the results Murdock found (see Figure 2.7).

Of course, if the rehearsal-prevention task were made more difficult, more re- sources would have to be devoted to the task and retention would suffer. A number of experiments show that short-term retention varies as a function of the difficulty of the rehearsal-prevention task (e.g., Posner and Konick, 1966; Watkins, Watkins, Craik, and Mazuryk, 1973). For example, assume that the rehearsal-prevention task involves count- ing forwards rather than backwards. Because counting forwards is a more familiar and automatized activity, fewer resources would have to be devoted to this activity, and more could be devoted to rehearsing the information to be remembered. Retention should therefore be better when the rehearsal-prevention task is easy. In general, therefore, a person's previously acquired skills and knowledge affect the resources necessary to (1) rehearse the information to be remembered and (2) perform the rehearsal-prevention task. The use of previously acquired information to form meaning-ful chunks of information can also help us retain information that might otherwise exceed the capacity of our "short-term store."

The preceding discussion has offered important examples of factors that determine why some people do better than others on tasks of short-term retention. Figure 1.1 illustrates many of these factors. Differences in short-term memory performance there-fore need not imply that people's short-term memories have different absolute ca-pacities. Some people may simply be better able to use what they know to encode information into meaningful chunks and patterns. This would improve their performance in short-term retention tasks.

As an illustration of this argument, consider studies by Perfetti and Goldman (1976) and Perfetti and Lesgold (1977). They studied people who were usually categorized as good or poor at school tasks involving comprehension and memory. Some of their experiments compared these people on short-term memory tasks. In one experiment, the experimenters used a memory-probe procedure like the one developed by Waugh and Norman (see our earlier discussion of this procedure). When numbers were used as the items to be remembered there were no short-term memory differences between the good and poor students. This suggests that their short-term capacities were the same. When sentences were used as the items to be remembered, however, the good students performed better on the short-term memory task.

In explanation of these results, Perfetti and Lesgold argue that all the students they studied were familiar with numbers (all of them could readily activate the names of each number); hence, the students were equally proficient at holding them in short-term memory. When the stimulus materials were sentences, however, the good students were able to understand many words more quickly and combine them into phrases and sentences, and this helped their performance on the short-term retention tasks. As Perfetti and Lesgold (1977) state,

> One possible explanation of the discourse memory effect [the study using sentences] is that the task requires rapid decoding and encoding of linguistic units. Words and phrases are decoded and must be kept alive in memory to be rearranged and encoded into full sentences or propositions. A rapid shifting of attention among coding operations is a constant demand in discourse [sen-tence] processing. (Pp. 155–56)

Note that although Perfetti and Lesgold suggest that poorer students can have difficulty holding information in short-term memory, this is not because the students have less short-term memory capacity (see also Chi, 1976; Huttenlocher and Burke, 1976). Rather, these students are slower at using what they know to identify words and phrases that they encounter. In other words, they must utilize more resources to identify words and phrases and hence are more easily disrupted by other attention-demanding events. With many types of materials their short-term retention therefore seems to be impaired. Note that this orientation has an important implication; it suggests that the performance of poorer students can be improved (whereas if they really differed in short-term memory *capacities,* it's not clear that they could be helped). As Perfetti and Lesgold (1977) suggest, "Aside from those individuals who suffer intellectual retardation, most of those who are poor specifically in verbal comprehension are simply not as practiced in the skills of verbal encoding and decoding" (p. 173). This argument is similar to ideas expressed by LaBerge and Samuels (see our discussion in Section 2). Certain processes must become automatized in order to permit efficient performance, and the degree of automaticity can have important effects even in short-term memory tasks.

Summary of Section 3

In summarizing this section on short-term retention, it is useful to begin with the information-processing model outlined in Figure 2.6. The model postulates a hypothetical short-term memory assumed to have properties that distinguish it from the sensory registers and from long-term memory. The most important properties are that information must be actively rehearsed in order to remain in short-term memory and that short-term memory is limited in capacity. Short-term memory is also assumed to play an especially important role in understanding and learning: we must be able to keep various ideas in mind in order to solve problems and understand sentences that we hear or read.

The idea that information must be actively rehearsed was supported by a number of studies. For example, Peterson and Peterson (1959) showed that forgetting can be very rapid when rehearsal is prevented by the task of counting backwards. Additional studies confirmed that this forgetting is strongly influenced by interference from other information: Information processed *after* receiving the information to be remembered can produce *retroactive* interference (e.g., Waugh and Norman, 1965), and previous trials on similar materials can produce *proactive* interference (e.g., Keppel and Underwood, 1962). Investigators have also found that some situations permit a release from proactive interference (e.g., Wickens, Born, and Allen, 1963). This release from interference presumably depends on the learner's ability to use previous knowledge to differentiate a particular set of items to be remembered (for example, numbers) from those experienced during earlier test trials (for example, letters).

We also reviewed evidence suggesting that short-term memory is limited in capacity. For example, a list of six letters or numbers is easy to remember, but lists of ten or more items frequently exceed our capacity for short-term memory. When incoming information exceeds our capacity, we generally experience a breakdown in our abilities to understand and learn.

Evidence suggesting that short-term memory has a limited capacity becomes especially significant when we realize that some people perform better in short-term retention tasks than others; it is possible that some people have a greater short-term *capacity* than others. Speaking metaphorically, it is possible that some people's short-term memories are larger than others or have more space than others. This might explain why some people experience learning difficulties; if they have less short-term memory capacity, they should be more likely to be overwhelmed by incoming materials because they can't keep all the necessary information in mind.

It was emphasized that assumptions about capacity differences must be evaluated in terms of our organizational framework (Figure 1.1). This framework suggests that there are many reasons why people differ in short-term retention tests. One is that people may not spontaneously perform certain activities like rehearsal (note the study with first-graders by Keeney, Cannizzo, and Flavell, 1967). Another is that they may lack the skills and knowledge necessary to chunk information into meaningful units. For example, chess masters seem to have a greater short-term memory capacity when presented with potentially meaningful chess configurations; but when chess positions are randomized so that masters cannot utilize their knowledge, their short-term retention is no better than that of people who are less skilled in chess.

The importance of utilizing previously acquired knowledge was linked to our earlier discussion of attention (Section 2). It was suggested that most studies of short-term retention measure people's abilities to coordinate several activities. For example, people may try to rehearse the information to be remembered and count backwards at the same time. If either the information or the rehearsal-prevention task is familiar and auto-matized, performance should be relatively good, whereas the performance of people who are less familiar with the information or the prevention task should be poorer. But this need not mean that poorer students have less short-term memory capacity. Perfetti and Lesgold's (1977) studies of "poor" and "good" students were cited as evidence that this is not necessarily the case. When good and poor students were presented with materials that were presumably equally familiar to all of them (lists of numbers), they did not differ on tests of short-term retention. When presented with sentences, however, the two groups did differ. If the poorer students were less adept at recognizing individual words (and hence had to devote more resources to this subtask), this could explain the difference in performance. Note that the latter hypothesis is very different from a view that assumes difference in capacity.

In conclusion, short-term retention seems to be a function of various activities performed by the learner. These include activities like rehearsing information and identifying inputs as meaningful chunks or patterns. The ability to perform these ac-tivities effectively has powerful effects on short-term retention tasks. From this per-spective the box in Figure 2.6 labeled "short-term memory" should be viewed as a convenient fiction. People do not really have short-term memories; instead, they perform certain activities that allow them to retain information for certain periods of time. As we shall see, however, activities that permit short-term retention are not necessarily equivalent to those that facilitate long-term retention. This aspect of the active nature of learning is explored in Section 4.

Section 4: Long-Term Retention

The purpose of this section is to explore the types of learning activities that facilitate long-term retention. As you probably realize, activities sufficient for short-term retention are not necessarily sufficient for long-term retention. For example, there are many instances where we may remember a phone number long enough to dial it yet have to look it up again when placing a call the next day. If the information were stored in long-term memory (see the information-processing diagram in Figure 2.6), we should be less likely to have to look the number up again.

Note further that although there are constraints on the amount of information we can hold in short-term memory (see Section 3), there are no such constraints on long-term memory. For example, although a list of fourteen randomly selected numbers will usually exceed our short-term capacity, we can nevertheless learn such lists eventually; we simply need to study them a number of times rather than once. One way to think about the effects of repeated study trials is to assume that they help us move information from a limited-capacity short-term memory to an unlimited-capacity long-term memory (see the information-processing model in Figure 2.6). This possibility is discussed below.

Rehearsal and Long-Term Retention

The information-processing model sketched in Figure 2.6 provides one framework for thinking about the processes necessary for long-term retention. Some theorists (e.g., Atkinson and Shiffrin, 1968; Waugh and Norman, 1965) have argued that long-term retention depends on rehearsal processes. The more an item is rehearsed, the greater the probability that it will be retained. Experiments by Rundus and colleagues provide support for this position (e.g., Rundus and Atkinson, 1970; Rundus, Loftus, and Atkinson, 1970; Rundus, 1971). For example, Rundus (1971) presented students with relatively long lists of words to remember (twenty words). Examples of some of the words presented are illustrated in Table 2.1. Students were also asked to *rehearse out loud* as the words were presented, and they were tape-recorded as they did so. An example of one possible set of rehearsal outputs is presented in Table 2.1.

Table 2.1 An Illustration of Rehearsal Patterns in Rundus's (1971) Experiment	
Items Presented	Items Rehearsed (Rehearsal Set)
1. Reaction	Reaction, reaction, reaction, reaction
2. Hoof	Hoof, reaction, hoof, reaction
3. Blessing	Blessing, hoof, reaction
4. Research	Research, reaction, hoof, research
5. Candy	Candy, hoof, research, reaction
6. Hardship	Hardship, hoof, hardship, hoof
7. Kindness	Kindness, candy, hardship, hoof
8. Nonsense	Nonsense, kindness, candy, hardship
. . .	. . .
20. Cellar	Cellar, alcohol, misery, cellar

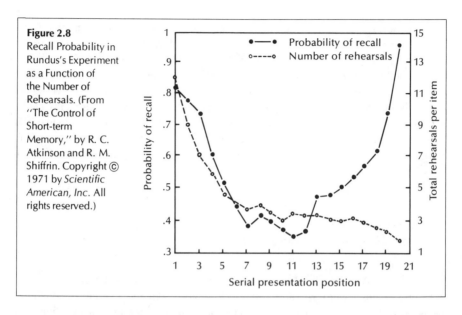

Figure 2.8
Recall Probability in Rundus's Experiment as a Function of the Number of Rehearsals. (From "The Control of Short-term Memory," by R. C. Atkinson and R. M. Shiffrin. Copyright © 1971 by *Scientific American, Inc.* All rights reserved.)

From the tape recordings, Rundus was able to compute the number of times each word was rehearsed during learning. He could then measure the effects of number of rehearsals on students' abilities to recall the words. Figure 2.8 illustrates the relationship between recall and rehearsal. For the first twelve to fifteen words there is a strong relationship between recall and the number of rehearsals: The greater the number of rehearsals, the higher the probability of recall. For the last five or so words on the list, however, recall is high despite a small number of overt rehearsals. Why is this the case? One possibility is that the last words on the list were heard the most recently, so that they still reside in, and can still be recalled from, short-term memory, whereas the words presented earlier must be recalled from long-term memory. Because the number of overt rehearsals is especially important for long-term retention, we might therefore expect a strong relationship between rehearsal and retention for the first fifteen words in a twenty-item list. In general, Rundus's (1971) results confirm this idea.

Types of Rehearsal Processes

The preceding experiment suggests that acts of rehearsal are important for long-term retention. Nevertheless, that concept of rehearsal needs to be more clearly defined. For example, we know that participants in Rundus's studies said the words out loud, and this was recorded on tape. However, did these people merely rehearse the sounds of the words, or did they also do other things like thinking about the meaning of each word, making images of the words, and so on? Note further that the rehearsal pattern illustrated in Table 2.1 shows that people frequently reviewed earlier items in the list when they rehearsed. For example, given the word *research* (the fourth item in the list), most people did not simply say, "Research, research, research, research," but instead rehearsed previously presented words ("Research, research, hoof, reaction," for example). There are many possible ways to rehearse information. Are they all equally effective, or are some better than others for long-term recall?

A number of theorists argue that there are different types of rehearsal processes and that some are more effective for long-term retention than others. Craik and Watkins's (1973) distinction between *maintenance* rehearsal and *elaborative* rehearsal (also called primary versus secondary rehearsal) represents a case in point. Maintenance rehearsal is assumed to be sufficient to maintain information in short-term memory, but not to guarantee long-term retention. The experiment described below provides an illustration of this point.

Maintenance Rehearsal versus Elaborative Rehearsal

Craik and Watkins (1973) examined the degree to which the act of simply rehearsing inputs (saying a word over and over, for example) is sufficient to establish long-term memory. They asked their participants to perform a particular type of acquisition task. Imagine that you participated in their experiment. You would be presented with a list of words like those illustrated in Table 2.2. Your task is not to try to learn the words, however, but to report the last word on the list that begins with the letter *P*.

As a participant, you do not know how many *P*-words will occur in the list. You must therefore maintain each *P*-word in short-term memory until you encounter the next *P*-word. In the list illustrated in Table 2.2 the first *P*-word (*peach*) occurs in Trial 5. This word is maintained by rehearsal until Trial 11, when the second *P*-word (*plum*) occurs. In Trial 12 a new *P*-word occurs, so the word *plum* receives only a single rehearsal. The word *pen* is then rehearsed from Trial 12 to 24. At this point you are asked to recall the last *P*-word, *pen*.

Note that the aforementioned procedure allows the investigator to control the number of rehearsals received by each item. In the list illustrated in Table 2.2, for example, the word *plum* receives one rehearsal, *peach* receives six rehearsals, and *pen* receives thirteen rehearsals. This control enables the investigator to test the hypothesis that long-term recall is determined by maintenance rehearsal. Assume that this is true, that the ability to recall information after relatively long periods is a function of the number of rehearsals. Assume, next, that having been exposed to several lists of words (like Table 2.2), you are given the unexpected instruction to recall all the words you have experienced. If recall is determined by the number of rehearsals each item received, then the more numerous the rehearsals, the more efficient the recall. In the case of the list in Table 2.2, for example, recall for *pen* should be highest; recall for *peach*, next highest; and recall for *plum*, lowest. Craik and Watkins (1973) found that this was not the case; they found that the probability of relatively long-term recall was *not* a function of the number of rehearsals received by particular items. In general, they found that words receiving only minimal rehearsal (like *plum* in the foregoing list) were recalled as well as those receiving frequent rehearsal (*peach*). On the basis of these results, Craik and Watkins argue for a difference between maintenance and elaborative rehearsal (see also Woodward, Bjork, and Jongeward, 1973). Their task induced maintenance, rather than elaborative, rehearsal. The former may be sufficient for activities like dialing a phone number after reading or hearing it, but in order to be able to recall this phone number at a later point in time, one must engage in elaborative or less superficial rehearsal processes. Differences between "superficial" and "deep," or "elaborative," processes are discussed below.

Table 2.2   Sample List Used to Study Maintenance Rehearsal

Words Presented	People's Rehearsals
1. Dog	———
2. Rock	———
3. Match	———
4. Tree	———
5. Peach	Peach
6. King	Peach
7. Grass	Peach
8. Window	Peach
9. Fence	Peach
10. Sky	Peach
11. Plum	Plum
12. Pen	Pen
13. Smoke	Pen
14. Tie	Pen
15. Fork	Pen
16. Bed	Pen
17. Rope	Pen
18. Dress	Pen
19. Lake	Pen
20. Chair	Pen
21. Cow	Pen
22. Orange	Pen
23. Cup	Pen
24. Bell	Pen

After Craik and Watkins (1973).

Levels of Processing

The experiment by Craik and Watkins (1973) suggests that maintenance rehearsal is not sufficient for long-term retention. We therefore need a more refined analysis of the types of activities that learners might perform. In a classic paper, Craik and Lockhart (1972) argue that information can be processed and rehearsed at various levels and that deeper levels of analysis result in superior long-term retention. Given a word like *Boy*, for example, one might concentrate on relatively superficial or shallow levels of analysis —on what the letters look like, for example, on whether the word has a capital *B*, on what the word sounds like, and so on. In contrast, a deeper level of analysis would include activities like thinking about what the word means. A number of studies provide support for the importance of the depth of processing. Some illustrations are provided below.

Imagine that you will be asked to listen to approximately thirty-five words played over a tape recorder. One word occurs every five seconds on the tape. If you are in Group 1, you will be asked to perform what is termed an orienting task, or acquisition activity, that requires you to state, as you receive each acquisition word, whether or not the letter *e* is contained in the word. For example, if you hear *boy* you should respond no; if you hear the word *bed*, you should say yes. Clearly, this task requires hearing the word and then making a decision about its letter structure. Since all words are being attended to, shouldn't they be stored and hence later remembered? Craik and Lockhart (1972) argue that this type of task involves a superficial level of analysis, so that retention should be relatively poor. It is easy to imagine other types of tasks that involve superficial levels of processing. Instead of stating whether or not each word contains the letter *e*, you might be asked to state whether each is composed of one, two, or three syllables; or you might be asked to generate a rhyme for each word presented on the tape recorder. Once again, in order to perform these tasks, you must clearly attend to the acquisition information on the tape; and once again the tasks involve relatively superficial levels of analysis, so that retention might be poor.

A series of experiments by Jenkins and his colleagues (e.g., Hyde and Jenkins, 1969; Johnston and Jenkins, 1971; Till and Jenkins, 1973; Walsh and Jenkins, 1973; Jenkins, 1974a, 1974b) has investigated the effects of various orienting tasks, such as e-checking, syllable counting, rhyme generation, on people's abilities to learn and remember lists of words. Generally these experiments involve *incidental* learning. At the beginning of the experiment, participants think that their only task is to rate the acquisition stimuli (the presence or absence of an *e*, the number of syllables, the potential for rhyme); they do not know that they will later be asked to recall the acquisition words. The purpose of this incidental procedure is not to trick the people in the experiment, but to investigate how particular types of acquisition activities affect learning and subsequent recall.

How effective are acquisition activities like e-checking, syllable counting, and rhyming? If you are asked to perform one of these activities and then asked to recall as many of the acquisition words as possible, how well do you think you would do? The studies by Jenkins and his colleagues reveal a consistent finding: Orienting tasks like those discussed above result in poor recall, even when participants clearly have to attend to each word.

Table 2.3   Recall as a Function of Orienting Tasks

Orienting Tasks	Average Number of Words Recalled
Pleasantness rating	16.3
E-Checking	9.4
Counting number of letters	9.9
Intentional instructions	16.1

From Hyde and Jenkins (1969). Copyright 1969 by the American Psychological Association. Reprinted by permission.

Of course, the notion of poor recall must be defined relative to some other standard. What types of orienting tasks produce better performance on the recall task? Jenkins and his colleagues have studied the effects of orienting tasks in which subjects are required to "rate each word as pleasant or unpleasant," "rate each word as important or unimportant," and so on—tasks in which people must think about the meaning of each word in order to make their ratings. These incidental orienting tasks provide high levels of recall; in general they are as effective as intentional learning conditions, where people explicitly try to learn a list of words because they know they will later be asked to recall it (see also Postman, Adams, and Bohm, 1956). Data from a study of levels of processing by Hyde and Jenkins (1969) are presented in Table 2.3.

Results similar to those of Jenkins and his colleagues have also been found in studies of recognition memory. The following example is from Craik and Tulving (1975). During acquisition one group of people was asked to decide whether a target word, or acquisition word, *rhymed* with another word (e.g., "Say yes or no; _____ rhymes with regal: eagle"). Another group was asked whether a target word fitted into a sentence frame (e.g., "Say yes or no; _____ has feathers: eagle"). People's subsequent abilities to recognize acquisition items (like *eagle*) were affected by the orienting task at acquisition. The rhyme task resulted in poorer recognition performance than did the more meaningful sentence-frame task. The level at which information is processed therefore seems to have important effects on memory for verbal materials. Can various orienting tasks also influence memory for visual information? This question is addressed in the next group of experiments.

Prerequisites for Visual Imaging

Try to create an image of an aspect of the environment with which you are familiar; for example, your parents' living room or the place in which you now live. Most people are able to do this quite readily. Can you see windows, plants, rugs, the location of a couch, piano, or chairs? Clearly, you were not born with such visual information. You had to acquire it. What factors influenced such learning? The simplest explanation is that you have looked at this information hundreds of times. Perhaps the mere frequency of exposure accounts for your ability to image. An important proviso, of course, is that you actually *looked at* the information rather than somewhere else. However, reflections on everyday experiences cast doubt on the idea that the act of looking at objects is in itself sufficient to allow one to image them later. How many streets have you frequently traveled yet are unable to precisely image? How many times have you seen certain friends' faces yet find yourself unable to answer whether their sideburns fall above, in the middle of, or below their ears? Simply looking at visual objects may not be sufficient to permit the types of learning necessary for precisely imaging what was seen.

Nitsch, McCarrell, Franks, and Bransford (see Bransford, Nitsch, and Franks, 1977) designed a series of studies to investigate factors involved in learning to image a particular visual situation. As their experimental material they chose a colored picture of a living room from a magazine. All participants were allowed the same amount of exposure to the picture (one minute). The question of interest was whether equal amounts of exposure to the picture would result in equivalent abilities to image it. The purpose of the experiment was to vary the way in which participants interacted with the picture. All of the experimental manipulations involved participants' looking at the objects in the picture. If effective learning involves nothing more than looking at visual objects, participants in all of the experimental groups should have been equally proficient at imaging what they had seen.

Participants in Group 1 were informed that the picture contained from zero to three extremely small inked-in x's. They were asked to scan the picture horizontally, then vertically, then horizontally, and so on, until told to stop; they would then be asked to report on the number of x's they had detected. In actuality, the picture contained no inked-in x's. The participants in the experiment did not know this, however. In scanning for the x's they had to look at (sweep their eyes over) everything in the picture. Is this type of activity sufficient to allow a person to acquire the visual information? For example, if asked to image the picture after the one-minute acquisition period and to report the contents of the image, would these participants be able to perform the task?

Participants in Group 2 were given similar instructions. However, they were told that any x's that appeared would occur on the *contours* of objects in the picture. They therefore moved their eyes around contours until told to stop. Like Group 1, they were allowed one minute for their search.

Group 3 received a different type of acquisition instruction. They were told that the major question of interest involved the kinds of *actions* they might perform on objects in the living room. Discussions conducted after the experiment indicated that participants in this group thought of acts like sitting on things, cleaning things, drinking from things, moving things, fixing things. They, too, had one minute of exposure during the acquisition task.

Note that none of the participants in Groups 1, 2, and 3 was aware that he or she would later be asked to image the picture. As noted earlier, this is called incidental learning. In contrast, Group 4 received *intentional* learning instructions. These instructions explicitly stated that they would be asked to image the picture after the one-minute exposure. Participants therefore spent their acquisition time trying to learn as much about the picture as they could.

Following the one-minute exposure, all participants were given a surprise test (of course, the test was no surprise for Group 4). All were asked to attempt to image the living room, verbally recall as many aspects of it as they could, and indicate on an answer sheet the relative positions of each object recalled.

The results were quite dramatic. There were extremely large differences between Groups 1 and 2 versus 3 and 4: Groups 1 and 2 recalled and located from three to eight objects; the range for Group 3 and Group 4 participants was from twenty-five to thirty-two, and the average number of items recalled was the same for these two groups. After this recall task, all participants were asked cuing questions like the following: "Was there a fireplace (and if so, where)?" "Was there a wine glass (and if so, where)?" Even when the groups were provided with those cuing questions, the large differences between groups persisted. On the average, all participants correctly remembered three additional objects when the prompting questions were read.

These results suggest two important conclusions. First, merely looking at something (sweeping one's eyes over it or around its edges) is not sufficient to produce the kinds of learning necessary for effectively imaging the information. More active modes of processing are necessary for remembering the scene. Secondly, our data indicate, one does not have to intentionally try to learn something in order to perform adequately (see also Hyde and Jenkins, 1969). The third of our incidental groups (Group 3) did just as well as the intentional group (Group 4). This latter conclusion is confirmed by our everyday experience, too. It is doubtful that many of us have ever explicitly tried to learn the visual layout of, for example, our parents' living room or the rooms of our present dwelling, but what we *have* done is live in these rooms. We walk around objects, sit on objects, move objects, clean objects, and so on, and it is these meaningful types of interactions that appear to promote effective learning and retention.

Orienting Activities and Face Recognition

Experiments by Bower and Karlin (1974) shed further light on relationships between visual inputs and acquisition activities. They presented two groups of people with a set of unfamiliar faces like those you might see in someone else's high-school or college yearbook. The first group was asked to determine whether each face was male or female; the second group, to rate the faces according to their "likeableness" and "honesty." Ratings of likeableness and honesty presumably involve deeper or more complex levels of analysis than determining whether a face is male or female. After acquisition, all participants were given a surprise recognition test and asked to indicate which faces they had seen during acquisition and which they had not. Despite equivalent amounts of exposure to the acquisition faces, people in Group 2 did much better than those in Group 1.

Bower and Karlin's data allow us to view in a different light the experiments of Shepard (1967) and Standing (1973) discussed in Section 1. The latter experiments involved intentional learning, whereas Bower and Karlin studied incidental learning.

People intentionally attempting to process pictures may frequently perform a greater number of appropriate acquisition activities than those instructed simply to classify each face as male or female. For example, if participants in Shepard and Standing's studies were simply asked to judge each picture on the basis of whether or not it contained a building, they might well perform much more poorly on a surprise recognition task.

Bower and Karlin also used sets of stimuli (the faces) that were much more similar to one another than were the pictures used by Shepard and Standing. Furthermore, those stimuli that were presented to Bower and Karlin's participants during the recognition test but had *not* been seen during acquisition (called recognition *foils*) were also faces, and hence similar to the acquisition stimuli (called recognition *targets*). As you might expect, greater degrees of similarity between targets and foils generally lead to poorer recognition performance. Shepard and Standing purposely used targets as well as foils that were relatively distinct or dissimilar. The extremely high levels of recognition accuracy found in their experiments therefore need not imply that every detail of each acquisition picture was perfectly retained.

The Bower and Karlin study also illustrates that the level of processing affects memory for visual as well as for verbal information. People do not operate like audio or visual tape recorders that passively store information; rather, they must actively perform certain types of activities in order to learn. Acquisition activities, then, are something we must consider if we are to understand why some people do better than others in learning tasks and memory tasks.

Some Implications of the Role of Acquisition Activities

Many people speak of their poor memories. What do they mean? Are they limited by inferior "storage capacity" because of the makeup of their brain? The following experiments suggest that it is the types of processing activities performed at acquisition that are important for learning and remembering. As these acquisition activities are changed, the ability to remember seems to follow suit.

An experiment by Koh, Kayton, and Peterson (1976) provides a powerful illustration of the role of particular types of acquisition activities. Koh has investigated the basis of many psychological disorders, of schizophrenia in particular. There are of course many varieties of schizophrenic disorders, but for present purposes it is sufficient to oversimplify and to note that schizophrenics generally exhibit extreme deficits in typical learning and memory experiments (for example, recalling a list of words presented during acquisition). It is easy to assume that these deficits reflect a lack in memory capacity. But Koh and colleagues (1976) question the adequacy of this point of view. In one experiment they instructed schizophrenics to process each acquisition item according to its "pleasantness" or "unpleasantness." Under these conditions, schizophrenics' abilities to remember improved dramatically. These results suggest that psychological disorders do not necessarily involve the loss of learning and memory capacities. Instead, it may well be that capacities remain intact and that inability to remember is due to the manner in which people process the inputs that they receive (see also Cermak, 1978).

An emphasis on the importance of acquisition activities also has implications for understanding why some students do better than others in school-related situations. Many students may not know how to process information effectively. They may simply rehearse information at a superficial level (maintenance rehearsal) rather than process it at deeper levels (elaborative rehearsal). If so, one would expect their long-term retention to be poor. This orientation is much more optimistic than the view that explains learning and memory problems in terms of storage capacity, because it suggests that learning and retention are a function of skills that can be developed. In short, it is possible that people can *learn to learn*. The possibility of learning to learn is highly consistent with our theoretical framework in Figure 1.1 and will be an important theme throughout the rest of this book. We must simultaneously consider additional factors before we can fully understand the problem of learning to learn, however, and these will be introduced in subsequent chapters. Meanwhile, our immediate task is to summarize this fourth section of Chapter 2.

Summary of Section 4

The present section has focused on the question of the types of learning activities necessary for long-term retention. One approach to the question is to assume that rehearsal processes allow us to transfer information from short-term memory to long-term memory. From this perspective, the greater the number of rehearsals, the higher the probability that information will be retained for relatively long periods of time. The levels-of-processing framework developed by Craik and Lockhart (1972) provides a somewhat different perspective on the question of long-term retention. There are many levels at which information can be processed, and the probability of long-term retention depends on the depth of processing involved.

We reviewed a number of studies that illustrate the importance of levels of processing. For example, some types of rehearsal processes may be sufficient for short-term retention but not for long-term retention (Craik and Watkins, 1973). Different orienting tasks that prompt various levels of processing also have powerful effects on subsequent recall. For example, orienting tasks like e-checking and letter counting prompt relatively superficial levels of processing, whereas tasks like rating an item as pleasant or unpleasant prompt much deeper processing. The deeper levels of processing result in superior retention both for verbal materials (e.g., Hyde and Jenkins, 1969) and for visual materials (recall the x-scanning studies, for example, and the experiments on face recognition).

The levels-of-processing framework is valuable because it suggests that poor learners and rememberers, far from suffering some inherent storage or capacity deficit, may simply need help in selecting learning activities that involve deeper levels of processing. Work with schizophrenics, for example, suggests that memory can be improved when appropriate orienting tasks are used (Koh, Kayton, and Peterson, 1976). As we shall see, however, a particular set of learning activities may be more or less valuable depending on the nature of the testing environment. This issue is explored in Chapter 3.

Chapter 3
Memory and Retrieval Processes

This chapter will emphasize another aspect of our framework illustrated in Figure 1.1, the types of testing contexts or retrieval environments used to assess learning. As we shall see, learning and remembering cannot be understood unless we consider processes of retrieval, as well as those of acquisition (discussed in Chapter 2). The present chapter is divided into four sections, which are briefly sketched below.

Overview

Section 1 discusses *why retrieval is important*. The section begins with a demonstration experiment that illustrates the importance of retrieval processes, and it then describes some classic experimental work on retrieval. The basic conclusion will be that long-term storage does little good unless we can retrieve stored information when we need to use it. We shall also discuss several types of testing or retrieval environments. In order to assess whether people have learned something, we must design tests that measure their degree of learning. Various tests provide different types of retrieval environments, so estimates of learning will vary as a function of the testing context.

Section 2 explores *relationships among learning activities and retrieval environments*. It will be argued that the value of particular learning activities must be defined in relation to the nature of the testing or retrieval environment. This argument will involve a reassessment of the levels-of-processing framework discussed in Chapter 2, Section 4.

Section 3 analyzes *theories of retrieval processes*. Why do particular retrieval cues sometimes facilitate retention yet at other times have no effect? Our discussion will emphasize the principle of encoding specificity (e.g., Tulving and Thomson, 1973), which stresses the importance of relationships between initial learning activities and retrieval-cue effectiveness at the time of testing.

Section 4 considers *some implications of focusing on retrieval processes*. For example, an emphasis on retrieval has implications for what it means to forget previously acquired information. It also has implications for understanding good versus poor learners, because the ability to use what was learned depends on the construction of appropriate retrieval schemes.

Section 1: Why Retrieval Is Important

The purpose of this section is to illustrate the importance of retrieval processes. We begin with a demonstration experiment that should help clarify the concept of retrieval.

A Demonstration Experiment

The following demonstration experiment is useful for understanding the importance of retrieval. Instructions for the demonstration are as follows. Read each of the acquisition sentences in the following list at your own pace. As soon as you finish, turn the book over and write down as many of the sentences as you can. Please begin now.

A brick can be used as a doorstop.

A ladder can be used as a bookshelf.

A wine bottle can be used as a candle holder.

A pan can be used as a drum.

A record can be used to serve potato chips.

A guitar can be used as a canoe paddle.

A leaf can be used as a bookmark.

An orange can be used to play catch.

A newspaper can be used to swat flies.

A TV antenna can be used as a clothes rack.

A sheet can be used as a sail.

A boat can be used as a shelter.

A bathtub can be used as a punch bowl.

A flashlight can be used to hold water.

A rock can be used as a paperweight.

A knife can be used to stir paint.

A pen can be used as an arrow.

A barrel can be used as a chair.

A rug can be used as a bedspread.

A telephone can be used as an alarm clock.

A scissors can be used to cut grass.

A board can be used as a ruler.

A balloon can be used as a pillow.

A shoe can be used to pound nails.

A dime can be used as a screwdriver.

A lampshade can be used as a hat.

Most people recall between 40 and 60 percent of the sentences. For present purposes we are interested in those sentences that were *not* recalled. What happened to them? Did they fail to register in the memory? Did they register but somehow fade away? Are they still in the memory but unable to be found? Most people who participate in the experiment feel that they learned *more* than they can recall; they are simply unable to find all the information that has been stored. In short, there seems to be a difference between storing information and retrieving or reactivating it later.

The presentation of appropriate *retrieval cues* can facilitate one's ability to remember. Without looking back at the acquisition sentences, read the following instructions: The words in the list below are potential retrieval cues. They are subject nouns of each of the acquisition sentences you have just tried to recall. Look at each cue and see if it reminds you of a previous sentence. Keep track of how many sentences you now remember so that you can compare this performance to your initial attempt at *free recall* (recall without the cues). Please begin now.

Flashlight

Sheet

Rock

Telephone

Boat

Dime

Wine bottle

Board

Pen

Balloon

Ladder

Record

TV antenna

Lampshade

Shoe

Guitar

Scissors

Leaf

Brick

Knife   (Continued on page 58.)

Newspaper

Pan

Barrel

Bathtub

Rug

Orange

Most people are able to remember much more under cued conditions than they do on their first recall trial. Since the original sentences were rather unusual, it is unlikely that people recalled more simply because they guessed a response to each cue. This suggests that people can frequently store information yet be unable to retrieve it when needed. Experiments by Tulving and Pearlstone (1966) provide experimental support for this idea.

Experiments on Retrieval

Tulving and Pearlstone (1966) asked two groups of people to learn a list of forty-eight words. The words could be grouped into twelve categories, and there were four words per category. For example, a list of words like *chair, carrot, boat, couch, car,* could be grouped into categories like furniture, vegetables, and modes of transportation. Both groups of people received the same word lists, so that they should initially have learned equivalent information. However, each group received a different type of test.

People in Group 1 were asked simply to recall as many words as possible. Those in Group 2 were also asked to recall, but they received the names of the twelve categories as retrieval cues. People in Group 2 recalled many more words than those in Group 1. Analysis of the data revealed the following patterns: People in Groups 1 and 2 recalled the same number of words per category (an average of 2.6 words), but those in Group 2 recalled words from more categories (an average of 11.5 categories, compared with 7.3 for Group 1). These results show that people in Group 1 often failed to retrieve whole categories of information. If they recalled one word from a category (the word *chair,* for example), they tended to recall one or two additional words from the same category (*table* or *couch,* perhaps). Frequently, however, they failed to retrieve any items from a category. People in Group 2 received category cues, so that they were much less likely to miss whole categories of previously experienced words. They therefore exhibited superior recall, hence illustrating the importance of retrieval cues.

Further Illustrations of Retrieval

The importance of retrieval can be illustrated even further. It is not sufficient simply to learn and store information. Unless we can activate it when needed, it does us little good. Try to make sense of the following sentences:

The haystack was important because the cloth ripped.

The notes were sour because the seam split.

Attempt to solve the following riddles:

What has a thousand needles but cannot sew?

In what sense is an orange like a stadium?

In some sense you know the information necessary to answer all these questions. The problem is not that you have to acquire new knowledge in order to answer, but that you don't know *which* of a vast array of potential answers to choose. But if you are given the "answer cues" *parachute, bagpipes,* a *porcupine,* and *they both have sections,* you can use these to go back and understand the questions (*parachute* permits comprehension of the first sentence, *bagpipes* the second, and so on). Note, however, that each of the answer cues represents something already familiar to you. You have had previous experiences that were potentially useful, but you were unable to make use of this past knowledge until explicitly instructed. Simply having knowledge, then, is not enough.

A familiar and frustrating illustration of retrieval involves the "tip of the tongue" experience: You know someone's name but just can't think of it; you know you know what a particular type of tool or object is called, but the word escapes you for the moment. The answer is right on the tip of your tongue.

Brown and McNeill (1966) investigated the tip-of-the-tongue phenomenon. They read dictionary definitions of relatively uncommon words to college students and asked them to identify the words. One definition was "A navigational instrument used in measuring angular distances, especially the altitude of sun, moon, and stars at sea." Sometimes students indicated that they simply had no idea of the answer (which is *sextant* for the above definition). The interesting data came from those who felt that they could not produce the answer at the moment, but that it was on the tip of their tongue. Brown and McNeill asked such students questions about the word they were searching after. What letter did it begin with? How many syllables did it have? What was a word with a similar sound? Students could answer these questions with considerable accuracy. For example, in 51 percent of the cases, they knew the first letter of the word, and in 47 percent of the cases, they knew the exact number of syllables in the word. Nevertheless, they were unable to retrieve the whole word. The tip-of-the-tongue phenomenon is an excellent illustration of the difference between storing information and being able to retrieve it later.

Types of Testing or Retrieval Environments

The previous studies show that it is not sufficient simply to store information; for unless we can activate information when needed, it does us little good. They also show that presentation of appropriate retrieval cues can facilitate memory by activating information. Note that different testing situations provide different types of retrieval environments, so that assessments of learning can vary as a function of testing contexts. Consider the following example.

The noted anthropologist Margaret Mead (1964) discusses the aborigines of south Australia. Important aspects of their culture, she notes, are transmitted through myths that are passed from generation to generation. The myths are presented in an oral rather than written medium, so that they must be committed to memory in order to be preserved. Mead (1964) notes that the aborigines have to walk through terrains that are relevant to myths in order to be able to tell a long myth correctly. In short, they seem to rely on aspects of the physical environment which function as effective retrieval cues. Imagine, however, that a psychologist tested some aborigines in order to verify that they did indeed have excellent memories for long, complicated myths, and he or she brought them into a laboratory and asked them to recite as many myths as they could. Without the environmental retrieval cues the aborigines would probably do poorly, and the psychologist might then mistakenly write about the "myth of aborigines' memories for myths." Within the context of their cultural activities, however, the aborigines have a very thorough and adaptive knowledge of myths.

We shall be reviewing studies of learning and memory that employ a number of different test measures. Because assessments of what someone knows appear to depend on the testing context, we must take care to understand the types of test measures that are used.

Recognition Measures

One measure of memory is recognition. The study by Shepard (1967) cited in Chapter 2, Section 1, is a case in point. In this study, participants were presented with 600 acquisition pictures. They exhibited excellent memory for the pictures. But what is meant by *excellent memory* in this case? It seems that memory was excellent in relation to the measures of recognition that Shepard employed. After acquisition, all participants were shown two pictures: one that they had been shown during acquisition (a recognition target) and one that had not appeared (a recognition foil). The participants were therefore provided with a previously experienced item. They simply had to choose which of the two items presented on each test trial was the one they had actually seen.

To be more precise, Shepard's study utilized a forced-choice recognition procedure: On each test trial the participants had to give a yes-response; they were forced to say yes to one member of each test-trial pair. The recognition procedure could have been conducted in a different (non-forced-choice) manner. Each test trial might have consisted of only a single picture rather than a pair of pictures. On each test trial participants would respond *either* yes or no. Why use forced-choice recognition rather than single-item recognition? There is no simple answer to this question. Each method has advantages and disadvantages of its own.

Forced-Choice versus Single-Item Recognition

One advantage of the forced-choice method can be appreciated by imagining that Shepard did *not* utilize it. Assume that he utilized single-item recognition instead. Analysis of the data might reveal that 99 percent of the previously seen pictures (targets) received yes-responses. Could we then conclude that the participants responded with 99 percent accuracy? The answer is no. Participants' responses to pictures that were *not* seen during acquisition (to recognition foils) must also be considered. What if participants also said yes to foils 99 percent of the time? Under these conditions, one would not want to say that they had excellent memory for the pictures, but rather that they simply had a lax criterion for saying yes.

Criteria problems also arise when attempting to assess the differences between two (or more) participants' memory performances. Suppose that Person A participates in the Shepard study and says yes to 99 percent of the previously experienced pictures (targets), and Person B says yes to only 80 percent. Has Person A remembered better than Person B? Clearly, we must look at each person's responses to foils before attempting an answer. What if Person A said yes to 100 percent of the foils, whereas Person B said yes to only 1 percent? Who would exhibit the better memory? Again, what if Person A said yes to 80 percent of the foils and Person B to 60 percent? Statistical procedures have been developed to answer questions such as these (e.g., Bernbach, 1967; Lockhart and Murdock, 1970). In general, the statistical procedures attempt to assess the degree to which someone can differentiate between recognition targets and recognition foils.

Forced-choice measures of recognition eliminate some of the criteria problems inherent in single-item measures. In a single-item procedure, Person A may have a lax criterion for accuracy and hence say yes to 90 percent of all test items (to foils as well as to actually experienced items). Person B may have a more stringent criterion and say yes only 55 percent of the time. In a forced-choice procedure, *all* participants must say yes to an item on *each* test trial. Because of this, differential criteria for saying yes do not play a role. One can then circumvent the problem of having to use certain statistical tests in order to analyze results like those found in the single-item method. The advantage of this circumvention is not that one is freed from having to perform statistical computations, but rather that one need not accept certain statistical *assumptions* that are necessary in order to utilize the statistical test appropriately.

What are the potential disadvantages of using a forced-choice measure? One is the degree to which such a measure mirrors judgments that occur in everyday life. Imagine that you are walking through a shopping center and see someone who looks vaguely familiar. Your decision to walk up to her and begin a conversation depends on whether you think you recognize her or not. Note that this situation mirrors the single-item rather than forced-choice method of recognition testing. We are not always presented with *pairs* of people and asked to choose *which* of the two we recognize. In everyday situations, analogs to the forced-choice method are more the exception than the rule. Perhaps forced-choice methods can tell us more about the absolute accuracy of recognition, whereas single-item procedures are more valuable for studying the modes of recognition that occur in everyday life.

Recall Measures

Recall measures are quite different from recognition measures. In recall, one must produce the previously experienced items on one's own. Assume that the participants in the Shepard (1967) and Standing (1973) studies (Chapter 2, Section 1) were asked for recall rather than recognition of the pictures. To avoid the problem of having to draw the pictures, participants could partially describe each one verbally. Clearly, the level of recall would be much lower than the level of recognition. Participants asked to recall would presumably have learned as much as those asked to recognize. The testing situations differ greatly, however. In recall, one has to generate one's own cues for retrieval. This is generally more difficult than being presented with items and judging whether or not they were experienced during acquisition tasks (however, see Tulving and Thomson, 1973; Section 3).

There are important distinctions among different measures of recall. Measures of *free recall* assess people's ability to recall previously experienced acquisition items in any order they wish to recall them. In contrast, measures of *serial recall* assess their ability to remember items in the exact order in which they were originally experienced. Remembering someone's phone number is an act of serial rather than free recall. Our third recall measure is *cued recall*.

The term *cued recall* refers to situations in which an experimenter explicitly provides participants with retrieval cues that may help them remember. In the demonstration experiment at the beginning of this chapter, the first noun from each acquisition sentence was provided as a retrieval cue. Retrieval cues may also be events that are related to what was learned but that were not actually experienced during acquisition. For example, the cue *animal* may act as a retrieval cue for previously experienced items such as *dog* or *cow*. The cue *rhymes with boy* may act as a retrieval cue for the previously experienced word *toy*. Clearly, not all retrieval cues presented by an experimenter will be effective. A major challenge for the memory theorist is to understand the conditions under which cues facilitate remembering. This question is explored more fully in Section 3.

Relearning Measures

Measures of relearning are one of the oldest in the history of experimental psychology. They were introduced by Ebbinghaus in 1885. That year his classic book on memory was published. Ebbinghaus's book represents one of the first attempts to study processes of learning and memory experimentally. One of its unique aspects is that all the studies were based on experiments that Ebbinghaus conducted on himself. His most frequent measure involved the amount of time that it took him to relearn materials that he had previously studied. For example, he might practice one list (List A) of items twenty times, and another list (List B) only ten times. Twenty days later he might then attempt to relearn each list. Ebbinghaus was interested in the number of trials it would take to relearn each of these lists to perfection. Suppose it took five trials to relearn List A, but six trials to relearn List B. If so, one would not be inclined to add the extra ten acquisition trials originally spent in learning List A.

Today, measures of relearning are used relatively infrequently. It is not clear why this is the case. Such measures appear to be potentially very valuable. For example, it seems possible to fail to recognize a particular set of items (in which case one might conclude that they were forgotten) and yet to be able to relearn them relatively rapidly. It might be fruitful to take a new look at the relearning measures that Ebbinghaus introduced.

Summary of Section 1

We have reviewed a number of measures that can be used to assess learning. The most basic measures are recognition, recall, and relearning. There are also subvarieties of these measures. Recognition tests can include forced-choice or single-item procedures, and recall tests can include free recall, serial recall, and cued recall.

Different memory measures provide varying amounts of information at the time of testing, so that they involve different retrieval environments. Consequently people may look as if they failed to learn when asked for free recall yet may show evidence of learning when given tests of cued recall or recognition. Assessments of learning therefore depend on the nature of the testing context. This raises an important question: Are learning activities that are optimal for one type of test also optimal for other tests, or does the value of a particular type of learning activity depend on the nature of the testing environment? This issue is explored in Section 2.

Section 2: Relationships among Learning Activities and Retrieval Environments

The discussion in this section will focus on relationships between two of the factors presented in Figure 1.1, namely, relationships between particular learning activities and subsequent retrieval environments. The basic argument will be that the value of particular learning activities must be defined relative to the nature of the testing or retrieval context. Consider first how this argument applies to the ease of learning and remembering visual forms.

Memory for Visual Forms

Figure 3.1 illustrates two different arrangements of the same set of visual elements. In Figure 3.1a these elements are arranged to form a coherent figure. In Figure 3.1b the same elements are more or less randomly arranged. Assume that you can have the same amount of time to study either 3.1a or 3.1b in order to prepare for a memory test. Which

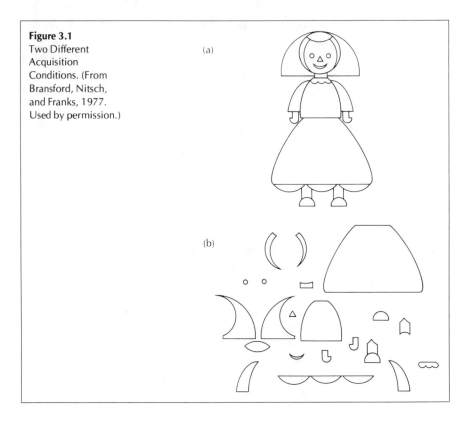

Figure 3.1
Two Different
Acquisition
Conditions. (From
Bransford, Nitsch,
and Franks, 1977.
Used by permission.)

(a)

(b)

figure would you choose? Most people are drawn toward Figure 3.1a. Because it represents a meaningful figure, it appears to be easier to learn and hence remember later. Note, however, that there are a number of possible ways to assess memory (see Section 1). Can you imagine a memory test where time spent studying Figure 3.1a would be less valuable than time spent studying Figure 3.1b?

Nitsch, McCarrell, Bransford, and Franks (see Bransford, Nitsch, and Franks, 1977) presented one group of people with Figure 3.1a, and another group with Figure 3.1b. All participants were given ninety seconds to study the visual pattern in order to prepare for a memory test. An important aspect of the experiment is that participants did not know the exact type of memory test they would receive. Figure 3.2 illustrates the memory test administered to participants. It is a forced-choice recognition test. Participants were asked to look at each pair of visual elements and circle the one they had seen during acquisition. Those who had studied Figure 3.1b were much more accurate than those who had studied Figure 3.1a.

This study provides a simple illustration of the importance of considering relationships between types of acquisition activities and subsequent abilities to remember. People who studied Figure 3.1a apparently learned the overall figure (the drawing of the girl) but were unable to identify the exact elements that made up the figure. Indeed, participants in this group frequently stated that they had to attempt to recall, or image, the

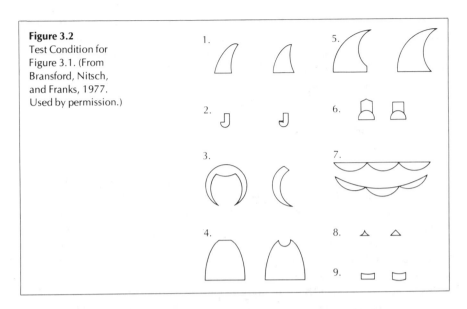

Figure 3.2
Test Condition for Figure 3.1. (From Bransford, Nitsch, and Franks, 1977. Used by permission.)

whole figure in order to decide whether a particular element could fit the overall visual pattern. When they failed to do this, they could not differentiate between the target and foil items. In contrast, participants who studied Figure 3.1b had processed each element and therefore performed quite well in the recognition test. If presented with a different type of test (free-recall, for example), participants who studied Figure 3.1a might have performed better than those who studied Figure 3.1b. The important point is that assumptions about the value of particular types of acquisition activities must be defined relative to the testing context. This argument has implications for the levels-of-processing framework that was discussed in Chapter 2, Section 4.

Levels of Processing Revisited

In Chapter 2 we discussed Craik and Lockhart's (1972) concept of levels of processing. Briefly, inputs processed at deeper, semantic levels of analysis were assumed to result in stronger and more durable memory traces than inputs processed at shallow or more superficial levels. Results like those reported by Jenkins and his colleagues (Chapter 2, Section 4) appear to be congruent with this hypothesis. For example, the task of rating words as pleasant or unpleasant is assumed to involve deep, semantic processing. In contrast, rhyming, syllable counting, and e-checking apparently involve superficial processing. The pleasant-unpleasant task resulted in much higher degrees of recall than did the other three types of tasks.

Note that we discussed levels of processing before considering the question of relationships between acquisition activities and particular types of testing contexts. We did show that levels-of-processing assumptions hold up under conditions of both recognition and free recall (see the Craik and Tulving study discussed in Chapter 2, Section 4).

Nevertheless, we are still left with the following question: Are there any testing contexts in which relatively superficial levels of processing can result in *better* performance than deeper levels of processing? If there are, we might need to revise assumptions about the inherently superior strength and durability of memory traces that result from deeper, semantic processing. This issue is explored below.

Levels of Processing versus Transfer-Appropriate Processing

Morris, Bransford, and Franks (1977) presented people with two different types of incidental orienting tasks. Task A involved deciding whether a target word fitted meaningfully into a sentence frame (e.g., "_____ has ears: dog"). Task B involved judgments about rhyme information (e.g., "_____ rhymes with log: dog"). After acquisition, participants received target items (in the preceding example, *dog*) plus foils in a single-item recognition test. Results indicated that semantic processing (Task A) resulted in better recognition performance than did more superficial processing (Task B). Note that these results replicate those found by Craik and Tulving (discussed in Chapter 2, Section 4).

The important aspect of the study by Morris and colleagues was the performance of a second group of participants. These people experienced identical acquisition situations but received a different type of test. They were presented with a completely new set of words and required to decide which of these words *rhymed* with targets heard during acquisition and which did not. Under these conditions people were better at recognizing rhymes of acquisition target words that had initially been processed in a rhyming rather than semantic mode. Subsequent experiments showed that the superiority of rhyme over semantic processing (given a rhyme test) persisted even when there was a twenty-four-hour delay between acquisition and test.

These results suggest that deeper levels of processing may not result in inherently stronger and more durable memory traces (see also Kolers, 1978). The value of particular levels of analysis seems to be relative to the types of test situations encountered later on. Morris and colleagues suggest that the concept of levels of processing might be replaced with one of "transfer-appropriate processing." They state that "transfer appropriate processing may sometimes involve the 'superficial' levels of analysis that are deemed less adequate by the levels of processing approach" (Morris, Bransford, and Franks, 1977, p. 29).

Further Investigations of Transfer-Appropriate Processing

A series of studies by Stein (1978) investigated transfer-appropriate processing from a different perspective. He employed two different types of orienting tasks and presented the target items in a visual rather than auditory mode.

The first orienting task was a visual-orthographic task, one that required that participants focus only on the more superficial visual characteristics of the target items (e.g., "Does this word have a capital *D*? *raDio*"). Each of the visually presented target items had different letters capitalized (e.g., *Car, treE, vAse*). The second orienting task was designed to prompt deeper, semantic levels of analysis. Hence, people might be asked, "Does this item use electricity? *raDio*." Note that particular letters were capitalized in each target word even when people were prompted to process the targets at deeper, semantic levels.

Like Morris and colleagues, Stein used two types of tests. The first was a forced-choice recognition test that required people to identify the actual target items presented during acquisition. Participants might see *raDio, ceDar, caDdy,* and *tiDbit* and be asked to choose which one of the four words was the target item. Note that if you only remembered having seen a capital *D*, you would be unable to distinguish the foils from the target. On the other hand, if you processed the meaning of the acquisition targets, you might choose *raDio* as the correct answer, even though you might not be able to remember whether you actually saw *raDio, Radio, radiO, rAdio,* or *radIo*. Using this test, Stein found that the deeper, semantic levels of processing led to superior recognition performance. These results are consistent with those of other studies that have compared semantic with visual-orthographic orienting tasks (see Craik and Tulving, 1975). However, do these data therefore imply that semantic processing leads to inherently stronger memory traces? It may be that the processing of visual-orthographic information can result in a very high degree of learning and that this learning is simply different from, and not inferior to, that which results from semantic processing. To explore this possibility, one needs to construct a test that more adequately taps the kind of information likely to be learned when processing in a visual-orthographic mode.

Stein's second type of test was also a forced-choice recognition test. This test, however, required people to identify the *visual* characteristics of the target items. For example, they might see *raDio, Radio, radiO,* and *rAdio* and be asked to indicate which one they saw during acquisition. Under these conditions deeper, semantic levels of processing led to performance that was *inferior* to that resulting from the more superficial, visual-orthographic levels of analysis. Once again, the value of particular types of acquisition activities appears to be relative to subsequent tasks one needs to perform.

The studies by Morris and colleagues and by Stein (see also Fisher and Craik, 1977) suggest that it is no longer profitable to assume that certain items' memory traces are less durable or adequate than others' simply because these items were processed at a shallow level. Indeed, others (e.g., Craik and Tulving, 1975; Baddeley, 1978) have noted that the original levels-of-processing hypothesis seems to fall short of really explaining memory phenomena. To say that something is more poorly retained because it was processed less deeply doesn't really help one understand *why* shallower levels of analysis are less beneficial. Furthermore, the data presented above suggest that shallower levels of processing can be superior to deeper levels if one designs test situations that assess the kind of information that actually results from shallower levels of analysis. Another way to highlight shortcomings of the originally proposed version of levels of processing is as follows: Imagine situations where different groups process items at deep, semantic levels, yet their memory performance differs. This would suggest that something more than deep processing of individual items is necessary for retention. An illustration of this type of situation is provided below.

Memory Differences despite
Deep Levels of Processing

Our present goal is more fully to understand why an emphasis on deep levels of processing is not sufficient to understand learning and memory. We have already noted that shallow levels of processing can be superior in certain testing contexts. The present discussion will focus on situations where all words are processed at deep, semantic levels, and yet memory performance differs. Memory performance will again be shown to vary as a function of the testing conditions used.

Stein (1977) conducted a series of studies that used the following incidental-acquisition procedure. Imagine that you are presented with a list of twenty-four similes, such as "A pin is like a nail," "A bumper is like a statue," "A pliers is like a crab." Your task is simply to indicate whether you can understand the simile. For example, you would respond yes to "A pin is like a nail" when you realize that they both have sharp points. Note that this task presumably involves a semantic level of analysis. You have to consider what each word means in order to adequately perform the task. After acquisition Stein presented participants with the subject noun of each simile (for example, *pin*) and asked them to recall the second member of each pair (*nail*). Cued recall reached an overall level of 59 percent accuracy. It reached 78 percent for those similes that participants indicated they had understood during acquisition, and 35 percent for those similes that they had not understood. These were the results for Group 1 in Stein's study.

The study included a second type of incidental orienting task. People in Group 2 heard the same similes in the same order but were asked to rate the two items in each simile in terms of their relative hardness or softness. For example, you would probably say "same" to "A pin is like a nail" because a pin and a nail are both hard objects. Note, however, that you would still have to process each word semantically in order to perform adequately in this acquisition task. After acquisition, people in Group 2 were given the subject nouns as retrieval cues and asked to recall the second pair member, the same procedure as was used in testing Group 1. Nevertheless, the cued-recall performance of Group 2 was vastly *inferior* to that of the Group 1. The overall level of cued recall reached only 21 percent accuracy. It reached a level of 36 percent accuracy for items that participants found to be the same in terms of relative hardness or softness, and 14 percent for those they found to be different.

It is instructive to note that in subsequent studies, Stein found that people in Groups 1 and 2 were equally proficient at recognizing *individual* subject and object nouns. (Did they recognize having heard *pin, bumper, nail,* for example?.) The two different types of processing, then, resulted in equivalent performances in individual-item recognition, but very different performances in cued recall. One implication of these results is that both types of processing (understanding similes versus rating in terms of hardness and softness) are equally good for individual-item recognition. If one's goal is to remember which items went together, however (for example, *pin* and *nail*), understanding the simile produces superior results. In Section 3 we shall discuss some possible reasons for this superiority. At present, it is useful to consider some additional illustrations of relationships between acquisition activities and subsequent abilities to remember what was learned.

*Organizing and Retrieving
Information*

Our previous discussion suggests that different types of semantic orienting tasks may be equivalent on some memory measures yet result in differences on other measures. An important implication is that people must learn to perform learning activities appropriate to the subsequent memory tasks they will perform. Our present discussion will focus on relationships between initial acts of organizing information and our ability measured in terms of free recall.

Imagine a list of sixty words. Groups of words belong to various categories (for example, animals, vegetables, professions), and the list includes fifteen members of four different categories. During the acquisition task, the words are grouped, not according to category membership, but randomly (the first item might be an animal, the second a vegetable, and so on). To what extent will people make use of these category relationships during learning and recall, and how could we tell whether they did or not? Bousfield (1953) studied how people learn and recall lists of categorizable words, and noted that an important pattern occurred: Although the acquisition words were presented in a random order, people did not recall them in a random order; rather, they tended to recall a set of words from one category, then from another category, and so on. This is called clustering. The existence of clustering suggests that people may be using information about categories as a retrieval scheme during recall. By recalling general categories, they may be generating their own retrieval cues that help them remember acquisition words.

Of course, people's retrieval schemes are not necessarily perfect. They may fail to consider whole categories of information, especially when there are large numbers of categories in a list. As an illustration recall the study by Tulving and Pearlstone (1966) discussed in Section 1 of this chapter. Here two groups of people received a list of words belonging to twelve categories. One group received explicit cues at the time of the test that reminded them of the overall categories. Students in this group exhibited a much higher level of recall than those in the group that received no cues.

The potential importance of organized retrieval schemes is also illustrated in a study by Bower, Clark, Lesgold, and Winzenz (1969). They presented students with a list of 112 words, like *limestone, common, brass, minerals, masonry.* The words could be organized into four general categories or structures, but they were presented randomly during acquisition. An example of an organizational structure for part of the list is illustrated in Figure 3.3. Two groups of students each received four presentation trials of the list and were asked to recall the list after each presentation trial. Group 1 received all 112 words on each presentation trial. After the fourth trial, they could recall approximately 65 words. Students in Group 2 received a different type of acquisition procedure, which was designed to help them acquire a coherent, organized structure. During the first trial they received only the words in Levels 1 and 2 (see Figure 3.3), words that emphasized a higher-order organizational structure. During the second trial they received the words in Levels 1, 2, and 3 (see Figure 3.3). During the last two trials all 112 words were presented. After the fourth trial, students in Group 2 recalled an average of about 100 words (compared with 65 for Group 1).

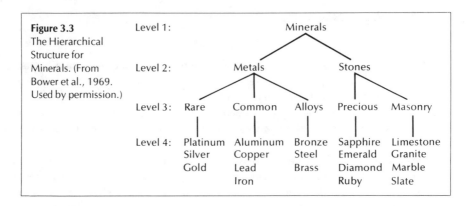

Figure 3.3
The Hierarchical Structure for Minerals. (From Bower et al., 1969. Used by permission.)

This study suggests that the development of organizing structures can have powerful effects on retention. Presumably these structures serve to guide retrieval at the time of recall. Assume, however, that a list of words does not have any apparent organizational structure. Will people create their own organizational structures, and will these structures affect their recall performance?

Experiments by Tulving (1962) suggest that effective learners do indeed impose their own organizational structure on lists of unrelated items (this is called subjective organization). To test the idea, Tulving first needed a way to measure the degree of subjective organization that each person employed. Because the organization was subjective and could vary from person to person, an experimenter would have no way to measure it from only one recall trial. In order to measure subjective organization, Tulving gave people a number of presentations of a list of words, presenting the words in a different order on each trial. He also asked them to recall the words after each trial. If participants were forming subjectively organized structures, one would expect to see a consistency in the order in which they recalled information across a series of trials. For example, if a person formed a subjectively organized structure from the words *tree, dog,* and *car,* one would expect these words to be recalled together on a number of recall trials. This type of intertrial consistency constituted Tulving's measure of the degree of subjective organization. He was then able to explore the relationship between degree of subjective organization and the absolute number of words recalled. Tulving found that people with higher scores on the subjective-organization measure also recalled a greater number of words (see also Mandler, 1967).

How to Perform Some Memory Feats

The previous discussion emphasized that certain types of organizing activities facilitate free recall of items to be remembered. The experiments reviewed focused on the *amount* recalled, but not always on the *order* of recall. Assume that you receive only a single exposure to acquisition lists yet want to perform memory feats like the following, singly or in combination.

1. Remember a long list of words in the exact order in which they occurred

2. Remember a long list of words in the reverse order from that in which they occurred

3. Remember a long list of words in any order that may be required

Since many learning strategies do not preserve information about the order in which items were presented, they will not permit you to perform memory feats like those listed above. However, there are mnemonic techniques that will permit the performance of such feats.

Assume that you hear the following list of words read at a rate of one every five seconds: *chicken, tree, pepper, truck, ear, mirror, fence, bucket, trumpet, nail*. Your goal is to remember these words in either their actual order of occurrence or the reverse order (the questioner will choose the task *after* you have heard the items to be learned). How could you learn this list in a manner that will permit you to perform either task (or both)? If this type of task seems trivial, attempt to recall the alphabet. Most people can easily recall it in the forward direction, but try recalling it backwards. Despite long exposure most people cannot easily recite the alphabet in reverse order.

To perform the feat of either forward or reverse recall, one needs to make use of previously acquired information that can facilitate retrieval. For example, the *method of loci* involves utilization of information about previously acquired spatial layouts or locations. The activation of information about the interior of a familiar house is often used. Imagine a familiar spatial layout, like your house or your parents' house, and perform the following activities: When you hear the first word to be remembered, *chicken,* imagine walking in the front door and seeing a chicken in a conspicuous location (in the hall closet, for example, on the nearest chair, playing the piano). The second word you hear, *tree,* should be imaged as a tree existing in the second conspicuous location you notice as you enter the familiar room. The same procedure should be repeated for each succeeding word to be remembered. Be sure to follow a natural path through the house and to create an image of each word's referent in a particular location. The images you create need not conform to expected reality but can be quite bizarre (a giant pepper shaker, perhaps, spilling on a lamp). To recall the words according to their order of input, you need only enter the front door of your imagined location, proceed in the natural direction, and perceive the items placed in particular locations. To recall the words in the reverse order, you need only reverse the direction in which you proceed through the house. The ability to effectively utilize this method of loci may require some practice, but most people find the technique quite easy to acquire and use.

Given sufficient practice, the method of loci is a very efficient technique for recalling information either forwards or backwards. Suppose, however, that you wish to be able to perform additional memory feats. In particular, if you are asked to recall the eighth item, then the third item, then the fifth item—you never know the order, it is up to the questioner—there exist memory techniques that are better suited to this task than the method of loci. Emphasis is now upon the speed with which you can remember a particular item. For this task, utilization of the method of loci would permit accurate performance, but one would first have to count the number of visually imaged locations traversed before one could remember the item by its number. If the word occurred late in the list, this counting process would take a long time.

An alternative mnemonic technique is the peg-word system. Here one must first acquire information that can then be utilized to remember subsequent events. It is possible to learn peg words numbering in the hundreds. The following illustrates peg words for the numbers 1 through 10:

One is a bun.

Two is a shoe.

Three is a tree.

Four is a door.

Five is a hive.

Six is sticks.

Seven is heaven.

Eight is a gate.

Nine is a line.

Ten is a hen.

The fact that each line rhymes should facilitate this acquisition process. Once the peg words have been learned, they can be used in the following manner. If the first word to be remembered is *airplane,* you might imagine an airplane wedged inside a bun. If the second word is *cup,* you could imagine a cup pouring coffee into the shoe. The same procedure is repeated for each additional item to be remembered. Essentially, the process is equivalent to the method of loci, except that peg words, rather than locations in a spatial layout, serve as the retrieval cues.

To remember the list of words, simply recall the peg words (for example, "one is a *bun*") and note what was imagined with each one (*airplane*). Clearly the peg-word system can be used to recall items both in the order of their acquisition and in the reverse order; the advantage of the peg-word system over the method of loci is that one can also recall any particular item quite readily. If asked to recall the sixth item, one need only remember that "six is sticks" and reactivate the object originally imaged with *sticks*. Note that both the method-of-loci and the peg-word systems provide an efficient means for retrieving information. Several books describe additional mnemonic techniques that can be used to facilitate memory and retrieval (e.g., Cermak, 1976; Higbee, 1977; Lorayne and Lucas, 1974). The techniques vary in usefulness depending on the material to be remembered as well as the memory feats one wants to perform.

Summary of Section 2

The purpose of this section was to illustrate how assumptions about the value of particular learning activities depend on the nature of the testing environment. This suggests that effective learners must be able to select acquisition activities appropriate to the memory feats to be performed. For example, paying attention to the sounds of words is beneficial if one wishes to recognize additional words that rhyme with those heard during acquisition (Morris, Bransford, and Franks, 1977), and noting whether certain letters are capitalized is more beneficial than deep, semantic processing in certain types of tests (Stein, 1978). Similarly, particular kinds of organizational strategies and mnemonic techniques are more or less valuable depending on the testing context. Note that each of the studies we discussed illustrates how remembering depends on processes of retrieval as well as storage. It is therefore important to examine the various theories of retrieval processes. What is known about the reasons why retrieval cues help?

Section 3: Theories of Retrieval Processes

Our goal in this section is to better understand processes of retrieval. Why do retrieval cues facilitate recall? How is cue effectiveness related to the kinds of learning activities performed during the acquisition task? Note that all tests of memory (free recall, cued recall, and recognition, for example) involve retrieval processes. In free recall people must generate their own retrieval cues. In recognition the original word, phrase, or sentence provides the retrieval cue (for example, "A pin is like a nail"). In cued recall, only a subitem of the originally presented information (*pin* in "A pin is like a nail") is presented as the retrieval cue. Processes of retrieval are important for all types of testing situations. It is therefore important to ask, Why do self-generated and experimenter-provided cues facilitate retrieval?

Retrieval Cues, Guessing, and Generation-Recognition

A simple hypothesis regarding the effectiveness of retrieval cues is the guessing hypothesis. Assume, for example, that you either generate or are presented with information stating that you had experienced acquisition words that were examples of animals and furniture. From your previously acquired knowledge you might proceed to guess words like *dog, cat, chair, couch.* Some of your guesses might match actual words presented during acquisition, so that your recall scores would be raised. Can a guessing hypothesis account for the high scores that result from self-generated and experimenter-provided cues? There is a major problem with the guessing hypothesis as a general explanation of retrieval. It suggests that people "recall" many words that were not presented during acquisition yet are members of previously experienced categories. This does happen on some occasions, but the occurrences are much rarer than a guessing hypothesis would predict.

The guessing hypothesis can be modified to yield a more plausible account of retrieval-cue effectiveness. Assume first that people use a cue (such as *animal*) to guess, or generate, plausible candidates (*dog, cat, wolf,* and so on). Now assume that people ask themselves whether they recognize any of the words that they generated on the basis of the cue. For example, assume that people encountered acquisition words like *dog* and *cow* and are then given the cue *animal* when tested. They may generate words like *dog, cat, cow,* and *wolf* but, on the basis of recognition, realize that only *dog* and *cow* occurred during acquisition. This *generation-recognition hypothesis* (e.g., Bahrick, 1970) could account for increased recall scores, as well as the lack of intruding words (*cat, wolf*) that are related to previously acquired categories but did not occur during acquisition. In short, the generation-recognition hypothesis assumes that retrieval cues facilitate recall because they help turn a free- or cued-recall situation into a recognition test.

The Principle of Encoding Specificity

Experiments by Tulving and his associates (e.g., Flexser and Tulving, 1978; Tulving and Osler, 1968; Tulving and Thomson, 1973; Tulving and Wiseman, 1975; Tulving, 1978) raise serious questions about the adequacy of generation-recognition theories of retrieval. They argue that retrieval-cue effectiveness is much more dependent on people's initial learning activities than a theory of generation-recognition would suggest. For example, imagine that you hear a list of words like *cold, slow, strong, white, small, low, good, hate.* It is unlikely that words like *ground, elephant, sun,* will be effective cues. However, if you originally study word *pairs* like *ground-cold, elephant-slow, sun-strong,* and so forth, it is highly likely that *ground, elephant, sun,* will act as effective retrieval cues for the words with which they were paired (see Tulving and Osler, 1968). Tulving and associates argue that retrieval-cue effectiveness is governed by the encoding-specificity principle. Cue effectiveness is a function of the degree of overlap between information received at the time of acquisition and retrieval information available at the time of testing. In other words, it is helpful if the cue given at the time of testing be a cue encoded at the time of acquisition.

Tulving and Thomson's (1973) data provide a striking illustration of encoding specificity. Assume that you study a list composed of noun pairs like *ground-cold.* You are told that *cold* is the word to be remembered, but that you should also study *ground* because it may provide a useful retrieval cue later. After acquisition, you are presented with a word like *hot* and asked to generate other words that go with it. As you can imagine, the probability of generating *cold* (one of the words to be remembered) is quite high given a cue like *hot.* After this generation phase, you are asked to look at all the words you have just generated and to circle those that occurred during the acquisition portion of the experiment. In short, this is like a recognition test, so that you should circle the word to be remembered, *cold.* Surprisingly, people do quite poorly on this recognition test and average only 24 percent accuracy. If people are given retrieval cues that were received during acquisition, however, like the cue *ground,* they can recall target words like *cold* 63 percent of the time. In short, cued recall is better than recognition in this situation.

The foregoing results present problems for a generation-recognition theory of retrieval. That theory assumes that retrieval cues are helpful because they permit one first to generate and then to recognize particular target items (for example, *cold*). People's recognition scores for target items (such as *cold*) should therefore never be lower than their cued-recall scores (for example, recall for *cold,* when they are given the cue *ground*). And yet Tulving and Thomson's data show that recognition *can* be inferior to cued recall; the word *ground* was shown to be a better retrieval cue for *cold* than was the word *cold* presented as a recognition item. In other words, retrieval-cue effectiveness is context dependent. It depends on similarities between the context at time of learning and the retrieval context at time of test.

The context-dependent nature of retrieval-cue effectiveness is also illustrated by the following. Barclay, Bransford, Franks, McCarrell, and Nitsch (1974) presented students with a list of acquisition sentences that included either 1 or 2:

1. The man lifted the piano.

2. The man tuned the piano.

Note that one tends to think about the weight of a piano in the context of the first sentence, and its sound in the context of the second. Will these different interpretations of the word *piano* influence the effectiveness of retrieval cues?

After students had heard the list of sentences, they were presented with a set of retrieval cues like "Do you remember hearing about something heavy?" "Do you remember hearing about something that makes nice sounds?" Results indicated that a cue like *something heavy* was effective for people who had heard a sentence like Sentence 1 but not for those who had heard Sentence 2. Similarly, the cue *makes nice sounds* was more effective for Sentence 2 than for Sentence 1. This suggests that retrieval-cue effectiveness is indeed influenced by the information acquired during the acquisition task.

As a final example of relationships between learning activities and retrieval-cue effectiveness, consider an experiment by Jacoby (1974). He presented college students with a long list of words that could be categorized. For example, two items might be birds (*robin, sparrow*), two might be modes of transportation (*car, boat*), and so forth. Generally, members of the same category were not presented together but in different places in the acquisition list (*robin* might be the fifth item and *sparrow* the eighteenth).

For present purposes the most relevant of Jacoby's acquisition conditions are the following. All participants were informed that many of the items on the list shared a category membership with another item and that their task was to make judgments about the category memberships. Group 1 were asked to judge whether each item shared a category membership with the item immediately preceding it. For example, if they encountered *robin* and the immediately preceding item was *rock,* they would probably say, "No, they are not members of the same category." This is called the one-back condition, because it involves category judgments made for only one item back in the list. Group 2 made the same category judgments and had the same exposure time, but they were asked to judge whether each item shared a category membership with *any of* the previous items in the list. This is called an n-back condition, because it imposes no limit on the number of previously experienced items one can access.

After the judgment task, all participants were given a surprise recall test. Group 2 did much better than Group 1. Group 2 also tended to recall both members of each category together (their outputs revealed clustering). The n-back instructions apparently prompted people to interrelate and organize the acquisition items. The one-back condition prompted no such activity, and recall was relatively low. The importance of the active nature of acquisition is also revealed by Jacoby's cued-recall data. In a cued-recall test, students were supplied with one member of each category (*robin*, for instance) and asked to recall the other item (*sparrow*). Once again the n-back condition prompted much better performance than did the one-back condition.

Jacoby's data suggest that clustering and cued recall are a function of the types of learning activities people are prompted to perform during acquisition. In order for *robin* to retrieve *sparrow*, for example, people must have actively interrelated them during the learning task (note that the n-back condition prompts this type of activity). In this context, it is useful to reconsider some studies in Chapter 2, Section 4, that explored relationships between rehearsal and long-term retention. Studies by Rundus and colleagues (e.g., Rundus, 1971) suggested that long-term retention was directly related to the number of rehearsals. In contrast, Craik and Watkins's (1973) study of maintenance rehearsal suggested no relationship between rehearsal and long-term recall. If you look back at Table 2.1, you will see that people in Rundus's experiment tended to rehearse *groups* of words (for example, *blessing, hoof, reaction*) rather than each word individually. This may have helped them form organized substructures that facilitated retrieval during free recall. Craik and Watkins's procedure, on the other hand, prompted people to rehearse each word individually, rather than relate it to previous words. Because retrieval processes seem to be especially important for free recall, we might expect this type of maintenance rehearsal to have little systematic effect on long-term recall. Note, however, that maintenance rehearsal may have effects on other measures of long-term retention. For example, the amount of maintenance rehearsal may affect recognition memory, because the construction of elaborate retrieval schemes is usually less important for recognition memory. Experiments by Woodward, Bjork, and Jongeward (1973) provide support for this hypothesis. It was found that greater amounts of maintenance rehearsal did increase recognition memory, despite their having no effects on long-term recall.

Further Explorations of Retrieval-Cue Effectiveness

The preceding discussion suggests that the effectiveness of retrieval cues depends on the types of learning activities performed during acquisition, as is emphasized by the principle of encoding specificity (e.g., Tulving, 1978). In order for a self-generated or experimenter-provided cue to be effective, it must be congruent with information acquired during the initial learning task. For example, *ground* will be an effective cue for *cold* if the words were encoded together during learning, but it will be ineffective if they were not.

We are now in a position to raise additional questions about retrieval-cue effectiveness. In particular, what does it mean to say that words are encoded together? Are there different types of encoding processes that influence the effectiveness of cues? In this context it is useful to reconsider the study by Stein (1977) discussed in Section 2 of this chapter. Remember that he presented students with statements like "A pin is like a nail" and varied the orienting activities used to direct processing of the information. Group 1 focused on the solution to each simile, whereas Group 2 rated the items in the similes according to their relative hardness or softness. Both groups presumably processed the items (like *pin* and *nail*) in relation to one another. Nevertheless, the cued-recall scores for Group 2 were much lower than those for Group 1.

Stein's results suggest that we need a better understanding of notions like "processing two items together" and of encoding processes in general. Noting that a pin and a nail are both relatively hard objects results in low cued-recall scores, whereas understanding a simile like "A pin is like a nail" permits excellent cued-recall performance. Why is this the case? One hypothesis is that the simile prompts a high degree of *elaborative* processing; it prompts one to consider that in addition to being hard objects, a pin and a nail are both relatively small, have sharp points, are made of metal, look somewhat similar, and so on. To consider the relative hardness and softness of the items in the simile, however, is to consider only one relationship. (Remember that the same relationship was considered for the remaining sentences on the acquisition list, too.) This suggests that retrieval-cue effectiveness may depend on the elaborateness of the encodings that people form during the learning task.

The Concept of Elaboration

Many theorists have emphasized the importance of elaborative encoding activities (e.g., Craik and Tulving, 1975; Anderson and Reder, 1978; Bransford, Franks, Morris, and Stein, 1978). An experiment by Craik and Tulving (1975) illustrates some of the evidence used to support this claim. They manipulated elaboration by varying the amount of information expressed in acquisition sentences. For example, participants were asked to state whether a particular target noun (*watch,* for example) fitted into sentence frames that varied in complexity. A relatively simple frame might be "He dropped the _____," and a more complex frame might be "The old man hobbled across the room and picked up the valuable _____ from the mahogany table." Of course, each participant heard each target noun only once.

After acquisition, participants were supplied with the sentence frames originally heard during acquisition and were tested for cued recall of the target nouns. There was an increase in cued-recall accuracy as the complexity or elaborateness of the sentence frames increased. It is important to note, however, that the elaborateness of the sentence frame increased recall only when the target noun was congruous with, or applicable to, the sentence frame. Craik and Tulving also included conditions where the sentence frame and target word were not congruous (e.g., "He dropped the _____: house"), and under these conditions cued recall did not increase with the complexity of the sentence frame. Craik and Tulving therefore argue that target-sentence congruity is an important determinant of retrieval-cue effectiveness: If the target and sentence are congruous, however, cued recall, they argue, will increase as the elaborateness or complexity of the sentence frames increases.

Craik and Tulving's demonstration of elaboration is important. Nevertheless, it is doubtful that elaboration can be equated with the complexity of the information expressed in semantically congruous sentences. Experiments by Stein and Bransford (in preparation; see also Stein, Morris, and Bransford, in press) illustrate this point. They investigated people's retention of target words under three types of acquisition conditions. Group 1 heard a list of *base sentences* like those illustrated in Table 3.1. Note that each of the base sentences is comprehensible and hence semantically consistent, but it is easy to confuse the adjectives during recall. For example, given a retrieval frame like "The _____ man read the newspaper," people have difficulty remembering whether the original adjective was *bald* or *old* or another word.

Groups 2 and 3 heard the base sentences followed by additional, elaborative phrases that were different for each group. For example, Group 2 heard "The tall man bought the crackers *that were on sale*," and Group 3 heard "The tall man bought the crackers *that were on the top shelf*" (see Table 3.1). Note that the elaborative phrases for Groups 2 and 3 both represent semantically congruous continuations of the base sentences. Nevertheless, people's abilities to recall the appropriate adjectives when given the base-sentence frames as retrieval cues (e.g., "The _____ man bought the crackers") were strikingly different. Group 3's cued-recall scores were excellent; those of Group 2, very low.

These results suggest that effective elaboration depends on the quality, rather than the quantity, of semantically congruous information. Stein and his colleagues have also shown that certain types of semantically congruous elaborations of base sentences (e.g., Group 2 in Table 3.1) can actually make recall worse than conditions where people receive the base sentences alone. Effective elaborations, they argue, are those that describe situations in which certain target concepts become especially relevant or nonarbitrary. For example, knowledge that the crackers were on the top shelf helps people understand why being tall is relevant in the context of buying crackers. (In contrast, knowledge that the crackers were on sale is not particularly relevant to the

Table 3.1 Examples of Effective and Ineffective Elaborations

Group 1 Base Sentences	Group 2 Ineffective Elaborators	Group 3 Effective Elaborators
The tall man bought the crackers	that were on sale	that were on the top shelf
The bald man read the newspaper	while eating his breakfast	to look for a hat sale
The old man purchased the paint	from the clerk	to decorate his cane
The short man put up the tent	in order to stay dry	that was two feet high

From Stein and Bransford (in preparation).

concept of tallness.) In other words, retention may be strongly influenced by the degree to which elaborative phrases help people use what they know to understand more precisely the significance of particular concepts; to understand, for example, why tallness is relevant in a particular context. In sum, retrieval-cue effectiveness is strongly influenced by processes of comprehension. This topic will be discussed more fully in Chapters 4 and 5. For present purposes, it is sufficient to note that effective elaboration cannot be equated with the mere quantity of semantically congruous information.

An ingenious series of experiments by Auble and Franks (1978) provides additional insights into elaborative processes. It is easy to assume that supplying learners with cues that permit effective elaboration is the best way to facilitate learning and retention. However, Auble and Franks suggest that initial inability to elaborate can also facilitate recall. They conducted a number of studies to support their argument. Only the essence of their results can be presented here.

A sentence like "The haystack was important because the parachute ripped," is easy to comprehend. As noted in Section 1 of this chapter, a sentence like "The haystack was important because the cloth ripped" is usually not so readily comprehended. Memory for the first sentence will therefore be superior to memory for the second (see Bransford and McCarrell, 1974). Imagine, however, that people hear sentences like the second and then receive the appropriate cue *parachute* five seconds later. This will allow them to comprehend eventually, but not before they have engaged in a process of problem solving. Most of their learning time will thus have been spent in efforts at comprehension. Meanwhile, people hearing sentences like the first may have spent their time in postcomprehension elaborations. Which type of situation will result in better free recall?

Auble and Franks report that efforts toward comprehension (for example, when one hears incomprehensible sentences and then cues five seconds later) result in better free recall than elaborations following comprehension (for example, when one hears readily comprehensible sentences). Provided that learners eventually reach a solution, it appears valuable that they spend their time trying to determine what must be assumed in order for the sentences to make sense. It is possible that people remember their initial attempts at problem solving, and that memory for these processes affords effective schemes for retrieval. In any event, it appears that initial inability to elaborate can be beneficial, provided that obstacles to comprehension are eventually removed.

Summary of Section 3

We reviewed several hypotheses concerning the effectiveness of retrieval cues. The guessing hypothesis was considered unsatisfactory because it predicted too many intrusions during recall. The generation-recognition hypothesis provides a more plausible account of cue effectiveness. Nevertheless, there are reasons for questioning its adequacy as a general account of retrieval. One reason is that cued recall (for example, recall of *cold* when one is given the cue *ground*) can be more effective than recognition (for example, recognition of *cold* when it is presented as a recognition item). (E.g., Tulving and Thomson, 1973.) Since a generation-recognition hypothesis assumes that cues work because they permit one to generate target words (like *cold*) and then recognize them, it has difficulty explaining why the probability of recognizing a target item can be lower than the probability of retrieving it during cued recall (given an appropriate cue like *ground*).

The principle of encoding specificity (e.g., Tulving, 1978) is perhaps the most plausible account of retrieval-cue effectiveness. This principle emphasizes that remembering depends on the degree of overlap between information acquired at the time of acquisition and retrieval information available at time of test. We reviewed several studies indicating that cue effectiveness varied as a function of initial encoding processes. For example, *robin* is an effective cue for *sparrow* only if these concepts were actively interrelated during the acquisition task (e.g., Jacoby, 1974).

We also examined the question of what it means to interrelate actively or to encode information during acquisition. One possibility is that greater degrees of elaboration permit more effective cued recall. However, effective elaboration cannot simply be equated with the amount of semantically congruous information presented during acquisition (e.g., Stein, Morris, and Bransford, in press). Effective elaboration involves the activation of knowledge that helps one realize the unique significance or nonarbitrary nature of target items (such as *tall*) relative to certain activities (such as buying crackers). Questions about effective encoding processes therefore lead us into an examination of processes of comprehension, a topic that will be more fully explored in later chapters. At present, it is useful to turn to some additional implications of our current focus on retrieval processes and remembering.

Section 4: Some Implications of Focusing on Retrieval Processes

The concept of retrieval has several important implications. It has implications for the question of forgetting, for example. We cannot be said to have forgotten something unless we learned it initially; forgetting therefore involves the loss of our ability to do something that we could do earlier. Is forgetting due to changes in previously stored memory traces, due to decay, for example, or to partial erasure? Theoretically, it is possible that everything we have ever experienced is still stored in memory. Perhaps forgetting is simply due to loss of the ability to *retrieve* information that is already stored. What types of factors are responsible for the fact that we do indeed seem to forget? These are some of the questions we shall be considering. We shall also consider the importance of retrieval processes to our understanding of learning activities.

Interference Theories of Forgetting

One of the best-known theories of forgetting is *interference theory* (e.g., see Postman and Underwood, 1973). A basic assumption of the theory is that learning additional information can interfere with the ability to remember information that was previously acquired. In Chapter 2, Section 3, we discussed interference theories as part of our treatment of short-term retention. Similar theories seem to be applicable to long-term retention.

Table 3.2	A Paradigm for Studying Retroactive Interference		
Experimental Group:	Learn A	Learn B	Test A
Control Group:	Learn A	No new learning	Test A

Jenkins and Dallenbach (1924) conducted a classic study of interference. All participants learned a list of nonsense syllables, like *FUB, TOL, TEZ*. One group then carried out their normal activities of the day, while the remainder went to sleep. The ability to recall what had been learned was then tested at one-, two-, four-, or eight-hour intervals. The results indicated that less forgetting occurred under conditions of sleep, suggesting that those participants who went about their everyday activities were more likely to encounter and learn new sets of information that interfered with what they had previously learned.

As noted in Chapter 2, interference theorists distinguish between two general types of interference: retroactive and proactive. The Jenkins and Dallenbach (1924) study investigated retroactive interference. Information learned after initial acquisition interfered with the ability of people to remember what they had learned. Table 3.2 schematizes the general form of a retroactive interference study. The purpose is to compare the performance of the experimental group with that of the control group in order to examine the interference effects of the intervening tasks. The design for studying proactive interference is outlined in Table 3.3. Proactive interference is the interference of previously learned information with one's ability to remember new information. Note that the issue is not whether previously acquired information interferes with the initial speed of learning subsequent inputs, but how it interferes with the ability to remember. The experimental group (see Table 3.3) might learn a set of inputs (A) as quickly as the control group, yet the prior learning of the experimental group may later cause interference and hence increase the extent to which forgetting takes place.

Studies by Underwood (1948a, 1948b, 1949) illustrate the importance of the concept of proactive interference. He noted that Ebbinghaus (1885), the psychologist who conducted memory studies on himself, reported forgetting about 65 percent of the materials (nonsense syllables) he had learned twenty-four hours earlier. In contrast, Underwood noted that a typical college student in his laboratory forgot only 20 percent of the nonsense syllables after twenty-four hours. Ebbinghaus had had a great deal of practice in learning nonsense syllables, whereas Underwood's college students had had almost none. Was Ebbinghaus simply unusually forgetful? Underwood hypothesized that memory may actually be hampered by having previously learned a number of lists in a laboratory context. Underwood (1964) tested his hypothesis in the following manner:

Table 3.3	A Paradigm for Studying Proactive Interference		
Experimental group:	Learn B	Learn A	Test A
Control group:	No particular learning task	Learn A	Test A

We give the subject a second list to learn and test him on this list 24 hours later. This time his performance is not quite so good as it was in [the first list]: he forgets more than 20 percent. We go on in the same way with a third list, a fourth, a fifth and so on up to 20 lists. Plotting his successive performances on a graph, we find a startlingly sharp rise in his rate of forgetting. . . . In the case of the 20th list, 24 hours after learning it he has forgotten 80 percent of the items. (P. 5)

In short, Underwood found evidence for proactive interference; prior learning can decrease people's abilities to remember a subsequent list. Note again that this prior learning need not decrease the speed with which people can learn the acquisition lists (e.g., see Jenkins, 1974a), but it does affect the probability of their forgetting these lists.

How Does Interference Occur?

Experimental demonstrations showing *that* interference occurs do not necessarily indicate *how* it occurs. Suppose you learn a list containing the sentence "A ladder can be used as a bookshelf." You then learn a number of subsequent lists, each containing different sentences about a ladder (for example, "A ladder can be used for firewood"). The act of learning the subsequent sentences may interfere with your ability to recall the first sentence when you are given the cue *ladder*. What is the cause of this interference? Did learning the subsequent sentences about a ladder degrade or erase the memory trace of the earlier sentence? Or is it possible that the memory trace of this sentence is still intact but cannot now be retrieved? Interference could operate by hindering retrieval rather than by actually erasing traces that were previously stored.

Tulving and Psotka (1971) explored the degree to which forgetting might depend on retrieval failures. They constructed lists of twenty-four words. Each list contained six conceptual categories with four words per category. One of the lists was as follows:

Hut, cottage, tent, hotel

Cliff, river, hill, volcano

Captain, corporal, sergeant, colonel

Ant, wasp, beetle, mosquito

Zinc, copper, aluminum, bronze

Drill, saw, chisel, nail

The words in the same category were always grouped together in order to make the conceptual categories quite clear. All participants in the experiment learned an initial target list of twenty-four words. They read the word list three times, after which they recalled as many of the words as they could. This provided a measure of original learning. Some of the participants were then required to learn one additional list; others, two additional lists; others, three; others, four; and the remainder, five. What effect

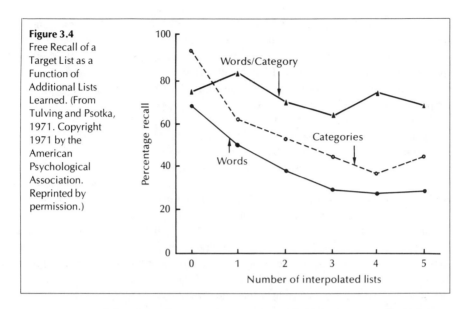

Figure 3.4 Free Recall of a Target List as a Function of Additional Lists Learned. (From Tulving and Psotka, 1971. Copyright 1971 by the American Psychological Association. Reprinted by permission.)

should these additional lists have had on the ability of the subjects to recall the original, target list they had learned? According to assumptions about retroactive interference, the greater the number of additional lists, the greater the interference that should occur. Figure 3.4 illustrates the results of Tulving and Psotka's (1971) study. The average number of words recalled from the original, target list decreased as a function of the number of subsequent lists learned. These data are consistent with expectations about retroactive interference. Did learning the subsequent lists change or degrade the actual memory traces of the target list, or did it decrease the probability that this information could be retrieved under conditions of free recall?

Tulving and Psotka sought to answer the preceding questions by means of a second test that differed from the first insofar as it supplied participants with category retrieval cues appropriate to the target list. Category cues for the sample list noted above were as follows: *types of buildings, earth formations, military titles, insects, metals, and carpenter's tools*. When these cues were supplied, even those people who had learned five additional lists did extremely well at recalling the target list. The number of additional lists learned hurt cued recall of the target list slightly, but the differences were small. Tulving and Psotka's results suggest that forgetting took place because of the lack of appropriate information in the retrieval environment rather than some change in, or degradation of, the memory traces. Although it is possible, of course, that traces can be changed by certain activities, it should be stressed that at least some forgetting is to be explained by the lack of information adequate to retrieve what has been learned.

Learning to Create Retrieval Schemes

The concept of retrieval also has implications for understanding the nature of acquisition activities that facilitate retention. We have already seen how certain learning activities may or may not be valuable depending on the type of testing or retrieval environment (e.g., see Section 2 of this chapter). Effective learners must therefore learn how to select learning strategies appropriate to the type of test they expect. There is evidence that college students study differently when they expect tests of recognition rather than recall (e.g., Tversky, 1973). Nevertheless, even college students can be helped to improve their learning activities.

An experiment by Wilson and Bransford (unpublished) provides an illustration of the preceding argument. They presented different groups of college students with a list of thirty unrelated nouns to be recalled. Group 1 were told that they would be asked to free-recall the nouns, so that one would expect them to use their "best" learning strategies. Groups 2 and 3 did not know about the memory test and therefore acquired the list incidentally rather than intentionally. As shown in Chapter 2, Section 4, certain types of incidental orienting tasks can result in free-recall scores that are as good as those resulting from intentional memory conditions (e.g., see the results of the Hyde and Jenkins study in Table 2.3). Wilson and Bransford used two types of incidental orienting tasks. The task of Group 2 involved rating each word according to its pleasantness or unpleasantness. This is one of the tasks used by Hyde and Jenkins (1969), and it was assumed that the task would enable Group 2 to exhibit recall scores equivalent to those of Group 1 (the intentional group). For Group 3 Wilson and Bransford tried to design an orienting task that would actually result in better recall than that achieved by the intentional group. Group 3 were asked to rate whether each word represented something that would be "important or unimportant" if they were stranded on a deserted island. Note that information about a deserted island provides a unifying theme or contextual structure that can facilitate organization and hence retrieval. People in this third group may therefore exhibit superior recall.

The results of the experiment were as expected. Students in Groups 1 and 2 showed equivalent levels of recall, but they remembered fewer words than students in Group 3. In short, incidental learning (Group 3) can sometimes be superior to intentional learning (Group 1). These results suggest that many college students in the intentional group did not know how to optimize their learning processes in ways that facilitate subsequent retrieval. Even among college students there appears to be much room for improvement of learning and retrieval skills.

An experiment by Hogan and Kintsch (1971) provides further information about the types of learning experiences that facilitate subsequent retrieval. Two groups of students were presented with a list of forty words. Those in Group 1 heard the list four times and

Table 3.4   The Effects of Study and Test Trials on Recall versus Recognition

Session 1						Session 2 (48 hr later)	
Group 1:	Study	Study	Study	Study	Recall 15.6	Recall 8.2	Recognition 34.0
Group 2:	Study	Recall	Recall	Recall	Recall 12.0	Recall 8.2	Recognition 30.4

From Hogan and Kintsch (1971). Used by permission.

then were asked to recall. Their recall scores averaged 15.6 items. When tested again after forty-eight hours, they recalled an average of 8.2 items. The degree of forgetting was therefore 47 percent. Group 2 heard the forty words only once. They then practiced recalling the words for four more trials (but never again were presented with the words). On the fourth trial their recall scores averaged 12 words. After a forty-eight-hour interval they, too, recalled an average of 8.2 words, so that they had forgotten only 32 percent of the information they had originally learned (compared with 47 percent for Group 1). These results suggest that practice at recall helps people establish retrieval schemes that are less likely to be forgotten. The results of the Hogan and Kintsch experiment are illustrated in Table 3.4.

Hogan and Kintsch (1971) also presented both groups of students with a recognition test after the forty-eight-hour interval. Group 1 correctly recognized an average of 34 words, and Group 2 an average of 30.4 (see Table 3.4). This time the score for Group 1 was consistent with their having initially learned more than Group 2. Remember, however, that recognition does not usually require so elaborate a retrieval scheme as free recall. Group 2 had received more practice at recall and hence showed evidence of less forgetting in the delayed-recall test.

Summary of Section 4

The purpose of this section was to consider some implications of retrieval processes; first, for questions regarding the nature of forgetting. It seems clear that we all forget things that were previously learned (our phone numbers from previous dwellings, for instance) and that forgetting is partially due to additional information we have learned (we have acquired new phone numbers). It is reasonable to assume, then, that forgetting is frequently due to interference, but even this assumption remains ambiguous. Does interference involve erasure of previously stored memory traces, or does it involve changes in the retrieval environments necessary to reactivate previously acquired information? The experiments by Tulving and Psotka (1971) suggest that at least some forgetting is due to retrieval failures. For example, people may prove forgetful under conditions of free recall and yet be able to remember when provided with appropriate retrieval cues.

An emphasis on retrieval processes also has implications for understanding learning activities. In many types of situations, it is not sufficient simply to process each item to be learned at a deep, semantic level (e.g., see Chapter 2, Section 4); it is necessary to interrelate items and form effective retrieval schemes. Even college students do not necessarily know how to do this efficiently. For example, incidental orienting tasks that prompt people to consider items from a common thematic perspective (for example, that of a deserted island) can result in better recall than intentional learning tasks. Practice in retrieving information may also reduce the amount of forgetting that occurs when free recall is tested after an interval of several days (Hogan and Kintsch, 1971). One can imagine students' reviewing for a forthcoming essay test by rereading the material rather than by attempting to recall it on their own. Hogan and Kintsch's data suggest that the latter type of activity may be more beneficial.

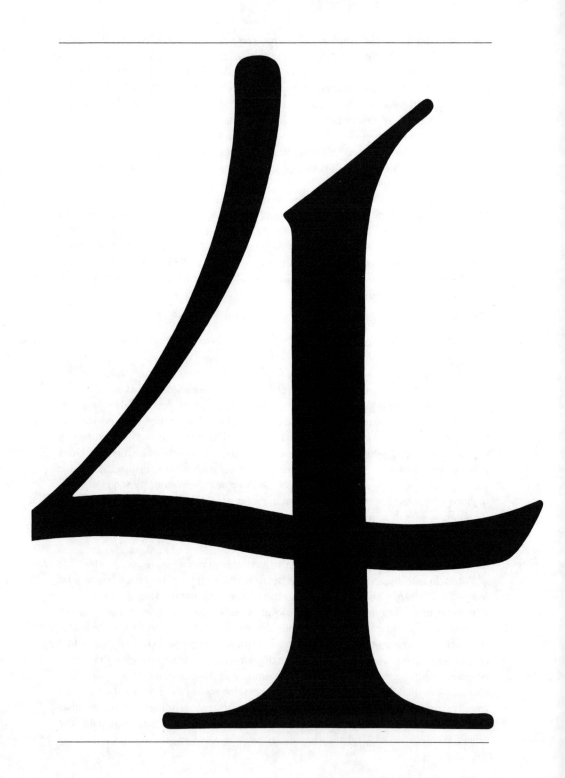

Chapter 4
Analyzing the Nature of
Learning Materials

The experiments discussed in Chapters 2 and 3 utilized sets of materials like word lists, sentences, and pictures, which recipients were asked to learn, understand, and remember. The goal of the present chapter is to analyze the nature of these materials more carefully. As we shall see, people's abilities to learn and remember are strongly influenced by the nature of the materials presented (see Figure 1.1).

Overview

Section 1 discusses *properties of individual items* that influence the ease of learning and retention. Variables like meaningfulness, imagery, and frequency of occurrence will be explored. These variables will be shown to have important influences on learning and memory tasks.

Section 2 explores *the nature of linguistic structures*. Most of the linguistic information we encounter is in the form of sentences, rather than word lists, and it is therefore important to understand the structure of sentences. There are various levels of sentential structure, which have important influences on people's abilities to understand, as well as to remember, what was learned.

In Section 3 we examine the question of *learning from sets of semantically related sentences*. Some types of texts are easier to learn than others, and some parts of texts are more likely to be remembered than others. It is therefore important to analyze the types of text structures that facilitate comprehension and recall.

Section 4 focuses on *some implications of analyzing the nature of materials*. For example, some theorists try to predict the readability of various materials so that they can be geared to the current level of knowledge and skills of the learner (a text of college-level readability is not appropriate for third-graders). Other theorists try to assess people's abilities by seeing how they perform given certain types of materials. Unless we have a better understanding of the structure of materials and the way they influence learning, it is easy to reach erroneous conclusions about what people can and cannot do.

Section 1: Properties
of Individual Items

It probably seems obvious that some things are easier to learn and remember than others. In this section, we examine several hypotheses about properties of individual items (words, for example) that make them easy or difficult to retain. In their classic book on verbal learning and memory, Underwood and Schultz (1960) emphasize the importance of this problem:

> The central empirical problem of our work can be illustrated very simply. If we construct one list made up of items such as GIZ and QZD, and another of such items as CAT and IBM, why is the second list learned so much more rapidly than the first? If a layman is asked this question, he may be insulted because of the obviousness of the answer, for he will say that the second list is learned more rapidly than the first because it is made up of more meaningful items than the first. Yet, in spite of the dimension per se being obvious, just how the characteristics of attributes which make up or are associated with this dimension, and which make it so obvious—just how they lead to such large differences in learning is not so easy to "come by." At least, we have not found it so. (Pp. 4–5)

Underwood and Schultz (1960) note that the meaningfulness of items facilitates and accelerates learning. They are not satisfied with this level of analysis, however. To fully understand meaningfulness, we need to know *why* items are meaningful and devise ways to measure this variable. One way of measuring meaningfulness is described below.

Measuring Meaningfulness

How can one measure the meaningfulness of items? For example, what differentiates the meaningfulness of items like *gojey* and *kitchen*? Intuitively one would say that the meaningful item *kitchen* is more readily relatable to other aspects of one's knowledge than is the less meaningful item *gojey*. In 1952 the psychologist Noble proposed the following measure for the meaningfulness of items: Present people with stimulus items (like *kitchen, gojey*) and ask them to generate as many verbal responses (additional words) to these items as they can within a specified time (for example, one minute). He reasoned that the greater the number of responses one could generate, the more meaningful an item should be. Table 4.1 illustrates some of Noble's meaningfulness ratings (M-values) for a list of words.

It is one thing to claim that a certain procedure measures meaningfulness; how can one test the validity of the claim? The first step is to measure the reliability of the procedure. Suppose that two groups of people are presented with identical sets of words and asked to generate responses to them for one minute per word. Will the resulting meaningfulness ratings of these two groups correlate positively with each other? For example, will both groups exhibit low measures for *gojey*, medium measures for *pallet*, high measures for *kitchen*? Studies indicate that Noble's procedure produces a very high degree of reliability (e.g., Noble and McNeely, 1957). The second step in clarifying Noble's measure is to ask whether the variable of meaningfulness (as measured by Noble) actually affects the speed and ease of learning. Will a list of highly meaningful words, for example, be learned more easily than a list of moderately meaningful words?

An experiment by Cieutat, Stockwell, and Noble (1958) utilized lists composed of pairs of stimuli such as *chair-rock*. The test, a cued-recall test, consisted of presenting people with the first member of each pair (*chair*) and asking them to recall the second member (*rock*). (A common name for this procedure is *paired-associate* learning, where the first word in each pair is considered the *stimulus* item and the second is considered the *response*.) The critical aspect of the study was the way in which the experimenters manipulated meaningfulness of the stimulus and response items, meaningfulness (hereafter abbreviated M) being defined according to Noble's (1952) norms. One list consisted of pairs whose stimulus and response items were both high in M (high-high pairs). A second list consisted of pairs whose stimulus and response items were both low in M (low-low pairs). A third list was composed of low-high pairs, and a fourth of high-low pairs.

Results indicated that M affected the speed and ease of learning. The high-high pairs were learned best, and the low-low pairs worst. The low-high pairs were second easiest to learn, and high-low pairs were third. This suggests that M has stronger effects on the *response* side than on the stimulus side. If you consider that one has to generate the response but need only recognize the stimulus, these results are understandable. When

Table 4.1   An Illustration of Meaningfulness Ratings

M-Value	Word
0.99	Gojey
1.26	Quipson
1.54	Icon
1.84	Tumbril
2.26	Carom
2.73	Rostrum
3.62	Pallet
5.33	Fatigue
6.57	Uncle
7.91	Heaven
8.98	Money
9.61	Kitchen

After Noble (1952).

you have to generate something, meaningfulness (M) seems to play an especially important role.

Note that the effects of meaningfulness depend on how learners process the words at time of acquisition (see Chapter 2). An experiment by Seamon and Murray (1976) illustrates this point. They varied the meaningfulness (M) value of the words in an acquisition list as well as the types of acquisition activities that learners were asked to perform. People in Group 1 were asked to attend to word meanings, and those in Group 2 to attend to the position of their lips while they vocalized each input. Overall, Group 1 recalled more words than Group 2. Furthermore, Group 1 recalled more high-M than low-M words. In contrast, the meaningfulness of the words had no effect on the recall scores of people in Group 2.

Imagery and Learning

In 1971, Alan Paivio published a very provocative book that dealt with variables affecting the ease of learning and remembering. He proposed that the ability to create *images* of words affects the ease with which they can be learned and remembered. What types of evidence could be used to support such a claim? Clearly, one of the first things Paivio needed was some measure of the ease and speed with which particular words evoked concrete images. One of his procedures was to ask people to rate words on a seven-point scale. A score of 7 would indicate that a word was extremely easy to image, a score of 1 that it was difficult to image. Table 4.2 illustrates imagery values for some of the words listed in the Paivio, Yuille, and Madigan (1968) norms.

Given appropriate norms, Paivio was able to assess the degree to which imagery affected learning and remembering. In one study (Paivio, Smythe, and Yuille, 1968), Paivio and his coworkers adopted a procedure similar to that used by Noble and his colleagues. Lists of paired associates were varied in terms of high or low levels of imagery for both the stimulus and response members. Thus, different lists included high-high, high-low, low-high, and low-low pairs. Results were as follows: high-high better than high-low better than low-high better than low-low. Note in particular that high-low pairs were better remembered than low-high pairs. This contrasts with Cieutat, Stockwell, and Noble's (1958) findings for M-rated pairs, that low-high pairs were better remembered than high-low pairs. According to Paivio (1971) images are especially easily retrieved and serve as conceptual pegs to which one can more easily attach response items. With regard to imagery, he predicts that high-low pairs will produce better cued recall than low-high pairs.

To explain why imagery facilitates retention, Paivio (e.g., 1971, 1975, 1976) proposes a *dual-code theory*, which postulates two separate but interconnected memory systems. One system is verbal in nature, and the other system is visual. A word like *alligator* that evokes images can be stored both verbally and visually; a word like *agreement* that does not so readily suggest an image will be stored only verbally. If people have two codes for information (verbal plus visual) rather than one, retention should be enhanced. Many people have questioned the adequacy of Paivio's dual-code theory (e.g., Anderson, 1976; Anderson and Bower, 1973; Friedman, in press; Kintsch, 1976; Pylyshyn, 1973), and these criticisms will be discussed in Chapter 6. For present purposes it is important to note that the imagery value of words does have powerful

Table 4.2   An Illustration of Imagery Ratings

Noun	Mean Imagery Rating
Abasement	2.03
Abbess	2.97
Abdication	3.57
Abdomen	6.00
Abduction	4.93
Aberration	2.27
Ability	2.67
Abode	5.07
Abyss	5.17
Accordion	6.50
Acrobat	6.53
Adage	2.77
Admiral	6.20
Advantage	2.37
Adversity	2.80
Advice	3.13
Affection	4.87
Afterlife	2.40
Agility	4.57
Agony	5.43
Agreement	3.33
Air	4.17
Alcohol	6.47
Algebra	5.17
Alimony	4.47
Allegory	2.13
Alligator	6.87
Amazement	4.47

After Paivio, Yuille, and Madigan (1968).

effects on retention. Most people accept Paivio's findings, even though some question the adequacy of the theory that he uses to explain these data.

Additional Variables That
Affect Learning and Memory

Clearly, meaningfulness and imagery are not the only variables that might affect the ease of learning and remembering. For example, Carroll and White (1973) suggest that the age at which you acquired particular words is a powerful predictor of remembering. They asked people to state the age at which they felt they had first learned certain concepts (and compare, for example, the ages at which they had learned *cup* and *atom*). Those words learned earliest appear to be easier to remember in a typical learning and memory test.

One might also hypothesize that the frequency of previous experience with words is an important variable underlying learning (e.g., see Underwood and Schultz, 1960). Indeed, the frequency of usage of items correlates with meaningfulness, imagery, age of acquisition, and so forth. Of course, our discussion in Chapter 2 indicated that frequency of exposure is not sufficient to guarantee learning. People must actively process information in order to benefit from particular types of exposure. Nevertheless, the greater the frequency of exposure, the higher the probability that they will have actively attended to and processed such inputs in appropriate ways.

A number of experiments illustrate the importance of the frequency of prior experience. In the following experiment imagine that words are flashed on a screen for fractions of a second. Your task is to attempt to read each word. You will be able to read high frequency words more readily than low frequency words (e.g., Solomon and Postman, 1952). It is unclear whether high frequency words are actually more easily *perceived* or whether one is more likely to respond with high frequency words (e.g., Goldiamond and Hawkins, 1958; Massaro, 1975). Whatever the mechanisms, it seems clear that frequency of prior exposure can facilitate performance. The importance of frequency was also evident in our discussion of automaticity (see Chapter 2).

Frequency of prior experience also affects the ability to remember. For example, high frequency words like *boy* and *tree* are more readily recalled than low frequency words like *aardvark* and *kumquat* (e.g., Bousfield and Cohen, 1955; Hall, 1954). However, assume that people receive a long list composed of high and low frequency words and are then tested for *recognition*. Under these conditions low frequency words are often recognized better than high frequency words (e.g., Shepard, 1967; Gorman, 1961; Kinsbourne and George, 1974). If this seems puzzling, consider the fact that recognition memory tests ask people whether a particular word occurred in the context of the experiment. One must distinguish this occurrence from other occurrences of the word prior to the experiment. As Gough (1977) notes, high frequency words are likely to have occurred more recently. Given a recognition test, we may be able to differentiate the occurrence of low frequency words in the test from earlier occurrences more easily than we can differentiate the occurrence of high frequency words.

The Problem of Correlations
among Stimulus Properties

We have shown that meaningfulness, imagery, and frequency influence learning and remembering. We have also noted that such variables are positively correlated. Words rated higher in meaningfulness also tend to be more readily imaged, learned at an earlier age, more frequent. If we find that high-M words are easier to learn than low-M words, how do we know that this is due to meaningfulness rather than frequency or imagery or both?

Christian, Bickley, Tarka, and Clayton (1978) obtained measures of free recall for each of 900 nouns in the Paivio, Yuille, and Madigan (1968) norms. They did this, not by presenting people with 900 nouns and asking for free recall, but by asking individual participants to recall lists of 25 nouns, different participants receiving different lists. By obtaining measures from a large number of lists and people, it was possible to obtain estimates of the recallability of each of the 900 nouns. The experimenters were then able to assess the degree to which recallability was influenced by such variables as meaningfulness, imagery, frequency. They estimated the effects of each variable, such as meaningfulness, independent of the effects of the other variables, such as imagery and frequency. (They did so by means of a statistical technique called partial correlation; for the details of this technique, see, for example, Kirk, 1968.)

The results were as follows. Frequency and imagery were approximately equal in their influence on free recall. (Frequency was measured by the Thorndike-Lorge, 1944, frequency count as well as the more recent Kucera and Francis, 1967, norms.) Meaningfulness, however, (measured by means of Noble's procedure) was essentially unrelated to recall (see also Paivio and Smythe, 1971). The effects of meaningfulness shown by previous studies may therefore have been due to imagery, frequency, or some combination of these and additional variables. Christian and colleagues also note that a great deal of recall performance is *not* accounted for by frequency or imagery. Additional factors must also be operating. Some of these factors will become apparent in Section 2.

Summary of Section 1

The purpose of this section was to ask why some items are easier to learn and retain than others. This is an important question because our answers can be used to design instructional materials that are easier for people to learn (we shall discuss this issue in Section 4). The major variables discussed were meaningfulness, imagery, and word frequency. When measured and tested individually, each of these variables has important effects on retention. Nevertheless, the variables are to a large extent correlated with one another; for example, words with high meaningfulness values tend also to have high values in terms of imagery and frequency. Christian and colleagues (1978) find that imagery and frequency appear to be more important than meaningfulness. These authors also suggest that additional variables must be operating, because imagery and frequency are only partially related to retention. Some of these variables are discussed in Section 2.

Section 2: The Nature of Linguistic Structures

Our discussion in Section 1 centered on the question of why some items (individual words, for example) are easier to learn and retain than others. Variables like meaningfulness, imagery and frequency of usage were presented as potential explanations for differences in the ease of learning. Note, however, that in everyday life we often encounter words that are structured to form sentences and paragraphs. To what extent do these structures affect our ability to learn and remember?

An Illustration of Linguistic Structures

One way to appreciate the importance of structure is to consider the following word strings.* Read them once and then try to recall them. Please begin now.

1. That that is is not that that is not is that it it is

2. Mary where Jane had had had had had had had had had had had the teacher's approval

Most people find it very difficult to recall these two word strings. In the second example, many readers have to count the number of *hads* in order to achieve accurate recall. It is instructive to try to read each word list aloud. To what extent does your reading reflect normal sentence intonation and rhythm? Many people sound as if they are reading word by word.

The word strings can be structured into sentential units. It is easiest to demonstrate this for the first. The use of appropriate punctuation can facilitate apprehension of its linguistic structure: "That that is, is not that that is not. Is that it? It is!"

The potential structure of List 2 is more difficult. If you fail to grasp it at first, don't give up. Imagine a situation where Mary and Jane are taking an English grammar test. They are asked to fill in the blank with the correct word or words. Mary fills in the blank with the words *had had,* but Jane fills it with *had.* The first part of the word string can therefore be paraphrased as follows: "Mary, where Jane had written the word *had,* wrote the words *had had.*" This idea can be stated as follows: "Mary, where Jane had had *had,* had had *had had.*" Work on this until it makes sense.

The second part of this word string has to do with the correctness of Mary's and Jane's answers. Mary had written the words *had had,* and the answer "had had" was correct. In short, the answer "had had" had received the teacher's approval (*had had* had had the teacher's approval). Now put the two parts of the word string together: "Mary, where Jane had had *had* had had *had had; had had* had had the teacher's approval." It may take some work to reach the point where you can perceive this structure. Once you do, however, the second word string, like the first, will seem organized and coherent. Intuitively, this should facilitate your retention. Note also that it changes your sentence intonation and rhythm when you read the lists.

---

*These examples were common "lab lore" when I was a graduate student at the University of Minnesota. Someone must have invented them, but I do not know who.

Some Effects of Linguistic Structure

A number of experiments demonstrate that linguistic structure has powerful effects on learning and retention. A classic study by Miller and Selfridge (1950) represents an excellent case in point. They manipulated the degree to which lists of words approximated the kinds of structures found in normal English. For example, imagine constructing a list of thirty words by randomly selecting them from a dictionary. This would represent a zero-order approximation to English. A first-order approximation might involve randomly selecting words from a popular book or magazine. Note that unlike a dictionary, popular books and magazines use individual words more than once and tend to include a greater number of high frequency words. Therefore a first-order approximation will include more frequently used words.

To construct a second-order approximation to English, imagine presenting someone with a single word (for example, *ever*) and asking that person to generate a subsequent word (the person might say *more*). A different person is then given the word *more* and asked to generate another word (*food,* perhaps). This procedure is continued, each person seeing only the preceding word and generating another. In this way, one can construct a second-order list.

Miller and Selfridge also used lists of third-, fourth-, fifth-, sixth-, and seventh-order approximations. To construct a third-order list, people see two previous words and generate another; for a fifth-order list each person sees four previous words and then adds his or her own. The following word strings (from Miller and Selfridge, 1950) are ten-word lists of varying orders of approximation to English.* Miller and Selfridge read individual lists like these to groups of people and then asked for immediate recall. People recalled a greater number of words as the lists' approximation to English increased.

Zero-Order Approximation:	By way consequence handsomely financier flux cavalry swiftness weatherbeaten extent
First-Order Approximation:	Abilities with that beside I for waltz you the sewing
Second-Order Approximation:	Was he went to the newspaper is in deep and
Third-Order Approximation:	Tall and thin boy is a biped is the beat
Fourth-Order Approximation:	Saw the football game will end at midnight on January
Fifth-Order Approximation:	They saw the play Saturday and sat down beside him
Seventh-Order Approximation:	Recognize her abilities in music after he scolded him before

---

*G. A. Miller and J. A. Selfridge, "Verbal context and the recall of meaningful material," *The American Journal of Psychology,* 63 (1950), 176–85. Reprinted by permission of The University of Illinois Press and the author.

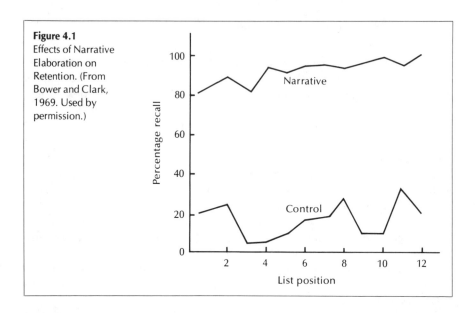

Figure 4.1
Effects of Narrative Elaboration on Retention. (From Bower and Clark, 1969. Used by permission.)

Experiments by Bower and Clark (1969) provide additional evidence for the importance of linguistic structure. In their experiment, twelve lists, each of ten words, were presented to two groups of students. Those in Group 1 were simply told to study the first list until they had learned it. They recalled the first list and then proceeded to the second, recalled the second and then studied the third, and so forth. Students in Group 2 went through the same study-test procedure, but they were instructed to make up stories that linked the individual words. Given words like *dinner, nerve, teacher,* for example, they might generate a sentence like "One night at *dinner,* I had the *nerve* to bring my *teacher.*" This sentence might then be linked to others that elaborated additional words. Both groups of students were able to recall each list right after they had studied it. The important data are the measurements of the students' abilities to go back and recall all twelve lists after completion of the experiment. Figure 4.1 illustrates the results of the experiment. The advantage for the narrative group (Group 2) is clear.

Note that Bower and Clark's results may help clarify discussion in Section 1 of this chapter. Christian, Bickley, Tarka, and Clayton (1978) showed that the frequency and imagery value of individual words predicted recall to some extent. Nevertheless, they noted that there was still a great deal of variability to be accounted for. Remember that they presented people with lists of words yet tried to predict recall on the basis of individual word properties. If some people spontaneously formed sentences linking particular words, this might facilitate recall, but this could not be predicted on the basis of the individual words. Note, for example, that all participants in the Bower and Clark experiment received the same set of target words (hence the words would be equated in terms of frequency, imagery, and so on). Nevertheless, there were large differences between the narrative and nonnarrative groups. This suggests that the ability to form linguistically appropriate structures is also an important determinant of recall.

Exploring the Nature
of Linguistic Structure

The preceding studies illustrate that linguistic structure has powerful effects on learning and retention. However, what does the term *linguistic structure* suggest? One might assume that perceptions of appropriate linguistic structures are based on the frequency with which certain words have followed one another in previously encountered sentences. For example, a word string like *John is a mystery* seems linguistically appropriate. In contrast, *John was is a mystery* sounds like a medium-order approximation to English. Perhaps the word string seems ungrammatical because the word *is* rarely follows the word *was* in English speech. Consider the following sentence, " 'Wherever John was is a mystery to me,' said Sally." This sentence seems perfectly grammatical. Note, however, that it too contains the word *is* preceded by *was*. Judgments of grammaticality cannot simply be based on the probability of one word following another. Something else must be involved.

The linguist Noam Chomsky (1957, 1965, 1972, 1975) has greatly influenced the way people think about linguistic structure. He argues that one's knowledge of language could not possibly be equivalent to word-by-word or even phrase-by-phrase probabilities based on prior frequencies of experience. For example, a string of words like *colorless green ideas sleep furiously* makes little sense, but it is clearly more grammatically acceptable than a string like *furiously sleep ideas green colorless*. You have probably never encountered either of the foregoing sentences unless you are familiar with the linguistics literature, but you can nevertheless make judgments about linguistic grammaticality. Similarly, you can make sense of *the two-headed horse sipped mint juleps from a straw while dangling from a rope tied to the moon* despite the novelty of the situation. Chomsky argues that one of the most important aspects of linguistic knowledge is that it is *generative*. We can understand an unlimited number of "novel but linguistically appropriate" sentences. The goal of a theory of language is to explain how we can accomplish such a seemingly miraculous feat.

Some Illustrations
of Linguistic Structure

It is impossible to do justice to theories of language within the space of a single chapter. More detailed discussion can be found in Chomsky (1975); Clark and Clark (1977); Foss and Hakes (1978); Glucksberg and Danks (1975); Langacker (1967), Palermo (1978). Our present goal is to discuss reasons why a concern with linguistic structure is important for understanding how people learn and comprehend.

Consider the sentences "They are flying planes" and "They are eating apples." These sentences are structurally ambiguous. For example, the first sentence can refer to people who are doing the flying or the flying planes. One task of an adequate theory of language is to characterize the nature of ambiguities such as this. For example, linguistic theories assign *structural descriptions* to sentences that reflect the organizational structure of various constituents. Ambiguous sentences therefore require more than one

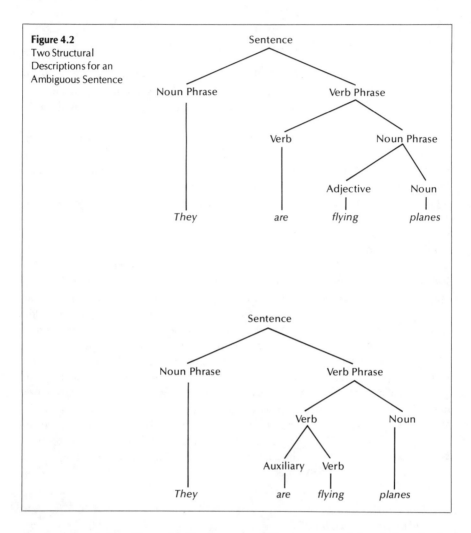

Figure 4.2
Two Structural Descriptions for an Ambiguous Sentence

structural description. Figure 4.2 illustrates two different structural descriptions for the ambiguous sentence "They are flying planes."

Experiments by Johnson (1965) illustrate how the organizational structure of sentences can affect retention. He presented people with sentences like "The tall boy saved the dying woman," "The house across the street is burning," and measured recall. Johnson reasoned that most recall errors would occur between, rather than within, major syntactic units in the organizational structure of the sentences. Figure 4.3 illustrates simplified structural descriptions for the sentences noted above. Note that the major syntactic break for "The tall boy saved the dying woman" occurs between the noun phrase and verb phrase (between *boy* and *saved*). Johnson assumed that the highest percentage of errors occurs between syntactic breaks like this. He therefore measured the probability that people could recall the next word in a sentence given that they

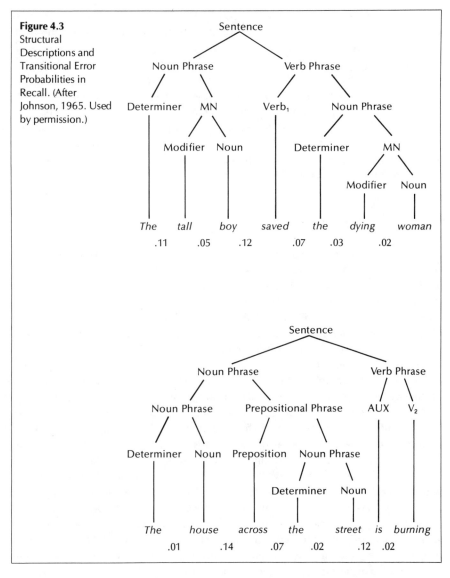

Figure 4.3 Structural Descriptions and Transitional Error Probabilities in Recall. (After Johnson, 1965. Used by permission.)

recalled the preceding word. The probability of a failure to recall the next word is called the transitional error probability (TEP). For the "tall boy" sentence, the highest TEP was indeed between *boy* and *saved* (12 percent). In contrast, the TEP between *dying* and *woman* (which represent a closely knit syntactic unit) was only 2 percent (see Figure 4.3). Note that the TEP between *The* and *tall* is higher than would be predicted from the syntactic structure illustrated in Figure 4.3. One reason is probably that the concept of tallness is not particularly relevant to the rest of the sentence, and this is why people had difficulty remembering the correct adjective. In Chapter 3, Section 3, our discussion of effective elaboration emphasized the importance of understanding nonarbitrary relationships between concepts and the contexts in which they occur. Viewed in this light, Johnson's sentence is like the sentence "The tall man bought the crackers that were on sale" in Chapter 3.

Johnson's sentence about the house (Figure 4.3) has a somewhat different organizational structure. Major syntactic breaks occur between *street* and *is* (transition from noun phrase to verb phrase) and *house* and *across* (transition from noun phrase to prepositional phrase). The TEPs for these transitions were 12 percent and 14 percent respectively. In contrast, TEPs between *the* and *street* as well as *is* and *burning* were only 2 percent. In general, Johnson's data support the hypothesis that the organizational structure of sentences has important effects on recall.

Levels of Linguistic Structure

Our previous discussion of structural descriptions has emphasized only one level of linguistic structure, namely, the *surface structure* of sentences. Another important aspect of linguistic structure is the *deep structure* (cf. Chomsky, 1957, 1965), or *conceptual structure* (cf. Langacker, 1967), of sentences. Sets of sentences can have similar surface structures, yet very different conceptual structures. Conversely, some sentences can have dissimilar surface structures, yet similar conceptual structures. Relations between surface structures and conceptual structures are discussed below.

Consider the sentences "John is eager to please" versus "John is easy to please," examples given by Chomsky. These sentences have similar surface structures; they both contain an initial proper noun followed by a verb (*is*), an adjective (*easy, eager*), and so forth. Nevertheless, the deep or conceptual structures underlying these two sentences are quite distinct. As a speaker of English, you in some sense know that *John* is the logical subject in "John is eager to please" (it is John who does the pleasing). In contrast, *John* is the logical object in the sentence "John is easy to please" (other people please John). In other words, it is appropriate to say "It is easy to please John" but not "It is eager to please John." Sentences like "John is eager to please" and "John is easy to please" therefore illustrate similar surface structure but distinct conceptual structure. On the other hand, sentences like "John is easy to please" and "It is easy to please John" have dissimilar surface structures, yet similar conceptual structures. Prior to Chomsky (1957) many people concentrated only on the surface structure of sentences. Chomsky's analysis made it clear that this type of approach would not suffice.

At present, linguists and psychologists seem to agree on the importance of deep or conceptual structures. No one would argue that sentences like "John is easy to please" and "John is eager to please" are understood in the same way. Nevertheless, there is much disagreement about how best to characterize the conceptual structures that represent people's understanding of language. For example, some linguists (e.g., Ross, 1974) argue that deep structure is much "deeper" (more complex) than Chomsky imagined; others, that Chomsky's analysis is much too syntactically based (for example, it emphasizes logical subjects and objects of sentences) and hence fails to capture psychologically important aspects of meaning (e.g., Fillmore, 1968, 1971a, 1971b; Halliday, 1973; Searle, 1969). Fillmore (1968, 1971a, 1971b) prefers to characterize conceptual structures in terms of more semantically based roles that particular entities play in an event structure. His case grammar includes roles like *agent* (the instigator of an action), *experiencer* (a person or an object on whom or which an action has an effect), *instrument* (an inanimate object used by the agent to perform an action). Thus, the statement like "John is eager to please" would involve *John* as the agent who wants to do the pleasing. In contrast, "John is easy to please" would involve an assumed "someone" as the agent who does the pleasing. In the latter sentence, John might be characterized as the experiencer, the person on whom the action has an effect.

The problem of characterizing conceptual structures is not simply a problem for linguists. Psychological models of understanding and memory must deal with this issue as well, and they, too, reflect a number of different assumptions about the best way to characterize people's understanding (see especially Anderson, 1976; Anderson and Bower, 1973; Kintsch, 1972, 1974, 1976; Norman and Rumelhart, 1975; Schank, 1972). Many of these models draw heavily on Fillmore's analysis of case grammar (e.g., Kintsch, 1974; Norman and Rumelhart, 1975). For present purposes it is not necessary to understand the precise details of the models, but it is important to realize that all of them are concerned with the problem of characterizing the nature of organized structures. None of them assumes that sentence understanding and memory is equivalent to the storage of word strings. Think back to the demonstration experiment illustrated in Figure 4.1. Most people can feel the change that occurs when initially unorganized sequences of words become structured. A major goal of psychological theories of understanding and memory is to characterize explicitly the nature of the organized structures that underlie our feelings of comprehension. The importance of this goal will become clearer in the discussion below.

Some Implications of
Conceptual Structure

A number of studies illustrate the importance of analyzing the conceptual structure of sentences. For example, Blumenthal and Boakes (1967) presented students with sets of sentences like "John is eager to please" and "John is easy to please." After acquisition, participants received the first word of each sentence as a retrieval cue. Cued recall was better for sentences like "John is eager to please" than for "John is easy to please." Note that in the first sentence *John* is the logical deep-structural subject (according to Chomsky's analysis) or the principle agent (according to Fillmore's analysis). Blumenthal and Boakes argue that deep-structural relationships like these are more primary than relationships such as those in the second sentence, where *John* is the object or experiencer. They therefore suggest that the role a concept plays in the conceptual structure of a sentence will affect its usefulness as a potential retrieval cue.

Experiments by Wanner (1974) further clarify the roles played in the conceptual structure of sentences. He presented people with sentences like

1. The governor asked the detective to cease drinking.

2. The governor asked the detective to prevent drinking.

Note that these sentences have different underlying conceptual structures. Using Fillmore's (1971a, 1971b) analysis, the first sentence can be organized around three events: asking, ceasing, and drinking. In the first sentence the governor plays the role of "asker," and the detective is the "askee." Sentence 1 also specifies that it is the detective who should cease and the detective who drinks. A simplified version of an event-based analysis for Sentence 1 can therefore be represented as follows: (ASK, governor, detective, (CEASE, detective, (DRINK, detective))). The corresponding representation for Sentence 2 would be: (ASK, governor, detective, (PREVENT, detective, someone, (DRINK, someone))). (Cf. Kintsch, 1977.) Note that for Sentence 1, the concept of a detective plays a role in all three events, but it plays a role in only two events in Sentence 2. In contrast, the concept of a governor plays a role in only one event both in Sentence 1 and in Sentence 2.

Given this analysis, we can now ask more specific questions about the psychological effects of different types of conceptual structures. For example, to what extent will the effectiveness of retrieval cues like *governor* and *detective* be influenced by the number of events in which they played a role? Wanner (1974) found that a cue like *governor* was equally effective for sentences like Sentences 1 and 2. In contrast, a cue like *detective* was generally better than *governor,* and *detective* resulted in higher cued-recall for sentences like Sentence 1 than for those like Sentence 2. These results suggest that the effectiveness of a retrieval cue is influenced by the number of events in which it plays a role in the conceptual structure of sentences. *Governor* plays a role in only one event in Sentences 1 and 2 and is equally effective for both types of sentences. In contrast, *detective* results in higher cued-recall for Sentence 1 than for Sentence 2, presumably because it plays a role in three events in Sentence 1 but only two events in Sentence 2.

The preceding analysis can also be applied to the results found by Blumenthal and Boakes (1967) discussed earlier. They found that *John* was a better cue for (1) "John is eager to please" than for (2) "John is easy to please." An event-based analysis of these sentences might be the following:

1. (EAGER, John, (PLEASE, John, someone))

2. (EASY, someone, (PLEASE, someone, John))

The concept of "John" appears in two events in Sentence 1 and only one in Sentence 2. Retrieval-cue effectiveness was better for Sentence 1. Note that an emphasis on the number of events in which a concept plays a role is different from Blumenthal and Boakes's assumption that the logical subject of a sentence is the best retrieval cue. In Wanner's experiment *governor* was the subject of the sentence. Nevertheless, *detective* was a more effective retrieval cue, presumably because it played a role in a greater number of events.

Research by Kintsch and Keenan (1973; see also Kintsch, 1976, 1977) provides further evidence of the importance of analyzing the conceptual structure of sentences. They note that various sentences can contain equal numbers of words and yet differ in the complexity of their underlying conceptual structures. When word length was controlled, college students still took longer to read and master sentences whose underlying structures were more complex. Differential degrees of sentence and text difficulty therefore cannot be predicted solely on the basis of surface characteristics like the number of words in a sentence. An emphasis on conceptual structure is very important for understanding why some materials are more difficult to comprehend and retain.

Conceptual Structure and Paraphrase

An emphasis on conceptual structure also has implications for problems of paraphrase. We rarely recall complex materials word for word; instead we tend to remember the "gist" of messages. How might we account for this fact? As noted earlier, particular conceptual structures may be expressible by a number of different surface structures. For example, "It is easy to please John" is an acceptable paraphrase of "John is easy to please." In everyday comprehension situations, we may tend to focus on abstract meaning rather than the exact, surface-structure wordings of statements. This possibility has been explored by Sachs (1967).

Sachs asked students to read various passages. At intervals chosen by the experimenter but not disclosed to the students in advance, Sachs tested students' memory for some of the material they had read. As an example, imagine that a passage contained the following sentence: "He sent a letter about it to Galileo, the great Italian scientist." Sachs would test students' memory for this sentence at various intervals: immediately after reading it, about thirty seconds later (note that students had continued reading up to this time), or forty-five seconds later (again, students kept reading during the interval). Sachs's test involved recognition memory, and the foils were of two types. One type changed the surface structure without violating the meaning of the original sentence (for example, "A letter about it was sent to Galileo, the great Italian scientist"; "He sent Galileo, the great Italian scientist, a letter about it"). Other foils changed the meaning of the original sentence ("Galileo, the great Italian scientist, sent him a letter about it"). Sachs explored the degree to which recognition memory varied as a function of the interval between the original reading of the sentence and the subsequent test.

When the test sentence was heard immediately following the original sentence, students were very good at rejecting both types of foil sentences. They tended to remember the exact wording they had read. After the thirty-second delay, however, their performance changed. At this point, they mistakenly identified foils that changed the surface structure of the original sentence but that preserved the underlying meaning. Nevertheless, they were very good at rejecting foils that changed the meaning of the original sentence—even after the forty-five-second delay. These results suggest that although surface-structure features may frequently be forgotten, an understanding of the meaning of sentences may remain intact (see also Jarvella, 1971).

Summary of Section 2

The goal of this section was to demonstrate the value of linguistic analysis of materials. Our memory for sentences is not equivalent to memory for a mere list of the individual words that constitute a sentence. Sentences are organized or structured, and these structures have powerful effects on learning and retention. Linguistic theories attempt to characterize the nature of sentential structures, and all current psychological theories of sentence memory attempt to take certain linguistic concepts into account.

Although there are many levels of linguistic structure, our discussion focused on two major aspects of structure: surface structure and deep or conceptual structure. A set of sentences can have dissimilar surface structures yet similar conceptual structures. In the latter situation, the sentences are paraphrases of one another. For example, a statement like "John kissed Mary" is an acceptable paraphrase of "Mary was kissed by John."

We discussed several reasons why an analysis of deep or conceptual structures is important. For example, if a word from a sentence is later used as a retrieval cue, its effectiveness seems to vary according to the number of events in which it played a role in the conceptual structure of the sentence (e.g., Wanner, 1974). The complexity of conceptual structures also affects the difficulty of comprehension and hence the speed of reading (e.g., Kintsch and Keenan, 1973). An analysis of conceptual structures is also important for understanding why people frequently remember the basic meaning or gist of sentences but frequently forget the exact wording (e.g., Sachs, 1967); they have forgotten the surface structure of statements but have remembered the deep-structural relationships. When tested, they may therefore be unable to distinguish target sentences from foil sentences if the latter do not violate the deep-structural relationships that were originally acquired.

We must stress, however, that the problem of analyzing the nature of the materials that people are frequently asked to learn goes beyond an analysis of individual sentences. For example, some sets of sentences form a coherent text or discourse, whereas others are simply a list of unrelated statements. Questions about learning from sets of semantically related sentences are discussed in Section 3.

Section 3: Learning from Sets of Semantically Related Sentences

Our previous discussion emphasized some properties of individual sentences that influence learning, understanding, and remembering. Frequently, however, we need to acquire information that is expressed by two or more individual sentences, so that we must somehow combine sentential information into higher-order units or structures. Imagine that you read a book that describes many different escapades of a particular person. At the end of the book, you will probably have an overall impression of the person that was never expressed in any single sentence in the book. The notion of combining sentential information to form integrated structures should be clarified by the demonstration experiment below.

A Demonstration Experiment and Experiments on Linguistic Abstraction

Table 4.3 contains a list of sentences. Before looking at this table, please read the following instructions. Read each sentence in the table individually. As soon as you have read each one, close your eyes and count to five. Then look at and answer the question that follows each sentence. Begin now.

Table 4.3   Sample Experiment by Bransford and Franks (1971)

Acquisition Sentences: Read each sentence, count to five, answer the question, go on to the next sentence.

The girl broke the window on the porch.	Broke what?
The tree in the front yard shaded the man who was smoking his pipe.	Where?
The hill was steep.	What was?
The cat, running from the barking dog, jumped on the table.	From what?
The tree was tall.	Was what?
The old car climbed the hill.	What did?
The cat running from the dog jumped on the table.	Where?
The girl who lives next door broke the window on the porch.	Lives where?
The car pulled the trailer.	Did what?
The scared cat was running from the barking dog.	What was?
The girl lives next door.	Who does?
The tree shaded the man who was smoking his pipe.	What did?
The scared cat jumped on the table.	What did?
The girl who lives next door broke the large window.	Broke what?
The man was smoking his pipe.	Who was?
The old car climbed the steep hill.	The what?
The large window was on the porch.	Where?
The tall tree was in the front yard.	What was?
The car pulling the trailer climbed the steep hill.	Did what?
The cat jumped on the table.	Where?
The tall tree in the front yard shaded the man.	Did what?
The car pulling the trailer climbed the hill.	Which car?
The dog was barking.	Was what?
The window was large.	What was?

STOP. Cover the preceding sentences. Now read each sentence in Table 4.4 and decide if it is a sentence from the list given above.

Table 4.4   Sample Experiment by Bransford and Franks (1971)

Test Set: How many are new?

1. The car climbed the hill.   (old _____, new _____)

2. The girl who lives next door broke the window.   (old _____, new _____)

3. The old man who was smoking his pipe climbed the steep
   hill.   (old _____, new _____)

4. The tree was in the front yard.   (old _____, new _____)

5. The scared cat, running from the barking dog, jumped on
   the table.   (old _____, new _____)

6. The window was on the porch.   (old _____, new _____)

7. The barking dog jumped on the old car in the front yard.   (old _____, new _____)

8. The tree in the front yard shaded the man.   (old _____, new _____)

9. The cat was running from the dog.   (old _____, new _____)

10. The old car pulled the trailer.   (old _____, new _____)

11. The tall tree in the front yard shaded the old car.   (old _____, new _____)

12. The tall tree shaded the man who was smoking his pipe. (old _____, new _____)

13. The scared cat was running from the dog.   (old _____, new _____)

14. The old car, pulling the trailer, climbed the hill.   (old _____, new _____)

15. The girl who lives next door broke the large window on the
    porch.   (old _____, new _____)

16. The tall tree shaded the man.   (old _____, new _____)

17. The cat was running from the barking dog.   (old _____, new _____)

18. The car was old.   (old _____, new _____)

19. The girl broke the large window.   (old _____, new _____)

20. The scared cat ran from the barking dog that jumped on the
    table.   (old _____, new _____)

21. The scared cat, running from the dog, jumped on the table. (old _____, new _____)

22. The old car pulling the trailer climbed the steep hill.   (old _____, new _____)

23. The girl broke the large window on the porch.   (old _____, new _____)

24. The scared cat which broke the window on the porch
    climbed the tree.   (old _____, new _____)

25. The tree shaded the man.   (old _____, new _____)

26. The car climbed the steep hill.   (old _____, new _____)

27. The girl broke the window.   (old _____, new _____)

28. The man who lives next door broke the large window on
    the porch.   (old _____, new _____)

29. The tall tree in the front yard shaded the man who was
    smoking the pipe.   (old _____, new _____)

30. The cat was scared.   (old _____, new _____)

STOP. Count the number of sentences judged "old."

How many test sentences in Table 4.4 did you judge "old"? Many people judge about 80 percent of the sentences old. A few assume that only 5 percent were experienced during acquisition. In fact, none of the test sentences in Table 4.4 occurred in the list of acquisition sentences in Table 4.3.

A series of studies by Bransford and Franks (1971, 1972; see also Franks and Bransford, 1972, 1974a, 1974b) investigated processes of learning and remembering in situations like the preceding one. The acquisition and test procedures were similar to those in the demonstration experiment. However, all acquisition and test sentences were presented in an auditory rather than a visual mode. The experiments were designed to explore linguistic abstraction by considering the following question: Suppose people were exposed to a number of semantically related "pieces" that, if combined, could produce knowledge about "overall ideas" or "abstracted knowledge structures." Would they spontaneously integrate the pieces, thereby acquiring knowledge of the overall ideas?

An examination of the twenty-four acquisition sentences in Table 4.3 reveals that each relates to one of four overall ideas. For example, one idea can be expressed by the sentence "The girl who lives next door broke the large window on the porch." A second idea is "The old car pulling the trailer climbed the steep hill." The overall ideas in the experiment were each defined as involving four simple propositions. For example, the overall idea "The girl who lives next door broke the large window on the porch" can be analyzed into four simple ideas or propositions: "The girl lives next door"; "The girl broke the window"; "The window was on the porch"; "The window was large."

Further examination of Table 4.3 will reveal that although it contains sentences related to four different overall ideas, no individual sentence mentions all four propositions that express these overall ideas. Consider the overall idea "The old car pulling the trailer climbed the steep hill." The sentences in Table 4.3 include two sentences expressing single propositions, called Ones ("The hill was steep," "The car pulled the trailer"); two sentences containing two propositions, called Twos ("The old car climbed the hill," "The car pulling the trailer climbed the hill"); and two sentences containing three propositions, called Threes ("The old car climbed the steep hill," "The car pulling the trailer climbed the steep hill"). Each of the three remaining idea sets illustrated in Table 4.3 is composed of the same types of acquisition sentences: two Ones, two Twos, and two Threes. Note once again that none of the sentences in Table 4.3 is composed of four propositions. Nevertheless, the overall ideas to be acquired were always Fours (composed of all four simple propositions).

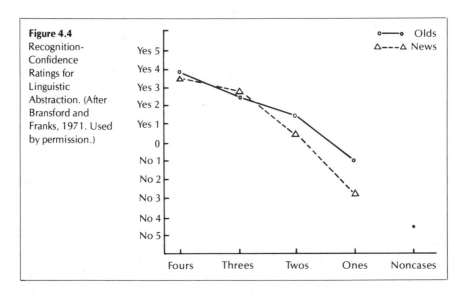

Figure 4.4 Recognition-Confidence Ratings for Linguistic Abstraction. (After Bransford and Franks, 1971. Used by permission.)

Figure 4.4 illustrates the results found by Bransford and Franks (1971). Three aspects of these results should be noted. First, people are likely to think that they recognized new Fours (sentences like "The old car pulling the trailer climbed the steep hill"), Fours that had never occurred during acquisition. This suggests that people combined information from two or more acquisition sentences in order to gain the knowledge of the overall ideas. Secondly, people were accurate at rejecting *noncases*; they knew they had not experienced these during the acquisition task. Noncases were formed by combining units from two or more idea sets that were heard during acquisition. For example, a sentence like "The old man who was smoking his pipe climbed the steep hill" is a noncase (Sentences 3, 7, 11, 20, 24, and 28 in Table 4.4 are also noncases). It is important that people accurately rejected noncases, because it suggests that they acquired a relatively precise understanding of the overall ideas communicated during the acquisition task. Thirdly, consider the recognition ratings for old sentences (hereafter, Olds) in Figure 4.4. In the demonstration experiment at the beginning of this section, only new sentences (hereafter, News) and noncase sentences were presented during testing. In some experiments, Bransford and Franks included Olds, test sentences that had actually been heard during acquisition. As Figure 4.4 illustrates, people were generally unable to distinguish between Olds and News that were consistent with the overall ideas presumably learned during acquisition.

It is important to note, however, that the generality of the Old-New results is questionable. For example, if acquisition sentences are presented visually rather than auditorily, people seem to remember some of the visual cues and hence can distinguish Olds from News (e.g., Katz and Gruenewald, 1974; Flagg, 1975). In addition, Bransford and Franks used a single-item rather than a forced-choice recognition procedure (see Chapter 3, Section 1). When a forced-choice procedure is used, people are also better able to distinguish Olds from News (e.g., Anderson and Bower, 1973; Griggs and Keen, 1977). In retrospect, it seems that Bransford and Franks overstated their case when they claimed that people store *only* the overall ideas and lose all memory for specific sentences heard during acquisition (e.g., see Reitman and Bower, 1973; James and Hillinger, 1977). However, these experiments do suggest that people acquire something more than a mere list of the individual sentences experienced during acquisition. There are ways to study this type of phenomenon more precisely. Some of these are discussed below.

Acquiring Knowledge
of Linear Orderings

Experiments by Barclay (1973) illustrate that people frequently acquire something more than a stored list of sentences heard during acquisition. A nice feature of Barclay's work is that he manipulated the types of activities people were asked to perform during acquisition. Different types of learning activities had powerful effects on the nature of the information that was acquired. In one of his studies, Barclay presented people with lists of sentences like the following (from Barclay, 1973):

1. The lion is to the left of the bear.
2. The lion is to the left of the giraffe.
3. The bear is to the left of the moose.
4. The bear is to the right of the lion.
5. The moose is to the left of the giraffe.
6. The moose is to the right of the lion.
7. The giraffe is to the left of the cow.
8. The giraffe is to the right of the bear.
9. The giraffe is to the right of the moose.
10. The cow is to the right of the giraffe.
11. The cow is to the right of the bear.

All participants heard the acquisition list three times. Group 1 were explicitly instructed to imagine an integrated representation of these sentences. If you study the sentences in the list, you will see that they express a consistent linear ordering of the animals, namely, *lion, bear, moose, giraffe, cow*. Group 2 were told to explicitly remember each acquisition sentence. There were large differences between these two groups in a subsequent recognition test.

Consider the results for Group 1. They were likely to recognize test sentences like "The lion is to the left of the cow," "The bear is to the left of the cow." Such sentences never occurred during acquisition but are consistent with the overall, integrated array. At the same time, these people were very unlikely to recognize (mistakenly) an incorrect, or noncase, sentence like "The bear is to the right of the cow." Contrast the performance of Group 1 with that of Group 2, who had attempted to memorize each acquisition sentence. Group 2 made many errors and frequently thought

they recognized noncases like "The bear is to the right of the cow." Even more important, only three of twenty people in Group 2 realized that a consistent array (a consistent
ordering of the animals) was possible. By concentrating on each sentence, Group 2
were generally unaware that any overall gist or semantic structure existed. Barclay's
experiments therefore provide strong evidence for the notion that integrative abstraction
depends on the types of acquisition activities that learners employ.

Experiments by Potts (1972, 1974) provide further support for the notion that people
frequently combine sentential information to form more holistic or integrated structures.
He used materials that were similar to Barclay's (1973) in that various sentences
expressed information about linear orderings. Rather than use a memory measure,
however, Potts measured the speed with which people could judge various statements as
true or false. To use Barclay's materials as an illustration, people could be presented with
test statements like "The bear is to the left of the cow" (a true statement) and "The bear is
to the right of the cow" (a false statement). Their task would be to say "true" or "false" as
fast as they could.

Potts found that people were often faster at verifying true information that had never
been explicitly presented during acquisition (like "The lion is to the left of the cow") than
they were at verifying information that had actually been presented during acquisition
("The lion is to the left of the bear"). In general, Potts found that people were faster at
verifying remote pairs than adjacent pairs. In an ordering like *lion, bear, moose, giraffe,
cow,* for example, *lion* and *cow* are remote pairs, and *lion* and *bear* are adjacent pairs.
Reaction times therefore seemed to be faster as the "distance" between the pairs
increased. Like Barclay's, Potts's results lend strong support to the notion that people
constructed integrated structures rather than merely stored a memory representation of
the original sentences presented during the acquisition task.

Prerequisites for Linguistic Abstraction

The preceding studies suggest that people's abilities to learn from sets of semantically related sentences involve the construction of relatively holistic, integrated structures. This seems to be very important because it permits people to make inferences (for
example, that the lion was to the left of the bear) that were not explicitly stated during
acquisition. We must now ask whether certain types of materials affect people's abilities
to form integrated structures. Experiments by Moeser (1976) are relevant to this point.

Moeser used measures of inference to investigate certain conditions necessary for
forming integrated structures. Imagine that you hear the following sentences: "The ants
ate the jelly"; "The jelly was on the table"; "The table was under the tree." Is it valid to
conclude that the ants were under the tree? It is, and the inference seems quite easy to
make. As noted earlier, measures of people's abilities to make certain types of inferences
are a useful index for assessing the degree to which integration has occurred. In the last
example, the three related sentences necessary to make the inference were presented
consecutively. Imagine a different type of presentation. The three sentences are presented during acquisition, but they are embedded in a list of other sentences (none of

which is semantically related to our example sentences). Furthermore, the example sentences never occur consecutively. For example, the first sentence ("The ants ate the jelly") may occur in the third position on the acquisition list; the second sentence ("The jelly was on the table"), in the seventh position; and the third sentence ("The table was under the tree"), in the eleventh position. Under these conditions, will integration (as measured by subsequent abilities to draw valid inferences) take place?

Moeser's (1976) data indicate that people can *not* integrate under these conditions (see also Flagg, 1976). People were excellent at recognizing the actual sentences heard during acquisition, such as "The ants ate the jelly." However, when presented with a potential inference sentence, such as "The ants were under the tree," they didn't know whether it was true or false. Like the group in Barclay's (1973) linear ordering experiments that explicitly memorized each individual sentence, participants could often remember the particular acquisition exemplars but had no notion of the overall integrated ideas. Note, however, that people in Barclay's group were explicitly told to remember each sentence, whereas those in Moeser's experiments did not receive such instructions. Note further that like Moeser's study, the demonstration experiment at the beginning of this section (see Table 4.3) also involved the nonconsecutive presentation of related sentences. Experiments analogous to the demonstration experiment provide evidence for integration, whereas Moeser's study indicates a breakdown of integration. What factors might be responsible for those differences in results?

One potentially important difference between the Moeser studies and the original Bransford-Franks experiments (the demonstration experiment and the abstraction experiments) involves the amount of information expressed in individual acquisition sentences. Moeser's acquisition list was composed only of single-proposition sentences (Ones). In contrast, the acquisition sentences in the Bransford-Franks experiments included Ones, Twos, and Threes. How might these differences affect whether or not integration occurs? Assume that integration involves the active interrelation of semantically similar, previously experienced acquisition information with the present input (see Jacoby's one-back and n-back experiments discussed in Chapter 3, Section 3, for a related argument). In order to interrelate present and past events, the present input must contain information sufficient to allow one to retrieve or reactivate relevant information from the past. If someone has previously heard "The ants ate the jelly" (followed by a number of unrelated sentences) and is now in the process of hearing "The jelly was on the table," there is only one cue (*jelly*) that can activate information about the previous sentence. This information may not be sufficient for retrieval. In lists composed solely of Ones, very little information is available for retrieving or activating previously acquired, related items.

Contrast this situation with one in which lists are composed of Ones, Twos, and Threes. If someone has previously heard a sentence like "The ants ate the sweet jelly" (a Two) and is currently processing "The sweet jelly was on the table" (a Two), there is a greater degree of specificity for activating previous, relevant information. Relationships between a current Two and a previous Three, or a current Three and a previous Three, are even more precisely defined. Under these conditions, integration should therefore be more likely to occur. Note that the Bransford-Franks experiments involved acquisition lists of Ones, Twos, and Threes.

If the preceding arguments have merit, there may be ways to permit integration even in Moeser's (1976) paradigm. One would need to find some way of helping people detect the relationships between present inputs and past acquisition events. Moeser (1976) conducted such a study. Before the participants heard the acquisition sentences, she had them memorize stories that could serve as frameworks for tying particular sentences together. The relevant story for the "ants" sentences described earlier was as follows:

> It was very hot inside the house, so the family planned to have dinner in their shady backyard. But after carrying out the food, they decided to go for a swim before they ate.

Given this meaningful framework as a reference point, people were able to integrate the individual acquisition sentences and make appropriate inferences during the subsequent test. These results highlight the importance of relating present and previous experiences. If the present and past are not interrelated, there is no integration. Appropriate knowledge frameworks such as Moeser's stories can act as reference points that make up for a lack of precisely specified relationships between one input and a related input (for example, between a One and another One). Under these conditions, integration can occur even with a list of Ones.

Further Illustrations of Intersentential Relationships

Our previous discussion suggests that the formation of integrated structures depends on the ability to relate present inputs to previously experienced, semantically related information. In order to make the inference that the ants were under the tree, for example, people in Moeser's (1976) experiment would have had to relate the statement "The table was under the tree" to the previously experienced statements "The jelly was on the table" and "The ants ate the jelly." There are therefore certain *intersentential dependencies* that must be realized in order to learn effectively from sets of semantically related sentences. It is instructive to explore these dependencies in more detail.

Experiments by Haviland and Clark (1974) show how certain intersentential dependencies affect the speed of comprehension. Consider a statement like "The beer was warm." As many theorists have noted, a word like *the* is usually used to refer to some previously mentioned concept or topic (e.g., Osgood, 1971; Chafe, 1972). The speed of comprehending such a sentence may therefore depend on the information previously stated in a text. To test this idea, Haviland and Clark presented people with such pairs of sentences as—

1. We got some beer out of the trunk. The beer was warm.
2. We checked the picnic supplies. The beer was warm.

The participants' task was simply to press a button as soon as they felt they understood each sentence. They were faster at understanding "The beer was warm" in Pair 1 than in Pair 2. Since the topic of beer had been introduced in the first sentence in Pair 1, it was easier to understand the statement "The beer was warm."

In subsequent experiments, Haviland and Clark (1974) investigated sentence pairs like the following:

3. Ed was given an alligator for his birthday. The alligator was his favorite present.

4. Ed wanted an alligator for his birthday. The alligator was his favorite present.

Once again, the question of major interest involved the speed of comprehending the second sentence in each pair. Results indicated that Pair 3 resulted in faster comprehension than Pair 4. Note that the initial sentences in both pairs mention an alligator. Nevertheless, the first sentence in Pair 3 suggests that Ed actually received the alligator, whereas the sentence in Pair 4 merely suggests the possibility of receiving one. Since the statement "The alligator was his favorite present" assumed that someone actually received the alligator, Pair 3 resulted in faster comprehension time.

Haviland and Clark discuss their results in terms of a *given-new contract*. Many statements assume that the comprehender has already been "given" certain facts, so that the statements express new information about these old facts. For example, when someone says, "The alligator was his favorite present," there is an assumption that the listener already knows who "he" is and that he, Ed, actually received an alligator. The new information about these old facts is that Ed liked this present best of all. If the listener doesn't know the old information, this may slow down comprehension. For example, if the listener simply knows that Ed *wanted* an alligator, he or she doesn't really know that Ed actually received one. It should therefore take longer to understand a subsequent sentence like "The alligator was his favorite present." This is precisely the type of results that Haviland and Clark found.

Haviland and Clark (1974) show that violations of the given-new contract can slow down the speed of comprehension. Can previously given information also affect people's abilities to remember what they hear or read? Experiments by Morris, Stein, and Bransford (in press) are relevant to this issue. They presented college students with target paragraphs like the following:

Target Paragraph 1   *The group discussed each man's experiences. The greatest praise went to the bald man for his resourcefulness. The tall man also received praise. The most severe criticism was leveled at the clever man who was told to rectify his activities. The rich man was also criticized for his acts. The group felt sorry for the fat man but couldn't help chuckling about the incident. They all agreed that the funny man had gotten what he deserved. . . . At the end of the meeting the men agreed to meet again next week.*

Target Paragraph 2   *The group discussed each man's experiences. The greatest praise went to the fat man for his resourcefulness. The rich man also received praise. The most severe criticism was leveled at the funny man who was told to rectify his activities. The clever man was also criticized for his acts. The group felt sorry for the bald man but couldn't help chuckling about the incident. They all agreed that the tall man had gotten what he deserved. . . . At the end of the meeting the men agreed to meet again next week.*

Note that both the paragraphs are comprehensible; nevertheless, they are not very specific. For example, both paragraphs begin with a statement about "the group" without providing any information about the nature of the group being considered. The paragraphs also refer to various people (like the fat man, the bald man) in a way that suggests that readers have already received some relevant knowledge about these men. The experimenters read the first paragraph to one group of college students, the second to another group, and then asked for free recall. Both paragraphs were recalled equally well.

Additional groups of students also received one of the target paragraphs but were *first* read one of two extra paragraphs like the following:

(Extra) Paragraph A (precise version)   *Six good friends got together to discuss the most significant event each had experienced or performed during the week. The men took turns describing their experiences. The funny man had offended people at the party. The bald man had made a fur hat. The fat man had gotten stuck in a cave. The tall man had painted the ceiling. . . . The clever man had cracked open the bank safe. The rich man had wrecked his sports car.*

(Extra) Paragraph B (less precise version)   *Six good friends got together to discuss the most significant event each had experienced or performed during the week. The men took turns describing their experiences. The tall man had offended people at the party. The fat man had made a fur hat. The bald man had gotten stuck in a cave. The rich man had painted the ceiling. . . . The funny man had cracked open the bank safe. The clever man had wrecked his sports car.*

The additional groups of students were asked to recall the target paragraph *and* the extra paragraph. They therefore had more information to learn and remember than those who had received the target paragraph alone. Note, however, that when the target paragraphs are preceded by the extra paragraphs, these extra paragraphs provide background information about the group, as well as about the men who are referred to in the target paragraphs. The major question of interest is, Will people who received both the extra information and the target paragraph exhibit better recall of the *target paragraph* than people who received the target paragraph alone?

Consider first the results for people who received Paragraph A and then Target Paragraph 1. Their recall of the target paragraph averaged 66 percent accuracy. This is much higher than the average score for people who received the target paragraph alone (43 percent accuracy). These results suggest that the presentation of prior information can have powerful effects on recall.

In order to understand why the extra information from Paragraph A may have facilitated recall of Target Paragraph 1, it is instructive to consider a sentence from the target paragraph; for example, "The group felt sorry for the fat man but couldn't help chuckling about the incident." As an isolated sentence this statement is not incomprehensible. Nevertheless, previously "given" information stating that "The fat man had gotten stuck in a cave" can be used to effectively elaborate the sentence in the target paragraph. People can now better understand the nature of the incident as well as reasons for the group's reaction (their chuckling). As was shown in Chapter 3, Section 3, the ability to elaborate information effectively (for example, to elaborate statements about a tall man buying crackers) can have powerful effects on retention. In the present study, however, the information used to elaborate statements in the target paragraph came from sentences that had previously been heard in the extra paragraph. Note, however, that people presumably must be able to retain and retrieve the previously experienced information in order to elaborate the sentences in the target paragraph effectively. It is instructive to explore this issue in more detail.

The preceding discussion compared recall of Target Paragraph 1 when learned in isolation with recall for the paragraph when preceded by information from Paragraph A. Consider now recall of Target Paragraph 2; first, when presented in isolation; then, when preceded by Paragraph B. As an isolated entity Target Paragraph 2 was recalled with a 36 percent level of accuracy (essentially the same as for Target Paragraph 1). When preceded by Paragraph B, Target Paragraph 2 was recalled *no better than when it was presented in isolation*. Why might this be the case?

If you examine the information in Paragraph B you will see that it contains statements like "The bald man had gotten stuck in a cave," "The tall man had offended people at the party." These statements are like the base sentences used in the study of effective elaboration discussed in Chapter 3, Section 3 (Table 3.1). Although the statements in Paragraph B are not incomprehensible, they lack information that helps people perceive nonarbitrary relationships between certain adjectives (such as *bald*) and the events in which they are embedded (such as getting stuck in a cave). People therefore become confused about which adjective went with which event. We shall refer to statements like those in Paragraph B as "less precise." In contrast, Paragraph A contained statements like "The fat man had gotten stuck in a cave." Here one can more readily perceive the relevance of the word *fat* for getting stuck. We shall therefore refer to these as "precise" statements. Morris and colleagues found that recall for the sentences in Paragraph A (precise) was much higher than for those in Paragraph B (less precise). Note once again that presentation of Paragraph A (precise) facilitated recall for Target Paragraph 1, but presentation of Paragraph B (less precise) did not facilitate recall for Target Paragraph 2. Presumably, people could not remember the less precise information in Paragraph B and hence were unable to use it to effectively elaborate the statements in Target Paragraph 2. Table 4.5 summarizes the results we have discussed so far.

Morris, Stein, and Bransford included an additional experimental condition that illustrates how memory for the target paragraphs depends on people's abilities to retain and retrieve previously experienced information (the information in Paragraphs A and B). In this condition, a group of students were given extra practice on Paragraph B (less precise), with the result that their level of free recall for this paragraph was equivalent to that of people who heard Paragraph A (precise) once. Both groups were therefore equal in their abilities to recall (the extra) Paragraphs A and B. The question of interest was, Would the two groups now be equivalent in their abilities to recall their respective *target paragraphs*? Morris and colleagues found that people who received extra practice on Paragraph B still did not significantly increase their recall of the target paragraph; recall of the target paragraph under these extra practice conditions was slightly higher than recall of the target paragraph presented in isolation (see Table 4.5), but the differences were not statistically significant. Why did these results occur?

In order to understand the results, we must reconsider earlier discussions of retrieval processes (Chapter 3) and of attention and automaticity (Chapter 2). Note that those people who had received extra practice on Paragraph B (less precise) could recall the statements from this paragraph as accurately as those who had heard Paragraph A (precise) only once could recall Paragraph A. Note also, however, that all students were given plenty of time during the recall test. In order to use the information from Paragraph A or B to elaborate the target paragraphs, the students needed to meet an additional criterion; they had to retrieve previously experienced information (from the extra paragraphs) within the time limitations imposed by the speed at which the target paragraphs were read to them. For example, imagine that students hear the following sentence from the target paragraphs: "The group felt sorry for the fat (or bald) man but couldn't help chuckling about the incident." In order to use previously given information to effectively elaborate this sentence, people must be able to retrieve quickly information about the fat (or bald) man getting stuck in a cave. If they cannot do this, the previously given information should do them little good.

We must now ask, Why might it be easier to quickly retrieve previously given information about a man getting stuck in a cave when a sentence states that the group felt sorry for the fat man (Target Paragraph 1) rather than the bald man (Target Paragraph 2)? One possibility is as follows: As a result of previously acquired knowledge, words like *fat* and *bald* automatically activate certain thoughts. When we hear *fat*, we think of large size, a love of food, and so on; when we hear *bald*, different thoughts come to mind heads without hair, for instance. These thoughts that are activated influence how we encode the potential retrieval information (*fat* and *bald*). Tulving's (1978) encoding-specificity principle (see Chapter 3, Section 3) suggests that retrieval-cue effectiveness is a function of the similarity between encoding at time of retrieval and encoding during

Table 4.5 Recall Scores for Target Paragraphs	
Acquisition Condition	Recall of Target Paragraph
Target Paragraph 1 alone:	43%*
Target Paragraph 2 alone:	36%*
Target Paragraph 1 when preceded by (extra) Paragraph A:	66%
Target Paragraph 2 when preceded by (extra) Paragraph B:	30%
Target Paragraph 2 when preceded by two trials on (extra) Paragraph B:	41%

After Morris, Stein, and Bransford (in press). Used by permission.

*These scores do not differ at a statistically significant level.

initial learning. In that the information to be retrieved involves a man getting stuck in a cave, it is more congruent with people's initial assumptions about fat men than with those about bald men. Given time constraints, people who hear that the group felt sorry for the bald man may therefore lack the advantage of relatively automatically activated knowledge that is congruent with the prior information to be retrieved (that the bald man had gotten stuck in a cave). Assume, however, that people heard the target sentence about the group feeling sorry for the fat (or bald) man but the information to be retrieved had been "The fat (or bald) man had lost his fur hat and frozen his head." Under these conditions, we should expect *bald* to be a more efficient cue than *fat* because our knowledge of the former is more congruent with the information to be retrieved.

It is important to note that the preceding suggestion is only one of many possible explanations for the results of the experiment, but it serves to illustrate how some of the concepts discussed earlier in this book may be applied to the present problem of text understanding. Note, for example, that the study by Morris and colleagues seems to illustrate how learning and understanding texts involves the coordination of several activities that require attention (see Chapter 2). When processing "The group felt sorry for the fat (or bald) man . . . ," for example, people must identify individual words and combine them into phrases. They must also retrieve or reactivate previously given information (about getting stuck in a cave) and use it to elaborate the target sentence. Text understanding therefore seems to involve concepts of retrieval and elaboration (Chapter 3). Furthermore, the automaticity of certain processes (Chapter 2) may play an important role in facilitating this retrieval within particular time limitations. Concepts like retrieval, automaticity, and elaboration therefore seem to play a role in a large number of learning tasks.

It is also instructive to note that the study by Morris and colleagues illustrates how the sentential structure and content of texts influences the ease with which they can be learned and remembered. If you reexamine the extra paragraphs and target paragraphs, you will see that Paragraph A (precise) contains the same individual words as Paragraph B (less precise), and Target Paragraph 1 the same words as Target Paragraph 2. The words are simply combined differently. Differences in the ability to learn and remember these texts therefore cannot be predicted on the basis of properties of the individual words themselves (properties like word frequency and word imagery; see Section 1 of this chapter). Furthermore, all sets of materials are syntactically well formed (see Section 2), so that differences in syntactic structure cannot account for the results. There are therefore many potential variables that can influence text difficulty. Additional factors are discussed below.

Additional Studies of Text Structure

Our previous discussion suggests that many aspects of the structure of paragraphs and texts can influence people's abilities to learn and remember. For example, paragraphs that violate the given-new contract (Haviland and Clark, 1974) can result in slower comprehension speed and poorer recall. The content of the information used to fulfill the given-new contract can affect retention as well (Morris, Stein, and Bransford, in press). There are many additional questions to be asked about text structures. One involves the degree to which some sentences in a text are more likely to be recalled than others. Is there any way to predict this on the basis of the structure of a paragraph or text? In an initial investigation of this question, Johnson (1970) asked one group of students to rate the degree to which each individual sentence or idea unit was important in an overall story. When their recall scores were compared with those of a different group of students who had simply read the story, without considering the importance of individual sentences, it was apparent that recall probabilities were a function of the first group's ratings of importance. The greater the degree of judged importance, the higher the probability of the sentences' being recalled.

Work by Meyer (1975, 1977) and Kintsch (1974, 1976) further explores the question of predicting what will be recalled. Each of them has developed a method for analyzing the structure of texts that is somewhat analogous to analyzing the structure of sentences (see Section 2 in this chapter). Their systems of text structures reveal the degree to which particular ideas are central or more peripheral to the main theme of a passage or story. For example, Kintsch proposes a method for analyzing a "text base" that utilizes concepts from Fillmore's (1968) case grammar (see Section 2). One aspect of his analysis is to assign propositions to various levels in the text-base hierarchy. Those propositions that are more central to the theme of the text are assigned a higher rank in the hierarchy (a rank of 1 being the highest). Figure 4.5 illustrates that the higher the level of a proposition, the greater the probability of recall (see also Meyer, 1977). Note that results like these also have implications for the best way to write texts and stories. If a writer wants a reader to remember certain ideas or propositions, these ideas should be high in the hierarchical structure of the text base.

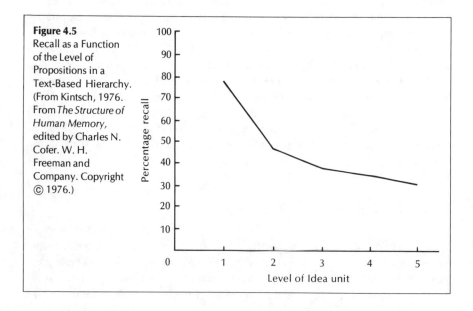

Figure 4.5 Recall as a Function of the Level of Propositions in a Text-Based Hierarchy. (From Kintsch, 1976. From *The Structure of Human Memory,* edited by Charles N. Cofer. W. H. Freeman and Company. Copyright © 1976.)

Texts can also vary in the degree to which semantically related sentences are organized. As an illustration, consider the following passage used by Danner (1976):

> *The fox looks like a dog. He has a long nose. His tail hangs down. He is red. The fox lives in the forest. He makes a home in the bushes. Sometimes he stays in a hole. He sleeps on the ground. The fox eats small animals. He catches birds for food. He sometimes eats fish. He even likes fruit.*

Note that this passage first discusses what a fox looks like; next, where it lives; and finally, what it eats. The passage is therefore organized around general topics. Danner also used passages containing the same sentences as the previous passage, but the topics were disorganized. For example, the first three sentences might be "The fox looks like a dog. He sleeps on the ground. He sometimes eats fish." When organized or disorganized passages were read to second-, fourth-, and sixth-graders, recall was strongly influenced by the degree of topical organization. Children at all three grade levels remembered the organized passages best.

In addition to variables like topical organization, the use of relevant *exemplars* can also have powerful effects on people's abilities to learn from textual information. An experiment by Pollchik (1975) represents a case in point. He presented college students enrolled in an introductory psychology course with written texts designed to help them acquire knowledge of seven psychological defense mechanisms. The concepts to be learned were denial, displacement, intellectualization, projection, reaction formation, regression, and sublimation. The total text comprised seven *basic texts,* each describing a different concept. The following (from Pollchik, 1975) is the basic text for the concept of projection:

> Projection *protects someone from disturbing and unacceptable impulses, desires, and attitudes by claiming that they are not the possession of the person; instead, it attributes them to sources external to the person—to other people or to the environment.*[1] *That is, in projection, personal characteristics or impulses that arouse anxiety in an individual are externalized by attributing them to others. By means of projection the person rids himself of the objectionable and also places the source of danger in the outer world, where he feels better able to cope with it. If the source of anxiety can be attributed to the external world rather than to the individual's own primitive impulses, or to the threats of his conscience, he is likely to achieve greater relief for his anxious condition. Projection often serves a dual purpose. It reduces anxiety by substituting a lesser danger (an external threat) for a greater one (an internal threat), and it enables the projecting person to express his impulses under the guise of defending himself against his enemies. Along with denial, projection achieves its success by the distortion of reality. In addition to distorting reality seriously, the individual whose primary defense is projection may also create new sources of anxiety by incurring the wrath of individuals he accuses of pos-sessing the undesirable projected impulse. In the general sense, whenever*

> an individual inaccurately attributes his own personal feelings or characteris-
> tics to others, he is projecting.[2] The use of projection is very characteristic
> of the paranoid personality, as is especially evident in cases of paranoid
> schizophrenia. When its defensive function is ignored or is not the prime
> concern, projection takes its place as one of the many aspects of the process
> of perception, and we find it entering into questions concerning the rela-
> tionship between perception and personality.

Students in one group read basic texts like the one just illustrated. Remember that the total text described six additional defense mechanisms. Students in a second group read the same text, but the text included two one-sentence examples for each of the seven defense mechanisms. The two examples for the basic text describing projection are as follows. Note that these examples were inserted at the points marked 1 and 2, respectively, in the basic text.

> **Example 1**   For example, imagine that you are very concerned about not being
> an incompetent store manager, so you tell your employees that they are re-
> sponsible for the month's drop in profits.
>
> **Example 2**   For example, imagine that you are very shy, but you describe
> vivacious, outgoing people as "scared, withdrawn individuals who are over-
> compensating for their weakness."

It is instructive to note that addition of two examples to each of the seven basic texts resulted in a difference of only fourteen sentences. Note further that the total text comprised about a hundred sentences; given this total, the addition of fourteen sentences is quite minimal. Is it realistic to assume that these additions will have measurable effects on students' abilities to learn?

Pollchik's results indicate that the presence of the fourteen examples had a powerful effect on learning. His primary measure tested students' abilities to identify novel examples of particular defense mechanisms. For example, students were presented with test statements like the following:

> Larry, who didn't dare strike back at his older sister when she gave him a
> tongue lashing, would try and pick fights during the weekend playground
> football games.

The task was to choose which of the following answers was correct:

  a. Denial

  b. Displacement

  c. Intellectualization

  d. Projection

  e. Reaction formation

    f. Regression

    g. Sublimation

    h. None of the above

Students who read the basic text and the examples were much more accurate than those who read only the basic text. Those who received examples answered 16.43 of 20 questions correctly, whereas those who received the text alone were correct on only 9.86 of the questions.*

    Research by Rothkopf, Frase, and others is also very important for understanding how learning is influenced by the nature of the materials (e.g., Anderson and Biddle, 1975; Frase, 1972; Frase and Kreitzberg, 1975; Rothkopf, 1966, 1970, 1972). Much of this work explores how learning can be influenced by providing students with instructional objectives about what they should learn from a text and by inserting relevant questions into texts so that students can evaluate their mastery of the material. A number of these studies suggest that students' learning and comprehension activities can be influenced by written objectives and embedded questions. This research is very valuable, then, because it shows how written documents—many of which are not optimally structured, and which are frequently written for purposes somewhat different from those of a teacher or instructor—can be improved upon. By providing students with goal statements and embedded questions, texts that would otherwise be extremely difficult can become much easier to learn.

Summary of Section 3

    The purpose of this section was to discuss how people learn from sets of semantically related sentences, including paragraphs and texts. It was argued that effective learners do not simply store individual sentences; instead, they combine information from semantically related sentences to form more holistic structures that capture the essence of a passage and that permit novel inferences. There are certain prerequisites for achieving such goals, however. For example, learners must be able to relate current information to relevant facts that were presented earlier in a passage. Failure to do this may hurt their ability to make inferences (e.g., Moeser, 1976), their speed of comprehension (e.g., Haviland and Clark, 1974), and their memory for statements that refer to previously experienced events (e.g., Morris, Stein, and Bransford, in press).

    Throughout our discussion it was noted that the structure of textual materials can affect the ease of forming holistic structures. For example, Moeser (1976) shows that a list of single-proposition sentences (such as "The ants ate the jelly") can be interrelated to permit valid inferences if they are presented consecutively. If the sentences are presented nonconsecutively, however, breakdowns in inference-making abilities can easily occur. Similarly, passages that violate the given-new contract (Haviland and Clark, 1974) can

---

*The answer to the test question is *b*.

affect memory and comprehension speed. We also noted that particular statements may or may not be recalled depending on their relationship to the overall text base (e.g., Kintsch, 1974, 1976; Meyer, 1975, 1977). In addition, ease of learning is related to the degree of topical organization in a text (e.g., Danner, 1976) and to the degree to which relevant examples of basic concepts are provided in a text (e.g., Pollchik, 1975). An important implication of these results is that researchers are becoming better able to analyze instructional materials and to improve them. This issue is explored more fully in Section 4.

Section 4: Some Implications of Analyzing the Nature of Materials

Discussion in the first three sections of this chapter emphasized how the ease of learning and remembering is influenced by properties of individual words (Section 1), the structure of sentences (Section 2), and the structure of sets of semantically related sentences (Section 3). Knowledge of these variables is important for designing instructional materials. Consider first how properties of individual words have been used to facilitate learning in school-related tasks.

Utilizing Word Properties to Facilitate Learning

During the early 1930s, Thorndike (e.g., see Hilgard and Bower, 1975) was concerned about the problem of teaching reading. What words should students be taught to read first? What words would children be likely to know already from their spoken language environment? Thorndike's answer to this question was simple and straightforward: Look at a word's frequency of usage and pick the most commonly used ones. He proceeded to tabulate thousands of words by counting the frequency with which they appeared in numerous sources (magazines, newspapers, books, and so on). He then made these tabulations available to teachers, so that children could begin reading those words that they presumably knew best. Thorndike and Lorge (1944) published norms indicating the frequency of usage of particular words. This simple and insightful procedure has affected the choice of the particular words that children are first taught to read.

Research by Marks, Doctorow, and Wittrock (1974) further illustrates the value of measures of word frequency. They created two versions of a story to be read by elementary-school children. Story comprehension and retention were nearly doubled by changing only 20 percent of the words in the story from less frequent items to more frequent items (for example, by changing *lad* to *boy*). The addition or subtraction of even a relatively small number of unfamiliar words can affect one's understanding and remembering of what one has read.

It should be noted that when Marks and colleagues varied words on the basis of their estimated frequency of usage, they were probably varying the words' familiarity, too. For example, words like *boy* are probably used much more frequently than are words like *lad*. Nevertheless, college students reading the passages presented by the researchers would undoubtedly be much less affected by changes from low to high frequency words than would elementary-school children. It is therefore reasonable to assume that the effects of absolute differences in frequency of usage will depend on the past experiences of the learners. For adults, words like *boy* and *lad* may differ greatly in terms of frequency of usage, but if both words are quite familiar, they may still result in roughly equivalent levels of learning and memory performance. For elementary-school children, however, absolute differences in frequency may reflect large differences in familiarity and hence have relatively powerful effects.

Utilizing the Power of Imagery

Research by Levin (1973) explores the value of imagery (see Section 1) in educational contexts. Rather than vary the imageability of the words in a story, however, he investigated the degree to which learners actually processed potentially imageable words. Recall that Seamon and Murray (see Section 1) showed that the effects of meaningfulness (M) depend on how learners process the inputs at time of acquisition. Similarly, Paivio's (e.g., 1971) studies of imagery usually involve instructions to image. Levin (1973) was concerned that many students (especially poor readers) do not make use of the potential for imagery when they attempt to learn.

Levin studied fourth-grade students' abilities to read and answer questions about stories. Some groups were explicitly taught how to image "pictures" of what they were reading. Other groups were told simply to read and understand as best they could. Results indicated that the imagery instructions facilitated students' abilities to remember.

An important aspect of Levin's results is the question of *which* students were helped by the imagery instructions. Students classified as good readers benefited from imagery instructions. Some of the students classified as poor readers also benefited, but others did not. Levin notes that there are many different reasons why one may be classified as a poor reader. Some people may simply hate school (yet be able to read well at home); some may be able to pronounce and identify each word they perceive, yet fail to utilize strategies (such as imagery) that could facilitate learning and memory; others may be unable to identify words seen in print. One would not expect the last group to benefit from imagery instructions, because word identification is a prerequisite for appropriate imagery (if students can't identify the word *dog*, they don't know what to image). However, imagery instructions should help people who simply fail to utilize learning strategies that facilitate later recall. This is the pattern of results that Levin found.

The Concept of Readability

The foregoing studies can be viewed as illustrations of work designed to clarify the general concept of comprehensibility and readability. The general question is, What types of factors make texts (especially those designed for children) more or less readable, and how might one develop measures of the readability of various texts? A number of researchers have worked on this problem (e.g., Flesh, 1945; Coleman, 1964). As Klare (1963) notes, three types of variables appear to have fairly consistent effects on readability. One is word difficulty, which usually correlates with word frequency (see Section 1 and the previous discussion in this section). The second variable is sentence length, with longer sentences leading to greater complexity. The third, related variable is sentence complexity (including such factors as the number of subordinate clauses or prepositional phrases). Note that sentences could be equally long yet differ in complexity (see the work by Kintsch and Keenan in Section 2), so that the second and third factors are not necessarily equivalent. On the basis of such data, some theorists have suggested that sentence length be kept at a minimum, prepositions, adjectives and adverbs used sparingly, and coordinating conjunctions replaced with periods. It seems straightforward that less complex sentences should be easier to understand and learn.

At this point, it is useful to reemphasize the previous discussion on learning from semantically related sentences (Section 3). It was argued that the acquisition of overall ideas involved something more than comprehension and storage of a mere list of acquisition sentences. Thus the ability to abstract the overall idea of a book or passage involves more than the ability to remember individual sentences. It follows that although a simple sentence like "The boy hit the ball" may be easier to understand than "The tall boy hit the red ball," comparisons of individual sentences may not be of major relevance when asking questions about readability. Instead, the relevant question might be as follows: If one wishes to convey an overall idea, what is the most effective way to do it? Is it more effective to say "The boy hit the ball; the boy is tall; the ball is red" or simply to say, "The tall boy hit the red ball"? As noted elsewhere (Bransford and Franks, 1971, 1972; Pearson, 1974), there may be a tradeoff between syntactic sentence complexity and semantic simplicity. Because of the constraints on integrating simple sentences (see the previous discussion of Moeser's experiments in Section 3), moderate levels of syntactic complexity may enable people to integrate information and hence to abstract overall ideas.

In an important series of studies, Pearson (1974) investigated questions of readability from the perspective of overall-idea acquisition. He compared children's comprehension of the same semantic content communicated in different manners; for example, (1) "The tall man liked the short woman," as compared with (2) "The man liked the woman; he was tall; she was short." In general, Pearson found that moderate degrees of syntactic complexity (as in Sentence 1) facilitated subsequent comprehension. Furthermore, additional studies demonstrated that children *preferred* moderate degrees of syntactic complexity to syntactic simplicity when asked which passages they would like to read in order to find the answer to certain questions (for example, "Which man liked the short woman?").

It is noteworthy that the critical comprehension questions Pearson asked required integration. For the sentence "The man liked the woman; he was tall; she was short," the critical comprehension question was not "Who liked the woman?" This could have been answered on the basis of a single acquisition sentence. Instead, questions like "Which woman was liked by the tall man?" were asked, whose answer necessitated a degree of intersentence integration. To the extent that effective comprehension involves acts of integration, these appear to be very appropriate types of comprehension questions to ask. Furthermore, the answers to such questions enable us to evaluate the notion of "simplifying" materials; sentences that are syntactically simple may actually make it harder for students to interrelate sentences and form more holistic, integrated structures. Additional questions about processes of simplification are discussed below.

Further Explorations of "Simplified Materials"

Questions about what it means to simplify materials have additional dimensions besides those so far discussed. For example, it is easy to believe that materials written for adults may contain extra details that are too complex for younger children. Although this assumption is probably true to some extent, there is a great need to examine the nature of the details that are omitted in texts simplified for children. If writers are not careful, they may omit information that is necessary for understanding the unique significance, or even the relevance, of the information in a story. Without this extra information, the stories children are asked to learn and read may seem to be no more than an arbitrary collection of facts.

As an illustration, consider once again statements like "The bald man had gotten stuck in a cave." As noted in Section 3, less precise statements like this are much more difficult to remember and retrieve than precise statements like "The fat man had gotten stuck in a cave." From a child's perspective, many of the stories he or she reads may also seem relatively arbitrary and nonprecise. For example, a story in a reading book for fourth-graders discussed Indian houses and contained statements somewhat like the following: "The Indians of the Northwest Coast lived in slant-roofed houses built of cedar plank. . . . Some California Indian tribes lived in simple earth-covered or brush shelters. . . . The Plains Indians lived mainly in tepees . . . ." The story provided no information about why certain Indians chose certain houses, and no attempt was made to explain how the area where Indians lived related to the kinds of houses they built. Adults reading this story might be able to make these assumptions on their own, but children are likely to have difficulty doing so. Without this extra information the relationships between particular Indian tribes and their houses seem arbitrary, and we should expect story comprehension and memory to suffer. In short, some attempts at simplification are not simplifications at all.

The importance of analyzing the information contained in stories takes on increased significance when it is realized that many researchers use various stories to make inferences about people's basic abilities. For example, Piaget (1969a) and Fraisse (1963) have read stories to young children and asked them to recall. The children frequently mixed up the order in which events occurred in the stories, prompting the researchers to claim that young children lack the *ability* to remember the temporal order of events. This is a strong claim to make, especially when the researchers made no careful analysis of the materials that the children were asked to learn and recall. Recently, researchers have begun to construct "story grammars" that characterize the sequence of events in stories and relate them to children's current levels of skills and knowledge (e.g., Mandler,

1978; Mandler, Johnson, and DeForest, 1976; Rumelhart, 1975; Stein and Glenn, in press). If age-appropriate stories are used, it appears that young children *can* recall events in their correct temporal order. By failing to analyze the nature of the materials used in various studies, many researchers have erroneously concluded that children lack certain abilities. As emphasized in our framework in Figure 1.1, however, performance is always a function of the nature of the materials in relation to the learner's current level of knowledge and skills.

As a final illustration of the need to better understand what it means to simplify materials and make them more readable and understandable, consider the structure of many novels. The following passage comes at the beginning of Joan Barthel's (1977) *A Death in Canaan*:

> When Barbara died, some of the news stories described her house as a little white cottage. The phrase made the place sound picturesque. . . . But the little house where Barbara and Peter lived was drab and boxy. . . . (P. 13)

Note that the novel begins with this passage, which violates many communication structures like the given-new contract (see Section 3). For example, it refers to Barbara and Peter without providing any information about who they are. Such novels arouse the readers' curiosity and interest, and challenge them to make assumptions. Many novels even seem to defeat readers' expectations deliberately, causing them to reinterpret old evidence later. For example, a natural tendency is to assume that Barbara and Peter are married. Later in the book, however, the reader realizes that Peter is Barbara's son. Are novels written in such a style harder to understand and remember because they violate principles like the given-new contract? Maybe they result in better comprehension because they engage readers' interest and attention. At present, little is explicitly known about the effects of various literary styles on comprehension and memory. This appears to be a promising area for future research.

Summary of Section 4

This section discussed why an analysis of the nature of the materials is important for evaluating people's abilities to learn and remember. For example, it was noted that such properties of individual words as their frequency of occurrence can have powerful effects on learning and memory, especially for elementary-school children. These properties are one of the major sets of criteria used to estimate the readability of school texts. Readability is also related to individual sentence complexity, but one must be careful not to exaggerate the significance of this variable. As isolated entities, syntactically complex sentences are indeed frequently more difficult to comprehend and remember than simpler sentences, but text understanding is not simply a matter of understanding and storing individual sentences. People must combine information from sets of semantically related sentences to form more holistic, integrated ideas. From this perspective, it is a mistake to assume that simplified syntax necessarily makes it easier to form the integrated structures that seem to underlie effective mastery of information in a text.

Misconceptions about what it means to simplify materials were also discussed from a different perspective. For example, many texts written for children tend to delete some of the details present in adult versions. One must be careful not to omit details that are important, however. Some details are necessary for understanding the significance of certain relationships, and their elimination may render the statements in the text arbitrary from the child's point of view. For example, if the temporal sequence of events seems arbitrary, one would expect children to have difficulty recalling these events in their correct temporal order. This does not necessarily mean that children lack the *ability* to perform such feats; in fact, when the nature of the materials is appropriate to children's current skills and knowledge, they seem to be able to recall events in the order in which they occurred. There is a great need for further research on the structure of materials, however. For example, many novelists purposely write in ways that violate certain expectations and conventions. There may be advantages to such styles; for example, they may challenge the reader. Here is an area where collaboration between cognitive scientists and literary scholars might provide important insights into factors that help people learn.

Chapter 5
The Role of Prior Knowledge

Our framework illustrated in Figure 1.1 suggests that performance is a joint function of learning activities (Chapter 2), testing or retrieval contexts (Chapter 3), the nature of the materials to be learned (Chapter 4), and the current level of the learner's skills and knowledge. It is the last topic that we shall explore in this chapter. Discussion is divided into four sections, which are outlined below.

Overview

Section 1 examines the issue of *cognitive prerequisites for comprehension*. The same set of materials may or may not be comprehensible depending on the learner's currently activated knowledge. This orientation is consistent with Buhler's (1908) "field theory" of comprehension, which assumes that effective understanding is a function of the relationship between present information and activated knowledge, and that effective communication therefore depends on the degree to which listeners and speakers share a common semantic "field."

Section 2 discusses *the role of inference in comprehension*. Most messages do not explicitly contain all the information necessary for effective comprehension. People must "fill in the gaps" in messages by making inferences and assumptions based on their general knowledge of the world. The same information may also be understood at many different levels, depending on the types of assumptions made by the reader or listener. People's abilities to make inferences are therefore extremely important. Sometimes, however, people may infer from messages ideas that are different from those that a speaker or writer intended to express.

In Section 3 we shall explore some *relationships between comprehending and remembering*. People's abilities to make assumptions that permit effective comprehension can sometimes help and sometimes hurt the accuracy of remembering. For example, people may sometimes think they heard or read information that they actually inferred. We shall also discuss two possible ways in which prior knowledge can affect remembering. The first possibility is that people *construct* inferences and interpretations at the time of comprehension and remember their constructions. The second is that people *reconstruct* details on the basis of general assumptions and expectations. They may therefore think they are accurately remembering yet be recalling information in a distorted form.

The goal of Section 4 is to discuss *some implications of focusing on the role of prior knowledge*. In particular, we shall reconsider some elements from our earlier analysis of the nature of materials to be learned (Chapter 4). It will be argued that the theme of Chapter 4 is important in itself but that materials must ultimately be evaluated in relation to the learner's current level of skill and knowledge. Our discussion will therefore emphasize relationships among some of the factors illustrated in our theoretical framework in Figure 1.1.

Section 1: Cognitive Prerequisites for Comprehension

The objective of this section is to demonstrate that the ability to understand and remember is always a function of relationships between present inputs and the currently activated knowledge of the learner (see Figure 1.1). Buhler (1908) emphasized the importance of this idea many years ago. His "field theory" focused on the interdependence between incoming information and the "field" or activated knowledge-base available to the comprehender. As Blumenthal (1970) states,

> Buhler's field concept was most important. Given two speakers of the same language, no matter how well one of them structures a sentence his utterance will fail if both parties do not share the same field to some degree. . . . There are inner aspects of the field, such as an area of knowledge, or outer aspects, such as objects in the environment. Indeed, the field can be analyzed into many aspects. The total field (Umfeld) consists not only of the practical situation (Ziegfeld) in which an utterance occurs, but also the symbol field (Symbolfeld) which is the context of language segments preceding the segment under consideration. . . . The structure of any particular language is largely field-independent, being determined by its own particular conventional rules, but the field determines how the rules are applied. . . . With a "rich" external field less needs to be specified in the sentence. (P. 56)

Buhler's emphasis on the relationship between incoming information and semantic "fields" is also characteristic of Lashley's (1951) theoretical position. He states:

> My principal thesis today will be that the input is never into a quiescent or static system, but always into a system which is already actively excited and organized. In the intact organism, behavior is the result of interaction of this background of excitation with input from any designated stimulus. Only when

we can state the general characteristics of this background of excitation, can we understand the effects of a given input. (P. 112)

One implication of the orientation adopted by both Buhler and Lashley is that the same materials may or may not be comprehensible depending on the currently activated "field" or knowledge of the reader or listener. This idea is illustrated by the studies described below.

The Balloon Study

Read the following passage once. Imagine that you will be asked to recall it after you have finished reading.

> *If the balloons popped, the sound would not be able to carry since everything would be too far away from the correct floor. A closed window would also prevent the sound from carrying since most buildings tend to be well insulated. Since the whole operation depends on a steady flow of electricity, a break in the middle of the wire would also cause problems. Of course the fellow could shout, but the human voice is not loud enough to carry that far. An additional problem is that a string could break on the instrument. Then there could be no accompaniment to the message. It is clear that the best situation would involve less distance. Then there would be fewer potential problems. With face to face contact, the least number of things could go wrong.*

Bransford and Johnson (1972) read this passage to a group of students (called the No Knowledge Context group). After hearing it, the group were asked to rate it for comprehensibility on a seven-point scale (where 7 indicates highly comprehensible) and then to attempt to recall it. As you might expect, people in this group rated the passage as very incomprehensible (the average rating was 2.3), and their recall scores were quite low (see Table 5.1).

The same passage becomes quite comprehensible if one is supplied with an appropriate knowledge framework or context, however. The picture in Figure 5.1 provides such a framework. Look at the picture and then read the passage again.

Table 5.1 Comprehension and Recall Scores for the Balloon Passage

	No Context (1 Repetition)	No Context (2 Repetitions)	Context After	Partial Context	Context Before	Maximum Score
Comprehension ratings:	2.30	3.60	3.30	3.70	6.10	7.00
Number of idea units recalled:	3.60	3.80	3.60	4.00	8.00	14.00

From Bransford and Johnson (1972). Used by permission.

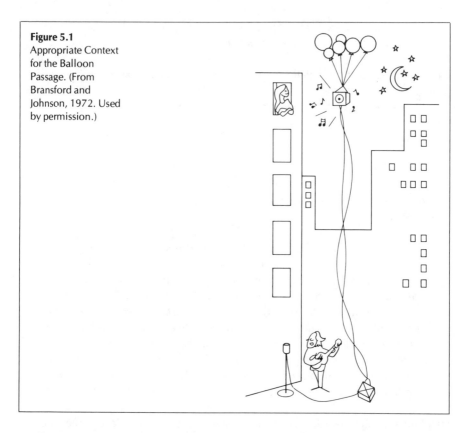

Figure 5.1
Appropriate Context for the Balloon Passage. (From Bransford and Johnson, 1972. Used by permission.)

People who first saw the appropriate picture and then heard the passage (called the Appropriate Context Before group) rated the passage as very comprehensible (the average rating was 6.1). Furthermore, their recall scores were over twice as high as the first group's (see Table 5.1). Note that the written passage was not simply a description of the appropriate-context picture. Instead, the picture provided a basis for allowing people to interpret meaningfully and to connect or organize sentences they heard. Bransford and Johnson also tested a number of control groups with the balloon passage. The overall design of the experiment is illustrated in Table 5.1.

People in the Appropriate Context After group *first* heard the passage and were *then* shown the picture in Figure 5.1. They then made their comprehension ratings and then recalled the passage. Seeing the picture after hearing the passage did not seem to help: this group also rated the passage as incomprehensible, and their recall scores were no better than those of the No Knowledge Context group (see Table 5.1). These results indicate that the superior recall of the Appropriate Context Before group was not due to their merely guessing and generating sentences that might relate to the picture they saw (the guessing hypothesis is discussed in Chapter 3, Section 3).

An additional control group was the Partial Context Before group. These people were shown the picture in Figure 5.2 *before* hearing the passage. Note that this picture

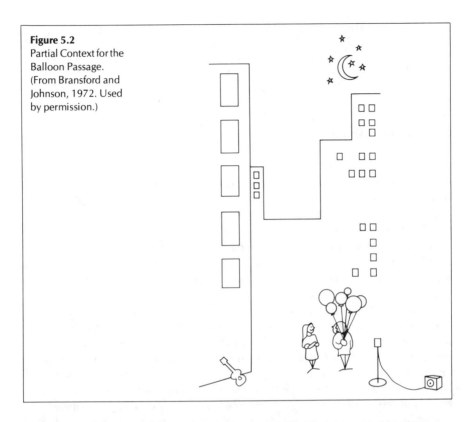

Figure 5.2
Partial Context for the
Balloon Passage.
(From Bransford and
Johnson, 1972. Used
by permission.)

contains all the objects in the appropriate picture, but the relations among the objects are different. In short, the overall structure of the knowledge context is not the same. This Partial Context Before group was included to ensure that a picture (even if it contained the same elements) was not in itself sufficient to facilitate comprehension and recall. As expected, the Partial Context Before group were clearly inferior to the Appropriate Context Before group in both comprehension ratings and recall (see Table 5.1).

Finally, consider the No Knowledge Context–Two Repetitions group. These people were read the passage twice in succession but never saw either picture. After hearing the passage twice, they performed comprehension ratings and then recalled. Table 5.1 indicates that these people also rated the passage as incomprehensible and showed very low recall. It is instructive to compare the performance of the No Knowledge Context–Two Repetitions group with that of the Appropriate Context Before group. The Two Repetitions group spent Time 1 trying to learn and understand the passage, and Time 2 performing the same activity. In contrast, people in the Appropriate Context-Before group spent Time 1 viewing the picture and devoted only Time 2 to trying to learn and understand the passage. In short, although the Two Repetitions group had twice as much exposure to the information to be learned, they performed much more poorly than the Appropriate Context Before group. These results suggest that the best way to spend one's time is not necessarily to focus only on the material that will eventually be tested; if

Table 5.2   Free Recall and Cued Recall for the Balloon Passage

	No Context	Context After	Context Before	Maximum Score
Free recall (no cues):	3.92	4.33	7.33	14.00
Keyword cues:	4.00	3.75	8.50	14.00

From Bransford and Johnson (1973). Used by permission.

certain information is needed to better understand the material to be learned, it is more beneficial to spend time learning the *prerequisite* material—even if it means spending less time on the actual material that forms the basis for a subsequent test.

The balloon experiment utilized measures of free recall. Suppose people were provided with key words from the balloon passage as retrieval cues at the time of the test (words like *balloon, window, wire, human voice, instrument, contact*). Would the No Knowledge Context group now perform at a level closer to that of the Appropriate Context Before group?

Nyberg and Cleary (see Bransford and Johnson, 1973) conducted such a study. They found that the presentation of retrieval cues increased rather than decreased the differences between the groups (see Table 5.2). One of the constraints on the effectiveness of retrieval cues (see Chapter 3, Section 3) is that potential cues must be actively and meaningfully encoded in terms of other items to be remembered. Without an appropriate knowledge context, the No Knowledge Context group presumably were less able to actively understand and encode the sentences in the balloon passage into meaningful events. This limited the capacity of potential retrieval cues to facilitate recall. Note further, however, that the cued-recall results of Nyberg and Cleary's study show that comprehension does not guarantee optimal free recall.

Further Studies of the Role of Activated Knowledge

The balloon study utilized a knowledge context that is unique and unlikely to have been previously experienced. Are such unique contexts necessary in order to demonstrate the intricate relationships between past knowledge and the materials to be learned? Read the following passage. Once again, imagine that you will be asked to recall it after reading it once.

> The procedure is actually quite simple. First you arrange items into different groups. Of course one pile may be sufficient depending on how much there is to do. If you have to go somewhere else due to lack of facilities that is the next step; otherwise, you are pretty well set. It is important not to overdo things. That is, it is better to do too few things at once than too many. In the short run this may not seem important but complications can easily arise. A mistake can be

expensive as well. At first, the whole procedure will seem complicated. Soon, however, it will become just another facet of life. It is difficult to foresee any end to the necessity for this task in the immediate future, but then, one never can tell. After the procedure is completed one arranges the materials into different groups again. Then they can be put into their appropriate places. Eventually they will be used once more and the whole cycle will then have to be repeated. However, that is part of life.

Bransford and Johnson (1972, 1973; see also Dooling and Lachman, 1971) read a group of people, the No Topic group, the previous passage and then asked them to rate it for comprehensibility and to recall it. Although a few were able to create their own contexts that permitted adequate comprehension, most rated the passage as incomprehensible and exhibited low levels of recall (see Table 5.3). A second group, the Topic Before group, were presented with a topic designed to activate relevant knowledge *before* hearing the passage. They achieved much higher comprehension and recall scores (see Table 5.3). The topic was "washing clothes." If you read the passage given this knowledge, it should make much more sense. A third group, the Topic After group, received the topic *after* hearing the passage but before making comprehension ratings and before recall. This procedure did little to facilitate either comprehension or recall (see Table 5.3). These findings indicate that simply having prior knowledge when making comprehension ratings or recalling is not necessarily sufficient to ensure adequate results. Previous knowledge must be activated in order to facilitate one's current abilities to understand and learn.

Prerequisites for Understanding Visual Objects

Relationships between current information and activated knowledge are important for understanding visual as well as linguistic inputs. For example, Bransford and McCarrell (1974) presented people with objects like those illustrated in Figure 5.3. These objects were meaningful to all participants at some level. However, most could not identify the objects nor decide what to use them for. Figure 5.4 illustrates appropriate functions for each of the objects. They become more meaningful when one understands and makes use of this additional information. The experiment illustrates that simply

	No Topic	Topic After	Topic Before	Maximum Score
Comprehension ratings:	2.29	2.12	4.50	7.00
Number of idea units recalled:	2.82	2.65	5.83	18.00

Table 5.3   Comprehension and Recall Scores for the "Washing Clothes" Passage

From Bransford and Johnson (1972). Used by permission.

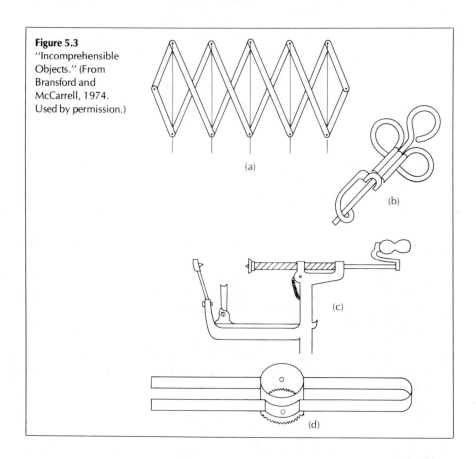

Figure 5.3
"Incomprehensible Objects." (From Bransford and McCarrell, 1974. Used by permission.)

(a)

(b)

(c)

(d)

seeing an object is not sufficient to ensure adequate understanding of it. As Dewey (1963) notes,

> To grasp the meaning of a thing, an event or a situation is to see it in its relations to other things; to note how it operates or functions, what consequences follow from it; what causes it, what uses it can be put to. In contrast, what we have called the brute thing, the thing without meaning to us, is something whose relations are not grasped. (P. 135)

Dewey's distinction between brute things and meaningful entities can be illustrated further. As an example, consider our understanding of something as "simple" as a five dollar bill. Searle (1969) notes that money has meaning only in the context of the larger system of social activities in which it is utilized; for "it is only given the institution of money that I now have a five dollar bill in my hand. Take away the institution and all I have is a piece of paper with various gray and green markings" (p. 51). In short, our understanding of particular objects (even something as simple as a five dollar bill) involves the ability to relate those objects to our knowledge of the social institutions characteristic of our culture.

It is also instructive to note that we can understand visual entities at a variety of levels. As an illustration, consider the five pairs of scissors illustrated in Figure 5.5 (see Bransford and McCarrell, 1974). Each of these is meaningful to us at some level because it is consistent with our general knowledge. Nevertheless, many people do not fully understand the differences among various pairs of scissors; they have not specifically considered how the physical features of particular pairs of scissors are related to their distinct functions. Table 5.4 lists the primary functions of each pair of scissors in Figure 5.5. Given this information, the particular structure of each pair becomes more meaningful. One can begin to appreciate the nonarbitrary relationship between particular

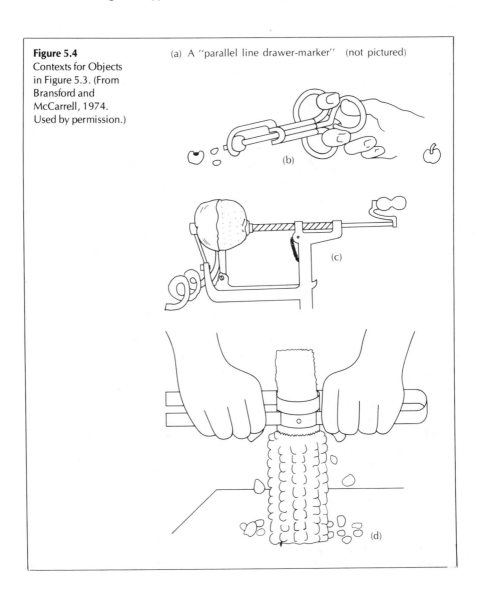

Figure 5.4
Contexts for Objects in Figure 5.3. (From Bransford and McCarrell, 1974. Used by permission.)

(a) A "parallel line drawer-marker"   (not pictured)

(b)

(c)

(d)

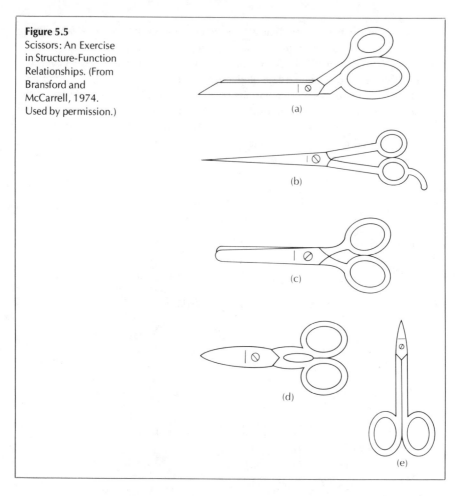

Figure 5.5
Scissors: An Exercise in Structure-Function Relationships. (From Bransford and McCarrell, 1974. Used by permission.)

(a)

(b)

(c)

(d)

(e)

structures and the functions for which they are used. Note that the importance of nonarbitrary relationships was also stressed in our discussion of effective elaboration (Chapter 3, Section 3); for example, elaborating the statement "The tall man bought the crackers" (in Table 3.1) with the phrase "that were on the top shelf" helps people appreciate the relevance of the word *tall*. Similarly, noting that the structure of the blades of dressmaker shears allows people to cut on a flat surface renders this physical feature nonarbitrary. With appropriate knowledge, people are therefore better able to understand reasons for physical as well as linguistic features.

In Chapter 3 we also noted that an increased understanding of the relevance of particular items (such as the word *tall* in our earlier example) facilitates retention. Improvement of understanding might affect problem solving as well. For example, people who understand the nonarbitrary relationship between the structure and function of pairs of scissors might conceivably use this understanding to invent a new pair that permits them to perform particular tasks more efficiently; they should certainly be better equipped to do so than people to whom the relevance of the scissors' structure is

Table 5.4   Functions for Pairs of Scissors Illustrated in Figure 5.5

	Structure	Function
a.	Dressmaker shears	
	heavy	because of heavy use.
	one hole larger than other	so that two or three fingers will fit in larger hole—allows greater steadiness as one cuts cloth on flat surface.
	blades off-centered and aligned with finger hole edge	so that blade can rest on table surface as cloth is cut—again, greater steadiness.
b.	Barber shears	
	very sharp	to cut thin material; i.e., hair.
	pointed	permits blades to snip close to scalp and to snip very small strands of hair.
	hook on finger hole	a rest for one finger which allows scissors to be supported when held at various angles—hence greater maneuverability.
c.	Pocket or children's scissors	
	blunt ends	so scissors can be carried in pocket without cutting through cloth; so children can handle without poking themselves or others.
	short blades	allows greater control by the gross motor movements of the child just learning to cut.
d.	Nail scissors	
	wide and thick at pivot point	to withstand pressure from cutting thick and rigid materials; i.e., nails.
	slightly curved blades	to cut slightly curved nails.
e.	Cuticle scissors	
	very sharp blade	to cut semi-elastic materials; i.e., skin of cuticles.
	small, curved blades	to allow maneuverability necessary to cut small curved area.
	long extension from finger holes to joint	as compensation for short blades, necessary for holding.

From Bransford and McCarrell (1974). Used by permission.

unclear. The following discussion illustrates how improved understanding facilitates problem solving.

Appropriately Activated Knowledge and Problem Solving

An experiment by Bransford and Franks (1976) illustrates the value of appropriately activated knowledge in a simple problem solving task. The six stimuli in Figure 5.6 are illustrations from a total set of twenty-four stimuli that were shown to participants. The task was to learn which stimuli belonged to Category A and which to Category B.

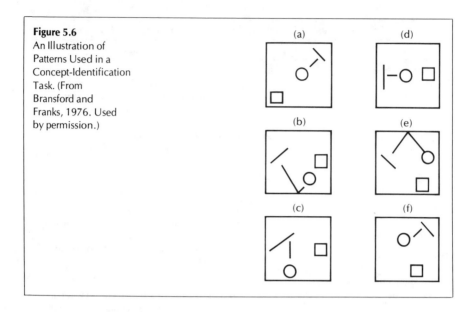

Figure 5.6
An Illustration of
Patterns Used in a
Concept-Identification
Task. (From
Bransford and
Franks, 1976. Used
by permission.)

Although Figure 5.6 shows six of the stimuli presented simultaneously, participants in the experiment saw only one stimulus at a time (successive presentation). During the first trial (a study trial), the experimenter presented each stimulus for four seconds and stated whether it belonged to Category A or Category B. On the second trial (called a test trial), the twenty-four stimuli were shown again (but in a different order), and the participants were asked to indicate whether each one was an A or a B. This procedure was repeated for four more pairs of study-test trials, so that all people received a total of five study trials and five tests. In Figure 5.6, Stimuli a, b, and d belong to Category A, and c, e, and f belong to Category B.

Two groups were tested in the study. They differed only in terms of the initial instructions they received. Before the first study trial, Group 1 were shown pictures of the individual elements constituting the stimuli (a circle, a square, and a long line; and a short line or two lines forming an angle), and they were told that these would occur in different organizations on each stimulus. Group 2 were also shown the individual elements but were told that they had to do with baseball: The circle was a ball, the square a glove, the long line a bat, and the short line (or the two lines forming an angle) the trajectory of the ball. Note that this latter information helped Group 2 to utilize their past knowledge to interpret more meaningfully each of the visual elements. However, this information did not explicitly tell them the answer to the subsequent problem solving task. Every stimulus contained a "ball," a "bat," "glove," and so on, but the task was to discover which stimuli were A's and which were B's.

The results of the study were clear. People in Group 2 were better able to solve the problem than those in Group 1. Through the use of appropriate knowledge, Group 2 were able to perceive each stimulus in dynamic terms (in particular, in terms of a ball moving somewhere) rather than in static terms (for example, in terms of a circle in a certain location). This dynamic orientation helped people focus on certain features designed to be relevant to the problem solution. For all stimuli in Category A, the "ball" was proceeding in a direction (sometimes after a bounce) that would permit it to be caught by the "glove." For Category B stimuli, the "ball" missed the "glove." Once one sees the solution, it becomes obvious. Before reaching the solution, however, it is difficult to know which features are important and which are not. As the experiment shows, previously acquired information (in this case, about baseball) that appropriately guides one's assumptions about what to look for in a set of stimuli also helps one notice how the stimuli may *differ* in important ways.

Summary of Section 1

The experiments discussed in the present section show that identical materials may or may not be understood and remembered depending on the activated knowledge of the learner. In Buhler's (1908) terminology, effective comprehension and communication depend on whether a speaker and listener share a common semantic "field." In other words, effective learning is always a function of relationships between the materials to be learned and the learner's currently activated skills and knowledge (see Figure 1.1). Appropriate knowledge is important for understanding visual objects, as well as linguistic materials. Depending on the nature of the materials to be learned, the presentation of information that helps people activate appropriate knowledge (the presentation of pictures or topics, for instance) can have powerful effects on their abilities to comprehend, to remember, and to solve problems that they confront.

It is instructive to consider how the discussion in this section relates to our analysis of the nature of the materials in Chapter 4. Note, for example, that both the balloon passage and the "washing clothes" passage could be said to violate the given-new contract (Haviland and Clark, 1974; see Chapter 4, Section 3) or to represent incomplete text bases (e.g., Kintsch, 1974, 1976; see Chapter 4, Section 3). Nevertheless, these materials could be understood and remembered when supplemented by appropriate background knowledge (the appropriate picture and the "washing clothes" topic). Many everyday conversations seem incomplete and fragmented when the utterances are analyzed in isolation, and yet they are meaningful when participants can use their shared background knowledge to fill in the gaps. Similarly, learners frequently acquire knowledge of a particular topic by reading or listening to two or more sources of information, so they must use their knowledge to blend sources of information. Because such diverse sources of information do not necessarily constitute a unitary, well-formed text or spoken presentation, learners must frequently fill in gaps and make connections on the basis of prior knowledge. This means, of course, that an analysis of the nature of various materials is valuable and can be used to improve written and spoken instruction (see Chapter 4). Nevertheless, it would be a mistake to restrict one's attention to this one issue. Effective learning and understanding is always a function of relationships among particular inputs and currently activated knowledge. Additional implications of this point are discussed in Section 2.

Section 2: The Role of
Inference in Comprehension

The purpose of this section is to discuss how everyday comprehension depends on people's abilities to make inferences and assumptions based on their general knowledge. Texts and oral presentations frequently leave out many details on the assumption that these can be supplied by the reader or listener (cf. Schank, 1972). Furthermore, identical words, phrases, and sentences may be understood differently depending on the assumptions made by the comprehender. These issues are explored in the following studies.

Lexical Ambiguity

Consider first a simple case of clarifying equivocal words. The sentences "She put the pig in the pen" and "She put the ink in the pen" require two different interpretations of the word *pen*. Many words are *homonyms* and have a number of distinct meanings. For example, *pen* may signify an "ink pen" or a "pig pen"; *cardinal*, a "chirping cardinal" or a "church cardinal"; *jam*, a "traffic jam" or "strawberry jam." The ability to interpret a word in a particular manner depends on linguistic as well as general knowledge of the world.

Researchers have shown that the way in which people originally understand homonyms affects how the homonyms are remembered. For example, assume you first hear a list in which one item includes the word *jam* in the context of *strawberry jam*. In a recognition test, you receive either *traffic jam* or *blueberry jam* and are asked whether you recognize the last word as having occurred during acquisition. Recognition for *jam* in the context of *blueberry* is much better than for *jam* in the context of *traffic* (cf. Light and Carter-Sobell, 1970). Memory is affected by the way in which people comprehend the words at the time of both acquisition and testing.

Differential Interpretations
of Nonhomonyms

Can differential activation of knowledge affect one's interpretation of nonhomonyms? For example, the word *ball* can refer to a sports object or an elegant party and dance. This word is therefore a homonym (see Katz and Fodor, 1963). However, suppose we focus only on the meaning of *ball* as a sports object. Sentences like "The girl hit the ball" and "The girl hid behind the ball" seem to induce different interpretations of *ball*, even when the word is understood as a sports object rather than as a dance. Intuitively, the first sentence suggests a small round object, whereas the second induces one to imagine a ball that is relatively large. Similarly, consider a word like *piano*. A sentence like "The man lifted the piano" seems to orient one to the weight of the piano. In contrast, "The man tuned the piano" focuses attention on a piano's sound but not necessarily on its weight.

As noted in Chapter 3, Section 3, Barclay, Bransford, Franks, McCarrell, and Nitsch (1974) presented people with sets of sentences like the foregoing. One group heard the target nouns (such as *ball* and *piano*) in one context (for example, with such words as *hit* and *lifted*), and a second group heard the targets in the alternative context. After acquisition, participants were presented with retrieval cues and asked to state whether a cue reminded them of target nouns they had heard. For example, they were asked questions like "Do you remember hearing about something heavy?" ". . . something that makes nice sounds?" ". . . a small round object?" ". . . a large round object?" After each cue, people wrote down their response. Results indicated that cues were differentially effective depending on how people had comprehended the target noun at acquisition. The cue *something heavy* was very effective for retrieving *piano* when people had heard "The man lifted the piano" but not when they had heard "The man tuned the piano." In contrast, the cue *something that makes nice sounds* was more effective for people originally hearing the "tuning" sentence than those hearing the "lifting" sentence. Similar results were found for other sentence types and cues. If one assumes that the effectiveness of retrieval cues is strongly influenced by the way in which inputs to be remembered were comprehended at acquisition (e.g., Tulving and Thomson, 1973; see Chapter 3, Section 3), these results suggest that even nonhomonyms are differentially interpreted depending on one's activated knowledge (which is influenced by the context in which the words occur).

Experiments by Anderson and Ortony (1975) provide further evidence for the notion that identical words are interpreted differently depending on context (see also Till, 1977). As an illustration, consider your interpretation of *container* in (1) "The container held the apples" versus (2) "The container held the cola." Anderson and Ortony found that a word like *basket* was a much more effective cue for a sentence like the first, but *bottle* was more effective for the second. This suggests that people's interpretations of *container* did indeed vary as a function of context and that these interpretations were guided by their general knowledge. At an intuitive level, variation in one's interpretations of the word *held* is also illustrated by the examples below (see Anderson, Pichert, Goetz, Schallert, Stevens, and Trollip, 1976):

The container held the cola.

The container held the door.

The brick held the door.

The policeman held the suspect.

The policeman held their attention.

Note the flexible interpretations of *held* as a function of the context in which it occurs.

One way to think about the previous illustrations of semantic flexibility is to assume that people interpret the general meaning of a term (such as *container*), but they don't halt their interpretation at this level. Instead, they *instantiate* (see Anderson and McGaw, 1973) a general term by making it more particular. Given a statement like "The container held the cola," for example, people do not simply think about all possible containers;

they tend to consider a more particular type of container (a bottle, perhaps) that is consistent with their knowledge of the types of vessels that cola is usually contained in.

Experiments by Anderson, Pichert, Goetz, Schallert, Stevens, and Trollip (1976) provide a particularly strong demonstration of processes of instantiation. They presented students with statements like (1) "The woman was outstanding in the theater," in which it seemed likely that most people would instantiate the general term *woman* by assuming that she was an actress. Given a statement like (2) "The woman worked near the theater," however, it seems less likely that the woman would be thought to be an actress. Anderson and colleagues found that a word like *actress* was an excellent retrieval cue for sentences like the first but not for those like the second. Even more important, *actress* was a better retrieval cue for Sentence 1 than the word *woman*. In short, a word that was not presented at acquisition (but was probably inferred) was a better retrieval cue than a word that students had actually heard.

Flexibility in Interpreting Visual Entities

It is instructive to note that flexibility of interpretation is characteristic of our understanding not only of linguistic but also of visual entities. As an illustration, consider your interpretation of the man illustrated in Figure 5.7a and then 5.7b (see Bransford and McCarrell, 1974). In the first case, the interpretation is of a man running; in the second, the man is viewed as chasing. Figure 5.8 provides yet another context and hence a new interpretation of the man.

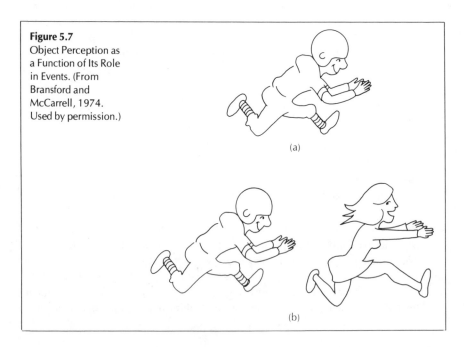

Figure 5.7
Object Perception as a Function of Its Role in Events. (From Bransford and McCarrell, 1974. Used by permission.)

(a)

(b)

Figure 5.8
Object Perception as a Function of Its Role in Events. (From Bransford and McCarrell, 1974. Used by permission.)

The flexibility of interpreting visual entities can also be appreciated by viewing the object illustrated in Figure 5.9. Most people attempt to use what they know to make this object meaningful. For example, many refer to it as a "bumpy lump" or "the back of a bear's head" (see Bransford and McCarrell, 1974). People's interpretation of this entity will vary as a function of the context in which it is embedded, however. Figure 5.10 illustrates three contexts that yield different interpretations of the object illustrated in Figure 5.9.

Comprehension and Inferences about Spatial Relationships

Our previous discussion illustrates how identical words and visual entities may be interpreted differently depending on contextual information and the general knowledge available to the comprehender. Effective comprehension involves much more than the use of prior knowledge to form more specific interpretations of information contained in a scene or message, however; people must also frequently "fill in the gaps" in messages. One example of this type of activity involves making inferences about spatial relationships among objects—inferences that go beyond the information explicitly mentioned in the particular inputs themselves.

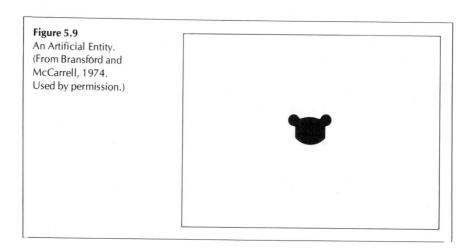

Figure 5.9
An Artificial Entity. (From Bransford and McCarrell, 1974. Used by permission.)

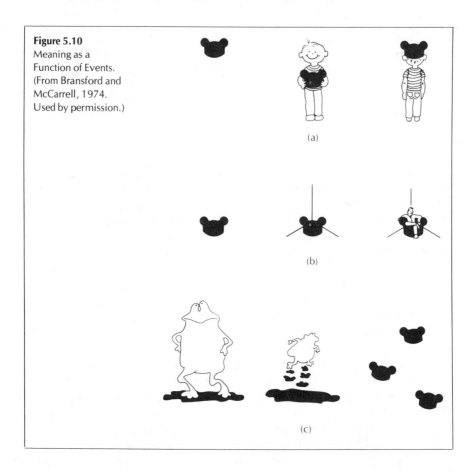

Figure 5.10
Meaning as a
Function of Events.
(From Bransford and
McCarrell, 1974.
Used by permission.)

(a)

(b)

(c)

Consider a sentence like "Three turtles rested beside a floating log, and a fish swam beneath them." Clearly, *them* refers to *the turtles,* and the sentence includes the information that a fish swam beneath the turtles. Compare the following sentence: "Three turtles rested on a floating log, and a fish swam beneath them." The only change in this sentence is the substitution of the word *on* for *beside.* Once again, this sentence explicitly contains the information that a fish swam beneath the turtles. On the basis of knowledge of spatial relationships, however, comprehenders can infer additional information that goes beyond what was explicitly stated. When the turtles were *on* the log, and the fish swam beneath them, the fish must have swum beneath it (the log) as well. Note that this inference regarding spatial relations is much less likely for the sentence containing the word *beside.* When the turtles were *beside* the log, the fish could swim beneath them without going beneath it (the log).

Bransford, Barclay, and Franks (1972) presented two groups with sets of sentences like those about the turtles. One group received the equivalent of the *beside* version of each sentence (the "noninference" version), and the other received versions like the *on* version ("potential inference"). The groups were simply asked to try to understand the sentences because they would be asked to answer questions about them later. After acquisition, participants were given a surprise recognition test. The critical test items included a change in the final pronoun of the original acquisition sentences (for example, "Three turtles rested beside a floating log, and a fish swam beneath *it*"; "Three turtles rested on a floating log, and a fish swam beneath *it*"). Note that if people had originally experienced a *beside* version, they also received *beside* in the critical test item.

Assume that people hearing the *on* version of the sentence did indeed make spontaneous spatial inferences during acquisition—that is, that when the turtles were on the log and a fish swam beneath them, it must also have swum beneath the log. These people might then erroneously believe that they had actually heard the critical test item (where the pronoun *them* was changed to *it*), even though it had not occurred during acquisition (this is called a false positive response or false recognition). In contrast, people who heard the *beside* version of the target item might be less likely to "falsely recognize" it, because the sentence would not be consistent with the information they had acquired. Results indicated that people originally receiving the potential-inference sentences were indeed likely to falsely recognize the critical test items. In short, people appear to make spontaneous inferences about spatial relations among objects when they comprehend.

Bransford, Barclay, and Franks (1972) reported a similar finding when sets of sentences were used to communicate an overall understanding of the spatial relationships among objects. For example, students heard several descriptions of the following type:

> There is a tree with a box beside it, and a chair is on top of the box. The box is to the right of the tree. The tree is green and extremely tall.

The reasoning was that students hearing such descriptions should know more than the information in the individual sentences. For example, they should also know that the chair is to the right of the tree or that the tree is to the left of the chair, even though this information was not presented. In a recognition task in which students were asked to choose which sentence they had actually heard from among a set of alternatives, students were much more likely to choose a sentence like "The tree is to the left of the chair" than they were to choose a sentence like "The chair is to the left of the tree," which violated the overall set of relationships.

Experiments by McCarrell, Bransford, and Johnson (see Bransford and Johnson, 1973) further illustrate the importance of making assumptions about spatial relationships among objects. They note that a sentence like "The haystack was important because the cloth ripped" is generally incomprehensible to most college students but that given the cue *parachute*, it becomes clear. It is easy to assume that presentation of the cue *parachute* simply provides a more specific referent for the word *cloth*. Note, however, that one must also assume that the parachute (and parachutist) was *above* the haystack in order for the sentence to become comprehensible. If one assumed that the haystack was above the parachute, the sentence would still be difficult to understand.

Assumptions about Instruments
Used to Perform Particular Acts

Read the following passage:

John was trying to fix the bird house. He was pounding the nail when his father
came out to watch him and to help him do the work.

What types of assumptions are made when understanding a simple passage like this?
One highly likely assumption involves the existence of some instrument (probably a
hammer) used to pound the nail. The passage doesn't mention a hammer, but it really
doesn't need to. This type of information can be supplied from one's general knowledge
of the world. Contrast the following passage:

John was trying to fix the bird house. He was looking for the nail when his father
came out to watch him and to help him do the work.

Only a few words are changed, but now assumptions about a hammer seem much less
likely. The act of looking for a nail and the act of pounding a nail require different types
of assumptions.

Johnson, Bransford, and Solomon (1973) presented groups of people with a set of
simple passages like those above. One group heard one version of each of the passages
and the second group heard the alternate version. After acquisition, both groups were
presented with identical sets of test sentences. Their task was to recognize whether each
test sentence was exactly like (contained exactly the same words as) sentences occurring
in the acquisition task.

A subset of the recognition test items was constructed to determine whether people
had made certain types of inferences during acquisition. The critical test item for the two
versions of the passage presented above was as follows:

John was using the hammer to fix the bird house when his father came out to
watch him and to help him do the work.

Results indicated that people who had originally heard the first version of the passage
were much more likely to falsely recognize the aforementioned critical test item than
were people who heard the second version of the passage. This suggests that assumptions about a hammer were indeed involved in understanding the first passage. When
you comprehend sentences like "The man was shot" versus "The man was stabbed,"
don't assumptions about different types of instruments come to mind (cf. Kintsch, 1972)?

Inferring the Consequences of Events

The Johnson, Bransford, and Solomon (1973) study also investigated whether
people spontaneously make a different type of inference. Imagine hearing a passage like
the following:

The river was narrow. A beaver hit the log that a turtle was sitting on, and the log flipped over from the shock. The turtle was very surprised by the event.

People who heard a set of acquisition passages including this one were very likely to falsely recognize the following critical test item:

A beaver hit the log and knocked the turtle into the water.

In contrast, consider the recognition performance of people who had heard the following acquisition passage:

The river was narrow. A beaver hit the log that a turtle was sitting beside, and the log flipped over from the shock. The turtle was very surprised by the event.

Although only one word had been changed (on to beside), people hearing the passage were now much less likely to recognize the critical test item. These data suggest that the comprehension process involves assumptions about the possible consequences of previously experienced events.

Creating Situations That
Justify the Relations among Events

Assume that you hear either Sentence 1 or Sentence 2 below:

1. John missed the bus so he knew he would have to walk to school.

2. John missed the bus because he knew he would have to walk to school.

The only difference between these two sentences is the inclusion of because or so. Do such connections affect the types of assumptions that comprehenders make? McCarrell, Bransford, and Johnson (see Bransford and Johnson, 1973) investigated the effects of comprehending phrases connected by either because or so. Note that a word like because can be viewed as an instruction to create a situation in which Phrase X follows from Phrase Y. In contrast, the connective so instructs one to make Y follow from X. People who hear Sentence 2 above frequently assume that John wanted to walk to school so he purposely missed the bus. Indeed, in subsequent memory tests this latter group stated that they actually heard test sentences like "John wanted to walk to school so he purposely missed the bus." However, people who heard Sentence 1 during acquisition did not falsely recognize such test foils.

As an additional example of the role of causal connectives, consider (1) "The mirror broke so the child grabbed the broom," and (2) "The mirror broke because the child grabbed the broom." In the latter case, most people assume that grabbing the broom resulted in the mirror's breaking. This assumption is not made in the first sentence. Clearly, connectives like because and so play important roles in guiding the assumptions people make in order to comprehend.

Sentences containing the connective and can also require assumptions that justify certain relationships (see especially R. Lakoff, 1971). Consider the sentence "The policeman held up his hand, and the cars stopped." Aren't assumptions that cars have drivers and drivers apply their brakes involved in understanding a simple sentence like this? Collins and Quillian (1972) suggest the following situation. Assume that there was an earthquake, which caused some parked cars to begin rolling down a hill. Now, given the sentence "The policeman held up his hand, and the cars stopped," one is forced to ask, How did he do that? The earthquake context rules out the possibility of assuming that drivers applied their brakes when viewing the policeman's hand signal. Under normal situations, however, assumptions about "drivers who apply their brakes" seem to be made.

The importance of making assumptions that justify relations among events is even more apparent in attempts to understand stories. Consider the following sentences:

1. Mary heard the ice cream man coming.

2. She remembered the pocket money.

3. She rushed into the house.

Rumelhart and Ortony (1977) note that these three sentences form a "snippet" of a story, which most people can interpret quite readily. Nevertheless, a number of assumptions are necessary in order to accomplish this feat.

> *Presumably this interpretation is along the lines that Mary heard the ice cream man coming and wanted to buy some ice cream. Buying ice cream costs money, so she had to think of a quick source of funds. She remembered some pocket money she had not yet spent which, presumably, was in the house. So, Mary hurried into the house trying to get the money by the time the ice cream man arrived. (P. 113)*

A similar example of assumptions necessary to connect sentences is provided by Schank and Abelson (1975).

1. John knew his wife's operation would be expensive.

2. There was always Uncle Harry.

3. John reached for the suburban telephone book.

Clearly, much information is involved in tying these sentences together; for example, assumptions about the need for money, that a relative might be likely to lend it, that the money could never be borrowed without contacting the uncle, that telephones can be used to make contact, and so on. Even children's stories require many assumptions to link sentences together to form coherent events (see Charniak, 1972; Rumelhart, 1975, 1977). The particular assumptions made are also guided by aspects of the story context. As an illustration, consider the story below (see Bransford and McCarrell, 1974):

> *The man was worried. His car came to a halt and he was all alone. It was extremely dark and cold. The man took off his overcoat, rolled down the window, and got out of the car as quickly as possible. Then he used all his strength to move as fast as he could. He was relieved when he finally saw the lights of the city, even though they were far away.*

Note that this passage is comprehensible in isolation. If you consider, however, you will probably realize that you made many assumptions that were not explicit in the text itself. To appreciate this, reread the passage, but this time with knowledge that the second sentence refers to a submerged car. Given this knowledge, many events seem to be understood differently. Even the addition of a single adjective can affect how one understands a set of events.

As a further example of how contextual cues affect one's assumptions while comprehending, assume that you do not read but, rather, are read the following passage; furthermore, imagine that you will be asked to remember what you heard. The title of the passage is "Watching a Peace March from the Fortieth Floor."

> *The view was breathtaking. From the window one could see the crowd below. Everything looked extremely small from such a distance, but the colorful costumes could still be seen. Everyone seemed to be moving in one direction in an orderly fashion, and there seemed to be little children as well as adults. The landing was gentle, and luckily the atmosphere was such that no special suits had to be worn. At first there was a great deal of activity. Later, when the speeches started, the crowd quieted down. The man with the television camera took many shots of the setting and the crowd. Everyone was very friendly and seemed glad when the music started.*

People who are told that this passage refers to a peace march are generally able to understand and remember all of the sentences except the one stating, "The landing was gentle . . ." They note that this sentence "jars" them. Under conditions of free recall, as well as cued recall, they are also unlikely to remember it (see Bransford and Johnson, 1973). Contrast this level of performance with that of people who are told that the passage is about a "Space Trip to an Inhabited Planet." This second group of people state that they are much less jarred by the landing sentence. Furthermore, they are much more likely to remember the landing sentence under conditions of free recall and cued recall (see Bransford and Johnson, 1973). The reference to the space trip presumably helped these people make assumptions that permitted them to make sense of the reference to a landing.

It is also instructive to examine the activities of those few people in the first group who were able to make sense of and remember the sentence that jarred upon them. Interpreting the passage in terms of watching a peace march from the fortieth floor, what assumptions did they have to make in order to make the "landing" make sense? Consider the response of one creative participant. In order to understand the "landing," she "moved" the whole peace march from the middle of a city to the airport, created a helicopter that landed with a famous person who was to be a speaker at the peace march, and assumed that *atmosphere* referred to the peaceful nature of the march, indicating that anti-Mace suits need not be worn. In short, the comprehender had to *invent* situations that would permit the passage to make sense.

The creative, problem solving aspect of comprehension activities is also illustrated by our final example. Bransford and Johnson (1973) presented people with the following sentence and asked them to try to understand it: "Bill is able to come to the party tonight because his car broke down." Most people indicated that they could comprehend this sentence by means of an invented context in which it made sense. A typical context is as follows:

> *Bill was originally going to leave town, but now he could not leave because his car broke down. Since he could not leave, he could come to the party since the party was in town.*

This act of creating an elaborate context in order to understand the *because* clause of the input sentence is a far cry from merely interpreting the meanings of the phrases "Bill is able to come to the party tonight" and "his car broke down." In some sense, *because* acts as a cue or instruction to elaborate an appropriate context. As noted in Section 1, if people cannot solve the problem of context creation, they cannot fully understand the input. Contextual cues in a passage can therefore either facilitate or hurt performance because they influence the types of assumptions that people make.

Comprehension and Communication

The examples discussed in this section illustrate that processes of understanding even simple sentences involve assumptions and inferences based on general knowledge. Clearly, we need to have a knowledge of language in order to make plausible assumptions about sentences that clarify their meaning. For example, if you have no knowledge of words like *because* or *so,* you will not know what kinds of additional assumptions to make when hearing sentences that contain them. Similarly, if you hear "The boy was found by the Nog," lack of knowledge of the word *Nog* limits precise understanding. If you knew that *Nog* referred to a famous landmark in some area, it would become clear that the boy was found in a certain geographic location. Suppose *Nog* refers to an animal with a very sensitive nose for tracking. Now the sentence might be paraphrased "The Nog found the boy."

The problem of distinguishing purely linguistic knowledge from general knowledge of the world is complicated, and it may be impossible to separate the two. Some linguists (e.g., Fillmore, 1971a, 1971b) have suggested that to understand language is to understand how to use words and sentences that express intended meanings and how to determine what others mean when they use them. It appears that effective comprehension involves more than merely linguistic knowledge. We use linguistic knowledge *in conjunction with* general knowledge to understand effectively (e.g., see Schank, 1972; Winograd, 1972).

This orientation toward processes of comprehension has some important implications for understanding human communication. As an illustration, consider the following demonstration story. It is entitled "The Prisoner."

> *Rocky slowly got up from the mat, planning his escape. He hesitated a moment and thought. Things were not going well. What bothered him the most was being held, especially since the charge against him had been weak. He considered his present situation. The lock that held him was strong but he thought he could break it. He knew, however, that his timing would have to be perfect. Rocky was aware that it was because of his early roughness that he had been penalized so severely—much too severely from his point of view. The situation was becoming frustrating; the pressure had been grinding on him for too long. He was being ridden unmercifully. Rocky was getting angry now. He felt he was ready to make his move. He knew that his success or failure would depend on what he did in the next few seconds.*

This paragraph seems quite straightforward. Did you notice anything special about it? Read it again, this time substituting the title "The Wrestler." Clearly, the passage can be understood in two quite different ways. In this procedure, you were given specific titles for the passage. What if ambiguous passages like this were read without titles? Would the past history and interests of listeners affect the kinds of interpretations they made?

Anderson, Reynolds, Schallert, and Goetz (see Anderson, 1977) used ambiguous passages to examine relationships between comprehension and people's knowledge and interests. For example, the demonstration story (without a title) was read to different groups of college students including those in weight lifting class. Similarly, a passage that could be interpreted in terms of playing cards or playing music was read to music students. Additional groups of people were tested, and biographical information about their interests and past experiences was obtained. Multiple-choice tests like the following were used to assess the interpretations they had made of the passages:

How had Rocky been punished for his aggressiveness?

a. He had been demoted to the "B" team.

b. His opponent had been given points.

c. He lost his privileges for the weekend.

d. He had been arrested and imprisoned.

Results indicated that people's interests and past experiences strongly affected the way in which they interpreted the passages. Furthermore, the majority (80 percent) of them were not aware that the passages could be interpreted in more than one way while they were reading them. They failed to detect even the most obvious ambiguity that these passages contained.

The use of general knowledge for understanding has both positive and negative aspects. On the positive side, speakers and writers can generally be understood without having to state explicitly all the details involved in comprehension. On the negative side, listeners can make assumptions that lead them to understand messages in ways other than those speakers or writers intend. An illustration is provided by the author Doris Lessing. In the preface to the third edition of her book *The Golden Notebook* (1973), she discusses the type of letters people have written to her concerning the book. Some see the book as dealing exclusively with women's liberation, others as dealing with politics, and still others view the main theme as mental illness. Yet it is the same book.

> *And naturally these incidents bring up again questions of what people see when they read a book, and why one person sees one pattern and nothing at all of another pattern, and how odd it is to have, as author, such a clear picture of a book, that is seen so very differently by its readers. (Lessing, 1973, p. xxi)*

Summary of Section 2

The purpose of this section was to illustrate how everyday comprehension involves inferences and assumptions based on general knowledge. If we hear a statement like "The container held the apples," for example, we generally assume that *container* refers to a basket or box rather than a bottle (e.g., Anderson and Ortony, 1975). We make similar assumptions about visual entities (see Figure 5.7–5.10). We also tend to make assumptions about spatial relationships among items (as in the "turtles" sentences); about instruments used to carry out various activities (for example, about the hammer used by the boy); about the motives of people (for example, John's motive in missing the bus). The assumptions we make are also guided by contextual clues contained in a message (a clue like the car's being *submerged*). There are therefore many levels at which we can comprehend a message, and our interpretations vary depending on our currently activated knowledge of the world.

The notion that comprehension involves active contributions on the part of the listener or reader has both positive and negative implications. On the positive side, speakers and writers need not impart a host of explicit details, because they can assume that various gaps will be filled in by the comprehender. On the negative side, listeners and readers can supply their own interpretations and hence misunderstand an intended message. Note that active contributions to comprehension can also affect the accuracy of remembering. People frequently think that they actually heard or read information (for example, that the boy used a hammer) that could only have been inferred. Relationships between comprehending and remembering are more fully explored in Section 3.

Section 3: Relationships between Comprehending and Remembering

The goal of this section is to explore carefully the relationships between comprehending and remembering. In Section 1 we noted that poor understanding resulted in poor memory performance (the balloon and "washing clothes" experiments). It might therefore be tempting to assume that the better the comprehension, the better memory performance will be. Note, however, that many of the studies in Section 2 suggested that the act of making assumptions while comprehending frequently resulted in errors in memory. People often thought they had actually read or heard information that they had only inferred.

In order to understand relationships between comprehension and memory, we must pay careful attention to the criteria used to assess memory. The different criteria we use, such as word-for-word accuracy or general paraphrase, will affect our conclusions. Note, for example, that in some situations it is sufficient for people to remember the gist of a message. They may also think they remember things that were only inferred. Frequently this does not matter, but there *are* situations where it is important to re-member what happened in as precise a manner as possible. In courtroom testimony, for example, the ideal goal is to remember exactly what a person said, rather than make inferences about what the person might have meant. The types of assumptions made while comprehending can therefore help or hurt performance, depending on the final testing or performance criteria (see Figure 1.1). Several investigations of relationships between comprehension and remembering are discussed below.

Understanding and
Remembering Deictic Elements

Consider first a situation where available information facilitates comprehension and memory for particular words or concepts. In particular, consider a class of words whose interpretations are particularly influenced by context; words that the linguist Fillmore (1966) calls *deictic* elements. Examples are words like *this, that, here,* and *there.* An experiment by Brewer and Harris (1974) shows how one's memory for deictic elements is influenced by contextual information that helps one understand them in more pre-cise ways.

Before we look specifically at Brewer and Harris's study, consider a typical memory experiment in which participants are presented with sentences like "Asparagus grows wild in this county" (note the deictic element *this*). This sentence is comprehensible to a certain extent. Note, however, that sentences presented in an experimental context are usually viewed as *examples* of utterances that *someone* might make at *some time* and in *some place.* Bransford, McCarrell, and Nitsch (1976) note that a sentence like "Bill has a red car" is deemed comprehensible by participants in a typical learning and memory experiment. It is viewed as an example of a potential English sentence. However, try walking up to a friend (or a stranger, if you dare) and simply uttering "Bill has a red car." The listener will know what you said but not what you mean. Listeners expect utterances to be relevant to their present situation. If they cannot understand the relevance, they fail to understand fully.

When Brewer and Harris presented sentences like "Asparagus grows wild in this county" in an experimental context, they found that participants made many errors in subsequent recall. The sentence was frequently recalled as "Asparagus grows wild in *the* (or *that*) county." It is tempting to conclude that words like *this* are simply abstract and hence relatively difficult to remember. Note, however, that the latter assumption fails to acknowledge that comprehension and memory are a function of *relationships* between linguistic knowledge and one's currently activated knowledge of the world (see Sections 1 and 2).

The ingenious aspect of Brewer and Harris's study was as follows. The experimenters presented the same sentences to a second group of participants but made it clear that they were saying things that were relevant to "this particular time and place." For example, participants in the second group knew that the phrase "this county" referred to the county in which the experiment was conducted. The ability to utilize contextually relevant information therefore helped participants to interpret words like *this* and *that* in a precise and nonarbitrary manner. Their memory for these deictic elements was thereby improved; for example, they accurately recalled *"this* county" rather than *the* (or *that*) county. The importance of making information nonarbitrary was also stressed in Chapter 3, Section 3 (for example, "The tall man bought the crackers that were on the top shelf"), and Chapter 4, Section 3 ("The group felt sorry for the fat man but couldn't help chuckling about the incident"). In the present example, however, the extra information that facilitated elaborative activities stemmed from knowledge of the relevance of the immediate environment rather than from extra phrases and sentences presented in a text.

Memory, Paraphrase, and Distortions

The experiments by Brewer and Harris (1974) suggest that contextually relevant information can facilitate people's comprehension and memory for acquisition sentences. Frequently, however, people use what they know to interpret messages in a way that changes their original meaning. In such instances, people's attempts to remember can result in distortions of the original message. Note that a distortion is different from a paraphrase. In Chapter 4, Section 2, we discussed how people may remember the deep or conceptual structure of sentences yet forget the exact surface structure (e.g., Sachs, 1967). A statement like "The ball was hit by the boy" might therefore be remembered as "The boy hit the ball." Paraphrases tend to preserve underlying meanings, whereas distortions change meaning. Some illustrations are provided below.

Bartlett (1932) was one of the first theorists to emphasize the importance of distortions in recall. He argued that memory is *reconstructive*. Even though we think we are accurately remembering, we frequently make errors because we are reconstructing details according to assumptions about "what must have been true." The following extract is a passage used in some of Bartlett's (1932) experiments. The story, entitled "The War of the Ghosts," is based on fairly mystical cultural assumptions that were unfamiliar to people in the experiments. Bartlett was interested in the degree to which their "efforts after meaning" would produce distortions in recall.

> One night two young men from Egulac went down to the river to hunt seals, and while they were there it became foggy and calm. Then they heard war-cries, and they thought: "Maybe this is a war-party." They escaped to the shore, and hid behind a log. Now canoes came up, and they heard the noise of paddles,

and saw one canoe coming up to them. There were five men in the canoe, and they said:

"What do you think? We wish to take you along. We are going up the river to make war on the people."

One of the young men said: "I have no arrows."

"Arrows are in the canoe," they said.

"I will not go along. I might be killed. My relatives do not know where I have gone. But you," he said, turning to the other, "may go with them."

So one of the young men went, but the other returned home.

And the warriors went on up the river to a town on the other side of Kalama. The people came down to the water, and they began to fight, and many were killed. But presently the young man heard one of the warriors say: "Quick, let us go home: that Indian has been hit." Now he thought: "Oh, they are ghosts." He did not feel sick, but they said he had been shot.

So the canoes went back to Egulac, and the young man went ashore to his house, and made a fire. And he told everybody and said: "Behold I accompanied the ghosts, and we went to fight. Many of our fellows were killed, and many of those who attacked us were killed. They said I was hit, and I did not feel sick."

He told it all, and then he became quiet. When the sun rose he fell down. Something black came out of his mouth. His face became contorted. The people jumped up and cried.

He was dead.

Bartlett found that there were indeed distortions in recall, and that they tended to be systematic. For example, many of the proper names (*Egulac* and *Kalama*) and other unfamiliar details would not be remembered; Bartlett called this *flattening*. Some details were also *sharpened* or elaborated. For example, the reference to "my relatives" might become "an old mother at home who is dependent on me." Bartlett also noted a third type of recall change, which he called *rationalization*. People made the story shorter, more coherent, and more consistent with their cultural expectations. In short, they seemed to be *reconstructing* the story according to their expectations about what must have been the case.

Experiments by Carmichael, Hogan, and Walter (1932) provide further evidence for Bartlett's view of memory. Participants were presented with twelve pictorial figures like the four illustrated in Figure 5.11. They also heard a verbal label while they viewed each picture. For example, some heard that the first picture in Figure 5.11 resembled eyeglasses, others that it resembled a dumbbell. Results indicated that the labels heard at the time of acquisition influenced people's drawings at time of recall (see Figure 5.11). As in Bartlett's (1932) experiments, people tended to interpret information in terms of previously acquired knowledge and concepts, which in turn influenced their recall of the material. Note once again that people frequently felt they were accurately remembering when, in fact, they were systematically distorting the information they had originally seen.

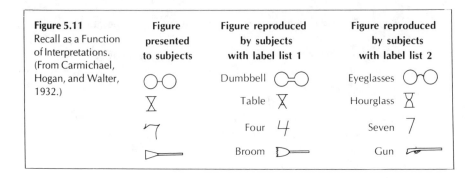

Figure 5.11 Recall as a Function of Interpretations. (From Carmichael, Hogan, and Walter, 1932.)	Figure presented to subjects	Figure reproduced by subjects with label list 1	Figure reproduced by subjects with label list 2
	⊙–○	Dumbbell ⊙–○	Eyeglasses ⊙–○
	X	Table X	Hourglass X
	7	Four 4	Seven 7
	▷—	Broom ▷—	Gun ↠

Investigations of Reconstructive Processes

Bartlett's (1932) approach to remembering is consistent with Buhler's approach (see Section 1) to comprehension. These theorists emphasize the importance of focusing on the relationships between the materials to be learned and the preexisting knowledge and skills of the learner (see Figure 1.1). Both comprehension and memory are strongly influenced by what the learner already knows.

It is instructive to note, however, that there are at least two general ways that previously acquired knowledge can affect comprehension and remembering. One is that people may use their knowledge to make certain assumptions and interpretations during the time of initial learning. We shall call this the *constructive hypothesis* (e.g., Bransford, Barclay, and Franks, 1972). From this perspective, comprehension involves the construction of meanings and inferences that may differ from the original message. Memories may prove inaccurate because people remember their constructions rather than the original information presented during the acquisition task. For example, they may think they remember that the boy used the hammer to pound the nail, although *hammer* was only inferred (see Section 2).

In contrast, the *reconstructive hypothesis* (e.g., Bartlett, 1932) assumes that remembering is not simply the retrieval of previously stored constructions; it is more like problem solving. People remember only the general idea of what was presented and then reconstruct the details according to their expectations of "what must have been true." They think they are accurately remembering when, in fact, they are not.

Of course, both constructive and reconstructive processes could (and probably do) influence remembering. It is often difficult to know whether memory distortions are due to one process or the other. For example, the results of the experiments by Bartlett (1932) and by Carmichael, Hogan, and Walter (1932) could be due to constructive processes during learning, reconstructive processes at the time of testing, or a combination of the two. Nevertheless, it merits attention that these two views of the role of prior knowledge have different implications. The major implications of a constructive hypothesis are sufficiently illustrated by our experiments relating to inference in Section 2 of this chapter. The major implication of the reconstructive hypothesis is that new information about a previous topic may affect one's memory for the topic by providing a different basis for reconstruction. The remainder of this section explores the possibility in detail.

The reconstructive hypothesis suggests, then, that new information can influence one's memory for previously experienced information. At first glance this possibility seems to be ruled out by experiments discussed earlier. In particular, the balloon and "washing clothes" studies (see Section 1) showed that information (the picture and the topic) presented *after the fact* did not facilitate comprehension and recall. Note, however, that the balloon and "washing clothes" passages were not comprehensible without the activation of appropriate knowledge. Because of this lack of comprehensibility, there is no coherent information to reinterpret in the light of the information presented after the fact (see Bransford and Johnson, 1973). A more appropriate test of reconstruction would involve messages that are initially comprehensible but can also be reinterpreted in the light of subsequent information. Experiments that meet this criterion are discussed below.

Experiments by Spiro (1977) provide evidence for the importance of reconstructive memory processes. A major aspect of Spiro's work is that he discusses the conditions under which a reconstructive theorist would expect systematic memory distortions to occur. Note, for example, that reconstructive theory does not assume that distortions will occur for all types of materials; if stories and pictures are consistent with people's knowledge and expectations, recall should be relatively accurate (in this context, we are assuming that paraphrases which do not drastically change meanings represent accurate recall). What reconstructive theory does assume is that when knowledge and experience change systematically over time, recall, too, will become systematically distorted. Spiro (1977) notes that the reason many theorists (e.g., Gomulicki, 1956) have argued against Bartlett's reconstructive hypothesis is that they have failed to find this relationship between systematic changes over time and systematic distortions; and he argues that their experimental tests have simply been inappropriate. Reconstructive errors should occur only with some sets of materials and in certain situations. In short, Spiro notes that memory performance will be a function of relationships among the types of materials, the nature of the learning activities, and the currently available skills and knowledge of the learner. His orientation is therefore consistent with our framework illustrated in Figure 1.1.

As an illustration of the types of studies conducted by Spiro (1977), imagine hearing a description of an engaged couple, Bob and Margie. The description refers to Bob's strong desire not to have children. He is reluctant to mention this to his fiancee, Margie, but finally does so. In one version of the story, Margie states that she feels the same way, and there are no conflicts of interest. In a second version of the story (heard by different people), Margie is horrified and states that children are very important to her. By changing a few sentences, Spiro created situations involving personal conflict versus no conflict. Near the end of the experiment, Spiro included a further experimental manipulation: He mentioned that (1) Margie and Bob married and are living happily together; or (2) they broke off their engagement; or (3) he said nothing about their current state. Through this manipulation, Spiro was able to create additional degrees of conflict between new information and previously stated facts.

In order to understand how these varying degrees of conflict could be used to predict reconstructive memory errors, consider the following. People who first heard that neither Bob nor Margie wanted children and were later told that they married received information that was consistent with their initial expectations. Contrast this with a situation where people receive information about Bob and Margie's disagreement regarding children and are later told that Bob and Margie married. If people in this second group used their knowledge that the couple is married to reconstruct the descriptions of the couple's earlier interactions, one would expect them to make systematic errors in reconstruction. For example, they might inadvertently minimize the fact that Bob and Margie had disagreed about having children, and elaborate those areas where the couple had reached agreements. In contrast, people who received consistent or "nonconflicting" information should recall more accurately.

Spiro's results lend strong support to the reconstruction position (see Royer, 1977, however). In general, systematic distortions increased as the degree of conflict between the couples' current state (married or unmarried) and their previous interactions increased. Distortions were also greater as the interval between initial learning and subsequent recall increased (the intervals were two days, three weeks, and six weeks). It is also noteworthy that people thought their memories were accurate. Spiro asked them to rate their confidence in the statements recalled and found no difference between ratings for those that were actually true and ratings for those that were false. People therefore believed they were accurately remembering when they were actually reconstructing details on the basis of their expectations.

Experiments by Snyder and Uranowitz (1978) provide further evidence for processes of reconstruction. They presented different groups of students with the same narrative, about the life of a woman named Betty K. The narrative provided information about Betty's birth, childhood, education, choice of profession, and so on. It also described her early home life, relationship with parents, and social life (for example, it stated that Betty dated occasionally). The crucial aspect of the study was the type of information students received *after* reading the narrative. Students in one group were told that Betty is now a lesbian; those in another group, that she follows a heterosexual lifestyle. This "after the fact" information was designed to activate different stereotyped assumptions about lesbians and heterosexuals. Would this affect how people remembered what they had learned about Betty earlier?

One week after all the students had read the case history, they were asked to remember as accurately as possible the details of Betty's life. Multiple-choice tests like the following were used to probe their memory for the events:

In high school Betty—

a. Occasionally dated men

b. Never went out with men

c. Went steady

d. No information provided

Results indicated that students' performance was strongly influenced by the degree to which earlier information was consistent with stereotyped beliefs about lesbian and heterosexual lifestyles. For example, although the original narrative stated that Betty dated occasionally, people who heard that Betty is a lesbian were likely to believe they had read that Betty never went out with men.

Snyder and Uranowitz note that their findings have important social implications. As an illustration, assume that you have known Betty for a long time and really like her. When told she is a lesbian, your ideal reaction would be to retain the same opinion of her, remembering all the things about her that you like. The reconstructive hypothesis suggests that this may not happen, however; social stereotypes about lesbians may influence memory and produce reinterpretations of previous experiences or information. In this way, reconstructive memories reinforce social stereotypes. As Snyder and Uranowitz (1978) argue, this may be one of the reasons many inaccurate stereotypes (including those involving sexuality) are so resistant to change.

The notion that remembering can be reconstructive has additional social implications. According to reconstructive theory, we can think we are accurately remembering when in fact we are not. For example, a person might be able to pass a lie-detector test and yet give faulty courtroom testimony because of errors in reconstructive memory. Furthermore, changes in concepts and expectations that serve as the basis of reconstruction might lead to exaggerated memory distortions. For example, if certain leading questions prompt changes in general expectations, we might expect memory to change as well.

An experiment by Loftus and Palmer (1974) provides an illustration of this argument. They showed students a film about an auto accident and then asked different leading questions to different groups. Groups 1, 2, and 3 received, respectively, the following leading questions:

1. About how fast were the cars going when they bumped?
2. About how fast were the cars going when they collided?
3. About how fast were the cars going when they smashed?

One week later, all participants were asked questions about the accident. One question was "Did you see broken glass?" (The film had not shown any broken glass.) The probability of saying yes to this question varied as a function of the leading questions asked earlier. In particular, people who had received Question 3 (which implies that the cars were going very fast) were more likely to think there was broken glass than people who had received Question 1 or 2.

Summary of Section 3

The purpose of this section was to explore some of the relationships between comprehending and remembering. Although contextual information that facilitates understanding may sometimes help memory (see, for example, Brewer and Harris's study of deictic elements), the use of prior knowledge to make information coherent and sensible (Bartlett's "effort after meaning") can sometimes result in distortions in recall.

These distortions can arise from constructive processes at time of comprehension and from reconstructive processes at time of recall. Gross distortions of recall should occur only under certain circumstances, however. If the materials to be learned are consistent with general knowledge and expectations, fewer reconstructive errors should occur (e.g., Spiro, 1977).

The concept of reconstructive memory is especially important because people can *think* they are remembering accurately and yet be failing to do so. Errors in reconstruction can also be magnified by leading questions that change those expectations that serve as the basis for subsequent reconstructive activities (e.g., Loftus and Palmer, 1974). People's confidence in their memories is therefore a questionable criterion for deciding whether these memories are accurate. To make better judgments about accuracy, we will need a more precise understanding of various types of relationships between to-be-learned information and the knowledge and skills of the learner. A detailed analysis of the types of situations that promote accurate and inaccurate memory must await further research.

Section 4: Some Implications of Focusing on the Role of Prior Knowledge

The three sections illustrated how currently available knowledge can affect understanding and remembering. Effective performance is a function of relationships between present inputs and what one already knows. This idea is simple but has some important implications, which require that we take another look at our previous discussion of the structure of materials (Chapter 4). As noted in the summary of Section 1 in this chapter, both the balloon and "washing clothes" passages violate certain norms of good text structure. Nevertheless, these passages can be understood and remembered if learners are able to activate appropriate knowledge that enables them to "fill in the gaps." Differences in text structure may therefore be of little or great importance depending on the current level of the learner's skills and knowledge. This issue is explored more fully in the studies below.

Relativistic Effects of Differences in Text Structures

An experiment by Raye (see Bransford and Johnson, 1973) explores relationships between current knowledge and text structures. She presented two different versions of the "washing clothes" passage (see Section 1) to different groups of college students. Passage 1 was identical with the one used by Bransford and Johnson. In Passage 2, Raye changed eleven of the abstract words and phrases to ones that were imageable or concrete. For example, *items* was replaced by *clothes,* and *somewhere else* by *laundromat* (see the passage in Section 1).

Some people in the experiment heard Passage 1, and some heard Passage 2, *without* being told the appropriate topic ("washing clothes"). Under these conditions, those who received the imageable passage, Passage 2, exhibited superior recall. According to Paivio (see Chapter 4, Section 1) this would be expected on the basis of the imagery ratings of the words that each passage contained (a word like *clothes* is more imageable than *items*). However, what happens if people are provided with knowledge of the topic before hearing the passage? Will this allow them to interpret words like *items* and *somewhere else* in ways that make them more meaningful and concrete? Raye's data suggest that the answer is yes. When the students received the "washing clothes" topic, their comprehension ratings for the abstract passage approached those for the concrete, imageable passage. The same was true of the recall scores (see Bransford and Johnson, 1973, for further discussion). In contrast, presentation of the "washing clothes" topic did not help those who received the concrete version of the passage (Passage 2). These results illustrate that providing information that establishes a shared "field" or area of knowledge (in this case, providing the topic of "washing clothes") may or may not be important depending on the nature of the materials that people are asked to learn (see also Ausubel, 1963). They also show that differences in the nature of materials to be learned (for example, abstract versus concrete) may or may not be important depending on the learner's currently activated knowledge and skills.

Pichert and Anderson (1977) provide additional arguments for the need to view text structures in relation to the activated skills and knowledge of the learner. In Chapter 4 (Section 3) we noted that theorists have attempted to predict which statements will and will not be recalled depending on their level in a text-base hierarchy (e.g., Kintsch, 1976; Meyer, 1977). Pichert and Anderson (1977) acknowledge the importance of such endeavors, but they argue that additional factors must be considered as well.

> *Mature readers are able to approach text with different purposes or perspectives that can override conventions a linguistic community ordinarily uses to structure a text. In other words, our hypothesis is that structure is not an invariant property of text, but rather that it depends on perspective. If, for whatever reason, people take divergent perspectives on a text . . . the relative significance of text elements will change. Elements that are important on one view may be unimportant on another. (P. 309)*

To support their arguments, Pichert and Anderson presented two groups of students with the same passage, describing two boys and the house in which they were playing. One group was told to read this story from the perspective of a potential home buyer, the other from the perspective of a burglar. Results indicated that recall was strongly influenced by the perspective from which readers viewed the story. For example, those viewing from the perspective of a burglar were likely to recall that there was a color television set but not that there was a leak in the roof of the house. When the story was viewed from the perspective of a home buyer, these recall probabilities were reversed. Pichert and Anderson therefore argue that recall is a function of an idea's significance to a particular perspective rather than of text structure per se.

As a final illustration of the need to evaluate text structure in relation to the activated knowledge and skills of the learner, consider the problem of writing texts for students of different educational levels—for example, second-graders, fifth-graders, high-school students. Because these groups possess varying degrees of knowledge, two different text structures may be equally well learned by some groups of students (high-school students, say) but result in large differences in learning for others (such as fifth-graders). More sophisticated learners may be able to "fill in the gaps" in some texts; less sophisticated learners may need a much more explicit structure in order to understand and learn effectively. In Chapter 4, Section 4, for example, we noted that a story composed of high frequency words like *boy* was much easier for fourth-graders to learn than one composed of low frequency words like *lad* (e.g., Marks, Doctorow, and Wittrock, 1974). If the same stories were read to high-school or college students, however, it seems much less likely that these large differences in learning and memory would be found (see also Mandler, 1978). We must therefore be extremely careful when attempting to generalize the results of any study. Differences in text structure that make no difference for some groups of people may result in large differences for others. Once again, questions about the nature of materials need to be considered in relation to the current level of the learner's knowledge and skills (see Figure 1.1).

Appropriate Knowledge and the Effects of Practice

The availability of appropriate past knowledge also has implications for evaluating the role of frequency of experience and practice. For example, given that learners actively attend to materials, it seems clear that three exposures to a list will result in better memory than two exposures, which will in turn be more effective than one exposure. However, the degree to which people benefit from exposure is affected by the relevant knowledge they have.

Johnson, Doll, Lapinsky, and Bransford (1974) presented students with lists of sentences like the following: "The streak blocked the light"; "The man saw his face in the body." The sentences were difficult for the students to understand unless they were provided with appropriate cues (*dirty window, new car*). After a single exposure to the list, students who received both the sentences and the cues showed higher recall than those who received the sentences alone. These results are congruent with those of Bransford and Johnson (in the balloon and "washing clothes" studies) reported earlier. For present purposes, the important consideration is the effects of presenting the materials a second time and then a third time. Both groups (those who received sentences and cues and those who received sentences alone) should improve. However, what is the *rate* at which they improve, from one trial to the next?

Johnson and colleagues found that the two groups improved at different rates. Students with appropriately activated knowledge (sentences and cues) improved more quickly than the others. Thus, by the end of the third trial, the recall difference between the groups was greater than it was on the first trial. The benefits of additional exposure therefore depend on the activated knowledge base that the learner already has.

As a final implication of ideas expressed in the present section, consider the question of educational applications. We have noted that variables like word frequency could be used to make passages easier for elementary-school children to understand and remember. Thus, low frequency words like *lad* could be replaced by high frequency words like *boy*. However, if students were only exposed to frequent and familiar words, they would learn no *new* vocabulary. How can they be helped to acquire new concepts and words?

An effective technique is to make use of what students already know, so that it serves as a basis for new learning. Experiments by Wittrock, Marks, and Doctorow (1975) provide an excellent illustration of this procedure. They selected a set of stories to be read by elementary-school children. The objective was to induce the children to learn some relatively infrequent and unfamiliar words that the stories contained.

Two groups of students participated in the study. During the first session students in Group 1 read the stories containing the new words. The stories were read once again during a second session, so that all students in Group 1 received two acquisition trials. Later they received a test to determine whether they had learned the meanings of the new words. Group 2 followed a different procedure. During the first session they read versions of the stories that contained *familiar* words similar in meaning to those studied by Group 1. During the second session they read the same stories, but these now contained the unfamiliar words. Group 2 therefore had only one trial in which to study the new words, whereas Group 1 had received two trials. Nevertheless, Group 2 did much better in the subsequent test. By first having better understood the stories, they were able to discover the meaning of the new words and hence to remember them later on. Note that these results are similar to some of those in the balloon study discussed in Section 1.

Summary of Section 4

The purpose of this section was to illustrate the need to consider the relationships among certain variables illustrated in our theoretical framework (Figure 1.1). In particular, we need to be mindful of the relationship between the nature of the materials to be learned and the skills and knowledge of the learner. Differences in text structure may or may not be important depending on the learner's ability to instantiate general terms and fill in the gaps in a message. Similarly, the likelihood of ideas' being recalled depends not only on text structure but also on the activated knowledge or perspective adopted by the reader or listener (Pichert and Anderson, 1977). Currently activated knowledge also affects the rate at which people learn from multiple exposure or practice. Sometimes it is better to spend a part of one's time building a basis for subsequent learning than to spend all of one's time on the materials to be learned (e.g., Wittrock, Marks, and Doctorow, 1975).

A major implication of this section is that we should be wary of overgeneralizing the results of a particular study. Variables that make no difference for one group of people may result in large differences for people with different levels of knowledge and skills. However, what does it mean to say that people have "knowledge," and how can we measure their current levels of skills and knowledge? These questions are explored in Chapter 6.

Chapter 6
Theories of the Nature and
Structure of Knowledge

The purpose of this chapter is to discuss experiments and theories that explore the nature and structure of people's knowledge. This is an extremely important topic because our abilities to learn, understand, and remember are strongly influenced by currently available knowledge. As shown in Chapter 5, effective comprehension involves the use of previously acquired knowledge to "fill in the gaps" in messages (see especially Section 2). If we are unable to do this we may experience a breakdown in our abilities to comprehend and remember. For example, unless provided with information that a passage was about washing clothes, students in Bransford and Johnson's study (Chapter 5, Section 1) were unable to use what they knew to make sense of the message. We shall now ask, What does it mean to say that people have knowledge of concepts and of events? How can we assess whether people have the prerequisite knowledge and concepts necessary to understand and remember certain materials? Questions like these will be the focus of the present chapter. Discussion is divided into four sections, which are sketched below.

Overview

Section 1 discusses some *investigations of semantic memory*. The term *semantic memory* refers to one's general knowledge, and this may be different from particular memories of past experiences (cf. Tulving, 1972). For example, one can *know* that *boy* is an English word yet not *remember* that it occurred in a particular list of materials to be learned. We shall explore studies and theories that deal with the nature of semantic memory, and we shall discuss how these studies differ from studies of remembering. Experiments on semantic memory are important because the structure of one's knowledge affects the speed and ease with which it can be utilized to learn and understand more effectively.

In Section 2 we discuss *schema theories of knowledge*. There are many varieties of schema theory, but all attempt to characterize our knowledge, both of concepts underlying individual words and of more complex concepts underlying the situations suggested by combinations of those words (for example, "going to a restaurant," "washing clothes") in terms of abstract systems of relationships. Schemata are assumed to be very important because they guide the types of assumptions we make while comprehending, learning, and remembering. Given a statement like "The ball broke the window," for example, people generally assume that some outside agent was responsible for throwing or hitting the ball. Our schematic knowledge of the verb *to break* includes information that may guide assumptions such as this.

The purpose of Section 3 is to examine the issue of *general knowledge and imagery*. When we acquire knowledge of a city, for example, we seem to develop a "cognitive map" that is partially visual in nature. We shall therefore ask whether aspects of our knowledge can be viewed as images and discuss some of the problems with a point of view that regards stored visual information in terms of stored pictures.

Section 4 explores the degree to which we have *knowledge about our own knowledge*. How do we know that we know something, even when we are unable to retrieve it at the moment? How can we tell whether or not we understand something and whether we have mastered it and can stop studying? It will be argued that many people do not spontaneously assess their current level of understanding and mastery. They therefore fail to perform such important activities as asking questions, rereading materials, monitoring their study time according to task difficulty. Becoming an effective learner involves the development of internal criteria that help one realize when information has been adequately understood and learned and when it has not.

Section 1: Investigations of Semantic Memory

The purpose of this section is to explore theories and research designed to clarify the nature and structure of general knowledge. Questions about what people *know* are not necessarily equivalent to questions about processes of *remembering* particular experiences. Tulving (1972) approaches the problem of distinguishing knowing from remembering by postulating two hypothetical types of memories: episodic memory and semantic memory.

Episodic memory refers to the storage and retrieval of personally dated, autobiographic experiences ("I remember encountering the word *boy* in this experiment"; "I remember the great shot I made in that tennis game"). According to Tulving, it is episodic memory that is tested in most laboratory experiments on remembering. Most of the studies we have discussed measure people's abilities to remember the information presented during the acquisition portion of an experiment. Thus, if we ask them to determine whether the word *rock* occurred in an experiment, we are asking them, not to decide whether *rock* is a meaningful English word, but to say whether they recognize a word as having been presented at a particular time, in a particular place, by a particular person. More generally, we are asking whether a particular input has been experienced during the experimental acquisition task.

Semantic memory refers to general knowledge of concepts, principles, and meanings that are used in the process of encoding or comprehending particular inputs. Questions regarding one's knowledge of concepts like "washing clothes," "triangle," "rock," involve semantic, rather than episodic, memory. It should be noted that Tulving's purpose was to postulate, not the existence of two physically separate memory systems (one located in section A of the head and one in section B), but a purely *conceptual* distinction that can guide one's thinking about certain types of research questions. In Tulving's terminology, discussion in the present section focuses on questions about semantic memory. We will begin with questions about the organization of the knowledge we have acquired.

The Organization of Knowledge

Imagine that you are asked to perform the following task as quickly as possible: Name a past president of the United States whose last name begins with *L*. Most people are able to answer, "Lincoln." What did you have to do to perform this task? While thinking about this question, try a few more examples: Name a piece of furniture that begins with *C*; name a make of car that begins with *F*; name a piece of clothing that begins with *S*.

You will probably agree that it is difficult to say exactly how you were able to arrive at the answers to the questions. One thing seems certain, however: You did not randomly search through everything you know until you finally stumbled on the correct answer. Asked the question about the president, for example, it's unlikely that you simply scanned a stored list of all possible names until you found *Lincoln*. Similarly, you probably did not think about furniture, makes of cars, clothing, while trying to answer the question about the president. We seem to have the ability to access selectively aspects of our knowledge that are relevant to a particular task or situation. This is extremely important for efficient performance. How can we account for this seemingly magical feat? A possible answer is that our knowledge is organized into certain categorical structures, into such categories as U.S. presidents, furniture, makes of cars, and clothing. In contrast, most of us probably don't have well-structured categories like words that begin with *b*, words containing *e*. The speed with which we can answer certain questions may therefore depend on the organizational structure of the knowledge we have acquired.

Experiments by Freedman and Loftus (1971) illustrate differences in the speed of accessing knowledge. They varied the order in which people received critical information. Some tasks were stated in the form "Name a fruit that begins with a *p*"; others, in the form "Name a word beginning with a *p* that is a fruit." People were faster on the first task than on the second (reaction times being measured from the *end* of each task statement). Given the first statement, people could presumably activate their knowledge of fruits while waiting for the letter cue. Given the second statement, they could not activate their knowledge of the relevant category until the end of the sentence. Because our knowledge of fruits beginning with a *p* seems to be organized in terms of fruits, but not in terms of words beginning with a *p,* people receiving the second task statement could not do much with the information about the initial letter until told the semantic category they needed to know.

A unique study by Loftus and Loftus (1974) provides further evidence for the notion that speed of question answering depends on the organizational structure of one's knowledge. They compared the ability of beginning and advanced graduate students in psychology to answer questions about psychologists. Students were given instructions either in the form "Name a developmental psychologist whose name begins with a *P*" or in the form "Name a psychologist whose name begins with a *P* and who is a developmentalist" (for example, Piaget). Advanced graduate students were faster at performing the first type of task, presumably because their knowledge of psychologists was organized into psychological subspecialties like developmental, memory, clinical, perception. In contrast, beginning graduate students were faster at performing the second type of task. They apparently knew the names of famous psychologists but did not have these organized in terms of the particular subspecialties for which each person was best known.

Organization and Priming

The preceding studies suggest that the ease of question answering depends on the way in which our knowledge is organized. An emphasis on the organizational structure of knowledge has additional implications as well. One involves the degree to which certain types of processing activities enable us to process subsequent inputs. Experiments by Loftus (1973) and by Loftus and Loftus (1974) illustrate this point. Imagine being asked to name a fruit beginning with the letter *a*; now name a fruit beginning with *p*. Loftus found that people could more quickly answer the second question when it was preceded by one asking about the same category. In short, knowledge of a category seems to become activated and hence facilitate subsequent processing (see also Collins and Quillian, 1970). Many theorists discuss this phenomenon in terms of "spreading activation" (e.g., see Collins and Loftus, 1975; Ortony, 1978). Activation of a concept like "apple" may spread to related concepts (such as "pear") and hence prime people for subsequent processing.

Note that the degree to which additional concepts become primed is assumed to depend on the organizational structure of one's knowledge. For example, if we assume that "apple" and "pear" are "stored close together," activation of "apple" should more quickly spread to "pear" because there is less distance to travel. In contrast, activation of "rock" should be less likely to prime one's concept of "pear" because the two concepts are stored in different places. Note that these ideas of "storage" and "distance" are meant to be metaphorical, and they involve no presuppositions that a concept is actually stored in a particular place in the brain. As metaphors, ideas about storage locations and distances are useful, however; they help us conceptualize certain types of results.

Experiments by Meyer, Schvaneveldt, and colleagues (e.g., Meyer and Schvaneveldt, 1971, 1976; Meyer, Schvaneveldt, and Ruddy, 1974) provide further evidence for the importance of priming. Imagine the following task: Strings of letters are flashed on a screen and your task is to indicate whether they are English words. You are to make this decision as quickly as you can. The letter strings occur in pairs, the second string appearing on the screen as soon as the response is made to the first string. Possible pairs of strings are illustrated below (the appropriate response is indicated in parentheses):

1. Nart (no) — Soam (no)

2. Wine (yes) — Reab (no)

3. Bread (yes) — Doctor (yes)

4. Nurse (yes) — Doctor (yes)

For present purposes, the most interesting data result from a comparison of pairs like Pair 3 and Pair 4. To what extent is the speed of saying that *doctor* is an English word (responding yes) a function of the immediately preceding word? Meyer and colleagues found that people were faster at saying yes to *doctor* given pairs like 4 than in pairs like 3. Since *nurse* and *doctor* are meaningfully related, processing of *nurse* seemed to prime people to process related words (like *doctor*).

Meyer and colleagues also included conditions where the visual stimuli were "degraded" (smudged, for example), and hence made more difficult to read. Under these conditions, priming effects were even greater than under "nondegraded" conditions; that is, differences between pairs like D and C were even greater. These results suggest that priming facilitated people's abilities to detect visual features of the words. The notion that appropriately activated knowledge can help one realize what to look for is perhaps most apparent when we try to read someone's sloppy handwriting. It may be difficult to identify particular words unless we are primed by having an idea of the concepts the person is writing about.

Experiments by Bruce (1958) provide additional evidence for the importance of priming. He presented people with sentences embedded in white noise. White noise is a continuous *shh* sound that makes the sentences harder to hear. The task is simply to report what one hears. Bruce presented sentences like "I tell you that our team will win the cup next year"; "You said it would rain, but the sun has come out now." For some sentences, people were first presented with appropriate key words that primed their processing. Appropriate key words for the preceding sentences were *sport* and *weather*, respectively. The presentation of appropriate key words facilitated performance in the identification task in the presence of white noise.

Organization and Inference

Consider a somewhat different aspect of the problem of knowledge activation. Assume that you hear the following two statements: (1) "Luckily, Aristotle was not blinded by the incident"; (2) "Luckily, the rock was not blinded by the incident." Statement 1 is readily understood by most adult comprehenders, but Statement 2 seems anomalous. If rocks don't have eyes, it's unclear why their being blinded should be of concern. Presumably, Statement 1 makes sense because we assume that Aristotle had eyes. But it is instructive to ask where an assumption like "Aristotle had eyes" might derive from. It is doubtful whether anyone explicitly told you that Aristotle had eyes (or a liver, stomach, heart, or big toe, for that matter). It seems more likely that you know that Aristotle was a person and that most people have eyes, big toes, and so forth. Certain aspects of our semantic knowledge seem to involve acquired knowledge of particular concepts (for example, that Aristotle was Greek, a great thinker). Other aspects of our knowledge seem to derive from inferences about relationships among concepts (for example, that Aristotle was a person, and most people have eyes). Collins and Quillian (1969) have proposed a model of semantic memory that addresses this issue.

Figure 6.1 illustrates a portion of a hypothetical semantic-memory structure as conceptualized by Collins and Quillian (1969). Note that concepts are assumed to be hierarchically organized; for example, birds and fish are stored under "animal," canaries are stored under "bird," sharks under "fish." Furthermore, only certain types of information are assumed to be stored at particular levels in the hierarchy. Thus, canaries eat and they have skin, but this type of information is not stored at the level of "canary"; it is stored at the level of "animal." Similarly, canaries have wings and can fly, but this information is stored at the level of "birds." Overall, Figure 6.1 illustrates a major assumption underlying the Collins and Quillian model, the assumption of *cognitive economy*. Characteristics of all birds are stored at the bird node, of all animals at the animal node, and so on. Only properties unique to canaries, sharks, and the like are stored at the lower levels of the hierarchy. This permits an economy of storage since information like "canaries, robins, wrens, bluebirds, have wings" needs only be stored once (at the level of birds) rather than a number of times (with each particular example of a bird).

Assume that knowledge really is represented in a form similar to that postulated by Collins and Quillian. What predictions could be made concerning people's abilities to answer questions regarding certain aspects of their knowledge? For example, consider questions like the following:

1. Does a canary sing?

2. Does a canary fly?

3. Does a canary eat?

How quickly should people be able to answer questions like these? Collins and Quillian conducted the following type of experiment. Participants were asked to say yes or no to various questions as quickly as possible, and the amount of time taken to respond (reaction time) was measured. Half the questions were designed to yield yes-responses (questions like "Does a canary fly?") and half were designed to yield no-responses ("Does a cadillac have rudders?"). The results indicate that questions like "Does a canary sing?" were answered more quickly than those like "Does a canary fly?" which were in turn answered more quickly than "Does a canary eat?"

Why should it take longer to decide that a canary flies than it does to decide that a canary can sing (for example)? According to the Collins and Quillian model, the time to

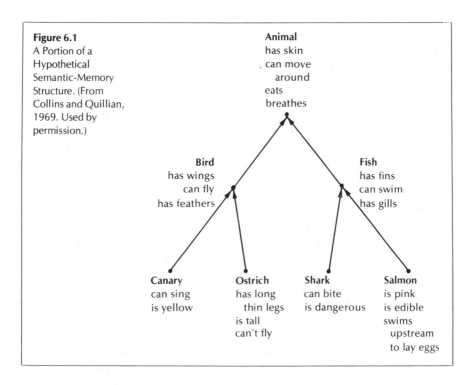

Figure 6.1
A Portion of a Hypothetical Semantic-Memory Structure. (From Collins and Quillian, 1969. Used by permission.)

respond depends on the number of steps necessary to make an inference. Because the singing of canaries is assumed to be stored at the level of "canary" (see Figure 6.1), this type of knowledge should be easily accessible, and reaction times should be relatively fast. In contrast, the ability to state that a canary can fly requires that one move up the hypothetical semantic-memory structure. The structure specifies that birds can fly, but one needs to realize that a canary is a bird in order to infer that canaries can fly. Similar arguments pertain to the time necessary to answer a question like "Does a canary eat?" The hypothetical semantic-memory structure specifies that animals eat, but one has to move two steps up the hierarchy in order to decide that canaries eat. Canaries are birds, and birds are animals; because animals eat, canaries must therefore eat too.

*Alternatives to the
Collins and Quillian Model*

The Collins and Quillian experiments had an important effect on cognitive theorists. Their data made people aware that different facets of our knowledge are not equally accessible. Furthermore, knowing cannot simply be equated with the retrieval of previously experienced (and currently stored) statements about particular facts. The ability to answer certain questions involves the ability to make inferences about what is most probably true, even though the inferences (for example, that Aristotle had eyes, canaries have skin) may never have been explicitly experienced in the individual's lifetime. In general, the greater the number of steps in making an inference, the greater the time it may take to respond.

It is important to note, however, that many of Collins and Quillian's insights can be accepted without the necessity of agreeing with their principle of cognitive economy and strict, logically based hierarchical storage. Collins and Quillian's emphasis on cognitive economy stems from their concern with computer modeling, where storage constraints are a primary issue. For humans, however, it is not clear that there are any appreciable constraints on storage (see Anderson and Bower, 1973). It seems more important for humans to be able to activate appropriate knowledge when needed. From this perspective, the organization of people's knowledge may therefore depend on the previous situations in which their knowledge has been used.

As an example of the preceding argument, assume that a chef had a special recipe for preparing canary skins, and that this was a great delicacy. The chef should therefore be very fast at verifying that "canaries have skin," even though under normal circumstances the principles of cognitive economy and strict, logical organization would thereby be violated. Similarly, a logically based knowledge structure would list *horse* under the concept "mammal" and *mammal* under the concept "animal." People should therefore be faster at verifying "A horse is a mammal" than "A horse is an animal" because the former involves fewer inferential steps. However, experiments by Rips, Shoben, and Smith (1973) show that the second sentence is verified more quickly than the first.

Experiments by Conrad (1972) raise further questions about the cognitive economy assumption. She asked people to describe a canary, a bird, an animal, and so forth. She then counted the frequency of occurrence of particular properties (such as color, presence of wings) and found that those properties that were frequently mentioned in conjunction with a concept ("canary," "bird") were ones that students in the Collins and Quillian study could verify quite rapidly. Conrad therefore repeated the Collins and Quillian study but included controls for familiarity or frequency. When frequency was controlled, the number of nodes or steps to be traveled in the logically based hierarchy (see Figure 6.1) had little effect on reaction time. In contrast, differences in frequency had very large effects on reaction time.

It is instructive to consider one final question regarding the Collins and Quillian model (Figure 6.1). What is the basis for deciding on the features to include at the bottom level of the hierarchy? For example, Figure 6.1 specifies the colors of the canary and the salmon; why not that of the shark, too? One possibility is that a shark's color is not so important for differentiating it from other fish, whereas a canary's color *is* an important distinguishing feature. Similarly, differences between a Chevrolet and a Cadillac are not based on their color but on their body style, degree of luxury, price. The bottom level of Collins and Quillian's hierarchy therefore reflects properties that seem especially characteristic or prototypic of particular concepts ("shark," "canary," "cadillac"). On the same line of reasoning, why shouldn't there be prototypic instances of higher-level concepts like "bird," and "furniture"? This issue is discussed below.

*The Internal Structure
of Conceptual Categories*

In an important series of articles, Rosch argues that many traditions of thought imply that concepts are Aristotelian in nature (e.g., Rosch, 1973, 1975). By *Aristotelian,* Rosch means the assumption that "categories are logical, clearly defined entities, whose membership is defined by an item's possession of a simple set of criterial features, in which all instances possessing the criterial attributes have a full and equal degree of membership" (1975). Rosch, however, argues that many natural categories are *not* of this type but are organized around prototypic exemplars, or "best representatives," of the category. Potential category members may vary in their distance from the prototypic exemplars, and category membership is not absolute but, rather, a matter of degree.

Note that assumptions about prototypes are different from the assumptions reflected in the Collins and Quillian model illustrated in Figure 6.1, where all exemplars of a concept are considered to be equally representative of the concept. Of course, the model could be modified to reflect varying distances between exemplars and a concept; some types of birds, for example, could be closer to the concept of "bird" than others (e.g., see Loftus, 1975). For present purposes, it is most useful to examine the types of data that Rosch uses to support her ideas.

Rosch's initial work dealt with color categories (e.g., Rosch, 1973). We classify things as red, green, blue, and so on, but what of all the shades in between? For example, some blues are bluer than others. Rosch found that various shades are organized around prototypic exemplars of colors (prototypic reds, greens, blues, etc.); other colors seem to be perceived in terms of their degree of similarity to the prototypic forms.

In subsequent work, Rosch extended her analysis to other types of categories, such as fruit, birds, vegetables (see Rosch, 1975). In one study, Rosch asked people to rate the degree to which particular exemplars were "good" instances of a category. Participants found this to be a meaningful task and generally agreed with one another. In the category "bird," for example, robin, sparrow, bluebird, and canary were the four top-ranked exemplars. In contrast, chicken, turkey, ostrich, and penguin were rated as much less prototypic of "birdness" (see Rosch, 1975, for additional ratings). Rosch has also shown that the "goodness" or "typicality" of examples has important effects on processing time. For example, people are faster at verifying that "a robin is a bird" than that "a turkey is a bird" (e.g., Rosch, 1973, 1975).

Rosch's emphasis on the importance of prototypes is also supported by experiments designed to teach new concepts (e.g., Posner and Keele, 1968, 1970; Franks and Bransford, 1971; Reed, 1972). Although the details differ, these studies generally involve the presentation of sets of visual patterns that represent examples of particular concepts. After acquisition, participants are tested on their abilities to recognize new examples of the concepts acquired. The results indicate that people frequently form prototypes that best represent the total set of acquisition stimuli. When asked to identify new examples of concepts, those which are closest to the prototype tend to be more quickly and accurately recognized.

The results of several experiments discussed earlier in this book can also be understood in terms of prototypes or typicality. For example, we noted that statements like "The fat man had gotten stuck in a cave" are much more easily remembered than "The bald man had gotten stuck in a cave" (see Chapter 4, Section 3). Similarly, Rosenberg (1968, 1969) has demonstrated that statements like "The doctor cured the patient" are better remembered than "The doctor fired the janitor." Statements like the preceding are comprehensible, but some are more prototypic or typical of concepts (like "fat man" and "doctor") than others. When statements express information that is relatively prototypic of previously acquired concepts, memory seems to be enhanced.

Rosch's arguments about prototypes also mesh nicely with Lakoff's (1973) discussion of "hedges." Hedges are linguistic devices used to express degrees of class membership. Imagine a surgeon who is extremely lazy, sloppy, and careless. We might say, "Technically speaking, he's a surgeon," but we should be unlikely to say, "Now, that's my idea of a good surgeon." Similarly we might say, "Loosely speaking, a chicken is a bird." Hedges like "technically speaking" and "loosely speaking" reflect the flexibility with which we assign category membership. Like Rosch, Lakoff argues that hedges illustrate that category membership is a matter of degree, and not absolute.

Models of Categorical Flexibility

Several authors have proposed models of semantic memory designed to take into account processes like hedging (e.g., Rips, Shoben, and Smith, 1973; Smith, Shoben, and Rips, 1974). These models characterize our knowledge of concepts in terms of sets of features. A critical assumption is that concepts are represented by two different types of features, those that are *defining* and those that are *characteristic*. Defining features are those that must be true of concepts. For example, a canary is animate, has feathers, has wings, has a head, and so on; the concept of "bird," too, suggests defining features like animation, feathers, wings, and so on. Note that this model does not assume the principle of cognitive economy (see our earlier discussion), for defining features are stored at the level of both "canary" and "bird." In addition to defining features, concepts may also have particular characteristic features. Characteristic features for "bird" include the ability to sing and fly, but flying and singing are not necessarily defining features of birds.

According to the Rips and colleagues' model, the speed of verifying statements depends on processes of feature matching. Consider the fact that "A canary is a bird" can be verified more quickly than "An ostrich is a bird." Why is this so? According to Rips and colleagues people first compare *both* the defining and characteristic features of the two concepts ("canary" and "bird" or "ostrich" and "bird") and respond very quickly if there is a sufficient degree of feature overlap. Because a prototypic instance like "canary" shares many features, both defining and characteristic, with "bird," reaction times should be fast. In contrast, Rips and colleagues argue, because "ostrich" and "bird" do not share so many common features—for example, flying and singing are not salient characteristics of ostriches—people must therefore proceed to a second stage of analysis. Here they compare only the defining features of the two concepts and then make their response, having realized, for example, that flying and singing (characteristic features of birds) are not necessary to qualify as an instance of "birdness"; and they therefore confirm the statement that an ostrich is a bird. This extra stage of analysis takes more processing time.

The two-stage model also helps explain differences in the speed of saying no to false statements (see also Meyer, 1970). For example, it is easier to reject "A canary is an apple" than "A canary is a robin." Because "canary" and "apple" have almost no features in common, one can disagree at the first level of processing; in contrast, "canary" and "robin" have many features in common, and so, Rips and colleagues argue, one must move to the second stage before making a response.

Smith, Shoben, and Rips (1974) also address the issue of hedges. Consider a statement like "Loosely speaking, a bat is a bird." Smith and associates assume that a phrase like "loosely speaking" orients people toward an analysis of characteristic, rather than defining, features. Thus, people might note that the ability to fly is a characteristic feature of both bats and birds, and would consequently agree with the hedged statement. When given a nonhedged statement like "A bat is a bird," however, they might disagree because the necessary defining features don't match. Hedged statements therefore resemble linguistic constructions like similes (such as "A pin is like a nail"), which people respond to on the basis of partial similarities rather than strict categorical identity (e.g., see Verbrugge, 1977). For example, most people will reject "A pin is a nail" but will accept "A pin is like a nail."

Further Considerations of Flexibility

The articles by Rips and colleagues represent elegant attempts to deal with some very complex issues. An extremely important feature of their model (and those of Collins and Quillian and others discussed earlier) is its precision, which permits evaluation of the model itself and helps focus attention on possible alternatives. The following discussion will consider some of the proposed alternatives to the notion of defining features.

Many people question whether concepts can be represented in terms of defining features. For example, a canary without wings or a head is still a canary (cf. Collins and Loftus, 1975). The noted philosopher Wittgenstein (1968) argues against the idea that concepts can be characterized by a fixed set of defining features. Consider his comments about the concept of "games":

> Consider for example the proceedings we call 'games'. . . . What is common to them all?—Don't say: There must be something in common, or they would not be called 'games'—but look and see whether there is anything common to all.—For if you look at them you will not see something that is common to all. (P. 31)

Wittgenstein argues that a word or concept has a "family" of meanings that may resemble one another like members of a human family. Members of a family may look similar and yet lack a clear set of defining features possessed by each individual member of the family. In an analogous manner, Wittgenstein's theory of "family resemblance" does not assume that there are particular defining features of concepts that must be common to all.

Research by Labov (1973) illustrates problems with assumptions about a fixed set of defining features. He investigated the degree to which people thought that various drawings represented a cup. The drawings ranged from prototypic to nonprototypic cups; the nonprototypic cups might lack a handle, have two handles, be oddly shaped, for example. Labov also manipulated the context in which the drawings appeared. The drawings portrayed both neutral contexts and contexts suggesting that the objects were filled with coffee, mashed potatoes, or flowers. Context had little influence on the degree to which people recognized prototypic cups, but great influence on their response to the less prototypic cups. When filled with coffee, for example, a medium-level prototypic cup might be called a cup, but not when filled with flowers. Wholly nonprototypic cups were almost never called cup, irrespective of the context in which they occurred.

It is important to note that certain features were constant across all the drawings used in Labov's experiments. For example, all the objects were upwardly concave and hence could serve as containers, and their contents might have suggested that they were nonleaking containers. One might therefore assume that such features constitute "defining" features of a cup. Note, however, that an upside-down cup is not upwardly concave, but it's still a cup. Similarly, a cup with a hole in it is still a cup; it's simply not very wise to fill it with liquid. When we combine these thoughts with Labov's findings that "cupness" is a function of context (for example, those suggested by coffee, mashed potatoes, flowers), assumptions about a static set of defining features become highly questionable. Prototypes (like a prototypic cup) may have particular *characteristic* features, but these are not necessary for an object to qualify as an instance of, for example, "cupness." Instead, the relative importance of features varies as a function of context (see also the discussion of semantic flexibility in Chapter 5, Section 2). For example, a somewhat narrow, tall container with two handles may be designated a noncup (more like a vase, perhaps) when filled with flowers. Features like tallness, narrowness, and two handles may therefore be very important in this context. When the cup clearly contains coffee, however, these features become less critical. Different concatenations of features become important as a function of the context in which items occur.

It is important to consider an additional point regarding issues of flexibility and defining features. It is one thing to argue that conceptual specification *can* be quite flexible. It is quite a different matter to argue that this is always ideal. Consider the following quotation from Lewis Carroll's *Through the Looking Glass* (1871):

"When I use a word," Humpty Dumpty said, in rather a scornful tone, "it means just what I choose it to mean—neither more nor less."

"The question is," said Alice, "whether you can make words mean so many different things."

"The question is," said Humpty Dumpty, "which is to be the master—that's all."

Alice was much too puzzled to say anything. . . .

Note that Humpty Dumpty stresses flexibility, but note further that too much flexibility can hinder communication. In order to communicate effectively, we must frequently agree on a particular set of defining features for the concepts we are discussing. For example, a speaker may say, "I'm using the term X in the following way for my discussion today." As ideas and theories become formalized (in systems of formal logic and in mathematics, for instance), terms must be defined precisely. An emphasis on defining features is therefore extremely important for precise communication and thought.

Note, however, that it is our conceptual flexibility that underlies this ability to choose particular sets of defining features depending on the context and purpose. If our conceptual knowledge consisted solely of a static set of defining features, we could not do so. The ability to be flexible in adopting a momentarily agreed-upon set of defining features therefore does not imply that there are *inherently* defining features. Within a given conversation (Wittgenstein, 1968, calls this a "language game") it is important to hold definitions constant (indeed, we frequently become confused because we inadvertently change the meaning of terms). When we change "language games," however, we often want to change definitions. This latter ability is very important because new ways of defining concepts (such as "learning," "memory") can lead to new insights about those concepts.

Some Implications of Work on Semantic Memory

Although psychological research on semantic memory is still in its infancy, many concepts and techniques from this research area are already proving to be important. An ongoing research project directed by McCauley and Sperber represents an excellent case in point. As an illustration of the questions they are pursuing, consider the task of assessing the nature and organization of the conceptual knowledge available to certain groups of people—to third-graders, for example, who seem to know more than most first-graders, or to individuals classified as retarded, who seem to lack certain concepts. Because people's ability to learn new information is strongly affected by what they already know (see Chapter 5), such an assessment is clearly very important.

A paper by Sperber, Ragain, and McCauley (1976) addresses the issue of assessing the conceptual knowledge available to retarded individuals. Sperber and colleagues note that retarded individuals perform poorly on tasks that require the use of conceptual information. (In fact, many aspects of standard intelligence tests require the use of conceptual knowledge for adequate performance.) On the basis of this poor performance, theorists have suggested that retarded individuals lack certain basic concepts. As Sperber and colleagues note, however, there are many possible reasons why certain individuals may perform poorly; they may not readily understand the particular task, for instance, or may have inappropriate strategies for using what they know. These possibilities are different from the notion that they have no knowledge of basic concepts or that these concepts are not organized in optimal ways.

Sperber and colleagues used a priming task to assess the conceptual knowledge available to retarded individuals. The advantage of this type of task is that it is simple and requires few strategies; if one's goal is to assess the nature of conceptual knowledge per se, it is best to find a relatively pure measure that is not complicated by additional processes that people must perform. In keeping with this goal, the researchers also used pictures, rather than words, as stimuli. The use of pictures therefore simplifies the task still further; for clearly it is possible to have the concept of "dog" and still be unable to read the word *dog*. The priming task was similar to that of Meyer and colleagues' study discussed earlier. Participants were shown pictures and asked to name them as quickly as possible. Sometimes a target picture (of a horse, for instance) was preceded by a conceptually related picture (such as a picture of a cat) and at other times by a conceptually unrelated picture (of a trumpet, perhaps). The purpose was to see whether the speed of naming target pictures would be increased as a result of priming by a previous, conceptually related picture. If retarded individuals lacked basic conceptual organization one would expect no priming effect. The retarded individuals clearly benefited from the priming, however, which suggests that their conceptual knowledge was in fact organized in appropriate forms.

Studies like the foregoing are important because they provide a refined analysis of why people have difficulties in activities that require the use of conceptual knowledge. It is regularly assumed that retarded individuals lack an adequate basis of conceptual organization for simple concepts, but Sperber and colleagues' study suggests that this may be a wrong assumption. Such a reevaluation encourages researchers to look at other reasons why certain people perform poorly in particular tasks. For example, priming seems to result in effective performance because it works relatively automatically and requires few conscious strategies. In contrast, a task like sorting a group of pictures into conceptual categories (for example, cat-horse, trumpet-guitar) seems to be more difficult because it requires conscious decisions and makes demands on short-term memory (e.g., people must remember what the task is). Questions about the differences between simply possessing knowledge and being able to use knowledge are therefore important to pursue.

Summary of Section 1

In Tulving's (1972) terminology, the research described in this section explored semantic, rather than episodic, memory; participants in the research were not asked to remember whether a word or picture occurred in a particular experimental context (episodic memory). Instead they were asked about general information (semantic memory): to "name a president whose name begins with an *L*," to verify statements (such as "A horse is a mammal"), to decide whether a word was a meaningful English word, and so forth. A number of issues regarding the nature of semantic memory were raised.

First, our knowledge or semantic memory seems to be organized. We do not need to search randomly through our knowledge, but instead can selectively access certain portions of it (makes of cars, for example). The organization of knowledge also affects priming and speed of verification. For example, it is easier to identify the word *doctor* when it is preceded by *nurse* than when it is preceded by *bread* (e.g., Meyer and Schvaneveldt, 1976); and it is easier to answer quickly the question "Is a canary yellow?" than "Does a canary eat?" (Collins and Quillian, 1969). However, concepts are not simply organized in relation to one another, they have internal organization as well. Thus, some examples of a concept are more prototypic or typical than others, and typicality greatly affects verification speed (e.g., Rosch, 1975).

We also explored the question of whether examples of a concept could be characterized by a fixed set of defining features (e.g., Rips, Shoben, and Smith, 1973). Some theorists have suggested that this is not the case, but that it is possible that category members share a "family resemblance" (Wittgenstein, 1968), and that different groupings of features become important as a function of context and purpose (Labov, 1973). Category membership appears to be flexible. When engaged in a particular language game, however, we must try to use concepts in a consistent way.

Concepts and techniques from semantic-memory research also have potential importance for assessing the nature of the knowledge available to certain groups of individuals. The study by Sperber, Ragain, and McCauley (1976) represents a case in point. There is a difference between simply having conceptual knowledge and being able to use and evaluate it consciously in appropriate situations. Different tasks require different degrees of conscious strategies and evaluations. For example, priming tasks seem to tap relatively automatic processes. A more refined analysis of task requirements should therefore help us increase our understanding of the reasons why performance may suffer in particular situations. It is equally important to strive for more refined analyses of particular aspects of people's knowledge. This topic is discussed in Section 2.

Section 2: Schema
Theories of Knowledge

The purpose of this section is to discuss a rapidly developing approach to questions about the nature of knowledge, which we shall call "schema theory" (the plural of schema is schemata). The schema concept derives from the work of such theorists as Kant (1787), Bartlett (1932; see Chapter 5, Section 3), and Piaget (e.g., 1969b); but recent theorists have attempted to characterize schemata in a much more precise manner than was previously considered. Most of the modern schema theorists are experts in computer science. Computers provide an excellent medium for working on problems of knowledge because they permit one to specify precisely complex hypotheses and to test them by computer simulation (for example, by building knowledge into the computer and then programming it to perform such tasks as comprehending and learning). When the computer simulation fails, one knows that something is wrong.

It is important to note that not all current theorists use the term *schema*. Kintsch (1976) and Rumelhart and Ortony (1977) use the term, but others refer to *frames* (e.g., Minsky, 1975; Charniak, 1977) and *scripts* (e.g., Schank and Abelson, 1977). These differences in terms reflect many differences in assumptions, but there are also some important concurrences. The most noteworthy is that each of these theorists has dared to tackle the complex problem of characterizing our knowledge of the world. We shall use the term *schema* to refer to the general class of theories noted above.

Some Illustrations of Schemata

As an illustration of the reasons why theorists postulate the existence of schemata, consider our knowledge of a concept like "move," as in the sentence "The dog moved." When the concept appears in this context, it is easy to believe that knowledge of "move" simply involves the assumption that something is momentarily nonstationary. Closer inspection of the problem, however, makes it clear that our knowledge of "move" is more complex. For example, a statement like "The house moved" seems anomalous. Why? One possibility is that our knowledge of "move" includes the constraint that there must be some agent or force that initiates the movement. Animate objects can initiate their own movement, but most inanimate objects cannot. However, if we make an assumption about external instigating forces (such as an earthquake), a statement like "The house moved" makes more sense (cf. Bransford and McCarrell, 1974).

The preceding example suggests that knowledge of events includes information about certain conditions that must be met before a situation may qualify as a particular type of event or action. Consider some additional examples of this general point. The sentences "The detective caught the criminal" and "The detective apprehended the criminal" are very similar in meaning. Perhaps "catch" is a synonym for "apprehend." Note, however, that it seems reasonable to say "The detective caught the ball," but not "The detective apprehended the ball." Our knowledge of "apprehend" involves the constraint that the object to be caught must be trying to get away (hence it generally must be animate). In contrast, the concept "catch," although it is appropriate in contexts where the object tries to avoid being caught, does not include this constraint. Schema theorists attempt to characterize our knowledge of situations such as these.

Figure 6.2 illustrates a schema for the concept "break," as constructed by Rumelhart and Ortony (1977). It specifies some of the knowledge that we have about the verb *to break*. We shall omit many of the details of this diagram (see Rumelhart and Ortony, 1977), although these details are important for cognitive science. To appreciate the value of precisely specifying various schemata, ask yourself the following question: What kinds of information would one need to build into a computer in order that it might simulate the comprehension and inference processes characteristic of human beings?

In essence, Figure 6.2 specifies that knowledge of "break" includes variables like (1) an *agent* that does the breaking, (2) an *object* that is broken, and (3) a *method* of doing the breaking. Note that these variables are specified relatively abstractly, so the "break" schema can apply to a wide variety of particular instances involving breaking. The encircled words in Figure 6.2 refer to other *subschemata* that would more precisely specify knowledge of concepts like "cause," "change," "do." For example, a "do" schema might place constraints on the types of methods or activities that are plausible given the particular agent involved. The notion of subschemata is important because we need not always consider all the details of a concept when it is activated. Given a concept like "face," for example, we probably activate general knowledge about eyes, ears, noses, and so on; but we do not necessarily think about each of these aspects in great detail. A general schema for "face" therefore makes reference to other sub-schemata for such features as eyes, ears, and noses. When we think more specifically

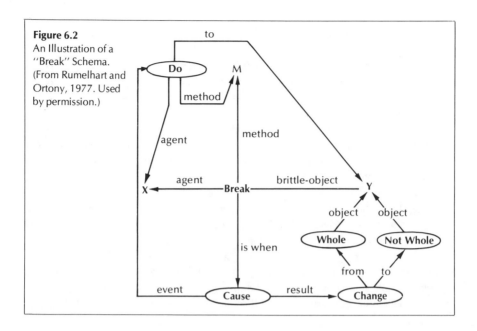

Figure 6.2
An Illustration of a "Break" Schema. (From Rumelhart and Ortony, 1977. Used by permission.)

about these latter features we may be consulting additional subschemata that are not explicitly defined in the "face" schema (cf. Rumelhart and Ortony, 1977).

As an illustration of the way the information specified in the "break" schema (Figure 6.2) might guide certain comprehension activities, imagine a statement like "The boy broke the window." The schema would describe the word *boy* as the agent and *window* as the object. The schema also specifies that the concept "break" involves some method instrumental in the breaking. Some set of plausible methods must therefore be assumed by the comprehender. If the context provides additional information, this may constrain the specific types of assumptions that are made. For example, if a preceding sentence states that the boy had a rock, this may affect one's assumptions about the particular method of breaking. An adequate schema theory must also include constraints on the plausibility of the method. A statement like "The boy broke the window with his thoughts" includes an agent, object, and method, but it is implausible. In contrast, a statement like "The Martian broke the window with his thoughts" seems a more plausible (though imaginary) event.

Rumelhart and Ortony (1977) also discuss contrasting statements like "The boy broke the window" and "The ball broke the window" (see also Bransford and McCarrell, 1974). The word *boy* can qualify as an agent, but the word *ball* cannot do so. In the second sentence the word *ball* is therefore interpreted as an instrument involved in the method of breaking, and it requires that a possible agent be assumed. Note that this is another example of sentences with similar surface structures and dissimilar conceptual structures (see Chapter 4, Section 2). One of the goals of schema theory is to characterize the processes by which conceptual structures are assigned.

Knowledge of More Complex Events

The ideas of Rumelhart and Ortony (1977) are representative of those held by a large group of theorists. As noted earlier, each of these theorists approaches this problem in different ways, and not all use the term *schema*. Their schemata are also of various kinds and of varying complexity. Even the schema for "break" (Figure 6.2) is relatively complex and makes reference to other subschemata like "cause" and "change." Now, consider the possibility that our knowledge includes information of still more complex concept sequences. For example, our knowledge of more complex concepts like "washing clothes," "going to a restaurant," and "attending a birthday party" seems to involve much more information than one can express by a single verb like *to break*.

As an illustration of more complex concepts, consider the following two sentences: "John went to the birthday party"; "First Bill opened the presents and then they ate the cake" (cf. Schank, 1976). As shown in our discussion of prior knowledge and comprehension (Chapter 5), we should need to make many assumptions in order to understand adequately even a simple scenario such as this. Many theorists argue that such assumptions are guided by complex schemata (or "frames" or "scripts") that characterize sequences of episodes. As an illustration, consider the following demonstration story:

> Jim went to the restaurant and asked to be seated in the gallery. He was told that there would be a one-half hour wait. Forty minutes later, the applause for his song indicated that he could proceed with the preparation. Twenty guests had ordered his favorite, a cheese soufflé.
>
> Jim enjoyed the customers in the main dining room. After two hours, he ordered the house specialty—roast pheasant under glass. It was incredible to enjoy such exquisite cuisine and yet still have fifteen dollars. He would surely come back soon.

You will probably agree that something seems to be wrong with the story. In the terminology of Schank and Abelson (1975, 1977) the story violates your knowledge of a "restaurant" script. Consider Schank and Abelson's analysis of the types of things most people know about going to a restaurant. Their analysis focuses both on the typical participants in a restaurant context and on the sequence of events involved in going to a restaurant and ordering a meal.

According to Schank and Abelson (1975), the participants, or cast of characters, for a "restaurant" script might be a customer, a waiter or waitress, chef, and a cashier (who might be the waiter or waitress). The sequence of events might involve *entering* the restaurant (which would involve selecting a table or being seated), *ordering* the food (receiving a menu, giving the order to the waiter or waitress), *preparing* the food (which involves someone communicating with the chef who then prepares it), *eating* the meal (brought by the waiter or waitress), and finally *exiting* from the restaurant (receiving the bill, leaving a tip, paying the cashier). Clearly, the "restaurant" script requires many specific concepts and events. A "restaurant" script (or schema) therefore seems more complex than a "break" schema, but even this doesn't exhaust the complexity of tasks like simulating human comprehension processes by means of a computer. Consider the discussion below.

Further Complexities
Involving Schemata

As noted earlier, a major goal of many theorists is to develop computer programs that can identify and utilize schemata (or scripts or frames) to comprehend inputs. For example, many theorists assume that comprehension consists of (1) finding a schema that fits a particular input (for instance, a "birthday party" schema), (2) discovering those entities that correspond to particular roles required in the schema ("John must be the birthday boy"), and (3) making inferences that fill in the gaps in the story ("John must have unwrapped the present in order to play with it"). Note that most stories involve a large number of schemata, so that the computer scientist's job is even more complex than one might imagine. As an example, consider the following story from Schank (1976):

> John went to New York by bus. On the bus he talked to an old lady. When he left the bus he thanked the driver. He took the subway to Leone's. On the subway his pocket was picked. He got off the train and entered Leone's. He had some lasagna. When the check came, he discovered he couldn't pay. The management told him he would have to wash dishes. When he left, he caught a bus to New Haven.*

Note that the preceding story could be said to include a "bus" schema, "subway" schema, "pickpocket" schema, and "restaurant" schema, not to mention all the possible subschemata for activities like talking, entering, discovering. The following represents the output of Schank's computer when utilizing preprogrammed schemata (actually scripts in Schank's terms) to make inferences and assumptions regarding the preceding story. Note the large number of explicit inferences that the computer program makes.

> John went to a bus stop. He waited at it a few minutes. He entered a bus. The driver got the ticket from John. He went to a seat. He sat down in it. While John was on the bus an old lady and John talked. The driver took John to New York. He went to the driver. When getting off the bus John thanked the driver. John got off it.
>
> He entered a station. He put a token into the turnstile. He went to the platform. He waited at it a few minutes. He entered a subway car. A thief went to John. The thief picked John's pocket. He went. John went to the seat. He left the subway car. He left the station.

---

*From *The Structure of Human Memory,* ed. Charles N. Cofer. W. H. Freeman and Company. Copyright © 1976.

He entered Leone's. He looked around inside it. He saw he could go to a table. He ordered some lasagna. The waiter indicated to the chef John would like him to prepare something. The chef prepared the lasagna. The waiter got it from the chef. The waiter went to the table. He served the lasagna to John. He ate it. He became full.

He asked the waiter for the check. John got it from the waiter. John read the check. John discovered he was unable to pay the check. He indicated to the waiter he was unable to pay the check. The management told John he would have to wash dishes. He entered the kitchen. He washed dishes. He left Leone's.

He went to the bus stop. He waited at it a few minutes. He entered the bus. The driver got the ticket from John. He went to the seat. He sat down in it. The driver took John to New Haven. He got off the bus.*

The work of Schank and other computer theorists is certainly impressive. The computer must have much "knowledge of the world" in order to make the inferences that it does. Note, however, that the inferences made are still quite arbitrary. Why not elaborate further? For example, the first sentence from the computer might read "John, who is a human with eyes, ears, etc., used his legs to go to the bus stop." On the other hand, why make all the assumptions that the computer does make? Humans generally do not make extensive sets of explicit inferences when recalling stories like these. One of the challenges facing computer models is to determine how comprehension processes (including inferences) vary as a function of context and purposes (see Chapter 5). This is a problem for further research. Nevertheless, the notion of abstract schemata (or scripts or frames) has important psychological implications. As an illustration, read once again the curious demonstration story about Jim in the restaurant. Some implications of this story are discussed below.

The Demonstration Story Revisited

As mentioned earlier, Schank and Abelson (1975) would claim that the demonstration story about Jim violates our "restaurant" script. One implication of their position is that the story could be more understandable if one's "restaurant" script could be changed. Assume, therefore, that Jim went to a very special type of restaurant. The owner allows people who can cook at least one special meal to compete for the honor of preparing their specialty for other customers who desire it. Those who wish to compete sit in the gallery rather than the main dining room (although a central stage is accessible to both).

The competition centers on the competitor's entertaining the crowd, by singing, for example, or dancing or playing an instrument. The approval of the crowd is a prerequisite for allowing the person to announce his or her cooking specialty. The rest of the crowd then has the option of ordering it, and the person receives a certain amount of money for each meal prepared. After doing the cooking and serving the meal to the customers, the person can then order from the regular restaurant menu and pay for it out of the money received for cooking. In general, this arrangement benefits the manager as well as the person. The manager obtains relatively inexpensive entertainment, and the person is usually able to make more than enough money to pay for an excellent meal.

Note that our scenario is quite different from our normal experiences with restaurants (probably for good reasons). Note further that you would probably have a very difficult time understanding this imaginary restaurant if you did not already have a normal "restaurant" script. For present purposes, the most important point is the relationship between scripts and comprehension. Given the modified "restaurant" script described above, reread the demonstration story and see if it doesn't make more sense (of course, you may have invented a modified script when first reading the story, in which case you were able to understand it the first time). Most people find that the modified "restaurant" script increases their ability to make sense of the demonstration story. This suggests that knowledge of abstract scripts and schemata may indeed be important for comprehension; they may guide the types of inferences and elaborations we make.

An increasing number of researchers are therefore beginning to emphasize the importance of characterizing the schematic knowledge available to people. Research on the nature of story schemata represents an excellent case in point (e.g., see Rumelhart, 1975; Mandler, Johnson, and DeForest, 1976; Stein and Glenn, in press). Consider such children's stories as "Once upon a time there was a friendly rabbit who lived in the forest. . . ." Many of these stories share a common abstract structure, including statements about an initial setting, the adventures of a main character, and so on. Through experience of various stories, children may develop schemata that help guide their abilities to comprehend and master stories that they hear and read. In a similar manner, people may develop schemata that guide their understanding of scientific articles (cf. Kintsch, 1976). It is also important to note that people from various cultures may have acquired different types of story schemata. In Chapter 5, Section 3, for example, we noted that Bartlett's (1932) story "The War of the Ghosts" involved many assumptions that were unfamiliar to the participants in his experiments; they therefore lacked certain schemata to help them understand the story in the way intended by the writer, and because they tried to adapt the story to inappropriate schemata, they exhibited major distortions in recall.

The analysis of story schemata is extremely important, especially in educational contexts where one needs to evaluate students' abilities and select educational materials accordingly. Note, for example, that a particular story may or may not represent a prototypic example of a learner's story schema (see Section 1 for discussion of prototypes). Those stories that are less prototypic may therefore result in more inaccuracies in understanding and recall. An emphasis on the degree to which particular stories conform to previously acquired schemata can therefore have important implications for assessing people's abilities. As noted in Chapter 4, Section 4, for example, Piaget (1969a) and Fraisse (1963) argue that young children lack the ability to recall events from stories in their correct temporal order. As Stein and Glenn (in press) note, however, no attention was paid to the degree to which the stories conformed to the types of schemata available to the children. Stein and Glenn show that children *can* recall events in their correct temporal order. However, the children must be presented with stories that are consistent with the internal schemata that they have acquired. This is just one example of the importance of taking schemata into account.

The concept of schemata can also help explain why people may remember different events in a story, depending on the perspective they adopt. As an example, reconsider Pichert and Anderson's (1977) study (discussed in Chapter 5, Section 4), in which groups of people read the same story from the perspective of either a burglar or a home buyer. Different types of information were recalled by the two groups. Note that "burglary" and "home buying" represent different schemata. Information that there was a color TV might therefore fit into a "loot" subschema of a "burglary" schema, but would be less likely to instantiate important variables in a "home buying" schema. Because schemata can presumably affect constructive aspects of comprehension and serve as a guide for reconstructive processes of recall (see Chapter 5, Section 3), Pichert and Anderson argue that one would expect people to recall information that is most consistent with their currently activated schemata. The results of their study support this claim (see also Bower, 1976).

Summary of Section 2

This section focused on a general approach to the problem of characterizing knowledge that we labeled "schema theory." Bartlett's theory (see Chapter 5, Section 3) emphasized the role of schemata, but he did not explicitly analyze the types of information that they might include. Recent theorists (e.g., Kintsch, 1976; Minsky, 1975; Rumelhart and Ortony, 1977; Schank and Abelson, 1977) have attempted to define schemata in more precise ways. We discussed only a few illustrations of schemata (also called frames and scripts). Examples included an analysis of our knowledge of "break" (see Figure 6.2) and "going to a restaurant." General schemata also make reference to more particular subschemata that may or may not be accessed depending on context and purpose; for instance, a generalized "face" schema contains reference to more detailed subschemata for such features as eyes, nose, and mouth. A particular story may require knowledge of numerous general schemata, such as "riding a bus," "eating at a restaurant," as well as knowledge of the subschemata that these general schemata contain.

Schemata are assumed to guide constructive comprehension activities as well as reconstructive processes at the time of remembering. At the time of comprehension for example, information about a restaurant may activate a "restaurant" script, or schema, which specifies that particular roles must be filled (such as those of customer, waiter or waitress, chef), and certain sequences of events must occur (such as entering, eating, exiting). This schematic information is only abstractly specified, so that the reader must instantiate (see Chapter 5, Section 2) these general variables with particulars ("Oh, Jim must be the customer"). If a schema specifies a variable that is not explicitly mentioned in a message, the comprehender must make assumptions; for example, that the ball broke the window because it was hit or thrown by some outside agent or force. Schemata may also guide reconstructive processes at the time of remembering. In a "burglary" schema, for example, people have information about the types of variables that are relevant (such as the need to avoid detection, the importance of loot). These general variables can therefore function as implicitly generated cues that help people retrieve previously experienced instantiations of the variables (cf. Pichert and Anderson, 1977).

An awareness of the potentially important role of schemata is also crucial for evaluating claims that certain groups of people, such as young children, lack certain basic abilities. If the information to be learned is not consistent with the schemata available to the children (or analogously, if the children adopt inappropriate perspectives on a story), one would expect to see distortions in recall (e.g., Stein and Glenn, in press).

It is important to add, however, that we must be wary of misuses of schema theory. Brown (1978) discusses some of the dangers of using schemata to explain what people do. It is easy to fall into the trap of saying, "People comprehended this story because they accessed their 'break' schema," or, "People failed to understand that passage because they lack a 'restaurant' schema." Unless we can independently measure what people know and then see how this affects performance in particular situations, explanations in terms of schemata can become circular. We are then left with pseudoexplanations that lead us into believing that we understand something that is not, in fact, adequately understood.

There is another potential problem with schema theory that needs to be noted. If effective comprehension depends on our abilities to activate previously acquired schemata, how do we ever acquire new schemata? How are we able to understand things that we could not previously understand? This issue will be explored in the chapter on acquiring new knowledge (Chapter 7). For present purposes, it is important to consider an additional question about the nature of previously acquired knowledge: To what extent are aspects of our knowledge visual in nature? This question is discussed in Section 3.

Section 3: General Knowledge and Imagery

Discussion in the two preceding sections focused on questions regarding our knowledge of objects (such as birds, human faces), of activities (such as breaking), and of complex episodes (such as going to a restaurant, home buying). These might be represented, respectively, by nouns, by verbs, and by phrases or combinations of phrases. All the models and theories we discussed involved what we shall call "propositionally based representations" of knowledge—representations like "X has wings," "X involves an agent," "X involves entering, ordering, preparing." We did not discuss the possibility that aspects of our knowledge include images. On subjective grounds, it seems obvious that our knowledge includes images. Think about your living room, your entire dwelling, a familiar restaurant, the route between your home and the nearest grocery store. For most people, something other than words comes to mind. Most people say that they visualize these types of events. Indeed, the ability to visualize familiar locations serves as the basis for many mnemonic techniques (see Chapter 3, Section 2).

As noted in Chapter 4, Section 1, Paivio has played an especially important role in rekindling psychologists' interests in imagery (e.g., Paivio, 1971, 1975, 1976). He proposes a dual-coding theory that postulates two separate but interconnected memory systems. In one system information can be stored verbally as discrete definitions, propositions, and the like. In the other system information is stored visually; it actually resembles the input and cannot be represented by definitions or propositions. Paivio has gathered an impressive array of data to support his position. For example, pictures are better remembered than words, and words that can be imaged are easier to retain than less imageable words (e.g., see Paivio and Csapo, 1973). Imagery therefore seems to have powerful effects in learning and retention tasks.

The problem of understanding imagery is more complex than one might assume, however. A particularly problematic question is, What might it mean to say that images are stored? Paivio insists that images are not pictures in one's head or snapshots. If not, then what are they? What the images are remains vague in Paivio's system, but there are good reasons to be vague; the problem is extremely complex. (See Anderson, 1978.) To explore this issue, it is useful to examine the hypothesis that images *are* snapshots and see what would be lacking in such a view.

Images as Snapshots

Suppose that people do indeed store images, and that these images are like snapshots or movie strips stored in the memory. The studies by Shepard and Standing (Chapter 2, Section 1), which demonstrated the possibility of accurate recognition memory for hundreds, and even thousands, of pictures, might seem to support this claim. However, contrast these findings with those of Goldstein and Chance (1971). They presented people with a series of slides of snowflake patterns, each of which was very distinctive. Nevertheless, people's ability to distinguish recognition targets from foils (which were also snowflakes) was very poor. To a camera it makes little difference whether the pictures are familiar scenes or snowflake patterns; to a human it matters a great deal.

Note that a major theme of our theoretical framework illustrated in Figure 1.1 is that the ability to learn is a function of an adequate knowledge base for interpreting and elaborating inputs. This applies to visual inputs as well as to verbal inputs. Without an appropriately refined knowledge base, snowflake patterns cannot be effectively encoded, and recognition memory cannot function adequately. This problem is analogous to that which we noticed in our discussion of chess masters and nonmasters (Chapter 2, Section 1). All participants saw the same visual patterns, but the ability to interpret these patterns meaningfully was crucial, even for short-term recall.

An emphasis on understanding pictures and visual scenes suggests additional problems for the notion that stored images resemble snapshots or movie strips. Like sentences, visual events can be coherent and comprehensible in varying degrees. For example, jumbled pictures, like jumbled sentences, are difficult to retain (e.g., Paivio,

1971; but also note the doll study in Chapter 3, Section 2). Similarly, a picture of a ball breaking a window is understood to represent the ball as part of the method for breaking, but some potential agent must still be assumed (see our discussion of the "break" schema in Section 2). In several experiments, investigators have presented people with a series of slides depicting such activities as making a sandwich, serving tea, getting a haircut (e.g., Jenkins, Wald, and Pittenger, in press; Kintsch, 1976). Particular slides can be left out of the sequence during acquisition, and yet participants will falsely recognize these slides at the time of testing. These results are analogous to those of the studies using linguistic materials that were discussed in Chapter 5, Section 2.

The preceding discussion suggests that people attempt to make sense of visual as well as linguistic inputs. This process includes the realization that certain visual entities are agents, objects, and so forth, as well as the realization that additional information must often be assumed in order to make the events sensible. In short, various schemata may guide our comprehension of visual as well as verbal events. It is for reasons like these that many theorists argue that a common, abstract form of representation under-lies our ability to comprehend and retain visual as well as linguistic inputs (e.g., see Anderson, 1976; Anderson and Bower, 1973; Friedman, in press; Kintsch, 1976; Pyly-shyn, 1973). The use of propositions to characterize abstract knowledge therefore need not imply that all knowledge is linguistic. Propositions can be used to represent knowledge that is assumed to be abstract and conceptual, rather than linguistic, visual, tactual. For example, many computer programs can create dynamic visual displays, but the basis of these programs is propositional (e.g., see Pylyshyn, 1973). Our ability to generate images of our home or our car, for example, need not therefore imply that we actually store images. By the same token, our ability to produce words and sentences need not imply that we store actual words and sentences. Indeed, the prevalence of paraphrase in memory experiments (see Chapters 4 and 5) suggests that we generate outputs on the basis of abstract representations of what was learned.

The Dual-Code Theory Revisited

The preceding discussion emphasizes that comprehending and learning is a func-tion of relationships between information and the currently available skills and knowl-edge of the learner. This applies to any type of input, irrespective of whether it involves language, vision, touch, smell, or taste (e.g., see Gibson and Gibson, 1955; Gibson, 1966). Paivio's dual-code theory (e.g., Paivio, 1971) does not help explain why mem-ory for visual information will vary as a function of the skills and knowledge of the learner. Similarly, the notion that there is a "linguistic system" that does things like store abstract sentences as word strings (e.g., Begg and Paivio, 1969) ignores issues about deep structures or conceptual structures that characterize our understanding of sen-tences (e.g., see Chapter 4, Section 2). In short, Paivio's model does not adequately address such problems as the way people utilize what they know to understand and learn effectively.

Note, however, that criticism of Paivio's particular theory does not necessarily imply that his basic insights should be discarded. For example, instructions to image can have powerful effects on learning and retention (e.g., see Paivio, 1971; Levine, Chapter 4, Section 4). Similarly, the advantages of experiencing something visually or tactually may be different from the advantages of hearing or reading a description of the same item or event. It is therefore important that we examine the role of such activities as verbalizing, visualizing, touching; but we shall do so without assuming that people store word strings or visual or tactual images. Some illustrations of this approach are discussed below.

Modes of Knowing

Note first that our present emphasis is on *activities* like verbalizing, visualizing, touching. The basis for these activities may be abstract knowledge that can be characterized propositionally, just as the basis of the computer's visual displays was propositional; but our emphasis is not on the ultimate form of storage, its propositional or nonpropositional nature, but rather, on the utilization of our knowledge to perform certain types of cognitive acts. Questions about our ability to perform certain activities should not be confused with questions about the ultimate form in which knowledge is stored.

As an illustration of the preceding argument, consider your ability to write your name. This activity involves kinesthetic and visual information. However, your ability to write your name need not imply that some stored visual-kinesthetic image is responsible for the feat. As an example, try the following: Hold a pen with your teeth or foot and try writing your name. You won't write as neatly, but you can still perform the task. Note, however, that the task involves a totally different set of muscle patterns from those involved in normal writing. There is no invariant kinesthetic image, but you can perform the task. Many theorists have argued that our knowledge of various skilled activities (for example, skills involving visualizing, verbalizing, writing) is abstract in nature (e.g., see Bartlett, 1932; Lashley, 1951; Turvey, 1977). Once again, questions about our ability to perform certain types of activities should not be confused with questions about the form in which knowledge is stored.

It should also be emphasized that facility in one class of activities, such as motor activities, is not necessarily translatable into facility in other classes of activities, like visualizing or verbalizing (e.g., see Bruner, 1968; Piaget and Inhelder, 1969). For example, you can *show* someone how you write your signature, but it is difficult to describe this in words. As a further illustration, consider a skilled typist who is asked to type the alphabet or is given a visual diagram of the keyboard and asked to fill in the alphabet. As Posner (1973) notes, the latter task is much more difficult. In a sense, the skilled typist's knowledge of the keyboard is in the typist's fingers, and not representable as a detailed visual image of the keyboard. Similarly, one may sometimes know how to travel from one place to another but be unable to represent this knowledge in the form of a map (cf. Posner, 1973).

The preceding illustrations demonstrate that people may perform motor activities without necessarily being able to verbalize or visualize the information. This suggests that some modes of knowing may prove more effective than others, depending on the activities we are engaged in. For example, researchers have shown that our ability to visualize can have important effects on our performance. Shepard and colleagues (Shepard and Metzler, 1971; Cooper and Shepard, 1973) show that people seem to be able to mentally rotate visual objects in order to perform certain comparisons. Similarly, Kosslyn (1976) presents data indicating that acts of visualizing affect reaction time. It is instructive to consider one of Kosslyn's studies in detail.

In one study, Kosslyn (1976) asked two groups of students to verify statements like "Cats have claws" and "Cats have heads." Students in Group 1 were asked to respond on the basis of their general knowledge and responded more quickly to sentences like the first than to those like the second. In contrast, students in Group 2 were asked first to image a cat and then to verify the statements. They verified statements like the second more quickly. Why? Kosslyn argues that in most people's images a cat's head is more prominent than a cat's claws. This would explain why people in Group 2, who were using their images as a basis for responding, should have been faster at verifying "Cats have heads." Kosslyn and colleagues provide additional data suggesting that activities like visualizing may have important effects on performance (e.g., Kosslyn and Pomerantz, 1977; Kosslyn, Murphy, Bemesderfer, and Feinstein, 1977; Kosslyn and Schwartz, 1977).

Activities like visualizing, verbalizing, and so forth also seem to have implications as distinct modes of acquiring new information. Different people may have preferences for different modes. Consider the comments of a mechanical engineering student who was interviewed by Tarka (personal communication). The student stated that he had to be able to visualize "the insides of devices" in order to understand how they worked. In contrast, many other engineering students seem to prefer more abstract forms of representation. For example, they are better able to understand the workings of mechanical devices in terms of mathematical formulas. Questions about different ways of acquiring information are clearly very important. People may visualize, verbalize, touch, and this can have major effects on their abilities to perform different types of tasks. For example, the act of imagining what something looks like may sometimes be a very effective way of learning; it is one form of elaboration that may facilitate comprehension. On the other hand, the act of verbally elaborating a visual input (explaining, for example, the appropriate functions of various pairs of scissors; see Chapter 5, Section 1) may also facilitate understanding and retention. The value of particular types of activities will undoubtedly depend on the nature of the information and the current level of the learner's knowledge and skills. Questions about preferred types of learning activities seem to be very important to pursue.

Summary of Section 3

The purpose of this section was to suggest the complexity of questions about imagery. It seems clear that most people have the ability to visualize certain scenes or events (e.g., their living rooms) and to imagine how things sound, what they feel like, and so forth. Activities like imaging are valuable because they can facilitate memory (e.g., Paivio, 1971, 1976). Nevertheless, there is a difference between assumptions about the value of performing such activities and assumptions about different forms of storing information. Paivio's (1971) dual-code theory states that some information can be stored both verbally and visually, but the assumption that we store pictures and strings of words is questionable. For example, computers can generate visual scenes even though they represent information in abstract propositional formats. Similarly, people can generate images and sentences, but this need not imply that images and strings of words are stored as such. Because similar processes of comprehension may be required for visual scenes and linguistic statements, abstract schemata (see Section 2) seem to play a role in visual as well as linguistic activities.

Despite the current controversy surrounding Paivio's dual-code theory, questions regarding the effects of activities like visualizing and verbalizing are very important. These are different types of activities, and some people may prefer one type over the others; for example, some seem to need information about what something looks like in order to learn effectively. This suggests that efficient learning also involves the ability to know what one further needs to know (to realize, for example, that one needs a picture or a formula) in order to understand and master materials. This topic is discussed in Section 4.

Section 4: Knowledge about Our Own Knowledge

In this section we discuss a topic that has been called the problem of *metacognition* (e.g., Brown, 1977a, 1977b; Brown and DeLoache, 1978; Flavell and Wellman, 1977). In general, metacognitive processes are assumed to underlie the ability to monitor our current level of learning and understanding. This monitoring requires knowledge about the current state of our knowledge. Without metacognitive processes we might fail to perform such crucial activities as asking questions, rereading difficult material, selecting the learning activities appropriate to a given task. As Brown and DeLoache (1978) state,

> *The basic skills of metacognition . . . include* predicting *the consequences of an action or event,* checking *the results of one's own actions (did it work),* monitoring *one's ongoing activity (how am I doing),* reality testing *(does this make sense) and a variety of other behaviors for* coordinating *and* controlling *deliberate attempts to learn and solve problems. (P. xxx)*

The topic of metacognition highlights the truly active nature of learning and understanding. We must learn what we as learners need to do in order to comprehend effectively and master information, and each of us may have somewhat different ways of optimizing our own learning.

The Development of Personal Criteria

Perhaps the most important factor underlying our ability to learn is the availability of criteria for evaluating the adequacy of our present level of understanding and mastery.

Without some feedback indicating that things are not quite right, we may fail to perform additional activities (to ask appropriate questions, for instance) that might correct our shortcomings and permit adaptive change.

A classic study by Thorndike (1931) illustrates the importance of feedback for evaluating the adequacy of one's performance. Two groups of students were blindfolded and given practice at attempting to draw a line exactly four inches long. One group was provided with feedback on each trial: "No, that's one inch too long," "Yes, that's right." The other was not. Only the people provided with feedback improved during the practice trials.

Some theorists (see Hilgard and Bower, 1975, for a review) interpreted Thorndike's results to mean that *reinforcement* was necessary for learning. However, to provide reinforcement like "Yes, that's right" is also to provide feedback or knowledge of results. In general, most theorists assume that external reinforcement is not necessary for learning (see especially Tolman, 1932); without some type of feedback, however, practice will not help one improve.

Thorndike's experiment involved *external* feedback provided by the experimenter. An extremely important aspect of learning is the development of personal *internalized* criteria that can help guide one's acts. As an example, consider a would-be musician who wants to learn to sing on key. It is not sufficient to simply supply this person with external feedback that permits the correction of voice quality. Musicians must be able to make such corrections on their own, and to do this they must know when they are off key and by how much. Similarly, many people claim to benefit from mental practice (e.g., see Hughes, 1915, who discusses mental practice by piano players). To benefit from mental practice one must have some internally derived criteria for correcting errors.

The Suzuki method of teaching children to play the violin is a particularly fascinating illustration of the development of internal criteria (cf. Pronko, 1969). Training begins soon after the child is born. The parents select a single piece of music by Mozart, Bach, or another classical composer and play a recording of it to the baby each day (the recording must be of very high fidelity). The piece is played for several months until there are indications that the baby recognizes the music, until the music has a very soothing effect on the infant, for example. Only at this point is a second piece of music played. This procedure continues until the child is three or four years old, when the child goes to violin school. These children learn to correct the movements of their bows until they can play the classical music. Presumably, they are able to compare the sounds they make with their previously acquired knowledge of the classical pieces and hence make corrections in their movements. The children thus learn to play by ear and only later are taught to read musical scores. This method is very successful and has produced some violinists who are now world-renowned.

Feelings of Knowing
and Understanding

Related to the ability to use internalized criteria is the ability to monitor one's feelings of knowing and understanding. If asked whether you know the meaning of *kursi* you will probably say no and let it go at that. If unable to recall the name of a relatively familiar person, however, you will feel frustrated. You know that you know the name but are simply unable to reactivate it at the time. (Recall our discussion of the tip-of-the-tongue phenomenon in Chapter 3.) Can we really know that we know something when we can't recall it at that time?

Experiments by Hart (1967) suggest that people's feelings of knowing can be very accurate. He presented people with general-knowledge questions like "Who wrote *Catch 22?*" When they could not provide the answer, they were asked whether they *felt* they knew the answer but simply couldn't produce it, and their replies were recorded. Later, Hart gave everyone a recognition test on the previously unanswered questions. Participants correctly recognized 76 percent of those items for which they had indicated a feeling of knowing but only 43 percent of those for which they had reported no feeling of knowing. These results indicate that people's feelings of knowing what they know can be monitored quite accurately.

Although Hart's data suggest sophisticated abilities to monitor feelings of knowing, it would probably be a mistake to accept this as a general conclusion. Hart tested college students' abilities to monitor their feelings about previously learned and fairly simple information. Contrast this with situations where we are attempting to learn new and complex information, in a college course, for example. How do we know whether we adequately understand, and understand sufficiently to meet certain performance criteria (for example, to answer test questions)? If something seems confusing, this feeling becomes a signal to request clarification. If we don't understand the intended point but feel that we do understand, we may fail to initiate the procedure (asking questions, for instance) by which we might progress beyond our current level of understanding; only when confronted with test questions will we realize that something is not quite right.

Consider once again the passage presented in Chapter 5, Section 2:

The man was worried. His car came to a halt and he was all alone. It was extremely dark and cold. The man took off his overcoat, rolled down the window, and got out of the car as quickly as possible. Then he used all his strength to move as fast as he could. He was relieved when he finally saw the lights of the city, even though they were far away.

You will probably recall that this passage can be understood as involving a submerged car. However, most people don't make this assumption when they hear it for the first time. Bransford and Nitsch (1978) read the passage to college students (none had heard it before) and asked them if they felt it made sense. All said yes. Their confident feelings of understanding could be dispelled quite easily, however. When asked, "Why did the man take off his overcoat?" "Why did he roll down the window?" students suddenly realized that they had not adequately evaluated the passage. Some made statements like "Now that I think about it, it does seem strange that the man took off his overcoat since the passage said the weather was cold." Without these questions, however, the students felt confident that the passage made sense. (If one assumes the car is submerged, the man's actions do make sense.) There are many levels at which we can evaluate our current understanding. Our feelings of comprehension may therefore vary depending on the goals we have.

The Flexibility of
Comprehension Criteria

The criteria used in assessing feelings of understanding seem flexible. They depend on our current knowledge, the present context, and the purposes we have (cf. Bransford and Nitsch, 1978). As an example, reconsider an experiment discussed earlier (Chapter 5, Section 3). When Bransford, McCarrell, and Nitsch (1976) presented the statement "Bill has a red car" in an experimental context, everyone said it was perfectly understandable. Consider in detail what happened when the same sentence was spoken in a social context. A colleague (hereafter C) was sitting in his office when a friend (hereafter E, the experimenter) walked in and said simply "Bill has a red car." C's reactions were quite interesting.

> He looked very surprised, paused for about three seconds, and finally exclaimed "What the h—— are you talking about?" After a hasty debriefing session C laughed and told E what had gone on in his head. First, C thought that E was talking about a person named Bill that C knew. Then C realized that E could not in all probability know that person; and besides, Bill would never buy a red car. Then C thought that E may have mixed up the name and really meant to say J (a mutual friend of C and E). C knew that J had ordered a new car, but he was surprised that it was red and that it had arrived so soon. C also entertained a few additional hypotheses— all within about three seconds of time. After that he gave up, thereupon uttering "What the h—— are you talking about?" (P. 340)

It is instructive to consider the activities of the would-be comprehender in the social situation. He had some well-specified criteria about what he needed to know in order to feel that he understood what the speaker meant. For example, it was not sufficient to assume that Bill was someone unknown to him; he needed to know which Bill the speaker had in mind. He even entertained the possibility that the speaker had not said what he meant. In short, the would-be comprehender entertained questions of clarification like "Wait a minute, I don't understand who Bill is. Did you mean to say another name, other than *Bill*?" In an experimental context, however, people hearing the sentence about the red car were perfectly comfortable with their relatively shallow level of understanding. The information they received was sufficient in view of the criteria that they used.

The preceding examples suggest that the sophistication of one's comprehension activities does not necessarily correlate with success or failure to understand at any particular moment (cf. Bransford and Nitsch, 1978). Indeed, the realization that one needs additional information in order to adequately understand represents a high degree of sophistication. By the same token, one cannot say that people in the experiment who stated that they understood the sentence "Bill has a red car" are superficial comprehenders. If someone in the latter group said, "No, this sentence is not comprehensible because I do not know who you're referring to by *Bill*," the experimenter would be likely to become frustrated and say, "You're reading too much into this situation; I'm only asking about the comprehensibility of this statement as an English sentence." The development of global comprehension skills seems to involve the ability to be flexible in adopting the particular types of comprehension criteria appropriate to the present situation (see especially Proffitt, 1976). Several theorists have argued that the ability to adopt such criteria is extremely valuable. For example, the development of abilities to monitor ongoing levels of comprehension seems to be an important factor in the cognitive development of children; it enables them to discover when they need additional information in order to understand effectively (e.g., Brown and DeLoache, 1978; Markman, 1977).

An experiment by Markman (1977) provides an excellent illustration of comprehension assessments. She asked children in grades 1, 2, and 3 to help her design instructions for new card games to be taught to other children. The instructions were incomplete, so that no one could actually understand the game unless they asked for more information. For example, the experimenter and child each received four alphabet cards along with the following instructions:

> We each put our cards in a pile. We both turn over the top card in our pile. We look at the cards to see who has the special card. Then we turn over the next card in our pile to see who has the special card this time. In the end the person with the most cards wins the game.

Note that the instructions contained no information about what the "special cards" were. Markman was interested in the degree to which the children would realize that they needed this information in order to understand the game. Results indicated that the younger children needed many prompts before they realized the gap in the instructions. Indeed, many had to try to perform the task before they realized they did not really know how to play the game.

The failure to adequately monitor current levels of understanding may underlie certain learning difficulties experienced by adults, too. Whimbey (1976) provides information relevant to this point. He cites the following passage from Gruber (1971):

> If a serious literary critic were to write a favorable, full-length review of How Could I Tell Mother She Frightened My Boy Friends Away, Grace Plumbuster's new story, his startled readers would assume either that he had gone mad, or that Grace Plumbuster was his editor's wife. (P. 85)

This passage was one used by Whimbey to assess the reading strategies of "poor comprehenders" (at college level). Whimbey (1976) states:

> This was the first sentence of a reading comprehension article, and I had to stop for a moment and reread a portion of it in order to understand its meaning

completely. Not so the low-aptitude student I was testing. He was halfway down the page by the time I had the details of the first sentence sorted out. I asked him if he had understood the sentence, and he answered, "No, not really." So I suggested he give it another try. (P. 85)

Whimbey goes on to note that good readers are much more systematic in their efforts to assess and update their ongoing sense of comprehension.

To the poor reader, however, the pattern of gradual, sequential construction of exact meaning is totally foreign. One-shot thinking (Bereiter and Engelmann's term) is the basis on which the poor reader makes interpretations and draws conclusions. (P. 86)

In short, poor learners may not only lack the skills to apply their existing knowledge to comprehension of new information; they may also be lacking in sensitive criteria for assessing their comprehension. Helping them learn to learn therefore involves changing their approach to comprehension tasks. However, even the ability to comprehend does not guarantee learning; we must also *master* the information that was understood.

Assessments of Mastery

The question of our ability to assess whether information has been mastered is somewhat different from the question of whether we have sufficient information to understand it. We can memorize information that we don't adequately understand, although it may take more learning trials to do so. Conversely, we can understand material and know that it has not yet been mastered; for example, we may realize the need to study more in order to do well on a test. Of course, comprehension and ease of mastery can also be interrelated; for example, increased difficulty usually requires increased study.

In Chapter 4, Section 3, we discussed an experiment by Danner (1976) involving passages that were topically organized or disorganized. Passages that were topically organized produced superior recall. Danner also assessed the degree to which various groups of children (second-, fourth-, and sixth-graders) realized whether differences in topical organization might affect their memory. The older children were more aware that differences in organization could affect their abilities to recall the stories they heard (see also Brown, 1977a, 1977b; Flavell and Wellman, 1977).

A series of studies by Owings, Petersen, Bransford, Morris, and Stein (in preparation) explored differences between successful and less successful fifth-graders. Would they spontaneously use their knowledge to evaluate the difficulty of stories and study longer for those that were harder? The students were therefore asked to read a series of "precise" and "less precise" stories (like those discussed in Chapter 4, Section 3, which included information about the fat [or bald] man getting stuck in a cave). The activities described in each story were simplified to ensure that all students knew the individual words, as well as the "precise" event sequences. Stories thus included such statements as "The hungry boy ate the hamburger" (precise) and "The sleepy boy ate the hamburger" (less precise).

Each student read a passage and studied it as long as he or she wished, and then read and studied another passage. (Each pair of passages contained one precise and one less precise story.) After each series of two passages, the students were asked to state whether one seemed harder to learn than the other and why. They then received tests on each passage; "What did the hungry boy do?" would be a typical test question. All students received the series of acquisition trials (reading, studying, and comparing) and test trials over a sequence of several sessions, so that they became familiar both with the procedure and with the nature of the tests. The data to be discussed came from their last session (involving two *pairs* of passages).

Two groups of fifth-graders participated; those in the top quarter of the class and those in the bottom quarter. Groups were chosen on the basis of teacher assessments and test scores. The upper-quartile students could readily distinguish precise from less precise passages. Furthermore, they studied longer for the harder, less precise passages than for the precise passages. In contrast, the lower-quartile students were quite poor at distinguishing between the two types of passages and, although they seemed highly motivated, exhibited absolutely no tendency to spend longer studying the harder, less precise passages.

It is also important to note that the test scores of the lower-quartile students were much higher for the precise than for the less precise passages (the same was true for upper-quartile students). These results suggest that the lower-quartile students had the appropriate knowledge and that it influenced their ability to learn and retrieve the information; but they seemed not to be *aware* of the degree to which the information they were reading was congruent with their existing knowledge, and that this increased learning difficulty. This became especially evident when their reasons for saying that something was difficult or easy to learn were analyzed. Even when they chose correctly (which might have been fortuitous, because they were asked to rate only two stories at a time), lower-quartile students would often say things like, "I think this one is longer, so it's harder," "This story mentioned dogs, and I like dogs, so it's easier." In contrast, the upper-quartile students almost always knew exactly why stories were easy or hard to learn.

In subsequent studies, Owings and colleagues found that lower-quartile students could be helped to notice the difference between precise and less precise stories. For example, they were eventually able to state how less precise stories should be rearranged to make them more precise (for example, "The hungry boy should eat the hamburger, not the sleepy boy"). These students were therefore capable of using what they knew to evaluate story difficulty, but they didn't appear to do so spontaneously unless explicitly instructed. They therefore failed to regulate additional activities like rereading and studying—activities that were necessary if they were to perform well on the tests.

It is instructive to note that even college students frequently have difficulty knowing whether they have adequately understood and mastered materials. Many students think that they have studied adequately and don't realize their mistake until confronted with a test. As an illustration, consider an actual case of a graduate student who studied for a test in statistics. The first test covered a number of chapters on probability theory, and the course instructor had provided study questions for each chapter. The graduate student demonstrated that he could easily solve each of the problem sets provided by the course instructor so he was convinced that he was ready for the test. At this point a fellow student stepped in, took out a pair of scissors to cut out the test questions from each problem sheet, and mixed them up. Under these conditions the first graduate student attempted to solve each problem and failed miserably. Why was he able to solve each of the problems on the study sheets yet unable to solve the same problems when presented randomly? It seems clear that this student's ability to do well when given the study sheets depended on his knowledge regarding which chapter the problems came from and hence which formulas were relevant. When the chapter information was no longer available, the student realized the need to study in a different way.

Personal Blocks to Effective Learning

The previous discussion illustrates the importance of using what we know to evaluate our current level of comprehension and mastery. If we fail to do this, we may neglect to pursue additional activities necessary for adequate performance later. Effective learning therefore seems to involve a critical attitude regarding our current level of knowing, which prompts us to ask questions, test ourselves, seek alternate opinions, and so forth. It is one thing to agree with assumptions about the importance of such activities; it is quite another actually to carry out such activities. The latter can often be anxiety producing. It is frequently less threatening to hold to one's current ideas than to explore alternatives and hence face being wrong.

Holt (1964) discusses how anxiety and fear of failure can impair learning. He notes that many students exhibit a "don't-look-back-it's-too-awful" pattern of behavior. For example, while reading aloud, one of Holt's students would consistently make wild guesses at relatively unfamiliar words rather than try to sound them out. Holt (1964) also notes that many elementary-school children are reluctant to ask questions because they are afraid they will seem stupid. Such fears are evident in many college students as well. Even college professors (the present author being no exception) experience such feelings when they ask colleagues for constructive criticism of a paper or book they have written. When colleagues return with valid criticisms, a frequent tendency is for the writer to become anxious and start defending his or her ideas. Happily, one can learn to identify and change such defensive reactions, at least to some extent. Unless people can begin to dissociate the worth of their ideas from their feelings of self-worth, however, they may be too threatened to test themselves or to learn from constructive yet critical interchanges such as those noted above.

It can be especially threatening if a colleague criticizes some basic assumptions that have implications for a wide range of endeavors. Members of the scientific community are continually giving and receiving criticism, so they must learn to deal with the emotional consequences of such interchanges if they wish to be critical of their own positions and hence learn. The physicist David Bohm (1969) discusses the emotional impact of receiving criticism. Consider his description of a scientist's reaction to some alternative assumptions proposed by another scientist.

>*His first reaction is often of violent disturbance, as views that are very dear are questioned or thrown to the ground. Nevertheless, if he will "stay with it" rather than escape into anger and unjustified rejection of contrary ideas, he will discover that this disturbance is very beneficial. For now he becomes aware of the assumptive character of a great many previously unquestioned features of his own thinking. This does not mean that he will reject these assumptions in favor of those of other people. Rather, what is needed is the conscious criticism of one's own metaphysics, leading to changes where appropriate and ultimately, to the continual creation of new and different kinds. (P. 42)*

If people are too defensive, they may fail to evaluate their current level of understanding and thereby lose many opportunities to learn.

Bohm's discussion involves a scientist, and our earlier discussion of fear of failure emphasized Holt's observations of children. Taken together, these observations suggest the overriding importance of the human element at all ages and in all kinds of occupations. We have discussed learning in terms of learning strategies, appropriate concepts and schemata, and the like, but important as these theoretical notions are, they should not blind us to the fact that it is people who learn, who change, who remember. The ability to learn and change is not simply a function of our factual knowledge; it depends on feelings about ourselves. Too often, it seems, we place the greatest emphasis on what people know at the moment, rather than on their ability to realize gaps in their current knowledge and hence learn effectively. Toulmin (1972) stresses the importance of the latter activity:

>*A [person] demonstrates his rationality, not by a commitment to fixed ideas, stereotyped procedures, or immutable concepts, but by the manner in which, and the occasions on which, he changes those ideas, procedures and concepts. (P. v)*

We may wish to better understand someone else's point of view or to develop a new one. In either case, the development of general learning and comprehension skills seems more closely related to the ability to ask relevant questions (of ourselves and others) than to the ability to state factual content. If the importance of these activities can be appreciated, people may feel less threatened and hence be more likely to learn.

Summary of Section 4

This section focused on the topic of metacognitive processes, which emphasizes the importance of being able to monitor accurately our current levels of understanding and mastery. If we could not detect any difference between things that seemed sensible and those that seemed nonsensible, we should be quite passive and have no idea of the need to ask questions, or follow other courses of action, that would raise our current level of understanding. Of course, most people have some notion of differences between understanding and not understanding. Nevertheless, there are many cases where people *think* they have understood and mastered information when, in fact, they have not (remember, for example, the statistics student).

It is doubtful whether we utilize a single criterion for assessing feelings of understanding. Thus, our ability to understand an utterance like ''Bill has a red car'' depends on the perceived purpose of the utterance. When it is used in a social context, for example, there are certain things we need to know in order to understand the intended meaning of the utterance. Sophisticated comprehenders know how to be flexible in adapting their comprehension criteria to particular situations. Many learning problems may be due to people's failure to make spontaneous use of what they know to assess their comprehension of new information, and to take appropriate steps to remedy deficiencies.

The act of monitoring our current level of understanding is not without its emotional implications. Fears of being thought foolish often keep us from questioning the adequacy of what we have heard or seen. Frequently, however, it is those people with the courage to ask seemingly naive questions who contribute most to a discussion or activity. The ability to detect gaps in our own knowledge should be viewed as a skill that is highly desirable.

Chapter 7
Acquiring New Knowledge and Skills

Our discussion in Chapters 5 and 6 suggests that the ability to understand and remember is strongly influenced by the learner's currently available skills and knowledge (see also Figure 1.1). The purpose of this chapter is to explore questions about the acquisition of *new* skills and knowledge. How do we understand and do things that we could not previously understand and do? For example, how do we acquire new concepts and schemata that will permit us to understand materials that at first seemed confusing? How do we develop skills that enable us to monitor more efficiently our current level of understanding and mastery? How do we learn to learn?

These questions involve a set of testing criteria different from those employed in earlier chapters. In Chapter 5, for example, we saw how appropriately activated knowledge, such as a "washing clothes" schema, facilitated people's abilities to comprehend and remember. The testing criterion involved people's abilities to remember information presented at the time of acquisition. Discussion in this chapter will emphasize a different set of criteria, namely, the ability to use what was learned to better understand and remember new information. In short, the focus of this chapter is on *transfer*. If you receive information about a new concept, you want to be able to do something more than simply remember the exact information heard during acquisition. You need to be able to identify new examples of the concept and to use this conceptual knowledge to understand material that you were at first unable to understand adequately. As we shall see, the ability to remember does not guarantee transfer. This chapter is divided into four sections, which are described below.

Overview

Section 1 discusses *some principles of concept identification*. There is a rich psychological literature on this topic. The major question concerns the types of variables that facilitate the identification of new examples (that facilitate transfer). This is different from questions about people's abilities to remember the exact exemplars presented during the acquisition task. There are also some possible limitations of traditional studies of concept identification that need to be considered. For example, the concepts studied are frequently arbitrary and not especially meaningful. Under these conditions, people may employ learning strategies different from those normally used. It will also be stressed that the problem of concept *identification* is different from concept *formation*. In concept identification one decides which of a set of previously acquired concepts represents the solution to a problem. This is different from acquiring a new concept.

Section 2 explores processes involved in *developing new skills and concepts*. These are different from processes of concept identification. We shall ask how people are enabled to understand and do things they could not previously understand and do. Like Piaget (1952), we shall stress that the development of new skills and knowledge involves processes of *accommodation* as well as *assimilation*. People assimilate new information to previously acquired schemata, but certain experiences can also help people modify previous schemata (accommodation). The availability of these new schemata can then help people understand subsequent events more completely.

The purpose of Section 3 is to examine *the role of practice in schema development*. We frequently need more than one learning trial in order to master new skills, concepts, and schemata. We learn by practicing; for example, by attempting to see how concepts and schemata apply in new contexts. Some ways of practicing facilitate memory, but not transfer; others help us develop skills and knowledge that permit flexible transfer; and still other ways of practicing frequently result in confusion because they require a level of development that has not yet been reached by the learner. It is for reasons like these that it is important to understand how different types of practice affect the development of knowledge and skills.

In Section 4 we discuss an aspect of the learning problem that represents a major challenge for cognitive science. The emphasis in this section is on *experiences that help people learn to learn*. Where Section 3 focuses on the types of practice situations that an experimenter or teacher might use to facilitate knowledge development, Section 4 asks how people learn to plan and structure their own learning activities. These skills of self-regulation seem to be a hallmark of intelligent activity. How do they develop, and how can people be helped to improve upon the skills of self-regulation that they already have?

Section 1: Some Principles of Concept Identification

The purpose of this section is to analyze some of the psychological literature on concept identification. This is an especially important topic because the ability to identify concepts is not simply equivalent to the ability to remember previously experienced examples and definitions; although people may be able to do the latter, they may fail to transfer their understanding to examples that are novel but related.

As an illustration of the type of problem to be considered, imagine being in a foreign country where people do not speak English and you don't know their language. People in that country may try to teach you their words for concepts by saying things like *medja* or *kursi* while pointing to appropriate objects and events; your task is to try to decide what the words mean. There is a large psychological literature on processes involved in identifying and acquiring concepts under conditions analogous to these. Aspects of the literature are discussed in this section.

Figure 7.1 illustrates examples of stimuli like those used in a classic study by Heidbreder (1946, 1947). Note that different labels are provided for each example shown. Each of these examples illustrates a fairly simple concept, and yet you will probably find yourself uncertain about the exact meaning of the linguistic labels. Does *ling* refer to socks, clothing, stripes, or to the concept of "twoness" or some other concept? Does *relk* refer to hair, eyes, beard, a man, a human face? *Fard* might be the name for a concept like "sixness," something bounded by a circle, something circular. Additional examples are needed in order to understand more precisely the meaning of each term.

Figure 7.2 provides additional examples for each of the three labels. Given this information, you should find that you are less uncertain about the precise meaning of each term. This increased knowledge should now help you transfer to the new set of test items (in the right-hand column in Figure 7.2). As noted earlier, the ability to transfer is an important criterion for assessing people's knowledge of concepts and schemata. Thus, it would be possible to rote-memorize previous examples of *ling, relk,* and *fard,* yet be unable to identify new examples of these concepts correctly on a transfer test.

Factors Affecting the Ease of Concept Identification

Researchers have investigated factors that make concept identification easy or difficult. Heidbreder (1946, 1947), for example, found that some types of concepts are easier to learn than others. Thus, when a concept to be learned was relatively concrete (as is "building" or "face"), most people acquired it fairly quickly. When concepts were more abstract ("twoness," "sixness"), however, they were harder to acquire. Similarly, Trabasso (1963) finds that people can more quickly identify concepts if they are based on salient characteristics like color than when they are based on less salient characteristics like the angle at which a stimulus appears on a page. Stimuli also differ in the degree to which they elicit thoughts about certain characteristic features. For example, *milk* and *snow* readily elicit *white,* whereas *fang* and *baseball* are less likely to elicit thoughts

Figure 7.1
Stimuli like Those Used in a Concept-Formation Study by Heidbreder. (From *Journal of General Psychology,* 1946, 35: 173–189. Used by permission.)

Ling   Relk   Fard

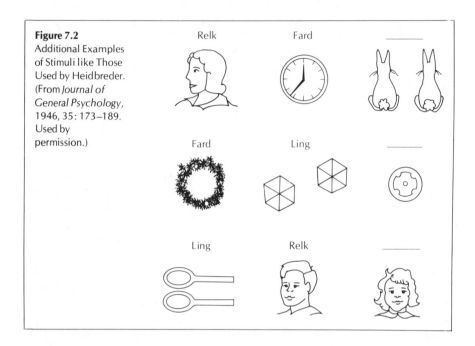

Figure 7.2
Additional Examples of Stimuli like Those Used by Heidbreder. (From *Journal of General Psychology*, 1946, 35: 173–189. Used by permission.)

Relk   Fard   _____

Fard   Ling   _____

Ling   Relk   _____

about whiteness. Underwood and Richardson (1956) therefore argue that features can vary in their *dominance level*. The feature "white" is highly dominant for the word *snow*, but not for *fang*. It should therefore be easier to identify the concept "white" when given exemplars like *milk* and *snow* than when given *fang* and *baseball*.

It is also possible to define concepts in terms of rules, and rule difficulty can affect the speed of concept solution. For example, the concept "red triangle" involves a *conjunction* of the subconcepts "red" and "triangle." A *disjunctive* concept would involve a rule like "all patterns that are red or triangular or both." Bourne (1970) has analyzed a number of rules for defining concepts and shows that the more complex the rule, the harder the concept problems are to solve.

The speed of concept identification also depends on the strategies used by the learners. A classic monograph by Bruner, Goodnow, and Austin (1956) explores various strategies in great detail. For example, some people seem to use a *wholist strategy*, which involves trying to remember all the features or attributes common to examples of a particular concept (for example, hair, eyes, freckles, a boy, a human face) until some of these features can be ruled out. Other people adopt a *partist strategy*, which involves forming a single hypothesis ("The critical feature might be freckles") and persevering with it until it is disproved. At this point a new hypothesis would be tried until it could be confirmed or disproved.

Levine (1971, 1975) has conducted a series of studies that convincingly demonstrate that people actively form and test hypotheses in tasks of concept identification. Levine's book (1975) is an excellent source for more detailed information than we can discuss here. In many of Levine's studies students were presented with two letters (a capital *X* or *T*) and asked to find the concept to be discovered. The letters differed in color (black or white), size (large or small), position on a stimulus card (on the left or right), besides their form (either *X* or *T*). If you received a stimulus card with a large black *X* on the left and a small white *T* on the right, for example, you might guess that the concept was "X" or "T" and then be told that the correct answer was "X." Given this information you would still not be certain of the correct solution. Since the *X* was also large, black, and on the left, any of these features could be the eventual solution to the concept task. To be certain of the correct solution, you would need a series of trials in order to rule out features that are not relevant to the problem at hand.

In general, Levine (1975) finds that people actively generate and test hypotheses about potential problem solutions. In some experiments, for example, he gave people four different trials on various stimuli; for example, a large black *X* on the left and a small white *T* on the right for one stimulus, and a large white *T* on the left and a small white *X* on the right for another stimulus. Levine asked people to respond on each trial ("I think it's a *T* on this stimulus card") but did not tell them if they were right or wrong. By analyzing the way people responded to the four different stimulus patterns he was then able to determine the particular hypothesis they were considering. This allowed Levine to predict people's choices on the fifth trial with an accuracy of 97 percent (almost a case of mind reading). Levine's arguments that people actively generate and test particular hypotheses (see also Restle, 1962; Trabasso and Bower, 1968) has important implications; in particular, that people can be prompted to consider very complex hypotheses and therefore be unable to solve a concept problem that is very simple (see Levine, 1975). Because it is the nature and adequacy of their current hypothesis that is of major concern to the learners, they can become blind to simple information that is right before their eyes.

Some Limitations of Concept-Identification Studies

The literature on concept identification provides valuable information, especially about active strategies of hypothesis testing and about the types of variables that make concept identification easy or difficult. It is instructive to consider some of the possible limitations of these studies, however. This should provide a better understanding of the types of processes that eventually need to be explained.

One potential limitation of traditional studies of concept identification is the arbitrary nature of many of the concepts studied. Logically, an experimenter could choose any set of features or attributes and combine them to form a concept; for example, "all five-letter words that begin with a vowel and contain at least one *p*." From a psychological perspective, however, some concepts are more meaningful and useful than others. Philosophers like Cassirer (e.g., 1923) and Dewey (1963) argue that there are reasons for forming concepts, and these reasons involve the function or use of concepts in relation to a particular cultural context. Similarly, Toulmin (1972) argues that concepts have "survival values"; some persist throughout history and others fall by the wayside because they are not relevant to the current times.

Like Dewey (1963), we may find it helpful to view concepts as conceptual tools that we use to organize and clarify our experiences. Concepts are therefore analogous to actual tools. In Chapter 5, Section 1, we discussed how certain human-made tools like pairs of scissors are designed to perform certain functions. We could arbitrarily combine physical features from different pairs of scissors and create a new pair, but this new pair would not necessarily be useful. Groupings of physical features remain arbitrary unless they become related to appropriate activities. Similarly, many potential groupings of conceptual features are relatively arbitrary (cf. Cassirer, 1923). This is not to say that people cannot form arbitrary concepts; but when concepts are meaningfully related to other knowledge and purposes, processes of concept formation and identification may be facilitated.

As an illustration, consider once again the concept-identification study discussed in Chapter 5, Section 1. Some people were told that the stimuli (see Figure 5.6) depicted events relating to baseball, and these people were better able to solve the concept-identification task. The information about baseball did not provide the solution to the problem. It did, however, make the task more meaningful; it helped people realize what to look for, because certain features were potentially more important than others. Note that people who considered the stimuli in terms of the baseball context presumably generated and tested hypotheses, but the types of hypotheses were probably constrained by their assumptions regarding those features that are important in a baseball context. In contrast, the people with no knowledge of the baseball context were in a situation where the hypotheses to be considered were relatively arbitrary. Appropriately activated knowledge can therefore help us generate hypotheses that are plausible and meaningful. This aspect of concept identification was not explicitly addressed in the preceding studies. In many concept-identification studies, people are told the total set of possible hypotheses and asked to discover which one is true. In most everyday situations, however, people are not provided with the total set of potential hypotheses. They must generate them on their own, and their currently available knowledge can frequently help them generate the most plausible ones.

It is also important to note that the concept-identification studies we have discussed did not really involve the acquisition of new concepts. Participants had simply to identify which member of a set of known concepts ("human face," "red triangle") was the particular concept that the experimenter had in mind. If the experimenter had simply told people the answer or solution ("red triangle") the tasks would have been solved immediately (cf. Anderson and Kulhavy, 1972). Contrast this with the typical school situation, where students are provided with definitions of new concepts but still fail to understand adequately and to transfer their knowledge. The processes involved in *identifying* acquired concepts may be different from those that help people to understand concepts that they didn't understand previously. The latter topic is discussed in Section 2.

Summary of Section 1

The purpose of this section was to discuss some of the studies of concept identification. These are important because they focus on people's abilities to transfer, rather than merely remember previously experienced examples. The concept-identification litera-ture also helps clarify why some concept problems are more difficult than others (depending on the salience of critical features, for example, or the complexity of the conceptual rules), and it describes various processes and strategies people utilize. The idea that people actively generate and test hypotheses is especially important because it suggests that they don't simply passively absorb, but analyze, the information presented in concept-identification tasks (see especially Levine, 1975).

We also noted some potential limitations of traditional concept-identification studies. One is that the concepts studied are frequently arbitrary. People's approach to such problems may differ from their approach to the identification of more meaningful concepts. It is also instructive to note that the studies reviewed involved concept *identification* rather than concept *formation*. A major aspect of learning involves the acquisition of new concepts and schemata that were not previously known. This topic is the focus of Section 2.

Section 2: Developing New Skills and Concepts

This section focuses on the types of learning experiences that facilitate the de-velopment of new skills and concepts (also called schemata). The studies to be discussed therefore explore concept and schema *formation,* rather than *identification*. As noted in Section 1, experiments on concept identification do not really assess how people acquire new concepts. Typical concept-identification studies involve solutions like "red triangle," "human face," concepts that were already available to participants before they began the experiment. Our present emphasis is on studies in which the participants learn new concepts and schemata during the acquisition portion of an experiment. As in Section 1, the major testing criteria will involve people's abilities to transfer to new sets of materials, rather than merely remember information presented during the acquisition task. Note that this emphasis on transfer also involves a shift in what we mean by learning. It is one thing to use previous skills and knowledge to learn and remember specific bits of information (see Chapters 5 and 6). It is another thing to learn new skills and knowledge. These differences in the term *learning* should be clarified by the following discussion.

Developing New Memory Skills

As an illustration of differences in uses of the term *learning,* assume that you were asked to learn and recall (in any order) the following list of items (cf. Cermak, 1976, p. 53): *salt, grapes, apples, corn, oranges, pepper, peas, carrots, paprika*. By rehearsing these items in a number of trials, you would eventually be able to remember them flawlessly. You would have learned the list of items, but to what extent would you have learned to remember? For example, to what extent would experience with the preceding list facilitate your ability to learn and remember a list like the following: *fire engine, cotton, Christmas tree, nurse's cap, rose, frog, bathtub, tomato, grass?* Note that exposure to previous items frequently produces proactive interference (see Chapter 3, Section 4), so that attempts to learn the first list could actually hurt your performance on the second list. However, if proactive interference always occurred, greater amounts of past experience should result in poorer rather than better performance. We might therefore expect chess masters to show poorer memory for chess positions than less experienced persons, yet the reverse is the case (see Chapter 2, Section 3).

In order to learn to remember more effectively, one needs to acquire general knowledge and skills that allow one to approach memory tasks in new and more adequate ways. Previous exposure to various word lists will not necessarily permit such changes in memory activities. In order to facilitate changes, one has to understand how to use particular exposures as *exemplars* or *instantiations* of the types of memorizing activities to be acquired. Return to the first word list presented earlier. It is one thing to memorize this list. It is another matter to use the list as an illustration of how to carry out processes of remembering; for example, by organizing the list in a way that both permits greater efficiency of performance and is applicable to subsequent lists as well.

In his book *Improving Your Memory,* Cermak (1976) discusses the importance of learning to actively organize information. However, he doesn't simply say to the reader, "Actively organize your information." This statement is comprehensible, but most people cannot understand it at a level that is precise enough to permit them to change their current remembering activities. They need some examples of what it means to organize materials in adaptive ways.

The first list of words presented above is one of the examples Cermak uses to illustrate the notion of organization. He states, "Don't, whatever you do, try to remember them in that order" (p. 53). Cermak suggests that one should reorganize the list by categories; for example, by fruits (grapes, apples, oranges), vegetables (corn, peas, carrots) and condiments (salt, pepper, paprika). One then need only recall the three categories, which can serve as retrieval cues for the particular items to be retained.

Note that similar organizational principles can now be applied to the second list of items noted earlier, although the basis for organization may not seem as obvious. One possibility is to organize the list into the most likely colors of the objects; for example, reds (fire engine, rose, tomato), greens (Christmas tree, grass, frog), and whites (nurse's cap, cotton, bathtub). Related organizational strategies can also be applied to remembering lists of numbers (a list like 1, 4, 9, 2, 1, 6, 2, 0, 1, 9, 8, 4) or lists of desired activities (such as fixing a leaky faucet, going to pick up the dry cleaning, buying a paper, scrubbing the kitchen floor, getting a new belt, picking up the dog from the vet's, taking the garbage to the dump, buying a birthday present, picking up a package at the post office; cf. Cermak, 1976, p. 53). With each new set of exemplars, slightly new perspectives on what it means to organize may be revealed.

Consider the task of remembering the previous list of numbers. One possibility is to group them into familiar dates (1492, 1620, 1984). In contrast, the list of activities can be categorized according to the nature of the activities. Cermak (1976) suggests the following categories as a basis of organization: buying three things (belt, paper, birthday present), picking up three things (package, dog, dry cleaning), and doing three jobs (leaky faucet, kitchen floor, garbage).

It seems clear that the development of global organizational skills requires experience with a wide variety of lists of items to be remembered. Note, however, that these lists must be viewed as *exemplars* of the organizational principles to be acquired, in order to permit refinements in one's ability to organize. Two people could be exposed to the same set of lists and yet learn very different things; one person might use the same strategy (rehearsal, for instance) for acquiring each list, the other might learn *from* these experiences and hence increase his or her abilities to organize lists.

As an illustration of the preceding argument, consider once again our discussion of Ebbinghaus (Chapter 3, Section 4), one of the first theorists to study memory systematically. Ebbinghaus wanted to study pure learning and memory and tried to use the same strategy (mainly rote rehearsal) for acquiring each new set of materials. (He also used nonsense syllables in order to eliminate any effects due to prior knowledge.) Perhaps Ebbinghaus's reliance on a single learning strategy is one reason for his high degree of forgetting (see the discussion of proactive interference in Chapter 3, Section 4). It is interesting to contrast Ebbinghaus's approach with that of current books on improving one's memory (e.g., Cermak, 1976; Higbee, 1977; Lorayne and Lucas, 1974). Although these books suggest a variety of approaches, none of them suggests that one should use the same strategy for remembering all materials or for performing all remembering tasks. Furthermore, none of the authors suggests that one can improve one's ability to remember simply by memorizing what is said in the book. The purpose of these books is to help people change the way they process information. The authors therefore discuss general principles in conjunction with specific instantiations of these principles. Techniques like the method of loci and the peg-word system are illustrations of the methods that these authors teach (see Chapter 3, Section 2).

Developing New Schemata: Three Types of Acquisition Conditions

We have emphasized that learning a particular list of words is not necessarily equivalent to learning new sets of skills that permit transfer. Different people may be exposed to the same word lists, but what they learn will depend on their currently activated knowledge. If they are prompted to view the word lists as examples or instantiations of a more general concept like "organization," for example, they may learn something from this experience that helps them transfer to new sets of materials. It is important to consider this issue in more detail. Our previous discussion emphasized the development of new skills that can enable people to remember more efficiently. The study described below (Hannigan, 1976) explores factors necessary for developing a schema that facilitates comprehension of new, unfamiliar statements. We shall first discuss the types of acquisition conditions utilized by Hannigan and then consider her transfer test.

In order to understand Hannigan's (1976) study, imagine first that you participate in the following experiment. You hear a list of seventy sentences, each about a man doing things. The task is simply to rate each sentence according to ease of comprehension (on a three-point scale). Examples of sentences are as follows:

The man set up housekeeping in the airplane.

The man threw the curtain over the metal bar.

The man propped the door against the rock wall.

The man thrashed the leaves with his cane.

The man put the chair at the base of the tree.

The man piled the bricks under the oak.

The man opened his briefcase.

The man turned the bell upside down.

The man made a sack out of the sheet.

All these sentences are understandable. Indeed, Hannigan's students rated them as very easy to comprehend.

Hannigan called the group who received the acquisition list the No Framework group (Group 1). The meaning of *no framework* will become clear later. For present purposes, it is useful to note the similarity between this type of acquisition procedure and those used in most of the studies discussed in previous chapters: In those studies, participants were presented with individual words, sentences, pictures, paragraphs, or similar materials. They were asked to learn the materials, and learning was usually assessed by some test of memory. In the present chapter we want to go beyond the notion that learning involves simply encoding, storage, and retrieval. Our present goal is to understand how people learn to use their experiences with previous materials to better understand subsequent materials, that is, in ways that facilitate transfer.

Hannigan devised a second acquisition condition, in which the seventy acquisition sentences heard by Group 1 were presented as materials that might be learned *from* and might change the participants' understanding of a particular area of knowledge. She achieved this by directing people in a second group (Group 2) to perceive the sentences as exemplars of a more general principle or schema. It was the general schema she wanted them to acquire, not simply the sentences. Hannigan called Group 2 the Framework group. Her objective was that this group learn possible techniques for surviving "on a previously inhabited but now deserted island." All participants presumably had some knowledge of survival, but Hannigan wanted to lead them beyond their current, normative knowledge. She hoped to modify their understanding of subsequent "novel but appropriate" survival-related events.

Assume you were in Group 2, the Framework group. You would hear the same seventy acquisition sentences as Group 1. However, each sentence is to be understood as a description of "survival on a previously inhabited but now deserted island," and also as an illustration of one of seven subtopics of "survival." The seven subtopics were as follows: "obtaining a shelter," "reaching for food on a branch above one's head," "finding a container for carrying food," "finding a container for water," "administering first aid," "making clothing," and "trying to get help." The following list illustrates the relationship of the acquisition sentences we considered earlier to the subtopics:

Obtaining a shelter:

> The man set up housekeeping in the airplane.
> The man threw the curtain over the metal bar.
> The man propped the door against the rock wall.

Reaching for food on a branch above one's head:

> The man thrashed the leaves with his cane.
> The man put the chair at the base of the tree.
> The man piled the bricks under the oak.

Finding a container for carrying food:

> The man opened his briefcase.
> The man turned the bell upside down.
> The man made a sack out of the sheet.

Group 2, like Group 1, were asked to rate the comprehensibility of each sentence (this time in terms of the survival framework) on a three-point scale.

Consider the different experiences of the No Framework (Group 1) and Framework (Group 2) participants. In Group 1 the sentences are understandable on the basis of one's general knowledge. In Group 2 a particular knowledge context is activated, which helps limit *how* the sentences are understood. Thus, when heard in isolation, a sentence like "The man put the chair at the base of the tree," might lead one to assume that he planned to sit there and relax in the shade. Hearing this sentence in the context of "reaching for food on a branch above one's head," however, one is more inclined to assume that the man planned to stand on the chair. Activated knowledge places constraints on what must be assumed in order to make a sentence understandable in a particular situation. (Note our discussion of "Bill has a red car," in Chapter 6, Section 4.)

Our discussion has emphasized that activated knowledge affects one's comprehension of the individual sentences or exemplars. By the same token, exposure to particular exemplars can refine one's understanding of the activated knowledge; in Hannigan's experiment the exemplars suggest particular, and perhaps new, ways of surviving. In Piaget's (e.g., 1952) terms, the development of new skills and schemata involves processes of assimilation and accommodation. In general, *assimilation* refers to the use of preexisting knowledge or schemata to interpret information; *accommodation* refers to modifications of previous schemata in light of new information. To phrase it another way, currently activated knowledge can both clarify new information and be clarified by that information. The process by which current knowledge both clarifies and is clarified by new information has been called *abduction* (e.g., Bransford and Franks, 1976; Bransford and Nitsch, 1978). The concept of abduction emphasizes that the development of new skills and schemata requires both appropriately activated knowledge and experience with particular exemplars. Neither of these factors will suffice alone.

The assumption that activated knowledge can both clarify and be clarified by particular exemplars suggests the need for a third group in Hannigan's study—a Framework After group. Hannigan assumed that an acquisition procedure that *first* presented the individual sentences and *then* presented the "survival" schema and the seven subcategories should not be sufficient to permit the types of changes necessary for transfer (that is, changes that would serve to improve comprehension of subsequent statements about survival). In this Framework After condition, information about survival and subcategories of survival are simply additional facts that are stored along with individual sentences. According to the arguments presented above, one needs an active, ongoing interplay between knowledge and exemplar and between exemplar and knowledge. This active interplay allows the development of a new schema that should permit one to better understand the novel examples of survival to be presented during the transfer test.

Note further that Hannigan's Framework After group provides a way to ensure that her experiment explores concept or schema *formation,* rather than *identification.* As noted in Section 1, most problems of concept identification would be solved immediately if the experimenter simply stated the solution ("By the way, the correct concept is 'red triangle'"). In essence, Hannigan's Framework After condition also tells people the solution. Just before the transfer test (described later), participants are told that the acquisition sentences can be interpreted as dealing with "survival on a previously inhabited but now deserted island" and are also told the seven subcategories of survival. Furthermore, people in this Framework After group are told that most of the sentences on the transfer test are relevant to the survival theme plus one of the seven subcategories.

If people in the Framework After group performed as well on the transfer test as those in the Framework group, it would suggest that people in the Framework group did not learn anything new about survival but, instead, merely activated previously existing knowledge; the experiment would therefore test the effects of concept or schema *identification.* Hannigan assumed that the Framework group would show better transfer than the Framework After group, however. The reason is that at the time of acquisition, the Framework group could use their activated knowledge of survival to interpret each acquisition sentence (assimilation) and also modify their knowledge of survival in the light of the particular acquisition exemplars (accommodation). People in this group should therefore develop a new "survival" schema that can facilitate subsequent transfer. Hannigan's test of transfer is described below.

Assessing Transfer

Hannigan (1976) utilized an unusual test of transfer; she measured people's abilities to identify new survival-related sentences that were embedded in white noise. In Chapter 6, Section 1, we noted that white noise involves a continuous *shh* sound that makes statements harder to identify. We also discussed Bruce's (1958) study which indicated that appropriate priming can increase people's abilities to identify sentences embedded in white noise; priming with a word like *weather* increased the likelihood of participants' correctly identifying and repeating a statement like "You said it would rain, but the sun has come out now."

People's abilities to identify sentences embedded in white noise also depend on the degree to which the sentences are congruent with their current knowledge. For example, a syntactically well-formed statement like "The boy hit the ball" is more readily identified than one like "The hit ball boy the" (e.g., Miller, Heise, and Lichten, 1951; Miller and Isard, 1963). Similarly, statements that express typical or prototypic events (such as "The doctor cured the patient") are more accurately identified than less typical statements like "The doctor fired the janitor" (e.g., Rosenberg and Jarvella, 1970).

Note that the studies just cited varied the nature of the test materials and showed differences in ease of identification. In contrast, Hannigan presented the same test materials to all participants in her study. She wanted to show that sentence identification would be a function of differences in the types of knowledge that people had acquired. For example, a novel test sentence like "The man put the drapes over the rope" might be especially meaningful to people in the Framework group because their newly modified "survival" schema could be used to understand the sentence as an illustration of "obtaining shelter." People in the Framework group might therefore perform better on the white-noise transfer test. During the test, all participants listened to each sentence (embedded in white noise) and attempted to report each one immediately afterwards.

Recall that Hannigan investigated the effects of three different types of acquisition conditions: No Framework, Framework, and Framework After. A fourth group, called the Baseline group, was also included in the study. People in this group received no acquisition sentences; they merely performed the white-noise identification test. The important data indicate the performance of the other groups in relation to that of the Baseline group.

Three types of sentences appeared on test tapes: Olds, Novel Appropriates, and Novel Inappropriates. Olds were sentences that had actually been heard during acquisition. Novel Appropriates were new sentences that were appropriate to survival. Thus, the sentence "The man put the drapes over the rope" is a novel example of "obtaining a shelter." Similarly, "The man stretched with the spear" is a novel example of "reaching for food on a branch above one's head." Note that these sentences include totally new words except for the phrase "the man." The Novel Inappropriate sentences were unrelated to survival; for example, "The man disconnected the refrigerator" and "The man threw the pliers into the net."

The test results are illustrated in Table 7.1. For Old test sentences, the No Framework, Framework, and Framework After groups' identification rate surpassed

Table 7.1   Identification of White-Noise-Embedded Sentences as a Function of Acquisition Conditions

Acquisition Conditions:	Average Number of Test Sentences Identified		
	Olds	Novel Appropriates	Novel Inappropriates
No Framework:	16.9	8.4	12.6
Framework:	21.6	18.5	14.3
Framework After:	19.7	10.2	13.5
Baseline:	9.4	9.2	13.9

After Hannigan (1976).

that of Baseline subjects. In short, experiences with particular acquisition sentences facilitated performance on the transfer test. The most important data involved Novel Appropriate sentences. It was assumed that only people in the Framework group would significantly surpass the Baseline group on these sentences, because they alone had received the types of learning experiences necessary to go beyond a mere list of episodically experienced sentences. This assumption was confirmed. Furthermore, the Framework group was better on Olds than the other two groups, presumably because of the added benefit of the particular "survival" schema that had been acquired. Finally, all groups were expected to be equivalent to the Baseline group on Novel Inappropriate sentences. This result was also found. Note that Baseline subjects identified Novel Inappropriates better than they identified Olds and Novel Appropriates. It is assumed that the sentences used as Novel Inappropriates were simply easier to identify in general (that is, they were relatively simple and distinctive sentences to begin with). Hannigan's results have been replicated and extended by Lee (1978).

It is also instructive to note that in additional studies, Hannigan (1976) used different measures to assess learning. In one study she tested recognition memory for Old and Novel Appropriate test sentences. For example, she presented a statement like "The man put the drapes over the rope" (without white noise) and asked participants whether they had actually heard this sentence during the acquisition task. Interestingly, the Framework and No Framework groups performed very similarly in tests of recognition memory. People in both groups were able to recognize accurately Old sentences (those that had actually occurred during acquisition), and they also knew that Novel Appropriate test sentences had *not* occurred during acquisition. There were therefore large differences between Framework and No Framework groups in tests of transfer (identification in white noise) but not in the test of recognition memory. These results illustrate that the ability to remember does not necessarily guarantee transfer. This point is discussed more fully in the next section of this chapter. At present, it is helpful to consider some additional illustrations of ways in which people come to understand things that they could not previously understand.

Further Illustrations of Knowledge Acquisition

Our preceding discussion suggests that new schemata develop only under certain conditions. One must be able not only to assimilate information to relevant schemata but also to experience exemplars that permit them to modify these schemata appropriately (accommodation). Students in Hannigan's Framework group received acquisition tasks that met both these conditions, and they alone showed transfer to novel, schema-related sentences on the white-noise transfer test.

Note, however, that people rarely receive lists of acquisition sentences like those in Hannigan's experiments. It is therefore instructive to see how the previous arguments relate to everyday situations such as those encountered in schools and colleges. Assume, therefore, that two groups of students read a text. The text may be viewed as a set of acquisition statements like those presented by Hannigan. We can now manipulate the activated knowledge available to students by providing one group with prior learning activities designed to help them learn from the text; these would resemble the Framework group. A second group might read the same text but be given no experiences or be given experiences that might not permit them to learn from the text in an optimal manner (like the No Framework group).

Bransford and Nitsch (1978) report a study of conditions analogous to Hannigan's Framework and No Framework conditions. The experimenters asked two groups of students to read the same text but manipulated their activated knowledge by providing them with different types of learning experiences prior to their reading the passage. The study then assessed their ability to transfer; for example, to generate novel examples illustrating the ideas from the text. In the study, college students were presented with excerpts of an article written by the psychologist Karl Buhler (cf. Blumenthal, 1970). The task was to understand the article and to answer questions about it that would be asked later.

Prior to reading the text, two groups of students were provided with one of two different learning experiences. Both groups heard a potentially incomprehensible passage (the "washing clothes" passage noted in Chapter 5, Section 1) and then recalled the passage. However, people in Group 1 heard the passage *with* the topic, and they therefore did not realize that it could be incomprehensible. Students in the second group first heard the passage without the topic and then heard it a second time with the topic; they therefore experienced a feeling of incomprehension followed by the ability to comprehend. Students in Group 1 were instructed to notice the paraphrasing that occurred in their recall; those in Group 2, to notice their feeling of incomprehension and their subsequent ability to understand.

All students were next asked to think about their experiences with the "washing clothes" passage while reading the text by Buhler. The text discussed paraphrase (consonant with Group 1's experiences) but dealt mainly with prerequisites to comprehension (consonant with Group 2's experiences). The text was therefore more relevant to the experiences of Group 2. Students read the text at their own rates (overall reading times did not differ) and then answered essay questions about what they had read.

Group 2's essay scores were superior to those of Group 1. Group 2 were better able to generate novel examples of principles discussed in the text and to relate the passage to their everyday experience of communication. One of the essay questions asked students to comment on the degree to which the "washing clothes" experience affected their understanding of the Buhler passage. The following is an unedited comment by one of the students in Group 2:

> The idea of the shared field [a concept from the Buhler passage] especially struck me after the description [the "washing clothes" passage] we listened to earlier. The paragraph [the "washing clothes" passage] did not make sense to me but once I was given a context—sharing the same field as the person that wrote the description—it made sense. This idea of a shared field or experience seems obvious, but was one I had never really thought about.

> *I also knew what was meant by the separation of word perception and sentence comprehension because the same thing happened to me while listening to the clothes-washing passage. I understood every word yet was confused.*
>
> *Also, going through that experience helped me to understand the article. It was a very abstract article and if I hadn't had a concrete example to identify with, most of it would have been meaningless to me. As it was, when something was described that happened to me, the whole thing had more meaning. (Bransford and Nitsch, 1978, p. 292)*

The preceding comment suggests that experience with the "washing clothes" passage helped the student understand the Buhler article. Information from Buhler's article also seemed to help the student better understand the significance of the "washing clothes" experience, because it allowed her to view this experience from a broader perspective. Note, for example, that the student used concepts from the Buhler article to describe her previous experience with the "washing clothes" passage; she wrote of the importance of "sharing the same field as the person that wrote the description." In short, prior experience with the "washing clothes" passage helped the student clarify the Buhler article, and at the same time this prior experience was clarified by the article as well.

Experiments by Mayer and Greeno (1972) provide more dramatic evidence for the importance of considering the dynamic interplay between information to be learned and previously acquired knowledge. They instructed two groups of students in binomial probability and then assessed their abilities by means of transfer tests. Students in Group 1, the Formula group, learned the components of the binomial formula and were given practice at using it to solve problems. Students in Group 2, the Concept group, first learned general concepts like "trial," "success," and "probability of success." These concepts were made meaningful by helping students relate them to everyday experience of such things as batting averages and rain forecasts.

The transfer test included different types of questions. Some comprised problems that were easily solved if one knew the binomial formula; Mayer and Greeno describe these types of questions as assessing "near transfer." Other questions were more conceptual in nature and assessed "far transfer." Some of these were questions designed to measure students' understanding of various aspects of the binomial formula, others were problems that students ought to recognize as impossible to solve if they fully understood the formula. Mayer and Greeno found that the nature of the learning situation had powerful effects on subsequent transfer performance. The Formula group (who had concentrated on solving problems) did well on near-transfer problems but not on far transfer; the Concept group were poorer than the Formula group at solving straightforward problems but much better on the far-transfer questions that assessed their basic understanding of the information they had received.

In a subsequent study, Mayer (1975) investigated different ways of helping students learn a simple computer-programming language. This information was presented in the form of a standard ten-page text. Students in Group 1 were first taught about computers by means of a model relating computer concepts to everyday experiences; the memory was a scoreboard, the program a shopping list with a pointer arrow, the input a ticket window, and so forth. They used this familiar model while reading the text. People in Group 2 first read the text and then heard about the familiar model; this group is comparable to Hannigan's Framework After group. Both groups were then administered transfer tests.

The Model After group was better at writing simple programs (these had been taught in the text), but the Model Before group was better at dealing with problems that had not been explicitly taught. For example, Model Before people were better able to interpret what a new computer program would do, and could write programs different from those encountered previously. By activating appropriate knowledge that both clarified and was clarified by the textual material, people in the Model Before group were able to transfer to a broader series of tasks.

Children's Acquisition of
New Concepts and Schemata

The preceding experiments demonstrate that knowledge acquisition depends on the dynamic interplay between present information and currently activated knowledge. If groups of people differ in their available knowledge, they may experience the same situation yet learn different things. Similarly, we may reread the same material yet understand it differently each time because our knowledge and skills have changed. This general orientation is important for attempts to understand why children acquire some concepts and schemata before they learn others, and why they sometimes show remarkably rapid spurts in conceptual development. Some illustrations of these points are provided below.

Consider first the question of how young children begin to acquire concepts that are expressed linguistically. For example, how do they begin to understand utterances like "dog" or "wash your face"? One way to approach this question is to imagine that you try to teach a child language by doing the following. You sit down with the child each day and say, "OK, here are some more English words and sentences: *cow, cup,* 'Close the door.' . . ." It is doubtful whether children could learn effectively under these conditions. They need some guidance regarding the possible meanings of utterances. They need to be shown, for example, that we are referring to events that are relevant to their immediate environment.

MacNamara (1972) argues that young children must have some knowledge of what a particular input *could* mean before they can learn a particular linguistic meaning.

Infants learn their language by first determining independent of language the meaning which a speaker intends to convey to them, and by then working out the relationship between the meaning and the language. To put it another way, the infant uses meaning as a clue to language rather than language as a clue to meaning. (P. 1)

As an example, MacNamara cites Hoffman's (1968) analysis of some of the errors (errors from the adult perspective, that is) that frequently occur during initial language acquisition. A seventeen-month-old child used the word *hot* as the name for "stove." Perhaps as the child was about to touch the stove an adult had said, "Hot!" This might have suggested to the child that *hot* was the name for "stove." Children's understanding of their environment (in particular, their understanding of perceptual information, gestures, tones of voice) affects what they think people must mean by an utterance. Only in this manner could they grasp what a linguistic entity (such as the word *hot*) does mean. Initially, however, they make mistakes.

MacNamara's argument is very similar to that of the philosopher Wittgenstein (1968). Imagine that a speaker says, "Notice the sepia," while pointing to a complex painting (cf. Hester, 1977). Unless you know that *sepia* refers to a color (and more specifically, to a brownish color), you will have difficulty understanding what the speaker means. Wittgenstein argues that even learning by *ostensive definition* (for example, hearing "This is red" while seeing someone point to a red object) presupposes that one has some knowledge of what the ostensibly defined object is supposed to be an example of (in this case, color). Knowledge that a word refers to the category "color" affects one's understanding of the object of the pointing gesture, which in turn may increase one's understanding of what counts as "red."

Current theorists of language acquisition pay careful attention to relationships between linguistic inputs and the learner's current skills and knowledge (e.g., see Bates, 1976; Bloom, 1978; Chapman, 1978; MacNamara, 1972; Nelson, 1974, 1977). Nelson (1974), for example, argues that the concepts first acquired by children are those that are relevant to events or actions that are important for the children. Furthermore, it seems likely that certain concepts must be acquired before others can be effectively understood and mastered. The availability of relevant knowledge may therefore affect the rate at which new concepts can be acquired.

Miller (1978) discusses the rate at which normal children acquire vocabulary. He cites Templin's (1957) study showing that six-year-old children of average intelligence can recognize about 13,000 words. By age eight the estimate is 28,300 words, an incredible increase! The fact that new words can be related to old words seems to be responsible for this rapid spurt in development.

> *Children encountering a new word can usually bring to bear on it information already acquired about other words—that it is associated with knowledge in a field of practical knowledge they have already begun to learn other words for, that its use in sentences is similar to other words they know, and so on. In short, a particular word is easier to learn if other words related to it in various ways are already known. Learning the generic word* furniture *is surely easier if one already knows such more specific words as* chair, table, couch, bed. . . . *In such ways a child can transfer previous lexical learning to new lexical learning, and one is encouraged to believe that the rapid acquisition of a vocabulary might someday be explicable. (Miller, 1978, p. 395)*

Gentner (1975) provides data that are congruent with Miller's arguments. She asked children between the ages of three and eight to make dolls act out verbs like *give, take, buy,* and *sell.* Gentner assumed that the meanings of *give* and *take* are simpler than those of *buy* and *sell.* The first two words imply that something is transferred from one person to the other; the last two, that some medium of exchange (presumably money) is involved. Younger children could act out the simpler verbs, *give* and *take,* but only the older children could accurately convey *buy* and *sell.* The simpler concepts appear to provide a basis upon which more complex concepts can be built.

Studies by Siegler (1976) provide an especially informative illustration of how learning depends on previous learning. He investigated children's abilities to learn the principle of balance beams; in this type of investigation different numbers of weights are put on a balance beam at different distances from the fulcrum, and the child predicts whether the beam will balance. Siegler found that children's approaches to this task could be characterized by four sets of rules. Those children using Rule 1 appear to attend only to the number of weights on each side of the fulcrum. If there are equal numbers of weights, the children predict balance; otherwise, they assume that the side with the greater number will go down. Children following Rule 2 exhibit somewhat more sophisticated behavior. They consider distance from the fulcrum whenever the numbers of weights are equal; otherwise, they choose the side with the most weights and fail to take distance into account. Children using Rule 3 always consider both weight and distance. However, there are still instances where weight and distance come into conflict. In those cases children following Rule 3 must guess. Rule 4 represents the most sophisticated approach to the balance beam. Children following this rule reach the correct answer by calculating the sum of the products of weight and distance (see Siegler, 1976). They therefore never need to guess.

From our present perspective, the most interesting of Siegler's data relate to subsequent attempts to teach children to solve the balance problem. Why not simply teach all the children how to apply Rule 4? The answer is that what children can learn depends on their current state of skills and knowledge. Siegler's data suggest that children who spontaneously utilize Rules 1 and 2 are less likely to learn from Rule 4 instruction than are those who utilize Rule 3. Overall, the most effective instruction involved efforts to help people move one rule beyond their current level of knowledge and skills.

It is instructive to note how the preceding discussion relates to that in Section 1 of this chapter. There we noted that studies of concept identification frequently utilize concepts that are relatively arbitrary. In such situations, people may use strategies different from those they use in more meaningful tasks. Indeed, Nelson (1974) notes that young children frequently do poorly in traditional tasks of concept identification but still show a remarkable ability to acquire new concepts in everyday settings. If we used only arbitrary tasks and stimuli, it would be easy to reach erroneous conclusions regarding children's abilities to identify and acquire concepts. We need to ask how information in the environment, and from previously acquired concepts, helps children activate knowledge that both clarifies and is clarified by new inputs and experiences. The ability to learn is strongly influenced by what is already known.

Summary of Section 2

The major goal of this section was to distinguish between studies of concept or schema identification (Section 1) and schema formation. Our orienting question was therefore, What enables us to understand and do things that we could not previously understand and do? It was argued that the development of new skills and schemata depends on the interplay between current information and previously acquired knowledge. People's currently activated knowledge can both clarify and be clarified by new information. Through this reciprocal interplay of assimilation and accommodation (cf. Piaget, 1952), people can develop skills and schemata that they did not have before.

It was also stressed that the development of new skills, concepts, and schemata is not necessarily equivalent to the ability to remember previous acquisition experiences. In Hannigan's (1976) experiments, for example, people in the Framework and No Framework groups were equivalent in tests of recognition memory, yet differed greatly in transfer tests. The studies in this section emphasized transfer tests because these allow some measure of the degree to which people have developed new skills and schemata that permit them to deal with novel situations; for example, to learn and remember lists of items more efficiently, to identify novel schema-related statements, to solve problems, to acquire additional concepts. Note, however, that we frequently require more than one learning trial to master new skills and schemata. We practice them in various situations. What kinds of practice are most beneficial for increasing our abilities to transfer? The role of practice in schema acquisition is discussed in Section 3.

Section 3: The Role of Practice in Schema Development

The goal of this section is to analyze carefully some of the relationships between particular learning experiences and subsequent transfer. Our emphasis will be on the degree to which people develop adequate concepts and schemata as a function of the conditions under which they attempt to practice these concepts and schemata. We frequently require more than one learning trial in order to master new concepts. When attempting to learn a new mathematical concept, for example, we may need to practice applying it to a variety of problems before we have mastered it. Similarly, we may need to see how a concept like "retrieval" applies to a number of memory experiments in order to understand how the concept is used. As we shall see, conceptual development is strongly influenced by the ways in which initial conceptual knowledge is applied or practiced. People may increase their initial level of understanding, stay at the same level, or become confused depending on the contexts in which they attempt to use their knowledge. A series of experiments by Nitsch (1977) provides an excellent illustration of these points.

Changing Initial
Levels of Understanding

To understand the basis of Nitsch's (1977) experiments, imagine that you want to learn six new concepts. Examples are—

Crinch: To make someone angry by performing an inappropriate act

Minge: To gang up on a person or thing

Rell: To rescue someone from a dangerous or problematic situation

These definitions are designed to be understandable in isolation, and you could therefore decide to learn the concepts by studying until you knew the definitions. For example, you might make flash cards with the six definitions written on one side of each card and the correct concept name on the other. Eventually you would be able to look at each definition and supply the correct concept label. This would constitute one form of learning, but would you now be able to do well on a transfer test that asked you to identify novel examples of the concepts? For example, could you identify "The striking waitresses angrily approached the restaurant manager" as an example of the concept "minge"?

One of Nitsch's (1977) studies included an acquisition condition similar to the one just described. People in a group called the Definitions Alone group first heard all six concepts and their definitions and later received a series of four practice trials. At each practice trial the students received the six concept definitions (in a different order each time) and were asked to supply the correct concept label. The experimenter then told them the correct answer. By the end of the four practice trials all students exhibited perfect performance. When given the transfer task which asked them to identify novel examples of the concepts, however, students in the Definitions Alone group did poorly on the task.

Note that the practice trials can be viewed as situations where people are asked to apply previously acquired knowledge; after their initial exposure to a concept ("minge," for example) and its definition ("to gang up on a person or thing"), their first practice trial provides a context for application of this knowledge. They are presented with the definition ("to gang up on a person or thing") and their task is to identify this definition as an example of "minge." The second, third, and fourth practice trials provide the same contexts of application. The students clearly learn from these practice trials because they make fewer errors and in the fourth trial exhibit perfect performance. The important question, however, is, What is learned from these practice trials? People learn to identify each definition, but they seem not to increase their understanding of the concepts; for increased understanding would surely have resulted in excellent performance on the transfer test. Practice trials that help people remember concept definitions are therefore not necessarily equivalent to those that help them develop a fuller understanding of concepts or schemata. We must therefore ask, What kinds of practice trials would help people understand the concepts in ways previously unavailable to them?

As was shown in Section 2, changes in understanding seem to involve processes of accommodation and assimilation; currently available knowledge can both clarify and be clarified by new situations. Assume, therefore, that people hear concept definitions ("Minge: to gang up on a person or a thing") and then are asked to apply this knowledge to particular situations. This was the procedure followed by the Definitions plus Examples group. Thus, they might be presented with a statement like "The six cowboys fought against the rustler" and be asked whether it is an example of "minge." In this instance, knowledge of the definition should guide participants' comprehension of the example, but at the same time, the example should help them to better understand the precise meaning of the definition. By applying their knowledge to a number of potential examples, they should therefore increase their understanding of the concepts. Indeed, Nitsch (1977) found that even a brief exposure to relevant examples facilitated transfer. Recall that Nitsch's transfer test asked people to identify novel examples of the six concepts. The Definitions Alone group did poorly on this test, but the Definitions plus Examples group did quite well (see also Pollchik, Chapter 4, Section 3).

It is important to note that for the Definitions plus Examples group, none of the examples on the transfer test had been experienced during acquisition, so that the test did indeed measure transfer rather than remembering. Exposure to relevant examples therefore seemed to help people improve their understanding of the concept definitions. In other words, when people were able to see how the general concepts applied to particular situations, they were able to understand the concepts more completely. If you think about it, most definitions we hear or read are inadequate unless we already have some knowledge of potential contexts of application. For example, the *Merriam-Webster Dictionary* (1974) defines *truck* as a vehicle (as a strong heavy automobile) designed for carrying heavy articles. Clearly, this is an inadequate definition in itself; most readers can understand the definition only because they already have the knowledge that allows them to instantiate it in more detail. If this knowledge is not already available, however, examples or instantiations of concepts need to be supplied. As we shall see, there are many possible contexts in which we can practice or utilize our initial knowledge, and some are more valuable than others. This issue is explored in the studies described below.

Some Effects of Different Types of Practice

The last experiment can be viewed as an illustration of the effects of practice. There is an old adage that practice makes perfect, but we must ask, Perfect with respect to what? People may practice identifying concept definitions (the Definitions Alone group) until they can do this perfectly, but this doesn't necessarily help them increase their understanding of the concepts and perform well in a transfer test. In contrast, when people practice by applying current knowledge to particular examples or situations (the Definitions plus Examples group), they may thereby improve both their understanding of concepts and schemata and their ability to use this knowledge to understand novel events.

There are additional questions about practice that we must now consider. As we shall see, some attempts to practice or utilize knowledge may be problematic because they result in confusion during the initial stages of learning; others may produce only minimal confusion initially but permit only limited transfer. A challenge for cognitive science is therefore to understand the types of learning experiences that reduce initial confusion and also permit excellent transfer. Experiments by Nitsch (1977) provide important information regarding this point.

The study to be discussed here (Nitsch, 1977) examined people's abilities to learn and understand six new concepts identical with those we discussed earlier, and included the concepts "crinch," "minge," and "rell." In this experiment, however, all participants received practice trials in which they attempted to use their initial knowledge to understand and identify examples of each concept. All participants first heard the six concept definitions together with their "contexts of origin" (to be explained below). However, different groups received different types of examples during the practice trials. Participants in Group 1 received same-context examples, while those in Group 2 received varied-context examples during the practice trials.

Table 7.2 illustrates two sets of examples and the contexts of origin of the concepts "crinch" and "minge." (There were six concepts in all.) The hypothetical contexts of origin referred to the groups of people who had originally used the concepts; for example, "crinch" was originally used by waitresses. The same-context examples repeated one context of application for each of the concepts ("crinch" involved restaurants; "minge" involved cowboys). The varied-context examples included different contexts of application for each concept. Note that both sets of examples were meaningful in relation to the concepts. Furthermore, all students were told to learn the general concepts, not to attempt to remember the particular examples. All received one of the four possible examples for each concept on each of the four practice trials, but Group 1 (the Same Context group) received same-context examples, and Group 2 (the Varied Context group) received varied-context examples.

Nitsch sought to discover whether practice with same-context or varied-context acquisition examples for each of the six concepts would influence participants' abilities to identify novel examples of concepts (to transfer). In order to answer this question, she constructed three types of examples on her transfer test (and some instances that were not examples of any of the concepts). The following are three types of test items for the concept "minge":

Old context: The cowboys chased the runaway mare.

Cross context: The striking waitresses angrily approached the restaurant manager.

New context: The students surrounded the professor.

Items like these were used to test both the Same Context group and the Varied Context group. It is important to note several points about these transfer-test items. Remember that the previous test items refer to the concept "minge," and that all are novel examples; none of them had occurred during acquisition. Consider how they differ, however.

Old-context items involved old contexts of application; "The cowboys chased the runaway mare" is a novel example of "minge" couched in an old context of application (a cowboy context). This was true for all the participants. The Same Context group had heard all four "minge" examples in a cowboy context; the Varied Context group had heard one example of "minge" in a cowboy context (see Table 7.2).

Next consider cross-context test items. An example for "minge" is "The striking waitresses angrily approached the restaurant manager." These test items involved contexts of application that were used to exemplify *other* acquisition concepts, but none of the students had ever experienced an example of the concept in that particular context during acquisition. For example, our cross-context example for "minge" involves a restaurant context. Neither the Varied Context group nor the Same Context group had experienced "minge" in this context during the acquisition task (see Table 7.2).

Finally, consider the new-context test items. These included contexts of application that had never been used for any of the practice conditions in the acquisition task. Thus, a

---

Table 7.2   Same-Context and Varied-Context Examples

Same-Context Examples:

> Crinch: Originally used by waitresses
> > To make someone angry by performing an inappropriate act.
> > The diner failed to leave a tip.
> > The man argued about the prices on the menu.
> > The customer deliberately knocked the ketchup on the floor.
> > The man complained because the waitress was too slow.

> Minge: Originally used by cowboys
> > To gang up on a person or thing.
> > The three riders decided to converge on the cow.
> > Four people took part in branding the horse.
> > They circled the wolf so it could not escape.
> > All six cowboys fought against the rustler.

Varied-Context Examples:

> Crinch: Originally used by waitessses
> > To make someone angry by performing an inappropriate act.
> > The cowboy did not remove his hat when he went into the church.
> > The spectator at the dog races jumped up on his seat and blocked the view of the people seated behind him.
> > The customer flicked cigarette ashes on the newly refinished antique chest.
> > The man complained because the waitress was too slow.

> Minge: Originally used by cowboys
> > To gang up on a person or thing.
> > The band of sailors angrily denounced the captain and threatened a mutiny.
> > A group in the audience booed the inept magician's act.
> > The junk dealer was helpless to defend himself from the three thieves.
> > All six cowboys fought against the rustler.

Adapted from Nitsch (1977).

new-context item for "minge" is "The students surrounded the professor." Neither of the example groups received acquisition sentences utilizing this context of application for any of the six concepts to be acquired.

Table 7.3 illustrates the results for Nitsch's transfer test. Both groups were equally proficient at identifying novel examples that occurred in old contexts of application. However, people in the Varied Context group were better able to identify test examples that occurred in cross contexts and new contexts. People in the Varied Context group therefore exhibited a flexible ability to transfer. Those in the Same Context group could transfer to some extent, but they had problems identifying cross-context and new-context items.

Although these results suggest that it is better to practice with varied-context examples than same-context examples, it is important to consider additional data from Nitsch's study before accepting this conclusion. In particular, note that our previous discussion involved performance on the transfer test (see Table 7.3). The transfer test was not administered until all participants had received four sets of practice trials, in which they were presented with examples and asked to name the appropriate concepts. Furthermore, only those people who were correct at least eleven of twelve times on the last two practice trials were given the transfer test. (Nitsch told people the correct answers in the first two practice trials but not the last two trials.) The transfer data in Table 7.3 are therefore based on the performance of only those people who met Nitsch's initial learning criterion. The next important question is, How easy was it for people to meet Nitsch's initial learning criterion?

Nitsch found that all people in the Same Context group were able to meet the initial learning criterion within four practice trials, and most did this with little difficulty (that is, they made few errors on the first few trials). In contrast, people in the Varied Context group made a large number of errors, and many did not meet the initial learning criterion after four practice trials. Practice with varied-context examples therefore seems to facilitate transfer eventually, but it can result in errors and confusion during the initial stages of learning. Practice with same-context examples produces a minimum of initial confusion, but it restricts people's abilities to transfer (see Table 7.3). It is important to ask why we might expect these differences between ease of initial learning and subsequent transfer, and to attempt to design practice situations that facilitate transfer but also decrease initial confusion. These issues are explored next.

Table 7.3   Correct Identification as a Function of Acquisition Condition and Test Type

| | Hit Rate | | | |
	Old Context	Cross Context	New Context	False Positive Rate
Same-context examples:	89%	66%	67%	9.7%
Varied-context examples:	91%	82%	84%	7.6%

Adapted from Nitsch (1977). Used by permission.

*Ease of Initial Learning
versus Flexibility of Transfer*

Consider first why practicing same-context examples may result in less confusion during initial stages of learning than varied-context examples. In Chapter 3 we noted that learning and memory depend on processes of retrieval, as well as those that occur at acquisition. We also discussed the principle of encoding specificity (e.g., Tulving and Thomson, 1973; Tulving, 1978; Chapter 3, Section 3), which emphasizes that remembering depends on the degree of overlap between information encoded at acquisition and information available in the retrieval environment. If we view each practice trial as involving a retrieval environment, it becomes clear that there is more overlap across same-context trials than across varied-context trials. Thus, if people encode a concept like "minge" in a cowboy context and later receive new practice examples that also involve cowboys, there is a greater overlap between initial encodings and subsequent retrieval information than is available to people in the Varied Context group.

The encoding-specificity principle can help us understand why same-context examples facilitate initial learning. Ultimately, however, practice with same-context examples is less beneficial for transfer than practice with varied-context examples. Given same-context examples, people seem to become overly dependent on certain contextual cues (that all examples of "minge," for instance, involve cowboys) and hence experience difficulty when these cues are not available (for instance, in cross- and new-context transfer items; see Table 7.3). To put it another way, people who practice same-context examples do not really understand the concept at a general, abstract level; whereas their knowledge of the concepts is *contextualized,* the knowledge of people who receive varied-context examples has become relatively *decontextualized* (cf. Bransford and Franks, 1976; Bransford and Nitsch, 1978). A similar illustration of contextualized knowledge appeared in Chapter 6, Section 4, where we discussed a graduate student's studying for a statistics test. Although he didn't realize it initially, his ability to solve various problems depended on knowledge of which chapters the problems came from; only after changing his method of studying was he gradually able to decontextualize his knowledge and thereby solve problems when no information about relevant chapters was presented in the test.

Note that the concept of decontextualization illustrates one type of change in understanding that can occur as a function of certain types of practice. This emphasis on *changes* in understanding represents an important difference between the theme of the present chapter and those of previous chapters. For example, the principle of encoding specificity (see the discussion above) stresses the importance of retrieval environments for recreating information about previously experienced episodes, but it doesn't emphasize how we may change this previous knowledge by using it in particular retrieval or practice situations (cf. Bransford, Franks, Morris, and Stein, 1978). If retrieval environments overlap with previously encoded information, this may facilitate remembering yet do little to help us to better understand appropriate concepts and schemata. As we have seen, however, practice with retrieval environments that are too much at variance with previously encoded information (as may be true of practice trials composed of varied-context examples) can also produce confusion. It is therefore important to design practice situations that ultimately both permit flexible transfer and reduce initial confusion.

Facilitating Both Initial Learning and Transfer

A third experiment by Nitsch (1977) investigated three different acquisition conditions. In this experiment all participants received seven practice trials rather than four. The first group received same-context examples, and the second received varied-context examples. The third group received a hybrid acquisition procedure; their first four practice trials involved same-context examples, and the last three involved varied-context examples. Nitsch reasoned that initial practice with same-context examples would help people in the Hybrid group develop a firm, contextualized basis of knowledge that would then permit them to learn from practice on varied-context examples without becoming confused. (The Hybrid group were told the correct answers during their first two exposures to varied-context examples, so that they had a chance to correct their mistakes.)

Results indicated that people in all three groups met Nitsch's initial learning criterion (eleven of twelve correct on the last two practice trials). People in the Hybrid group were therefore able to deal with the varied-context examples (the last three practice trials) quite readily. (Contrast this with the great difficulty participants have with varied-context examples when they have not first developed a basis of knowledge through practice with same-context examples.) Equally important, people in the Hybrid group performed as well on the transfer test as people in the Varied Context group (see Table 7.4). Nitsch's hybrid procedure therefore permitted flexible transfer, but students were also spared the frustration and confusion characteristic of the Varied Context group during the initial practice trials. When Nitsch asked participants to rate their sense of confusion during the practice trials, those in the Varied Context group stated that they were very confused; those in the Hybrid group were not. Such feelings of confusion in educational contexts may cause students simply to give up the task rather than continue trying to learn.

Table 7.4   Correct Identification as a Function of Acquisition Condition and Test Type

	Hit Rate			
	Old Context	Cross Context	New Context	False Positive Rate
Same-context examples:	90%	60%	69%	15.9%
Varied-context examples:	92%	82%	82%	11.0%
Hybrid examples:	90%	85%	91%	12.0%

Adapted from Nitsch (1977). Used by permission.

Some Patterns of Language Acquisition

Nitsch's (1977) experiments highlight two factors that might provide important constraints for understanding the development of new concepts and schemata. On the one hand, it can be beneficial initially to acquire information that is restricted to a particular context. To state this in different terms, it can be helpful to learn by experiencing a few highly similar prototypic instances of a concept. (See our discussion of prototypes in Chapter 6, Section 1.) On the other hand, learning from similar prototypes can also reduce the possibility of flexible transfer. If these two points are valid, we might expect to see cases where people begin with a contextually restricted ability to understand and only later show evidence of flexibility. Some illustrations are discussed below.

Data reported by Bloom (1974) provide one example of contextually restricted comprehension. During her early stages of language acquisition, Bloom's daughter, Allison, seemed to recognize the meanings of the words *birds* and *music*. However, she did not *always* react in a manner indicating that she knew what these words meant. Bloom notes that Allison first recognized the word *birds* when it referred to a mobile above her dressing table, and the word *music* when it referred to the sound of the record player in her room. Bloom (1974) states that "she did not recognize the words *birds* and *music* in any situations other than her mobile and her record player for many months" (p. 289).

The possibility of contextually derived understanding of particulars is also discussed by Nelson (1977). She notes that an eighteen-month-old girl could identify the words *nose, hair, eyes, mouth,* and *ears* appropriately. When asked, "Where's your face?" however, the child did not respond. More important, Nelson continues, a request to "wash your face" *did* result in indications of understanding (that is, the child went through the motions of washing and wiping her hands all over her face). These results suggest that the ability to understand the word *face* depended on support from additional, contextually related events.

The preceding examples have focused on contextually derived *comprehension*. Data from Bloom, Hood, and Lightbown (1974) suggest that similar considerations are necessary for understanding linguistic *production*. Bloom and colleagues played a "Simple Simon" game of imitation with Peter (age thirty-two months, two weeks). They presented sentences such as "This is broken," "I'm trying to get this cow in here," "I'm gonna get the cow to drink milk," "You make him stand up over there." Peter's imitations were, respectively, "What's broken," "Cow in here," "Get the cow to drink milk," "Stand up there." As Bloom (1974) notes, these imitation data suggest that Peter had not yet developed certain levels of linguistic competence; for example, Peter apparently lacked a consistent use of the copula *is* and lacked connectives like *trying, gonna, make*. And yet, each of the sentences that the experimenters presented for imitation was a sentence that Peter himself had previously produced spontaneously. For example, Peter had said, "I'm gonna get the cow to drink milk" while returning to a toy cow with some toy barrels fetched from a sack; he had said, "You make him stand up over there" when asking the experimenter to spread an animal's legs so that it could stand in a spot Peter had cleared. These data provide a striking illustration of contextually derived abilities to know and act.

The importance of contextual support is also illustrated in a study by Olson (1974). He presented young schoolchildren with sentences like "John hit Mary" and asked them to decide whether they meant the same thing as other statements, such as "Mary hit John," "Mary was hit by John." Children's performance in this task was very poor. In other cases, Olson systematically increased the richness of the children's knowledge base, or internal context, and performance consistently improved. Performance was worst when arbitrary names (such as *John* and *Mary*) were used, but it was improved by simply including known characters (e.g., the names of classmates). The addition of a story context in which both characters and their relations were nonarbitrary further facilitated the children's performances. In short, the nature of the context in which the sentences were embedded affected the children's ability to understand relationships among the sentences they heard.

Consider one additional aspect of general patterns of language acquisition. Is there any evidence that children first acquire a firm *basis* of knowing that then enables them to deal with novelty? (The children would then be comparable to Nitsch's Hybrid group.) Data of Bloom, Lightbown, and Hood (1975) provide evidence that can be viewed as supporting this idea. They studied the development of children's linguistic abilities. At any particular stage of language acquisition, children seem to be experimenting with new means of linguistic expressions; they begin to utilize more complicated syntactic forms, for instance. Is there any relationship between their experimentation and what they already know? Bloom and colleagues suggest that the answer may be yes. They analyzed those utterances that included (for the children) new syntactic constructions. New constructions occurred in those utterances with whose components (especially the verbs) the children were already very familiar. If the children had tried to talk about unfamiliar events and had used unfamiliar verbs, it might have been too taxing to experiment with new syntactic constructions at the same time. When the content is familiar, however, the children seem able to experiment with more efficient ways of saying what they mean.

Summary of Section 3

Discussion in this section focused on the role of practice for developing new concepts and schemata. Some ways of practicing, such as rehearsal of concept definitions, facilitate remembering but do not increase understanding and, hence, transfer; other ways of practicing, such as studying varied-context examples, often result in confusion during the initial stages of learning but may facilitate transfer later. Nitsch's hybrid procedure illustrates a situation that facilitates not only the speed and ease of initial learning but also flexible transfer on subsequent tasks.

There are some intriguing analogs to Nitsch's Hybrid group that appear in the literature on language acquisition. Children sometimes seem to acquire concepts and schemata in certain prototypic contexts and then depend on this contextual support to perform adequately. Gradually, they increase their ability to perform without contextual support; their knowledge becomes decontextualized (cf. Bransford and Franks, 1976).

Nitsch's studies suggest some reasons why we might expect to see such patterns of development; here is an area that warrants further research.

Section 4: Experiences
That Help People Learn to Learn

The purpose of this section is to discuss an aspect of the learning problem that represents a major challenge for cognitive scientists: the problem of helping people learn to learn. This issue is different from the major issues of the earlier sections in this chapter. In Section 3 we discussed certain types of practice or study situations that could facilitate initial learning as well as subsequent transfer, and in particular, Nitsch's hybrid procedure. Note, however, that it was the experimenter, comparable to the teacher, who determined what should be studied and when it should be studied; students in Nitsch's Hybrid group were given materials of the experimenter's choosing, in the sequence chosen by the experimenter. As shown in Chapter 6, Section 4, truly active and efficient learners know what they themselves need to do in order to comprehend and master information. They know when to ask questions, when to reread, how to spend their study time, and so forth. In short, effective learners don't always need to rely on an experimenter, teacher, or programmed text to prescribe the best study procedure but can figure this out for themselves. Some theorists, in fact, argue that intelligence might be regarded as the ability to learn despite the absence of direct or complete instruction (e.g., Campione and Brown, in press; Resnick and Glaser, 1976). Our present question is, How do people develop the ability to plan and regulate their own learning activities? What kinds of experiences can help them learn to learn?

The Importance of Self-
Regulative Learning Activities

One way to appreciate the importance of learning to regulate one's own learning activities is to consider studies of people who tend not to do this. Children who are regarded as educable retarded individuals (with IQ scores of about 70) represent a case in point. Campione and Brown (in press) have studied such children and argue that an important aspect of intelligence is the ability to plan and coordinate learning strategies and activities (see also Brown, 1978; Flavell and Wellman, 1977); they suggest that the poor performance that is frequently exhibited by educable retarded children is strongly influenced by their lack of such planning skills. For example, these children generally do poorly when asked to learn and remember a list of items. If they are trained in techniques like rehearsal and "chunking" (see Chapter 2, Section 3), however, their performance can be improved (e.g., Belmont and Butterfield, 1971; Brown, Campione, Bray, and Wilcox, 1973). Comparing results such as these with what one knows of the performance of ordinary children, one may assume that a major difference between educable retarded children and ordinary children is that the latter are more likely to recognize the need to employ learning strategies and hence use them without explicit prompting. If we want to help educable retarded children learn to learn, we must therefore ask how they might be helped to plan and execute appropriate strategies without having to rely on explicit prompts.

Our discussion in Chapter 6, Section 4, included additional examples illustrating the importance of people's abilities to regulate their own learning activities. Fifth-grade children who tended to do poorly in school failed to realize that stories containing "precise" information ("The hungry boy ate the hamburger") were easier to learn and master than those with "less precise" information ("The sleepy boy ate the hamburger"); these children therefore failed to study longer for harder stories and hence did poorly on subsequent tests (cf. Owings, Petersen, Bransford, Morris, and Stein, in preparation). Whimbey's (1976) work with college students who have learning difficulties suggested similar problems. Unlike efficient comprehenders, the less successful college students simply continued reading difficult material without monitoring their current levels of understanding and rereading when necessary. Without actively regulating and planning their activities, one could hardly expect these students to perform well in school.

It should also be remembered that many of the fifth-graders and college students we discussed earlier were helped to improve their performance when they were explicitly prompted to evaluate new materials in the light of their existing knowledge and to employ efficient learning strategies. Ultimately, however, they need to progress to the point where they do this spontaneously, and in a wide variety of tasks. In other words, the problem of learning to learn involves the development of general skills of self-regulation and planning that permit transfer to a wide variety of new learning situations. This aspect of the learning to learn problem is discussed below.

The Problem of Transferring
Self-Regulatory Skills

Our preceding discussion suggested that many people can be taught particular strategies that will help them improve their performance. Training studies like those we have considered suggest that many learning problems can be modified; they don't solve the problem of learning to learn, however. That people may employ newly learned strategies in a particular series of experiments or with a particular set of materials does not mean that they will do this in new contexts and with different materials. Under these conditions the benefits of teaching particular strategies are very limited.

As an illustration of the preceding problem, consider once again the task of teaching new strategies to educable retarded children. Campione and Brown (in press) note that these children can be taught to use learning strategies, but most training studies find that the children fail to transfer or generalize these strategies to new situations. When faced with a new task or context, the children frequently fall back upon their earlier (pretraining) methods. Needless to say, such findings are very discouraging. It is possible that educable retarded children are simply unable to generalize; perhaps this ability is what we really mean by intelligence. Another possibility is that we need a better understanding of what it means to "teach new strategies." Perhaps researchers have approached this problem in less than optimal ways. Campione and Brown (in press) argue that this is so (see also Feuerstein, in press, a, b).

Campione and Brown suggest that children must be helped to realize the limitations of their own information processing systems and to see how various strategies can help them overcome these limitations. If a list of items exceeds their short-term memory capacity, for example, children need to recognize this to be able to do something about it. They also need to realize that they can test their own memory for the items, so that they will know when it is appropriate to continue studying. In short, children need to learn to evaluate a task's difficulty relative to their current knowledge and skills. Note that this discussion emphasizes the importance of developing metacognitive awareness or knowledge about one's own knowledge (see Chapter 6, Section 4). This orientation has important implications for the types of training tasks one should employ. For example, it is one thing to tell people to rehearse items in order to remember them, and to show that this can improve their performance; it is another matter to help them recognize when lists exceed their short-term capacity and to teach them how to evaluate their memory by means of self-testing.

Brown, Campione, and Barclay (1978) trained educable retarded children to use a simple strategy of "stopping, checking (self-testing) and studying (if you need to)." The children were trained to recognize when lists exceeded their short-term capacity and were taught to study until they could recall all the items. This training enabled them to improve their performance greatly. More important, the children spontaneously transferred to a new task and to a new type of materials. They were better at learning and remembering the gist of prose passages they heard than a control group (children without the training) tested on the same materials.

The work by Brown and colleagues illustrates a training program that results in spontaneous transfer. It is significant that this success was achieved with educable retarded children, for one might expect a high probability of failure with such children. Furthermore, that these children's abilities to learn can be enhanced suggests that others' abilities can be improved, too. It is also significant that success was achieved when Brown and colleagues focused on helping the children become aware of their own potentials for self-evaluation and correction; if the children tested themselves and could not answer correctly, they would know that they must study longer. This is different from simply teaching someone a strategy, such as rehearsal or chunking, that they mechanically apply to a particular task.

Note, however, that evaluation of one's memory for a list of items is only one rather simple example of self-monitoring activities. Campione and Brown (in press) note that there are many other aspects of self-evaluation and regulation that are important for effective learning. For example, it seems easier to evaluate our ability to recall a list of words than it is to determine whether we have understood and mastered the materials presented by a college professor. Indeed, college students frequently think they have understood and mastered information when, in fact, they failed to do so. How can one be helped to learn to better evaluate and regulate one's study activities? This question is discussed below.

The Problem of Evaluating
Current Levels of Understanding

The task of helping people learn to learn is a major challenge for cognitive science. This topic is extremely important because it suggests that efficient learning and high intelligence might involve sophisticated skills that some people have developed and others can develop (e.g., see Bartlett, 1932). This assumption about skills is apparent in a number of approaches to education; for example, in books designed to help people develop memory skills (e.g., Cermak, 1976; Higbee, 1977; Lorayne and Lucas, 1974) and in books discussing general strategies for problem solving (e.g., Newell and Simon, 1972; Polya, 1957, 1968; Whimbey, 1976; Wickelgren, 1974). There is a great need for more detailed theory and research on this question, however. For example, much of the work on problem solving involves presenting people with a problem and then suggesting some strategies for solving it. In many learning situations, however, people don't even realize that they are faced with a problem; for example, they don't realize that they have failed to adequately understand and master information. If people think they have understood and learned, they will not perform additional activities like asking questions, rereading, studying in new ways (cf. Bransford and Nitsch, 1978). An important aspect of helping people learn to learn therefore involves the development of internal criteria that can guide their processes of self-evaluation. How do people develop the ability to know when they have understood and learned and when they have not?

The present question can be clarified by considering additional data from Nitsch's (1977) experiments, which were discussed in Section 3. Recall that Nitsch asked participants to practice with same-context or varied-context examples and measured the ease of initial learning as well as the ability to transfer. People who received same-context examples performed more poorly in the transfer task. Our present question is, To what extent did people in Nitsch's study think they had adequately understood and mastered the concepts after receiving the practice trials (but before the transfer test)?

To answer this question, Nitsch asked people to rate their "feelings of mastery" just before and just after they were given the transfer test. Everyone had received seven practice trials before making the ratings. Before the first transfer test, Same Context participants' ratings of their feelings of mastery were equivalent to those of the Varied Context participants (all people in this Varied Context group had met the initial learning criteria by the time they made their ratings). The Same Context participants therefore thought they had adequately learned and understood the concepts. After taking the transfer test, however, they produced lower feelings-of-mastery ratings than people from the Varied Context group. (Note that participants received no information about whether they were right or wrong on the transfer test.) People from the Same Context group therefore were unable to evaluate the adequacy of their current level of understanding until they tried to use it in a new situation, that is, in the transfer test.

Nitsch's results suggest that information about the conditions under which knowledge must be utilized may play an important role in helping people evaluate their current level of understanding and mastery. It is doubtful whether we ever absolutely understand anything. Our current ideas, concepts, and schemata may seem sufficient until we try to apply them in new areas, answer questions about them, and so forth.

People who learn effectively may do so because they think about potential applications of information to new situations and hence realize when they need to know more. These points are further illustrated in the following example.

In Chapter 6, Section 4, we discussed Markman's (1977) study in which certain crucial information was left out of a set of instructions about how to play a new card game. Younger children frequently failed to realize that they needed this information; they thought they understood. When actually attempting to play the game, however, the younger children frequently recognized the need for the missing information. It is possible that as children get older, they *think about* playing a game when reading instructions. They may therefore detect gaps in the instructions without actually having to play the game. As people develop more knowledge of possible areas for applying information, they may therefore increase their abilities to monitor effectively their current levels of comprehension and mastery. Experience with different ways of using information may therefore be extremely important. The discussion below examines this possibility in more detail.

Learning from Testlike Situations

In Section 3 we noted that different ways of practicing information (such as practice at concept definitions and same-context or varied-context examples) resulted in different types of learning. Practice trials can be viewed as testlike situations where people attempt to apply their current knowledge. The emphasis in Section 3 was on the development of particular concepts and schemata as a function of various practice situations. For example, people receiving varied-context examples became capable of understanding Nitsch's (1977) concepts (such as "minge," "crinch") at a level permitting flexible transfer. There is another aspect of learning from practice or testlike situations that is important in the present context. Experience with certain types of testlike situations may help people better learn additional concepts because these people can now anticipate the types of situations in which this knowledge may eventually be used.

As an illustration of the present issue, assume that two groups of people study Nitsch's (1977) six concepts by practicing with same-context examples. One group (Group 1) then receives the transfer test, but the other (Group 2) does not. Will Group 1 learn something by taking the transfer test? For example, if both groups are presented with additional concepts to be learned and are told to study them any way they wish (and ask questions when they wish), will people in Group 1 do better because they can anticipate the types of testlike situations in which their knowledge must be used? Intuitively, one feels that information about potential ways of using knowledge (about the types of tests to be given in a course, for instance) is extremely important for evaluating our current levels of understanding and mastery and hence guiding study behavior. It is therefore beneficial to ask whether experience with certain testlike situations helps people improve not only their current level of understanding but also their abilities to learn subsequent material on their own.

At present there is little formal research on this question. We shall therefore discuss some semiformal studies that I conducted with college students taking a course on material similar to that of this book. The general design of these investigations was to ask students to study material until they felt they had mastered it. They were then asked to use what they had learned in certain testlike situations and were provided with feedback regarding potentially correct answers. The goal was to determine whether the testlike situations would help the students increase their understanding and mastery of the materials as well as help them learn to study new materials more efficiently.

Consider first a situation where students had studied materials like those discussed in Chapters 2 and 3 of this book and were therefore familiar with basic topics like short-term memory, long-term memory, levels of processing, retrieval, forgetting. There are a number of ways one might ask questions about these topics; for example, one might ask students to describe the levels-of-processing framework and cite an illustrative study, or one might present them with concepts or topics and ask for definitions, ask them to answer true-false or multiple-choice questions, and so on. It was assumed, however, that students could answer these types of questions without necessarily having mastered the material in ways that would permit efficient transfer. Ideally the students would be able to use concepts and principles from a course to better understand everyday experiences and situations, solve open-ended problems, and so forth, but it seems clear from previous discussions in this chapter that many methods of learning do not help students achieve such goals. The students were therefore given testlike situations that challenged them to use what they had learned to solve problems; for example, to evaluate the claims of a set of hypothetical studies.

The following description illustrates one of the problems posed to students: "A researcher wanted to show that 'poor' learners had a higher forgetting rate than 'good' learners. He therefore read a story to a group of 'good' versus 'poor' fifth-grade students and tested their memory twenty-four hours later. Because the poor learners exhibited a lower level of recall, the researcher concluded that 'poor' learners indeed forgot more rapidly than 'good' learners." The students were asked to use what they had learned to evaluate the researcher's claims.

Somewhat surprisingly, perhaps, over 60 percent of the students produced very weak answers to problems like the foregoing. Many agreed with the researcher's erroneous conclusions, others wrote criticisms that were not really to the point (for example, "You can't conclude much from only a single study"). After their initial attempts to react to the problems, students were then provided with hints or retrieval cues regarding the types of issues they might consider. After rereading the problem described above, for example, students were told, "Think about our discussion of forgetting, especially relationships between forgetting and learning." Under these conditions, many students were able to criticize the researcher's conclusions effectively, to point out, that is, that because the researcher had not adjusted for original degrees of learning, it was erroneous to conclude that slow learners have higher forgetting rates than fast learners. Most of the college students had therefore learned about forgetting but had failed to apply this knowledge spontaneously when first confronted with the hypothetical experiment and conclusions (without the explicit cues). The students were enthusiastic about this type of exercise as a valuable learning experience because it helped them better understand the significance of particular concepts. Furthermore, many of them had originally thought they had mastered the relevant material, but the aforementioned exercise helped them modify these feelings. Such exercises may therefore be important for developing more sophisticated criteria for evaluating the levels of comprehension and mastery that one has reached.

The problem of developing criteria that can guide one's efforts to understand adequately and master information was explored in another semiformal study I conducted with college students. The study was based on the assumption that knowledge of the situations in which information must be used has important effects on learning activities, and that students frequently do not get the opportunity to use what they have learned in interesting and challenging ways. The purpose of the study was to induce the students to respond in a classroom situation to the sorts of challenges faced by the practicing cognitive scientist.

Many courses are taught from the perspective of scientists imparting already discovered knowledge to students, and the students' role is to learn the information they receive. In contrast, the practicing scientist is in the role of an explorer. He or she wants to add to the development of the field. This means that the scientist must be able to motivate studies and theories and defend them against potential criticisms from colleagues. For example, colleagues may say, "But your data and ideas are just like X or Y or Z, and that's already well known in the literature." This type of dynamic interchange sensitizes scientists to certain types of criteria for evaluation. For example, scientists learn to focus on *relationships* among their ideas, concepts, and data and those that already exist in the literature. Contrast this with situations where people learn individual concepts and principles but fail to see how they interrelate. This contrast will become apparent from the following study.

The study to be described evaluated the potential advantages of simulating the types of dynamic interchanges that are characteristic of the everyday professional life of scientists. Students were first presented with a simple description (three typed pages) of studies illustrating three types of variables that affect retention. Part 1 described the concept of word meaningfulness (M) and the way it was technically defined and measured; students also read that high M-values facilitated recall (see Chapter 4). Part 2 described the concept of word imagery, the way it is measured, and its effects on retention (see Chapter 4, Section 1). Part 3 included a simplified discussion of the balloon study (only the No Knowledge Context, Appropriate Context Before, and Appropriate Context After groups were discussed; see Chapter 5, Section 1). Students were allowed to study the material until they felt they had mastered it.

The students were given a rating scale by which to indicate the degree to which they felt they had mastered the material. Because the material was simple and students had unlimited study time, nearly all said that they knew the material very well. Phase 1 of the experiment ended here.

In Phase 2, students read a brief discussion of scientists' responsibilities to defend their ideas and studies. They then read the following:

Assume that studies on meaningfulness (Study 1) and imagery (Study 2) are already in the literature. Now assume that you conduct the balloon study (Study 3). You think it contributes to the literature, but certain journal editors insist that you must first be able to answer some potential criticisms regarding the study. These potential criticisms are presented below. Try to counter them as best you can (write out your responses).

Students received four potential criticisms. The first is illustrated below:

Criticism 1   *The balloon study tells us nothing new. The same point is made by using lists of high- versus low-meaningful words and showing that the first list is better retained. This has already been shown.*

Students attempted to answer each criticism as best they could.

Some of the students did reasonable jobs of countering the potential criticisms. Most, however, had great difficulty with the tasks. With respect to the first criticism, for example, most felt that the point of the balloon study was somehow different from the point made by meaningfulness studies, but they weren't really sure why. Many failed to make obvious arguments like "All groups heard the same balloon passage, so that its word-meaningfulness value ought to have remained constant." In short, they failed to notice certain important distinctions between the meaningfulness studies and the balloon study. Students' inabilities to counter the criticisms helped them realize that they had not understood the material as well as they had thought originally. For example, their feelings-of-mastery ratings were now lower than before.

In Phase 3 of the study, students received examples of counterarguments to the potential criticisms. For example, distinctions between the balloon study and meaningfulness studies were pointed out. After reading the counterarguments, students again rated the degree to which they now felt they understood the materials; did they understand them much better, somewhat better, the same, less? The majority stated that they understood the studies much better. They were also enthusiastic about this type of learning experience. A final question asked students to explain why they felt their understanding had changed. Note that nearly all of them said that their understanding had greatly improved. Consider some of the comments:

Simply seeing the point that people had against it and then for it brought out the hidden meanings, constraints, and conditions for the experiment. Other people's insights and knowledge can add to your own and stimulate your own, helping you to see it in a new light.

Having to "defend" the study makes one think. One has to recall what was done, but also has to place this knowledge into a larger framework—seeing the facts but also applying them, and looking at them from different angles. This processing seems to increase understanding, for it is applying the material.

In writing essays, I had to think about what I'd just read, then write about it. In reading the counterarguments, I was exposed to ideas about the balloon study that I hadn't thought about before.

I understand it better mainly because of the given counterarguments. They made the study much clearer. Before I really didn't see that anything was detected that wasn't already known.

It is important to note that the previous studies are exploratory in nature. Nevertheless, they suggest some important points that should be further researched. For example, they emphasize the importance of analyzing the types of experiences that help people learn to utilize appropriate knowledge when needed. Many methods of teaching and testing (including self-testing) fail to develop such skills. Thus, attempts to answer factual questions about particular studies and concepts do not guarantee that people will be able to utilize their knowledge when needed; for example, they may have to rely on external prompts or cues. Furthermore, people can know the details of individual studies and concepts and yet fail to detect similarities and differences among them. The ability to understand similarities and differences between meaningfulness studies and the balloon study is a case in point. Our understanding is continually evolving. When our everyday interactions (which are often testlike situations) prompt us to evaluate or defend ideas, our knowledge seems to evolve into forms that enable us to deal with novel but related situations and events (see also Bransford and Franks, 1976).

Experience with testlike situations may also help us anticipate the types of situations in which knowledge must be utilized. If we can anticipate certain types of questions and criticisms, for example, we are better able to determine whether we are adequately prepared or need more information and practice. We may also increase our ability to evaluate other people's ideas and arguments because we can attempt to apply them in particular situations and see whether they break down. Note that the informal studies just discussed do not really address this latter issue. The studies suggest that experience with certain types of testlike situations can help people come to understand previously studied materials more fully, but we don't know whether they will help people better understand and master *new* materials. Our current hypothesis is that certain testlike situations *should* facilitate such transfer by enabling us to anticipate what we need to know in order to perform adequately. Here is an area where we need a great deal of research, for it seems to be an important aspect of learning to learn.

There is another aspect of the problem of learning to learn that warrants careful study: To what extent is it important that one *actively*, or *spontaneously*, practice dealing with new situations (for example, answering potential criticisms), as opposed to merely being told the correct answers? If effective learners are those who know what to do in order to understand and master information, it seems important to help people develop their own active learning skills. Note, for example, that the informal studies mentioned above first had students respond to certain problems and criticisms and then provided them with potentially correct answers or solutions. Is the first step important, or could we just tell people answers and find that learning is just as good?

The following discussion will emphasize the importance of the active role of the individual in processes of remembering, of understanding, and of learning. That memory may be facilitated by the individual's active generation of knowledge has been demonstrated in a number of experiments (e.g., Anderson, Goldberg, and Hidde, 1971; Bobrow and Bower, 1969). For example, Anderson and colleagues show that the probability of recalling *purse* from the cue *woman* is greater if students have initially received fill-in-the-blank frames for which they must generate their own responses (for example, "The woman put the lipstick back into her _____") than if they have received whole sentences ("The woman put the lipstick back into her purse"). Experiments by Olson

(1977) provide additional information. Two groups of elementary-school children received noun pairs to be learned (such as "chicken-rock"). One group heard these nouns in the context of a linking sentence (such as "The chicken perched on the rock"), whereas the other group were instructed to generate their own linking sentences. The important aspect of Olson's study is that it measured the children's abilities to learn a *new* set of noun pairs where no linking sentences were provided. The children who had initially generated their own sentences exhibited superior retention of the new set of noun pairs.

The preceding studies focus on activities that facilitate memory for previously experienced information. Are active attempts to utilize our knowledge also important for helping us understand and learn new information and recognize gaps in our abilities to understand? Experiments by Soraci (in preparation) and Kronseder (in preparation) provide interesting information regarding this question. They used a white-noise transfer procedure like the one employed by Hannigan (1976; see Section 2). Recall that Hannigan presented people with acquisition sentences about a man doing things. People in the No Framework group heard these sentences in isolation, whereas those in the Framework group heard them in the context of "survival" and one of its seven subcategories (such as "reaching for food on a branch above one's head"). The Framework group was better at detecting Novel Appropriate sentences on the white-noise test.

In their experiments, both Soraci and Kronseder included a different acquisition condition. Some students were told that all the acquisition sentences were about "survival on a previously inhabited but now deserted island," but they were given no information about the subcategories. It was assumed that this type of acquisition condition would require students to do more thinking on their own than was necessary in the Framework condition. Indeed, people in this new group (the No Subcategory group) rated the acquisition sentences as more difficult to understand than did people in the Framework group. However, the No Subcategory group were eventually able to see how most of the sentences could apply to the survival theme.

On the white-noise transfer test, both Soraci and Kronseder found that people in the No Subcategory group were even better than those in the Framework group at identifying Novel Appropriate sentences. (Soraci and Kronseder found that, as in Hannigan's studies, people in the No Framework group did least well.) People in the new group had been forced to be more creative during acquisition, and this may have helped them perform better on the transfer task. These results therefore seem consistent with arguments that many theorists have made concerning the value of *discovery learning* (e.g., Anthony, 1973; Bruner, 1959; Wittrock, 1974, in press). If people can discover things on their own, they not only acquire new knowledge but also develop skills for effectively utilizing what they already know. Note, however, that this argument requires some qualification.

It would be a mistake to assume that discovery learning requires that people should be given no guidance whatsoever. Certain types of guidance are often necessary, and a major goal of effective instruction ought to be to set the stage so that discoveries are more likely to be made. As an illustration, note once again that people in the No Framework group did poorly in the white-noise test of transfer. They, too, presumably had a chance to be creative, but they were given no guidelines for channeling their initial comprehension activities. In contrast, people in the new group (survival theme but no subcategories) were provided with a guideline from which to begin.

It should be stressed, however, that guided discovery learning must always take into account the current knowledge of the learner. Note that Soraci and Kronseder ran their experiments with college students. If the participants were third-graders, it is possible that the Framework group would be superior to the No Subcategory group. The reason is that third-graders may need more explicit prompts (such as information about subcategories) because their knowledge and skills are not as well developed as those of the college students. Assumptions about guided discovery must therefore be evaluated in relation to what the learner already knows.

It is useful to consider one additional reason why attempts to use knowledge actively in new situations may be beneficial. Our concluding discussion refers specifically to guided discovery learning but is for the most part applicable to discovery learning in general. If people are simply told the answer to a problem or potential criticism, they frequently think they knew the answer all along; the answer may seem so reasonable that people say, "Of course," and let it go at that. What is often overlooked, however, is that the ability to recognize a correct answer is not necessarily equivalent to being able to produce or generate it on one's own. By first trying to produce an answer, people may therefore become aware of certain limitations in their current level of understanding and mastery. In Chapter 3, Section 3, we discussed Auble and Franks's (1978) studies, which indicated that initial breakdowns in attempts to comprehend can be beneficial provided that one eventually reaches a solution. Although their studies assessed people's abilities to remember previous information, it is possible that these types of experiences have additional benefits as well. By becoming aware of limitations in their current level of understanding and mastery, people may become better able both to improve subsequent study activities and to appreciate the value of the new information, even though they may still think, "Of course," when the information is presented. In addition, when learners realize they have been helped to do something that, at the moment at least, they couldn't do on their own, they will of course better appreciate the contributions of those who have helped them.

Summary of Section 4

Section 4 discussed an aspect of learning that was not explicitly emphasized in the first three sections: the problem of learning to learn. The ability to plan and evaluate our own learning strategies seems to be a hallmark of intelligent activity. From this perspective, intelligence involves the development of skills for utilizing and modifying previously existing knowledge, rather than the possession of some fixed capacity. It is therefore important to analyze the types of learning experiences that help people learn to learn.

It was suggested that learning to learn involves an increased ability to understand our own limitations and to decide how to overcome these limitations. For example, we must recognize that a set of materials exceeds our short-term memory in order to plan ways of overcoming these limitations. We can also devise procedures for testing current levels of comprehension and mastery on our own. There seems to be an important difference between training studies that teach particular strategies and those that emphasize metacognitive procedures that help people learn to evaluate their current level of comprehension and mastery. For example, Campione and Brown (in press) find that the latter procedures are more likely to produce superior transfer than those that involve more mechanical applications of particular strategies. Apparently, people can learn to utilize strategies, such as rehearsal, in particular contexts or with particular types of materials and yet fail to transfer to a broader range of tasks.

It was also suggested that there are many different aspects to the problem of planning and evaluating our current levels of comprehension and mastery. Thus, it seems easier to determine whether we can remember a list of words than it is to assess our comprehension and mastery of a college professor's intended points. Experience with tests and testlike situations may increase our abilities to learn subsequent materials because we frequently have more adequate criteria for the ways in which we must utilize our knowledge. Effective learners may therefore spontaneously attempt to apply concepts to new situations and hence increase their understanding and be able to detect gaps in their knowledge. There is a great need for more research on this problem. If people can really learn to be intelligent (e.g., see Feuerstein, in press, a, b; Whimbey, 1976), this would be of immeasurable value to society. The challenge, of course, is to better understand the types of learning experiences that help people act more intelligently in future situations—that is, that help people learn to learn.

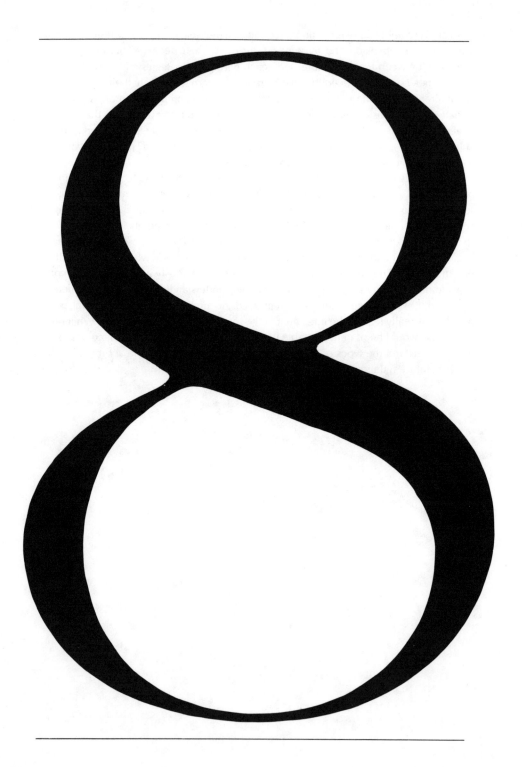

Chapter 8
Conclusions and Implications

We have discussed numerous studies designed to investigate processes of learning, understanding, and remembering. The purpose of this final chapter is to reemphasize some general principles that can be derived from the research presented and to suggest potential implications for future theorizing and research.

Consider first some factors involved in each of the studies reviewed in this book. They include the fact that (1) some type of learning material is presented; (2) some type of criterial task or tasks is selected by the experimenter; (3) learners engage in some type of activity while being exposed to the input information; (4) learners enter the experiment with some degree of available skills and knowledge. These factors are very general and are important aspects of any experiment on learning and memory; they are also present in any classroom situation. It is for these reasons that Figure 1.1 was chosen as our organizing framework (see also Jenkins, 1978). This framework seems deceptively simple, but it illustrates a complex set of relationships among factors that must always be taken into account when evaluating theoretical claims. We will first review how the framework can be used to guide evaluations of hypotheses about learning and then apply it to statements about people as learners. Implications for programs of intervention (in particular, ways to help people learn) will also be discussed.

Evaluating Claims about Learning

We have suggested that performance is a function of relationships among the major factors in our framework in Figure 1.1. These relationships must be taken into account when evaluating theoretical claims. For example, our framework emphasizes that assumptions about optimal learning activities should be evaluated in relation to the types of performance criteria or testing environments. This theme was emphasized at a number of points in this book. In Chapter 3, Section 2, for example, we discussed Craik and Lockhart's (1972) levels-of-processing theory, which assumed that deeper levels of processing were superior to shallower levels. Several experiments were cited that questioned this claim (e.g., Morris, Bransford, and Franks, 1977; Stein, 1978). For example, shallower levels of processing like paying attention to the sounds of words or noticing whether certain letters were capitalized frequently resulted in better performance than deeper levels of processing. The crucial variable was the relationship between the information acquired at the time of learning and the information necessary to perform well on the test.

The importance of considering relationships among acquisition activities and tests emerged again in Chapter 7. For example, it seemed to make no difference whether students processed information in terms of a "survival" framework (the Framework group) or received no such framework (the No Framework group) when their performance was measured by a recognition test; when the same groups were asked to use what they had learned, however, to identify Novel Appropriate sentences embedded in white noise, there were large differences between them (e.g., Hannigan, 1976; see Chapter 7, Section 2).

The experiments by Nitsch (Chapter 7, Section 3) provide further evidence for the importance of considering acquisition–test relationships. In her experiments, people's learning activities were strongly influenced by the nature of the materials provided by the experimenter. If we view the experimenter as a teacher who guides students' learning activities, Nitsch's results indicate that certain teaching sequences are better or worse than others, depending on the learning criteria one adopts. If the criterion is the speed and ease of initial learning, it is more efficient to present same-context examples. The presentation of varied-context examples, on the other hand, leads to a gradual refinement of people's initial understanding, making them better able to identify novel examples of the concepts they have learned. Similarly, one might present elementary-school children with stories that closely match their currently available story schemata (see Chapter 6, Section 2); stories of this sort may be recalled better, but they won't necessarily help children develop new story schemata that permit them to learn subsequent types of stories more effectively (least of all, those that are less prototypic of simpler schemata). Recall is therefore only one of many types of criteria by which learning may be assessed.

We also noted that the adoption of particular testing criteria involves assumptions about what one means by *learning*. The studies in Chapters 2 through 6 emphasized the act of learning the information presented. In Chapter 7 we stressed the importance of learning *from* information. Here the emphasis was on transfer, that is, the ability to use what was learned to better understand and master something new. The term *learning* is ambiguous, and an experimenter's choice of criterial tasks is an index of his or her current use of the term.

Another aspect of the many-faceted definition of *learning* is the degree to which certain types of experiences help people learn to learn. As noted in Chapters 6 (Section 4) and 7 (Section 4), effective learners know themselves what they need to know and do in order to perform effectively; they are able to monitor their own levels of understanding and mastery. These active learners are therefore likely to ask questions of clarification and more efficiently plan their study activities. Such activities are quite different from passively accepting (yet *momentarily* actively processing) the particular information that a person or text presents.

Note that an emphasis on learning to learn suggests a different set of criteria for evaluating learning activities from those cited previously. Imagine a programmed learning text that is ideal for step-by-step mastery of certain information (facts about genetics, say); again, imagine that an experimenter finds the optimal way to present information so that people can identify new examples of concepts (recall, for example, Nitsch's studies in Chapter 7). Even if by means of such procedures one manages to guide people's learning activities so that they can transfer to related-content areas, such learning activities are not necessarily optimal if one's goal is to help them learn to learn. In Chapter 3 (Section 3), for example, we discussed the concept of effective elaboration. It is one thing to provide people with elaborative information that helps them learn and remember a particular set of inputs (such as "The tall man bought the crackers that were on the top shelf"); it is a different matter to help them learn how to create their own effective elaborations and thereby help them more readily learn *subsequent* inputs (e.g., see Olson, 1977; Chapter 7, Section 4). The topic of learning to learn receives more detailed discussion later.

Evaluating Learning Activities in Relation to People's Current Knowledge and Skills

Our discussion above focused on relationships between optimal learning activities and desired performance criteria. Figure 1.1 emphasizes that statements about learning activities must also be evaluated in relation to the learner's current knowledge and skills.

As an example, consider questions about the value of intentional-learning as compared with incidental-learning activities. Experiments by Jenkins and colleagues (Chapter 2, Section 4) suggest that incidental learning can be as effective as intentional learning (see also Postman, Adams, and Bohm, 1956). In many studies with elementary-school children, however, incidental-orienting instructions often result in better performance than intentional instructions (e.g., see Brown, 1978). Younger children may not know what to do when told simply to try to learn. However, they may be able to perform such incidental-orienting activities as deciding whether inputs are pleasant or unpleasant. If incidental-orienting instructions prompt children to encode inputs more efficiently (relative to particular testing criteria) than they would if left to their own devices, incidental learning will seem more beneficial than intentional learning. Similar results can be found in tests of college students. As discussed in Chapter 3, Section 4, Wilson and Bransford asked one group of students to decide whether words represented something that would be "important or unimportant" if they were stranded on a deserted island. A second group were explicitly asked to learn the list of nouns but received no island context. The first group exhibited superior free recall, even though they had not expected the recall test.

Assume, however, that certain students are very sophisticated at effectively encoding and elaborating inputs (see Chapter 3, Section 3, for discussion of elaboration). Intentional instructions may prompt more effective elaborations from these students than certain incidental instructions ("Say whether each sentence is comprehensible"). In short, claims about the relative superiority of intentional and incidental acquisition activities must be evaluated in relation to the learner's available and activated knowledge and skills. As noted earlier, such claims must also be evaluated in relation to one's learning criteria. Providing people with incidental orienting tasks that optimize their ability to remember particular sets of inputs will not necessarily help them learn how to learn intentionally.

Particular learning activities must also be evaluated in terms of relationships between the information to be acquired and the learner's knowledge and skills; for different types of materials also promote different learning activities. Whenever we assume that people learn by being told relevant facts, concepts, definitions, and so forth, we are presupposing that they have the available knowledge and skills necessary to understand and master this new information. If they lack an appropriate knowledge base, however, simply telling them to learn will do little good. For example, two exposures to the balloon passage without the appropriate picture (which serves as an appropriate knowledge base) are much less effective than one exposure when preceded by a presentation of the picture (Chapter 5, Section 1). Similarly, varied-context examples are much more readily mastered by people in Nitsch's Hybrid group who have already developed a stable, contextualized basis of knowledge (Chapter 7, Section 3). Clearly, the value of presenting certain types of information must be defined in relation to the learner's currently available knowledge and skills.

The importance of presenting information in a form that is consistent with the current state of the learner's skills and knowledge has been emphasized by many theorists; for example, Ausubel (1968). As Novak (1977) notes, this basic idea seems intuitively obvious. Nevertheless, its implications are frequently overlooked. A particularly salient example involves people's attempts to test some of Ausubel's ideas.

Ausubel proposed the use of *advanced organizers* as a means of bridging the gap between information to be acquired and the learner's knowledge. Basically, the function of advanced organizers is to marshal and train learners' momentarily available skills so that they will be more readily able to learn. The balloon picture or the "washing clothes" topic can be viewed as advanced organizers (see Chapter 5, Section 1). As Novak (1977) notes, many researchers have found evidence for the value of advanced organizers, others have failed to find such advantages. But need this mean that Ausubel's notion is in error?

Note that an advanced organizer should be effective only if it prepares people to acquire information that they could not easily have acquired otherwise. If a particular passage is consistent with the learner's available skills and knowledge, an advanced organizer is not necessary and hence should do little good. As a simple example, consider Raye's study (Chapter 5, Section 4) comparing the effects of presence and absence of the "washing clothes" topic (an advanced organizer) as determined by whether people receive abstract or concrete versions of the passage. Knowledge of the topic was highly beneficial for people who received the abstract version, but not for those who received the concrete version. To evaluate Ausubel's theory properly, one must determine the degree to which the information to be acquired is congruent with the learner's available and activated skills and knowledge. It is only in those cases where some type of *cognitive bridging* seems necessary that Ausubel would expect advanced organizers to help.

The importance of considering relationships among instructional techniques (meaning both materials and activities) and currently activated skills and knowledge is further illustrated by research in observational learning. Researchers have found that the act of attending to visual and auditory models of people performing certain types of activities may result in better performance than simply attempting to perform such activities. The models may perform activities ranging from attempts at problem solving (e.g., Bandura, 1976), to participation in psychotherapy (e.g., Strupp and Bloxom, 1973). The results of such modeling experiments must be evaluated in relation to the current level of the learner's knowledge and skills. Strupp and Bloxom (1973) are careful to take this into account. Their data suggest that visual and auditory modeling of an actual therapy session can improve clients' abilities to learn from psychotherapy. Strupp and Bloxom note, however, that they focused only on certain types of potential clients; those whose initial expectations were most likely to *differ* from the therapeutic interactions that actually took place.

Bandura (1976) also acknowledges that the effectiveness of particular types of modeling must be defined in relation to the currently available skills and knowledge of the learner. It seems clear, for example, that a theoretical physicist could visually and auditorily model a mathematical proof; but one would not expect such modeling to be very helpful for most people. Similarly, consider the following illustration of a mother's attempt to be an appropriate language model for her child (cf. McNeill, 1966).

Child: Nobody don't like me.

Mother: No, say "Nobody likes me."

Child: Nobody don't like me.

Mother: No, say "Nobody likes me."

(Eight repetitions of this dialogue)

Mother: No, now listen carefully, say "Nobody likes me."

Child: Oh! Nobody don't likes me.

What the child learned from the model depended on his current level of knowledge and skills.

One aspect of Bandura's (1976) emphasis on modeling and observational learning warrants additional discussion. Consider the intuitively obvious claim that the best way to learn is to learn by doing. Bandura provides evidence in support of an alternative intuitively obvious pattern: It can be more beneficial to watch someone perform a task effectively than it is to jump in immediately and try to do the task oneself. Statements like "Learning by doing is always superior" must therefore be questioned. Need they be ruled out, however? The alternative viewpoint can also be supported. For example, it seems clear that active attempts to perform particular activities can improve one's ability to learn from observing models. A person who has first tried to perform a dance may notice things about someone modeling a dance that others fail to notice; attempts to draw an object may help one notice information not previously detected. Other examples are not hard to find. Indeed, Piaget (1970) summarizes experiments indicating that children learn more from actively doing than they do by observing. It seems clear that there is a time for watching and a time for doing. The value of these activities depends on the ever-changing state of the learner's knowledge and skills.

Evaluating Learners

We have emphasized that the value of particular learning experiences (with various materials and processing activities) must be defined in relation to criterial objectives (in particular, testing situations) and in relation to the current state of the learner's skills and knowledge. We noted that many theoretical statements are suspect because they fail to acknowledge relationships like these. Let us move from questions about the "goodness" of learning activities to questions about the "goodness" of learners. People frequently speak of fast and slow learners. Statements like "John is a slow learner" must also be evaluated in terms of systems of relationships like those illustrated in Figure 1.1. Consider this argument in more detail below.

Imagine a group of fifth-grade students who are slow learners compared with their classmates (one could just as easily imagine students at any grade level, and college level, too). That they do more poorly than their classmates is not in question; what's important is *why* their learning seems impaired. Society (parents, teachers, peers) proposes a variety of so-called explanations regarding slow learners: They lack intelligence (just look at their scores on intelligence tests), they have certain types of cognitive deficits ("John can't think abstractly"), learning deficits, and so on and so forth. These are powerful labels that can be used to pigeonhole people rather than help them.

It is important to note that some children do have particular types of problems that hamper their learning abilities. Some may be hyperactive and hence have difficulty settling down and focusing their attention (a problem that can sometimes be helped by a proper diet). Others may exhibit particular perceptual problems that restrict their ability to decode visually presented letters. It is extremely important to attempt to diagnose and remedy such particularized problems, and progress is being made in this area (e.g., Ross, 1977; Farnham-Diggory, 1978). However, it is equally important to be wary of the widespread use of labels that simply pigeonhole people and go no further. In particular, tacit assumptions that people lack certain capacities or abilities can be very damaging from the perspective of effective intervention. What factors other than some cognitive deficit might be responsible for the difficulties that slow learners seem to have?

Consider first our expectations about learners regarded as normal or good learners. What we expect them to learn is relative to their current level of knowledge and skills. For example, normal infants require much time to learn about themselves and their environment before they are ready to acquire language (e.g., see Bates, 1976; Bloom, 1978; MacNamara, 1972; Chapman, 1978; Nelson, 1974, 1977). As shown in Chapter 7, Section 2, children's available skills and knowledge determine their rate of language development as well (e.g., Miller, 1978).

The notion that learning depends on previous learning was illustrated by many of the experiments we have discussed. For example, in Nitsch's studies (Chapter 7, Section 3) college students could readily deal with varied-context practice trials provided that they had already acquired a firm, contextualized basis of knowing (Nitsch's Hybrid group). Without this previous level of learning, however (e.g., the Varied Context groups), they frequently looked like inefficient learners, especially on the early practice trials. It seems clear, therefore, that statements like "Mary is a good learner" are not meant to suggest that Mary can learn anything she chooses; if she is a third-grader we don't expect her to learn a college text on calculus. Tacitly at least, we seem to admit that the goodness of learners must be defined in relation to their currently available skills and knowledge. It seems reasonable that a statement like "John is a slow learner" must be evaluated on the basis of a similar context of constraints.

The previous argument becomes especially important when we ask whether certain tests (comprehension tests, intelligence tests, and others) tap basic abilities of people. It is easy to fall into the trap of assuming that tests measure basic abilities or capacities, and this can be a serious error. In Chapter 2, Section 3, for example, we noted that chess masters appeared to have a greater short-term memory capacity than other people when asked to remember meaningful chess configurations (e.g., Chase and Simon, 1973; deGroot, 1965). When presented with randomized chess configurations, however, estimates of chess masters' short-term memory capacities became equivalent to those of nonexperts. Similarly, Perfetti and Lesgold (1977; see Chapter 2, Section 3) found that successful students were better than less successful students when presented with short-term memory tasks involving memory for sentences. When they asked the students to retain lists of numbers, however, which were presumably equally familiar to both groups, no differences in short-term capacity were found. If we assume that short-term capacity is independent of the skills and knowledge of the learner, we may be making a serious error.

It is also easy to make erroneous assumptions about basic abilities or capacities when comparing children of various ages. In Chapters 4 (Section 4) and 6 (Section 3), for example, we discussed the claim by some researchers that young children lack the ability to recall information in its correct temporal order (e.g., Fraisse, 1963; Piaget, 1969a). These claims are backed by experimental data, but we must be aware of the conditions under which the results were obtained. Given certain types of materials, younger children may indeed perform more poorly than older children. When presented with materials that are consistent with their currently available schemata, however, they seem to be able to remember serial ordering (e.g., Stein and Glenn, in press). These results suggest that correct memory for serial ordering should not be viewed as a basic ability or capacity that children either have or don't have (see Odom and Mumbauer, 1971; Odom, Astor, and Cunningham, 1975, for related arguments).

The previous arguments are also relevant to the way one regards people from different cultures and subcultures. Once again, it is all too convenient to conclude that certain groups are more primitive or less intelligent by evaluating their performance on particular types of intelligence tasks. Cole and Scribner (e.g., 1974) have had a great deal of experience working with people from different cultures and they warn against such erroneous assumptions. Thus, they argue that many researchers have concluded that people from other cultures have various capacity limitations because of the following:

1. There is a great readiness to assume that particular kinds of tests or experimental situations are diagnostic of particular cognitive capacities or processes.

2. Psychological processes are treated as "entities," which a person "has" or "does not have" as a property of the person independent of the problem situation. They are also considered to operate independently of each other.

3. Closely related to (1) and (2) is a readiness to believe that poor performance on a particular test is reflective of a deficiency in, or lack of, "the" process that the test is said to measure. (P. 173)

Ideally, the framework illustrated in Figure 1.1 can help us avoid such erroneous assumptions, irrespective of whether we are concerned with slow or fast learners, children of different ages, or people from different cultures or subcultures. Our organizational framework also has implications for understanding processes of effective intervention. This topic is discussed next.

Intervention: Helping People Learn What They Need to Learn

So far, discussion in this chapter has explored how our organizational framework (Figure 1.1) can be helpful for evaluating claims about both learning principles and learners. The basic argument is as follows: It is easy to make erroneous assumptions about these topics because, in particular circumstances, one or more of the basic factors in Figure 1.1 have inadvertently been ignored. As noted in Chapter 1, cognitive scientists are attempting to understand processes of learning and ways to evaluate individual learners. A major reason is that this information should help us better understand the nature of effective learning environments. Consider, therefore, the task of helping a slow learner develop the ability to acquire new linguistic concepts.

Our current topic is illustrated by an intervention project conducted by Anita Willis; it was designed to help a slow learner (see Bransford and Nitsch, 1978). She attempted to teach new concepts and words to a boy (age three years, nine months) who had been diagnosed as developmentally delayed. Willis warned that her study was informal and that she lacked hard data to back up her observations. Nevertheless, her observations provide valuable hints about what someone might look for in order to understand learning processes in more detail.

Willis began by observing the thirteen children in her toddler group. All of these "delayed" children were being trained by behavior modification; in particular they were reinforced, or rewarded, for correct answers. Willis believed that as powerful a technique as this is, its success depended on the sophistication of its recipients. She therefore paid close attention to the children's reactions to the behavioral modification sessions to discern what they understood. Willis felt that the children did not really understand what the teachers were trying to teach them. The children might eventually learn to give the correct answers (for example, "Ball" to a spherical object), but something was not quite right. For example, Willis noted that the children frequently performed incorrectly and then clapped their hands. Hand clapping (social praise) was one of the reinforcers used by the teachers. These children seemed to be mimicking social praise yet appeared unaware of the relationship between social praise and their response.

Willis also noted that although children frequently performed a task correctly (said "Ball"), they remained uncertain about the adequacy of their answer. Her assumptions were based on the children's facial expressions. Their expressions would seem blank or suggest a questioning look even when they gave the correct response. Once the teacher praised the child (for example, by clapping hands and saying, "Good, good"), the look on the child's face would change dramatically, to a look of pleasure and increased confidence. Note, however, that this situation is analogous to relying totally on external feedback, rather than having acquired internal criteria of one's own (see Chapter 6, Section 4). Willis wanted to lead the boy she worked with to the point where *he* could judge the effectiveness of his own actions, independently of feedback from the experimenter. From her perspective, helping the boy learn to respond accurately was not necessarily equivalent to helping him realize that his responses were correct.

Willis attempted to help the child learn words like *comb, brush, mirror*. Even more important, she wanted the child to come to the point of realizing that his use of these words was appropriate. She therefore refrained from a teaching procedure that involved (for example) simply placing the referent of each of the words to be learned on a table and reinforcing the boy for an appropriate response to a request like "Hand me the comb." Instead, Willis fashioned a mini-environment that comprised a small room equipped with such items as a comb, a brush, and a mirror in which the boy could see himself. She wanted to help the boy come to understand this nonverbal environment and then to help him learn the meaning of certain words. In Chapter 5, Section 1, we noted that the ability to understand the significance of even nonlinguistic materials (remember the pictures of the corn cutter, Figures 5.3–5.4) depends on the ability to relate such entities to other aspects of one's general knowledge. If exemplars of concepts are not meaningful to a learner, how could one expect the concepts to be meaningfully acquired?

Willis noted that at first the boy she worked with exhibited extremely erratic behavior and was very inattentive. The comb, brush, and other items seemed to have little meaning to him, and he kept them in his mouth more often than not. With each session, however, the boy became more attentive. He kept the objects out of his mouth more and more, and became attentive to the way Willis used the comb and brush. After a while he began combing Willis's hair, as well as his own; he also became increasingly conscious of his own image in the mirror as he was using the objects. Throughout these sessions Willis would say things that were meaningful in the context of the child's activities ("You are using the comb very well") and praise him when he accurately responded to requests like "Where is the brush?" Note, however, that all this training was done in the context of a mini-environment that was becoming increasingly meaningful to the child.

In the final session of her training program, Willis evaluated the boy's ability to understand the words and requests she had taught him; could he respond appropriately to requests like "Please hand me the comb"? Rather than merely focus on the accuracy of performance, however, Willis chose a more global criterion: Did the boy know that his responses were correct? Willis was therefore more impressed by the look on the child's face when he performed the appropriate actions than she was by the mere correctness of his responses. The boy's facial expressions suggested that he knew he was performing well. He still enjoyed and responded to social praise from Willis, but the look of understanding occurred before any external reinforcement that she could provide.

Willis's approach to teaching reflects a sensitivity to various learning criteria—in particular, that the child's developing a sense of mastery was preferable to his simply making correct responses—and to the importance of gearing instruction to the current state of the learner's skills and knowledge. Her approach also has implications for understanding slow learners. They may be slow because the current level of their skills and knowledge is not sufficient to cope with the types of information they are expected to master. Their current state of knowledge and skills would affect their comprehension, short-term memory, and long-term retention. In many types of situations one would *expect* their learning to be impaired.

Imagine presenting normal third-graders with college textbooks on calculus. As noted earlier, they would also look like slow learners. What they *would* learn is that things are generally frustrating and confusing and there is not much they can do. Although the point seems intuitively obvious in this context, it is frequently overlooked in other situations. Thus, if Willis had simply attempted to teach her boy by presenting him with objects and saying their names, the situation might have been as much at variance with his current level of skills and knowledge as a college text on calculus would be to third-graders. An emphasis on relationships between materials to be learned and the skills and knowledge of the learner sets important constraints on the way we interpret the term *slow learner*.

Learning and "Simple Tasks"

Note that Willis attempted to help her boy learn by fashioning a mini-environment such that the child could first understand it and hence better understand linguistic meanings. Even this mini-environment was quite simple; it might have been difficult for the child to begin by attempting to understand an environment that was more complex. The notion of beginning with a simplified situation and building on it seems obvious. However, this use of *simplified* differs in important ways from other uses of the term (cf. Bransford and Nitsch, 1978).

McCarrell and Brooks (1975) provide a perceptive analysis of frequently expressed theoretical conceptions of simple and complex processes. Many theorists view development as progression from simple to more complex ways of dealing with information, and the simpler processes are assumed to be prerequisites for those that are more complex. The important question is, What is meant by *simpler processes*? For many theorists, these simpler processes are assumed to involve something like copying or rote-learning. Thus, the acquisition of unmeaningful connections is assumed to be a prerequisite for more meaningful and elaborative thoughts. For example, McCarrell and Brooks (1975) cite Gagne (1970), who identifies the representational copying of stimulus–response connections as a prerequisite for higher learning; Berlyne (1965), who claims that basic associations provide the building blocks for subsequent thought and actions; and Jensen (1970, 1972), who distinguishes between Level 1 and 2 abilities. Level 1 abilities are assumed to involve only minimal processing of data and establish simple and direct stimulus-response correspondences. Level 2 abilities involve more sophisticated elaborations of inputs.

It is important to think carefully about these basic assumptions underlying many theories of development. From the present perspective these assumptions are highly questionable. The present argument is not against intuitively important ideas like "building blocks" or prerequisites for further understanding but, rather, against equating these prerequisite processes with activities like copying or forming simple stimulus–response connections. Note, for example, that Willis attempted to eliminate the painstaking procedure of learning unmeaningful associations; she avoided simply training the child to make the response "brush" when shown a real brush. The notion of fashioning a mini-environment so that inputs can become meaningful is markedly different from the notion that processes like rote-learning are prerequisites for higher mental processes. The present approach emphasizes the importance of marshaling learners' available skills so that the learners make inputs more meaningful. What they can learn and do depends on the cognitive support that they currently have.

Cognitive Support Systems

It may be useful to develop a concept of *support systems* in order to aid our thinking about processes of learning. At a biological level, necessities like oxygen, food, and water constitute part of the support necessary for functioning. Similarly, currently available information may be an important aspect of our cognitive support systems. In other words, our ability to acquire, activate, or retrieve knowledge may well depend on the resources available to us from our environment as well as from previously acquired knowledge and skills.

As an example, consider the problem of language acquisition. It seems clear that information available in the environment provides a necessary aspect of the infant's support system for acquiring language (see Chapter 7, Section 2). Thus, it is doubtful whether infants could acquire language by hearing sentences played from a tape recorder in a dark, contextless environment; they need environmental support to discover what someone is talking about. An important aspect of understanding why infants develop their language in the ways they do is to look at those events in their environment that are important and salient for them (e.g., Bates, 1976; Bloom, 1978; Chapman, 1978; Lahey, 1978; MacNamara, 1972; Nelson, 1974, 1977). Willis's procedure further illustrates the importance of a cognitive support system that provides a basis for the acquisition of new knowledge. The boy she worked with began to show signs that he was indeed capable of learning. However, if Willis had not geared her instruction to the boy's current knowledge level, he might have appeared to be hopelessly slow.

The notion of cognitive support systems that affect the activation of knowledge was implicit in a number of other examples. Recall the study by Bloom, Hood, and Lightbown (1974; Chapter 7, Section 3) regarding Peter's ability to imitate sentences. He did poorly, even though the sentences to be imitated were ones that he had previously produced. He had produced the sentences in an environment that provided meaningful support, but was unable to activate his existing knowledge in the new environment. Again, the children in Olson's study (Chapter 7, Section 3) were unable to identify the similarities in meaning of sentences like "John hit Mary" and "Mary was hit by John" until provided with more information about *who* the people were and *why* they were interacting. The notion that remembering is a function of acquisition activities and retrieval conditions also suggests the importance of focusing on relationships between people and their environments (see, for example, Shaw and Bransford, 1977). For instance, the aborigines discussed by Mead (Chapter 3, Section 1) needed to walk through the forest in order to recall their complicated myths.

The preceding examples suggest that people may be better able to acquire, activate, and retrieve knowledge if tasks are designed to be consistent with their current skills and knowledge. Now we must consider an additional problem: Why have some people failed to develop the skills and knowledge necessary for dealing with the types of information that can be acquired by their age mates? How can their rates of development be modified? It seems clear that effective intervention involves something more than simply "mapping into" what the person already knows.

Figure 8.1 illustrates the present problem more graphically. It represents the hypothetical developmental curves of two individuals (it could also represent groups of individuals). The curves provide a simplified representation of the development of learners' skills and knowledge; hence, Person 1 is portrayed as developing more quickly than Person 2. The time scale can be interpreted very broadly. For example, it could reflect a person's lifetime, his or her development in the course of a year, development within a single experimental laboratory session. Note that learners' abilities to deal with new information are assumed to be a function of their current level of skills and knowledge. For example, imagine that Person 1 is an average child and Person 2 is the boy Willis worked with. Both are the same age. At Time T_2 assume that Person 1 can learn from normal types of language instruction but Person 2 lacks the appropriate skills and knowledge. Willis's procedure was specially designed to map into the skills and knowledge currently available to Person 2.

Note, however, that Willis's procedure was designed to do something more than simply move Person 2 farther along on his path of development. For example, by the time Person 2 reaches Point B on his developmental path, he has reached the level that Person 1 reached at Point A (see Figure 8.1). In terms of our simplified analysis, Person 2 (at Point B) should now be able to deal with the types of information that Person 1 dealt with at Point A. However, Person 1 is by now well beyond Point A (at Point C), so we still have differences between fast and slow learners. In terms of Figure 8.1, effective intervention means that the slope of the learner's developmental curve must be modified. For

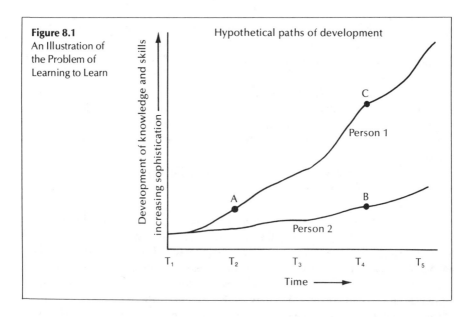

Figure 8.1
An Illustration of
the Problem of
Learning to Learn

example, Person 2 needs the kind of help that will set him on a path of development like that of Person 1. In short, Person 2 needs to be helped to learn to learn.

Learning to Learn

In Chapters 6 (Section 4) and 7 (Section 4) we noted that truly active learners have a sense of what they need to do in order to facilitate their own understanding (see also Bransford, Nitsch, and Franks, 1977; Bransford and Nitsch, 1978). They ask questions of clarification, know how to monitor their own comprehension and study activities, are able to critically evaluate and elaborate. In short, effective learners seem to have learned how to learn. Learning to learn appears to be an important aspect of helping someone change his or her path of development. As noted earlier, however, an emphasis on learning to learn involves different sets of performance criteria from other conceptualizations of learning (such as simply learning a set of facts by utilizing a programmed learning text). It is important to reconsider what some of these criteria might be.

Willis's procedure (see the previous discussion) reflects a sensitivity to the learning to learn problem. Her major criterion was based on the "look of understanding" reflected in the face of the boy she helped. Willis wanted to help him gain a sense of mastery, rather than merely allow him to rely on external feedback (such as social praise). Some knowledge of how it feels to really understand and master information would appear to be an important aspect of learning what it means to learn.

Feelings of comprehension and mastery can also affect people's assessments of themselves as learners. In talking with fifth-graders who are somewhat slow as compared with their classmates, my colleagues and I find that many of them have already pegged themselves as poor learners (see also Holt, 1964; deCharms, 1972, 1976). For example, after reading a story and then rating it as "easy to understand," many of these children still predicted that their test performance on the story would be poor. When asked about their predictions, a frequent response was something like: "Well, that is just the way that I do on stuff like this."

An emphasis on people's feelings about themselves as learners is also related to the problem of fear of failure. As noted in Chapter 6, Section 4 (see also Holt, 1964), it is frequently less threatening to run quickly through a task and get it over with than to proceed systematically. Activities like rechecking one's initial understanding or revising what one has written can easily be seen rather as admissions of failure than as sophisticated and effective strategies. An important aspect of helping people learn to learn is the problem of helping them appreciate the value of activities that allow them to clarify and revise previously held ideas and beliefs.

In Chapter 7, Section 4, we discussed some of the procedures that may be important for helping people change the way they approach learning situations. Campione and Brown's (in press) work on the development of plans for self-evaluation and self-testing is an excellent case in point. Experience with the types of situations in which knowledge must eventually be utilized may also be important for helping people evaluate their current levels of comprehension and mastery. For example, when college students were placed in roles that challenged them to evaluate and defend certain ideas, they became better able to understand previously read information (see Chapter 7, Section 4). Ideally, such experiences should also help them understand and master new sets of materials, but data are needed to verify this point.

One potential obstacle to the development of learning to learn skills may be the manner in which information is presented in many formal educational settings (see also Olson, 1977). In Chapter 7, Section 4, for example, it was suggested that many courses are taught from the perspective of teachers imparting already known information. The student's task is frequently to learn this knowledge for its own sake. We contrasted this situation with that of children learning language in the context of exploring their own environment (Chapter 7, Section 2). Similarly, the development of practicing scientists' knowledge may be greatly facilitated by day-to-day interactions with colleagues. Some very important papers contrast formal with informal educational settings (e.g., Brown, 1977a; Cole and Scribner, 1975a, 1975b, 1977; Scribner and Cole, 1973). In informal settings, people generally receive knowledge that is relevant to the present context; they therefore better understand its potential significance. In formal educational contexts, however, we frequently learn information without understanding its potential significance. For example, we may not be explicitly told how concepts can be applied to particular situations and areas of knowledge. Effective learners may spontaneously think of potential applications on their own; others may fail to do so. In order to learn new information effectively, one may therefore need guidance to consider the types of situations in which this information might be used.

The preceding arguments have some important implications. For example, many educators note that some children seem dull within the classroom yet sharp and intelligent outside the classroom. To paraphrase Holt (1964), these children seem to disconnect their intelligence from their schooling (see Holt, pp. 25–26). The work by Owings and colleagues with less successful fifth-graders (see Chapter 6, Section 4) is a potential example of this point. These children did not seem to evaluate spontaneously the degree to which information (like "The sleepy boy ate the hamburger") was congruent with their existing knowledge. They therefore failed to study longer for the materials that were harder to learn.

Assume, however, that one talks with these children about their everyday lives and activities. If someone said, "When you are sleepy, I'll bet you go home and eat a hamburger," the children would most surely have viewed this statement as strange. Procedures that prompt students to relate information to everyday social contexts and activities may therefore be important. As an illustration, recall Olson's study (Chapter 7, Section 3) that assessed children's abilities to detect similarities in meaning between sentences like "John hit Mary" and "Mary was hit by John." When the information was made relevant to the children's everyday life (they might be told that John and Mary were real classmates), performance greatly improved. Similarly, consider once again how everyday social contexts affect our criteria for assessing comprehension. When "Bill has a red car" was uttered in a social context, the comprehender performed very sophisticated activities in order to understand what was meant (Chapter 6, Section 4). The experiments by Brewer and Harris (Chapter 5, Section 3) are also important in this context. When students realized that the experimenter was talking about events relevant to their immediate environment, utterances like "Asparagus grows wild in this county" were understood more precisely and were accurately recalled. Finally, consider once again Willis's intervention procedure. She worked with the child in the context of a mini-environment with which the child had become familiar. This environment was simplified but not impoverished. In this meaningful cognitive–social context, the boy could presumably better understand the significance of the information he received.

Note once again, however, that the problem of learning to learn involves more than simply providing people with socially relevant contexts. Ultimately, people need to learn to learn in formal educational settings as well. As suggested earlier, many effective learners seem to generate their own relevant personal contexts ("Let's see, what can this story about Indians' houses tell me about relationships among life styles, geographical regions, and dwellings?" "How would I explain this complicated idea to a third-grader?"). Placing people in roles in which they must use school-learned concepts in give-and-take situations may facilitate both the development of skills and schemata and the development of criteria for guiding learning and comprehension activities (see Chapter 7, Section 4). Helping people become aware of differences in what they do in formal and informal contexts may be important as well. At present, these ideas are only hypotheses. What seems certain, however, is the need for more precise theorizing and research.

Concluding Thoughts

The problem of learning to learn is just beginning to be tackled by cognitive scientists. It is a very complex problem, but it is no less challenging than it is complex. It is hoped that the reader will be motivated to explore additional literature on the subject. The work of Brown, Campione, and colleagues (e.g., Brown, 1977a, 1977b, 1978;

Campione and Brown, in press) is excellent. Whimbey's book *Intelligence Can Be Taught* (1976) includes provocative ideas and many references. Bloom and Lahey (1978) provide an outstanding discussion of language intervention programs. The approach adopted by Feuerstein (in press, a, b) is very promising as well. Numerous studies involving learning strategies and problem solving skills are also extremely relevant to the problem of learning to learn (see especially, Reif, Larkin, and Brackett, 1976). There is a need to consolidate information from various literatures, to encourage communication across various fields.

The notion of interdisciplinary communication is particularly important; for the problem of learning to learn is not simply a problem for cognitive psychology, linguistics, or computer science. An increased understanding of the problem requires coordination among additional disciplines and subdisciplines as well. First and foremost, learning to learn is a *developmental* problem. Static models of how skilled adults perform certain tasks can be very helpful, but they don't necessarily clarify processes by which people develop new concepts and skills (e.g., see Bransford and Franks, 1976; Bransford, Franks, and Nitsch, 1977; Brown, 1978; Neisser, 1976).

An attempt to understand the problem of learning to learn also requires inputs from educational psychology, social psychology, clinical psychology, and related disciplines. For example, people's feelings of self-worth can affect learning and vice versa (see Chapter 6, Section 4). What is known about ways to deal with problems like this? Similarly, the social context of one's everyday interactions may have important effects on knowledge acquisition as well as on the development of criteria for assessing comprehension and mastery. There may be important differences in the degree to which people experience the types of challenging everyday conversations and interactions that enhance school-related comprehension skills. Furthermore, the general content of conversations may differ. Thus, some families and peer groups may spend much time discussing the types of concepts taught in school-related settings; others may focus on different sorts of topics. Processes affecting cognitive development surely are not confined to formal educational settings. Indeed, everyday social interactions are probably much more important than school per se. An analysis of learning to learn therefore necessitates a concern with the social environments in which people live and act (see especially McDermott, 1974).

An emphasis on learning to learn also represents a potential challenge to capacity theories of intelligence. In this context, it is interesting to note that the concept of learning to learn is most frequently discussed with reference to Harlow's (1949) work on "learning sets" in monkeys. This research was very important, because it illustrated that monkeys could learn to learn. Note, however, that subsequent researchers used the ability to form learning sets as a criterion for attempting to measure the intellectual *capacity* of various species (e.g., see Tarpy and Mayer, 1978, pp. 170–74). The static concept of capacity still dominated people's thinking. The challenge of work on *cognitive therapy* (Whimbey, 1976) or *cognitive modifiability* (Feuerstein, in press, a, b) is that it represents a potential alternative to notions of static capacity. A momentary assessment of someone's intelligence involves measurements at one point in development. The possibility of significantly *modifying* development is an exciting idea to pursue.

There have, of course, been attempts to modify intelligence. Operation Head Start is a case in point. More often than not, the beneficial effects of such programs have been only temporary (e.g., see Whimbey, 1976). However, both Whimbey (1976) and Feuertein (in press, a, b) argue that such programs have been based on naive ideas regarding development. For example, an emphasis on enriched environments is important yet insufficient. Unless people can be helped to develop the skills necessary to learn *from* experiences, exposure to enriched environments may do little good. The failure of previous attempts at cognitive modifiability should therefore not be taken as evidence against the potential importance of the concept. However, these failures should provide a challenge for more precise theorizing and research.

References

Anderson, J. R. 1976. *Language, memory, and thought.* Hillsdale, N.J.: Lawrence Erlbaum Associates.

———. 1978. Arguments concerning representations for mental imagery. *Psychological Review* 85: 249–277.

Anderson, J. R., and Bower, G. H. 1973. *Human associative memory.* Washington, D.C.: Hemisphere Press.

Anderson, J. R., and Reder, L. M. 1978. An elaborative processing explanation of depth of processing. In L. S. Cermak and F. I. M. Craik (eds.), *Levels of processing and human memory.* Hillsdale, N.J.: Lawrence Erlbaum Associates.

Anderson, R. C. 1977. The notion of schemata and the educational enterprise. In R. C. Anderson, R. J. Spiro, and W. E. Montague (eds.), *Schooling and the acquisition of knowledge.* Hillsdale, N.J.: Lawrence Erlbaum Associates.

Anderson, R. C., and Biddle, W. B. 1975. On asking people questions about what they are reading. In G. Bower (ed.), *Psychology of learning and motivation,* vol. 9. New York: Academic Press.

Anderson, R. C., Goldberg, S. R., and Hidde, J. L. 1971. Meaningful processing of sentences. *Journal of Educational Psychology* 62: 395–99.

Anderson, R. C., and Kulhavy, R. W. 1972. Learning concepts from definitions. *American Educational Research Journal* 9: 385–90.

Anderson, R. C., and McGaw, B. 1973. On the representation of the meanings of general terms. *Journal of Experimental Psychology* 101: 301–6.

Anderson, R. C., and Ortony, A. 1975. On putting apples into bottles—a problem of polysemy. *Cognitive Psychology* 7: 167–80.

Anderson, R. C., Pichert, J. W., Goetz, E. T., Schallert, D. L., Stevens, K. V., and Trollip, S. R. 1976. Instantiation of general terms. *Journal of Verbal Learning and Verbal Behavior* 15: 667–79.

Anthony, W. S. 1973. Learning to discover rules by discovery. *Journal of Educational Psychology* 64: 325–28.

Aristotle. *On memory and recollection.* Appendix to *On the soul, Parva naturalia, On breath,* trans. W. S. Hett. Cambridge: Harvard University Press, 1964.

Atkinson, R. C., and Shiffrin, R. M. 1968. Human memory: A proposed system and its control processes. In K. W. Spence and J. T. Spence (eds.), *The psychology of learning and motivation,* vol. 2. New York: Academic Press.

———. 1971. The control processes of short-term memory. *Scientific American* 224: 82–90.

Auble, P. M., and Franks, J. J. 1978. The effects of effort toward comprehension on recall. *Memory and Cognition* 6: 20–25.

Ausubel, D. P. 1963. *The psychology of meaningful verbal learning.* New York: Grune and Stratton.

———. 1968. *Educational psychology: A cognitive view.* New York: Holt, Rinehart and Winston.

Baddeley, A. D. 1978. The trouble with levels: A reexamination of Craik and Lockhart's framework for memory research. *Psychological Review* 85: 139–52.

Bahrick, H. P. 1970. Two-phase model for prompted recall. *Psychological Review* 77: 215–22.

Bandura, A. 1977. *Social learning theory.* Englewood Cliffs, N.J.: Prentice-Hall.

Barclay, J. R. 1973. The role of comprehension in remembering sentences. *Cognitive Psychology* 4:229–54.

Barclay, J. R., Bransford, J. D., Franks, J. J., McCarrell, N. S., and Nitsch, K. E. 1974. Comprehension and semantic flexibility. *Journal of Verbal Learning and Verbal Behavior* 13: 471–81.

Barthel, J. 1977. *A death in Canaan.* N.Y.: Dell.

Bartlett, F. C. 1932. *Remembering: A study in experimental and social psychology.* London: Cambridge University Press.

Bates, E. 1976. *Language and context: The acquisition of pragmatics.* New York: Academic Press.

Begg, I., and Paivio, A. 1969. Concreteness and imagery in sentence meaning. *Journal of Verbal Learning and Verbal Behavior* 8: 821–27.

Belmont, J. M., and Butterfield, E. C. 1971. Learning strategies as determinants of memory deficiencies. *Cognitive Psychology* 2: 411–20.

Berlyne, D. E. 1965. *Structure and direction in thinking.* New York: Wiley.

Bernbach, H. A. 1967. Decision processes in memory. *Psychological Review* 74: 462–80.

Bernstein, N. 1967. *The co-ordination and regulation of movements.* Oxford: Pergamon Press.

Bloom, B. S. 1976. *Human characteristics and school learning.* New York: McGraw-Hill.

Bloom, L. 1970. *Language development: Form and function in emerging grammars.* Cambridge, Mass.: MIT Press.

―――. 1974. Talking, understanding, and thinking. In R. L. Schiefelbusch and L. L. Lloyd (eds.), *Language perspectives: Acquisition, retardation, and intervention.* Baltimore, Md.: University Park.

―――. 1978. The integration of form, content and use in language development. In J. F. Kavanagh and W. Strange (eds.), *Speech and language in the laboratory, school and clinic.* Cambridge, Mass.: MIT Press.

Bloom, L., Hood, L., and Lightbown, P. 1974. Imitation in language development: If, when, and why. *Cognitive Psychology* 6: 380–420.

Bloom, L., and Lahey, M. 1978. *Language development and language disorders.* New York: Halsted Press.

Bloom, L., Lightbown, P., and Hood, L. 1975. *Structure and variation in child language.* Monographs of the Society for Research in Child Development, vol. 40, no. 2 (whole no. 160).

Blumenthal, A. L. 1970. *Language and psychology.* New York: Wiley.

Blumenthal, A., and Boakes, R. 1967. Prompted recall of sentences: A further study. *Journal of Verbal Learning and Verbal Behavior* 6: 674–75.

Bobrow, S. A., and Bower, G. H. 1969. Comprehension and recall of sentences. *Journal of Experimental Psychology* 80: 455–61.

Bohm, D. 1969. Further remarks on order. In C. H. Waddington (ed.), *Towards a theoretical biology,* vol. 2. Chicago: Aldine.

Boring, E. G. 1950. *A history of experimental psychology.* New York: Appleton-Century-Crofts.

Bourne, L. E., Jr. 1970. Knowing and using concepts. *Psychological Review* 77: 546–56.

Bousfield, W. A. 1953. The occurrence of clustering in the recall of randomly arranged associates. *Journal of General Psychology* 49: 229–40.

Bousfield, W. A., and Cohen, B. M. 1955. The occurrence of clustering in the recall of randomly arranged words of different frequencies of usage. *Journal of Genetic Psychology* 52: 83–95.

Bower, G. H. 1976. Experiments on story understanding and recall. *Quarterly Journal of Experimental Psychology* 28: 211–534.

Bower, G. H., and Clark, M. C. 1969. Narrative stories as mediators for serial learning. *Psychonomic Science* 14: 181–82.

Bower, G. H., Clark, M. C., Lesgold, A. M., and Winzenz, D. 1969. Hierarchical retrieval schemes in recall of categorized word lists. *Journal of Verbal Learning and Verbal Behavior* 8: 323–43.

Bower, G. H., and Karlin, M. B. 1974. Depth of processing pictures of faces and recognition memory. *Journal of Experimental Psychology* 103: 751–57.

Bower, G. H., and Trabasso, T. R. 1963. Reversals prior to solution in concept identification. *Journal of Experimental Psychology* 66: 409–18.

————. 1964. Concept identification. In R. C. Atkinson (ed.), *Studies in mathematical psychology.* Stanford, Calif.: Stanford University Press.

Bransford, J. D., Barclay, J. R., and Franks, J. J. 1972. Sentence memory: A constructive versus interpretive approach. *Cognitive Psychology* 3: 193–209.

Bransford, J. D., and Franks, J. J. 1971. The abstraction of linguistic ideas. *Cognitive Psychology* 2: 331–50.

————. 1972. The abstraction of linguistic ideas: A review. *Cognition: International Journal of Cognitive Psychology* 1: 211–49.

————. 1976. Toward a framework for understanding learning. In G. H. Bower (ed.), *The psychology of learning and motivation,* vol. 10. New York: Academic Press.

Bransford, J. D., Franks, J. J., Morris, C. D., and Stein, B. S. 1978. Some general constraints on learning and memory research. In L. S. Cermak and F. I. M. Craik (eds.), *Levels of processing and human memory.* Hillsdale, N.J.: Lawrence Erlbaum Associates.

Bransford, J. D., and Johnson, M. K. 1972. Contextual prerequisites for understanding: Some investigations of comprehension and recall. *Journal of Verbal Learning and Verbal Behavior* 11: 717–26.

————. 1973. Considerations of some problems of comprehension. In W. G. Chase (ed.), *Visual information processing.* New York: Academic Press.

Bransford, J. D., and McCarrell, N. S. 1974. A sketch of a cognitive approach to comprehension. In W. Weimer and D. S. Palermo (eds.), *Cognition and the symbolic processes.* Hillsdale, N.J.: Lawrence Erlbaum Associates.

Bransford, J. D., McCarrell, N. S., Franks, J. J., and Nitsch, K. E. 1977. Toward unexplaining memory. In R. E. Shaw and J. D. Bransford (eds.), *Perceiving, acting and knowing: Toward an ecological psychology.* Hillsdale, N.J.: Lawrence Erlbaum Associates.

Bransford, J. D., McCarrell, N. S., and Nitsch, K. E. 1976. Contexte, compréhension et flexibilité sémantique: Quelques implications théoriques et méthodologiques. In S. Ehrlich and E. Tulving (eds.), *La mémoire sémantique.* Paris: Bulletin de Psychologie.

Bransford, J. D., and Nitsch, K. E. 1978. Coming to understand things we could not previously understand. In J. F. Kavanagh and W. Strange (eds.), *Speech and language in the laboratory, school and clinic.* Cambridge, Mass.: MIT Press.

Bransford, J. D., Nitsch, K. E., and Franks, J. J. 1977. Schooling and the facilitation of knowing. In R. C. Anderson, R. J. Spiro, and W. E. Montague (eds.), *Schooling and the acquisition of knowledge.* Hillsdale, N.J.: Lawrence Erlbaum Associates.

Brewer, W. F. 1974. The problem of meaning and the interrelations of the higher mental processes. In W. Weimer and D. S. Palermo (eds.), *Cognition and the symbolic processes.* Hillsdale, N.J.: Lawrence Erlbaum Associates.

Brewer, W. F., and Harris, R. J. 1974. Memory for deictic elements in sentences. *Journal of Verbal Learning and Verbal Behavior* 13: 321–27.

Broadbent, D. E. 1958. *Perception and communication.* London: Pergamon Press.

Brown, A. L. 1977a. Development, schooling and the acquisition of knowledge about knowledge. In R. C. Anderson, R. J. Spiro, and W. E. Montague (eds.), *Schooling and the acquisition of knowledge.* Hillsdale, N.J.: Lawrence Erlbaum Associates.

———. 1977b. Knowing when, where, and how to remember: A problem of metacognition. In R. Glaser (ed.), *Advances in instructional psychology.* Hillsdale, N.J.: Lawrence Erlbaum Associates.

———. 1978. Theories of memory and the problems of development: Activity, growth and knowledge. In L. S. Cermak and F. I. M. Craik (eds.), *Levels of processing and human memory.* Hillsdale, N.J.: Lawrence Erlbaum Associates.

Brown, A. L., Campione, J. C., and Barclay, C. R. 1978. Training self-checking routines for estimating test readiness: Generalization from list learning to prose recall. Unpublished manuscript, University of Illinois.

Brown, A. L., Campione, J. C., Bray, N. W., and Wilcox, B. L. 1973. Keeping track of changing variables: Effects of rehearsal training and rehearsal prevention in normal and retarded adolescents. *Journal of Experimental Psychology* 101: 123–31.

Brown, A. L. and DeLoache, J. S. 1978. Skills, plans, and self-regulation. In R. Siegler (ed.), *Children's thinking: What develops.* Hillsdale, N.J.: Lawrence Erlbaum Associates.

Brown, R., and McNeill, D. 1966. The "tip of the tongue" phenomenon. *Journal of Verbal Learning and Verbal Behavior* 5: 325–37.

Bruce, D. J. 1958. The effect of listeners' anticipations on the intelligibility of heard speech. *Language and Speech* 1: 79–97.

Bruce, D. J., Evans, C. R., Fenwick, P. B. C., and Spencer, V. 1970. Effect of presenting novel verbal material during slow-wave sleep. *Nature* 225: 873–74.

Bruner, J. S. 1959. Learning and thinking. *Harvard Educational Review* 29: 184–88.

———. 1968. *Processes of cognitive growth: Infancy.* Worcester, Mass.: Clark University Press.

Bruner, J. S., Goodnow, J., and Austin, G. A. 1956. *A study of thinking.* New York: Wiley.

Buhler, K. 1908. Tatsachen und Probleme zu einer Psychologie der Denkuorgange. III. Ueber Gedankenerinnerungen. *Arch. f.d. ges. Psychol.*

Campione, J. C., and Brown, A. L. In press. Toward a theory of intelligence: Contributions from research with retarded children. *Intelligence.*

Carmichael, L. L., Hogan, H. P., and Walter, A. A. 1932. An experimental study of the effect of language on the reproduction of visually perceived form. *Journal of Experimental Psychology* 15: 73–86.

Carroll, J. B. 1963. A model of school learning. *Teachers College Record* 64: 723–33.

Carroll, J. B., and White, M. N. 1973. Age-of-acquisition norms for 220 picturable nouns. *Journal of Verbal Learning and Verbal Behavior* 12: 563–76.

Cassirer, E. 1923. *Substance and function.* Chicago: Open Court.

Cermak, L. S. 1976. *Improving your memory*. New York: McGraw-Hill.

———. 1978. Amnesic patients' level of processing. In L. S. Cermak and F. I. M. Craik (eds.), *Levels of processing and human memory*. Hillsdale, N.J.: Lawrence Erlbaum Associates.

Chafe, W. L. 1972. Discourse structure and human knowledge. In J. B. Carroll and R. O. Freedle (eds.), *Language comprehension and the acquisition of knowledge*. Washington, D.C.: V. H. Winston and Sons.

Chapman, R. S. 1978. Comprehension strategies in children. In J. Kavanagh and W. Strange (eds.), *Speech and language in the laboratory, school and clinic*. Cambridge, Mass.: MIT Press.

Charniak, E. 1972. Toward a model of children's story comprehension. Doctoral dissertation, Massachusetts Institute of Technology. (Also MIT Artificial Intellignce Laboratory Tech. Rep. A1-TR, 266, 1972.)

Charniak, E. 1977. A framed painting: The representation of a common sense knowledge fragment. *Cognitive Science* 1: 355–94.

Chase, W. G., and Simon, H. A. 1973. The mind's eye in chess. In W. Chase (ed.), *Visual information processing*. New York: Academic Press.

Cherry, E. C. 1953. Some experiments on the recognition of speech with one and two ears. *Journal of the Acoustical Society of America* 25: 975–79.

Chi, M. T. H. 1976. Short-term memory limitations in children: Capacity or processing deficits? *Memory and Cognition* 4: 559–72.

Chomsky, N. 1957. *Syntactic structures*. The Hague: Mouton.

———. 1965. *Aspects of the theory of syntax*. Cambridge, Mass.: MIT Press.

———. 1972. *Language and mind*. Enlarged edition. New York: Harcourt Brace Jovanovich.

———. 1975. *Reflections on language*. New York: Pantheon.

Christian, J., Bickley, W., Tarka, M., and Clayton, K. 1978. Measures of free recall of 900 English nouns: Correlations with imagery, concreteness, meaningfulness, and frequency. *Memory and Cognition* 6: 379–90.

Cieutat, V. J., Stockwell, F. E., and Noble, C. E. 1958. The interaction of ability and amount of practice with stimulus and response meaningfulness (m, m') in paired-associate learning. *Journal of Experimental Psychology* 56: 193–202.

Clark, H. H., and Clark, E. V. 1977. *Psychology and language: An introduction to psycholinguistics*. New York: Harcourt Brace Jovanovich.

Clayton, K. N. 1978. An analysis of remembering. Unpublished manuscript, Vanderbilt University.

Cole, M., and Scribner, S. 1974. *Culture and thought: A psychological introduction*. New York: Wiley.

———. 1975a. Theorizing about socialization of cognition. *Ethos* 3: 249–68.

————. 1975b. Developmental theories applied to cross-cultural cognitive research. Paper presented at the New York Academy of Sciences, October 1975.

————. 1977. Cross-cultural studies of memory and cognition. In R. V. Kail, Jr., and J. W. Hagen (eds.), *Perspectives on the development of memory and cognition.* Hillsdale, N.J.: Lawrence Erlbaum Associates.

Coleman, E. B. 1964. The comprehensibility of several grammatical transformations. *Journal of Applied Psychology* 48: 186–90.

Coles, R. 1970. *Uprooted children: The early life of migrant farm workers.* New York: Harper & Row.

Collins, A. M., and Loftus, E. F. 1975. A spreading-activation theory of semantic processing. *Psychological Review* 82: 407–28.

Collins, A. M., and Quillian, M. R. 1969. Retrieval time from semantic memory. *Journal of Verbal Learning and Verbal Behavior* 8: 240–47.

————. 1970. Facilitating retrieval from semantic memory: The effect of repeating part of an interference. *Acta Psychologica* 33: 304–14.

————. 1972. How to make a language user. In E. Tulving and W. Donaldson (eds.), *Organization of memory.* New York: Academic Press.

Conrad, C. 1972. Cognitive economy in semantic memory. *Journal of Experimental Psychology* 92: 149–54.

Conrad, R. 1964. Acoustic confusions in immediate memory. *British Journal of Psychology* 55: 75–83.

Cooper, L. A., and Shepard, R. N. 1973. Chronometric studies of the rotation of mental images. In W. G. Chase (ed.), *Visual information processing.* New York: Academic Press.

Craik, F. I. M., and Lockhart, R. S. 1972. Levels of processing: A framework for memory research. *Journal of Verbal Learning and Verbal Behavior* 11: 671–84.

Craik, F. I. M., and Tulving, E. 1975. Depth of processing and the retention of words in episodic memory. *Journal of Experimental Psychology: General* 104: 268–94.

Craik, F. I. M., and Watkins, M. J. 1973. The role of rehearsal in short-term memory. *Journal of Verbal Learning and Verbal Behavior* 12: 599–607.

Danner, F. W. 1976. Children's understanding of intersentence organization in the recall of short descriptive passages. *Journal of Educational Psychology* 2: 174–83.

deCharms, R. 1972. Personal causation training in the schools. *Journal of Applied Psychology* 2: 95–113.

————. 1976. *Enhancing motivation: Change in the classroom.* New York: Irvington.

deGroot, A. D. 1965. *Thought and choice in chess.* The Hague: Mouton.

Dewey, J. 1963. *How we think.* Portions published in R. M. Hutchins and M. J. Adler (eds.), *Gateway to the great books.* Vol. 10. Chicago: Encyclopedia Britannica, Inc. (Originally published by Heath, 1933, 1961.)

Dooling, D. J., and Lachman, R. 1971. Effects of comprehension on retention of prose. *Journal of Experimental Psychology* 88: 216–22.

Ebbinghaus, H. 1885. *Uber das Gedächtnis*. Leipzig: Duncker & Humbolt. (In English: *Memory*. Trans. H. A. Ruger and C. E. Bussenius. New York: Teachers College, 1913; Dover, 1964.)

―――. 1902. *Grundzüge der Psychologie*. Leipzig: Viet & Co.

Farnham-Diggory, S. 1978. *Learning disabilities.*Cambridge, Mass.: Harvard University Press.

Feuerstein, R. In press, a. *The dynamic assessment of retarded performers*. Baltimore, Md.: University Park.

―――. In press, b. *Instrumental enrichment*. Baltimore, Md.: University Park.

Fillmore, C. J. 1966. Deictic categories in the semantics of "come." *Foundations of Language* 2: 219–27.

―――. 1968. The case for case. In E. Bach and R. T. Harms (eds.), *Universals in linguistic theory*. New York: Holt, Rinehart and Winston.

―――. 1971a. Some problems for case grammar. In R. J. O'Brien (ed.), *Georgetown University round table on languages and linguistics*. Washington, D.C.: Georgetown University Press.

―――. 1971b. Verbs of judging: An exercise in semantic description. In C. J. Fillmore and D. T. Langendoen (eds.), *Studies in linguistic semantics*. New York: Holt, Rinehart and Winston.

Fisher, R. P., and Craik, F. I. M. 1977. The interaction between encoding and retrieval operations in cued recall. *Journal of Experimental Psychology: Human Learning and Memory* 3: 701–11.

Flagg, P. W. 1975. Semantic integration in sentence memory. Ph.D. dissertation, Dartmouth College.

―――. 1976. Semantic integration in sentence memory. *Journal of Verbal Learning and Verbal Behavior* 15: 491–504.

Flavell, J. H., and Wellman, H. M. 1977. Metamemory. In R. V. Kail, Jr., and J. W. Hagen (eds.), *Perspectives on the development of memory and cognition*. Hillsdale, N.J.: Lawrence Erlbaum Associates.

Flesh, Rudolf F. 1945. The science of making sense. *American Mercury* 60: 194–97.

Flexser, A. J., and Tulving, E. 1978. Retrieval independence in recognition and recall. *Psychological Review* 85: 153–71.

Foss, D. J., and Hakes, D. T. 1978. *Psycholinguistics: An introduction to the psychology of language*. Englewood Cliffs, N.J.: Prentice-Hall.

Fraisse, P. 1963. *The psychology of time*. New York: Harper & Row.

Franks, J. J., and Bransford, J. D. 1971. The abstraction of visual patterns. *Journal of Experimental Psychology* 90: 65–74.

————. 1972. The acquisition of abstract ideas. *Journal of Verbal Learning and Verbal Behavior* 11: 311–15.

————. 1974a. A brief note on linguistic integration. *Journal of Verbal Learning and Verbal Behavior* 13: 217–19.

————. 1974b. Memory for syntactic form as a function of semantic context. *Journal of Experimental Psychology* 103: 1037–39.

Frase, L. T. 1972. Maintenance and control in the acquisition of knowledge from written materials. In J. B. Carroll and R. O. Freedle (eds.), *Language comprehension and the acquisition of knowledge*. Washington, D.C.: V. H. Winston and Sons.

Frase, L. T., and Kreitzberg, V. S. 1975. Effect of topical and indirect learning directions on prose recall. *Journal of Educational Psychology* 67: 320–24.

Freedman, J. L., and Loftus, E. F. 1971. Retrieval of words from long-term memory. *Journal of Verbal Learning and Verbal Behavior* 10: 107–15.

Friedman, A. In press. Memorial comparisons without the "mind's eye." *Journal of Verbal Learning and Verbal Behavior*.

Gagne, R. M. 1970. *The conditions of learning*. Rev. ed. New York: Holt, Rinehart and Winston.

Gentner, D. 1975. Evidence for the psychological reality of semantic components: The verbs of possession. In D. A. Norman, D. E. Rumelhart, and the LNR Research Group, *Explorations in cognition*. San Francisco: W. H. Freeman.

Gibson, J. J. 1966. *The senses considered as perceptual systems*. Boston: Houghton Mifflin.

Gibson, J. J., and Gibson, E. J. 1955. Perceptual learning: Differentiation or enrichment? *Psychological Review* 62: 32–41.

Glucksberg, S., and Cohen, G. N., Jr. 1970. Memory for nonattended auditory material. *Cognitive Psychology* 1: 149–56.

Glucksberg, S., and Danks, J. H. 1975. *Experimental psycholinguistics: An introduction*. Hillsdale, N.J.: Lawrence Erlbaum Associates.

Goldiamond, I., and Hawkins, W. F. 1958. Vixierversuch: The log relationship between word-frequency and recognition obtained in the absence of stimulus words. *Journal of Experimental Psychology* 56: 457–63.

Goldstein, A. G., and Chance, J. E. 1971. Visual recognition memory for complex configurations. *Perception and Psychophysics* 9: 237–41.

Gomulicki, B. R. 1956. Recall as an abstractive process. *Acta Psychologica* 12: 77–94.

Gorman, A. N. 1961. Recognition memory for names as a function of abstractness and frequency. *Journal of Experimental Psychology* 61: 23–29.

Gough, P. B. 1977. Word frequency and word recognition. Invited paper, Midwestern Psychological Association.

Griggs, R. A., and Keen, D. M. 1977. The role of test procedure in linguistic integration studies. *Memory and Cognition* 5: 685–89.

Gruber, G. R. 1971. *Reading interpretation in social studies, natural sciences and literature.* New York: Simon and Schuster.

Hall, J. F. 1954. Learning as a function of word frequency. *American Journal of Psychology* 67: 138–60.

Halliday, M. A. K. 1970. Language structure and language function. In J. Lyons (ed.), *New horizons in linguistics.* Baltimore, Md.: Penguin.

———. 1973. *Explorations in the function of language.* London: Edward Arnold.

Hannigan, M. L. 1976. The effects of frameworks on sentence perception and memory. Ph.D. dissertation, Vanderbilt University.

Harlow, H. F. 1949. The formation of learning sets. *Psychological Review* 56: 51–65.

Hart, J. T. 1967. Memory and memory monitoring processes. *Journal of Verbal Learning and Learning Behavior* 6: 685–91.

Haviland, S. E., and Clark, H. H. 1974. What's new? Acquiring new information as a process in comprehension. *Journal of Verbal Learning and Verbal Behavior* 13: 512–21.

Heidbreder, E. 1946. The attainment of concepts: I. Terminology and methodology. *Journal of General Psychology* 35: 173–89.

———. 1947. The attainment of concepts: III. The process. *Journal of General Psychology* 24: 93–108.

Hester, M. 1977. Visual attention and sensibility. In R. E. Shaw and J. D. Bransford (eds.), *Perceiving, acting and knowing: Toward an ecological psychology.* Hillsdale, N.J.: Lawrence Erlbaum Associates.

Higbee, K. L. 1977. *Your memory: How it works and how to improve it.* Englewood Cliffs, N.J.: Prentice-Hall.

Hilgard, E. R., and Bower, G. H. 1975. *Theories of learning.* 4th ed. New York: Appleton-Century-Crofts.

Hoffman, M. 1968. Child language. Master's thesis. McGill University, Department of Psychology.

Hogan, R. M., and Kintsch, W. 1971. Differential effects of study and test trials on long-term recognition and recall. *Journal of Verbal Learning and Verbal Behavior* 10: 562–67.

Holt, J. 1964. *How children fail.* New York: Dell.

Hughes, E. 1915. Musical memory in piano playing and piano study. *The Musical Quarterly* 1: 592–603.

Huttenlocher, J., and Burke, D. 1976. Why does memory span increase with age? *Cognitive Psychology* 8: 1–31.

Hyde, T. S., and Jenkins, J. J. 1969. Differential effects of incidental tasks on the organization of recall of a list of highly associated words. *Journal of Experimental Psychology* 82: 472–81.

Jacoby, L. L. 1974. The role of mental contiguity in memory: Registration and retrieval effects. *Journal of Verbal Learning and Verbal Behavior* 13: 483–96.

James, C. T., and Hillinger, M. L. 1977. The role of confusion in the semantic integration paradigm. *Journal of Verbal Learning and Verbal Behavior* 16: 711–21.

James, W. 1890. *The principles of psychology*. New York: Holt.

Jarvella, R. J. 1971. Syntactic processing of connected speech. *Journal of Verbal Learning and Verbal Behavior* 10: 409–16.

Jenkins, J. G., and Dallenbach, K. M. 1924. Oblivescence during sleep and waking. *American Journal of Psychology* 35: 605–12.

Jenkins, J. J. 1974a. Can we have a theory of meaningful memory? In R. L. Solso (ed.), *Theories in cognitive psychology: The Loyola symposium*. Hillsdale, N.J.: Lawrence Erlbaum Associates.

———. 1974b. Remember that old theory of memory? Well, forget it! *American Psychologist* 29: 785–95.

———. 1978. Four points to remember: A tetrahedral model of memory experiments. In L. S. Cermak and F. I. M. Craik (eds.), *Levels of processing and human memory*. Hillsdale, N.J.: Lawrence Erlbaum Associates.

Jenkins, J. J., Wald, J., and Pittenger, J. B. In press. Apprehending pictorial events: An instance of psychological cohesion. In C. W. Savage (ed.), *Minnesota Studies in the Philosophy of Science*, vol. 9. Minneapolis: University of Minnesota Press.

Jensen, A. R. 1970. A theory of primary and secondary familiar mental retardation. In N. R. Ellis (ed.), *International review of research in mental retardation*, vol. 4. New York: Academic Press.

———. 1972. *Genetics and education*. New York: Harper & Row.

Johnson, M. K., Bransford, J. D., and Solomon, S. 1973. Memory for tacit implications of sentences. *Journal of Experimental Psychology* 98: 203–5.

Johnson, M. K., Doll, T. J., Bransford, J. D., and Lapinski, R. 1974. Context effects in sentence memory. *Journal of Experimental Psychology* 103: 358–60.

Johnson, N. F. 1965. The psychological reality of phrase-structure rules. *Journal of Verbal Learning and Verbal Behavior* 4: 469–75.

Johnson, R. E. 1970. Recall of prose as a function of the structural importance of linguistic units. *Journal of Verbal Learning and Verbal Behavior* 9: 12–20.

Johnston, C. D., and Jenkins, J. J. 1971. Two more incidental tasks that differentially affect associative clustering in recall. *Journal of Experimental Psychology* 89: 92–95.

Johnston, W. A., and Heinz, S. P. 1974. It takes attention to pay attention. Paper presented at the meeting of the Psychonomic Society, Boston.

Kant, E. *Critique of pure reason*. 1st ed., 1781; 2nd ed., 1787. Trans. N. Kemp Smith. London: Macmillan, 1963.

Katz, J. J., and Fodor, J. A. 1963. The structure of semantic theory. *Language* 39: 170–210.

Katz, S., and Gruenewald, P. 1974. The abstraction of linguistic ideas in "meaningful" sentences. *Memory and Cognition* 2: 737–41.

Keeney, T. J., Cannizzo, S. R., and Flavell, J. H. 1967. Spontaneous and induced verbal rehearsal in a recall task. *Child Development* 38: 953–66.

Keppel, G., and Underwood, B. J. 1962. Proactive inhibition in short-term retention of single items. *Journal of Verbal Learning and Verbal Behavior* 1: 153–61.

Kinsbourne, M., and George, J. 1974. The mechanism of the word-frequency effect on recognition memory. *Journal of Verbal Learning and Verbal Behavior* 13: 63–69.

Kintsch, W. 1972. Notes on the structure of semantic memory. In E. Tulving, and W. Donaldson (eds.), *Organization of memory.* New York: Academic Press.

———. 1974. *The representation of meaning in memory.* Hillsdale, N.J.: Lawrence Erlbaum Associates.

———. 1976. Memory for prose. In C. N. Cofer (ed.), *The structure of human memory.* San Francisco: W. H. Freeman.

———. 1977. *Memory and cognition.* 2nd ed. New York: Wiley.

Kintsch, W., and Keenan, J. M. 1973. Reading rate as a function of the number of propositions in the base structure of sentences. *Cognitive Psychology* 5: 257–74.

Kirk, R. E. 1968. *Experimental design: Procedures for the behavioral sciences.* Belmont, Calif.: Brooks-Cole.

Klare, G. R. 1963. *The measurement of readability.* Ames, Iowa: Iowa State University Press.

Koh, S. D., Kayton, L., and Peterson, R. A. 1976. Affective encoding and consequent remembering in schizophrenic adults. *Journal of Abnormal Psychology* 85: 156–66.

Kolers, P. A. 1978. A pattern analyzing basis of recognition. In L. S. Cermak and F. I. M. Craik (eds.), *Levels of processing and human memory.* Hillsdale, N.J.: Lawrence Erlbaum Associates.

Kosslyn, S. M. 1973. Scanning visual images: Some structural implications. *Perception and Psychophysics* 14: 90–94.

———. 1975. Information representation in visual images. *Cognitive Psychology* 7: 341–70.

———. 1976. Can imagery be distinguished from other forms of internal representation? Evidence from studies of information retrieval time. *Memory and Cognition* 4: 291–97.

Kosslyn, S. M., Murphy, G. L., Bemesderfer, M. E., and Feinstein, K. J. 1977. Category and continuum in mental comparisons. *Journal of Experimental Psychology: General.*

Kosslyn, S. M., and Pomerantz, J. R. 1977. Imagery, propositions, and the form of internal representations. *Cognitive Psychology* 9: 52–76.

Kosslyn, S. M., and Schwartz, S. M. 1977. A data-driven simulation of visual imagery. *Cognitive Science* 1: 265–96.

Kronseder, C. In preparation. Active modes of acquisition (working title). Vanderbilt University.

Kucera, H., and Francis, W. N. 1967. *Computational analysis of present-day American English*. Providence, R.I.: Brown University Press.

LaBerge, D., and Samuels, S. J. 1974. Toward a theory of automatic information processing in reading. *Cognitive Psychology* 6: 293–323.

Labov, W. 1973. The boundaries of words and their meanings. In C. J. Bailey and R. W. Shuy (eds.), *New ways of analyzing variation in English*. Washington, D.C.: Georgetown University Press.

Lahey, M. 1978. Disruptions in the development and integration of form, content and use in language. In J. W. Kavanagh and W. Strange (eds.), *Speech and language in the laboratory, school and clinic*. Cambridge, Mass.: MIT Press.

Lakoff, G. 1973. Hedges: A study in meaning criteria and the logic of fuzzy concepts. In P. M. Peranteau, J. N. Levi, and G. C. Phares (eds.), *Papers from the eighth regional meeting, Chicago Linguistics Society*. Chicago: University of Chicago, Linguistics Department.

Lakoff, R. 1971. If's, and's, and but's about conjunction. In C. J. Fillmore and D. T. Langendoen (eds.), *Studies in linguistic semantics*. New York: Holt, Rinehart and Winston.

Langacker, R. W. 1967. *Language and its structure*. New York: Harcourt Brace Jovanovich.

Lashley, K. S. 1951. The problem of serial order in behavior. In L. A. Jeffress (ed.), *Cerebral mechanisms in behavior*. New York: Wiley.

Lee, T. S. 1978. Episodic and semantic contributions to transfer. Paper presented at Midwest Psychological Association.

Lessing, D. 1973. *The golden notebook*. New York: Bantam.

Levin, J. R. 1973. Inducing comprehension in poor readers: A test of a recent model. *Journal of Educational Psychology* 65: 19–24.

Levine, M. 1966. Hypothesis behavior by humans during discrimination learning. *Journal of Experimental Psychology* 71: 331–38.

———. 1971. Hypothesis theory and nonlearning despite ideal S-R reinforcement contingencies. *Psychological Review* 78: 130–40.

———. 1975. *Hypothesis testing: A cognitive theory of learning*. Hillsdale, N.J.: Lawrence Erlbaum Associates.

Light, L. L., and Carter-Sobell, L. 1970. Effects of changed semantic context on recognition memory. *Journal of Verbal Learning and Verbal Behavior* 9: 1–11.

Lockhart, R. S., and Murdock, B. B., Jr. 1970. Memory and the theory of signal detection. *Psychological Bulletin* 74: 100–109.

Loftus, E. F. 1973. Activation of semantic memory. *American Journal of Psychology* 86: 331–37.

———. 1975. Spreading activation within semantic categories: Comments on Rosch's "Cognitive representations of semantic categories." *Journal of Experimental Psychology: General* 104: 234–40.

Loftus, E. F., and Loftus, G. R. 1974. Changes in memory structure and retrieval over the course of instruction. *Journal of Educational Psychology* 66: 315–18.

Loftus, E. F., and Palmer, J. C. 1974. Reconstruction of automobile destruction: An example of the interaction between language and memory. *Journal of Verbal Learning and Verbal Behavior* 13: 585–89.

Loftus, G. R., and Loftus, E. F. 1974. The influence of one memory retrieval on a subsequent memory retrieval. *Memory & Cognition* 3: 467–71.

Lorayne, H., and Lucas, J. 1974. *The memory book.* New York: Stein and Day. (Also published in paperback by Ballantine, 1975.)

MacNamara, J. 1972. Cognitive basis of language learning in infants. *Psychological Review* 79: 1–13.

Mandler, G. 1967. Organization and memory. In K. W. Spence and J. T. Spence (eds.), *Psychology of learning and motivation,* vol. 1. New York: Academic Press.

Mandler, J. M. 1978. A code in the node: The use of a story schema in retrieval. *Discourse Processes* 1: 14–35.

Mandler, J. M., Johnson, N. S., and DeForest, M. 1976. A structural analysis of stories and their recall: From "once upon a time" to "happily ever after." *Center for Human Information Processing Technical Report,* April 1976.

Markman, E. M. 1977. Realizing that you don't understand: A preliminary investigation. *Child Development* 48: 986–92.

Marks, C. B., Doctorow, M. J., and Wittrock, M. C. 1974. Word frequency and reading comprehension. *Journal of Educational Research* 67: 259–62.

Massaro, D. W. 1975. *Understanding language.* New York: Academic Press.

Mayer, R. E. 1975. Different problem-solving competencies established in learning computer programming with and without meaningful models. *Journal of Educational Psychology* 67: 725–34.

Mayer, R. E., and Greeno, J. G. 1972. Structural differences between learning outcomes produced by different instructional methods. *Journal of Educational Psychology* 63: 165–73.

McCarrell, N. S., and Brooks, P. H. September, 1975. Mental retardation: comprehension gone awry. Research colloquium sponsored by the John F. Kennedy Center for Research on Education and Human Development, Nashville, Tennessee.

McDermott, R. P. 1974. Achieving school failure: An anthropological approach to illiteracy and social stratification. In G. Spindler (ed.), *Education and cultural process: Toward an anthropology of education.* New York: Holt, Rinehart and Winston.

McKay, D. G. 1973. Aspects of the theory of comprehension, memory and attention. *Quarterly Journal of Experimental Psychology* 25: 22–40.

McNeill, D. 1966. Developmental psycholinguistics. In F. Smith and G. A. Miller (eds.), *The genesis of language: A psycholinguistic approach*. Cambridge, Mass.: MIT Press.

Mead, M. 1964. *Continuities in cultural evolution*. New Haven: Yale University Press.

Melton, A. W. 1963. Implications of short-term memory for a general theory of memory. *Journal of Verbal Learning and Verbal Behavior* 2: 1–21.

Meyer, B. J. F. 1975. *The organization of prose and its effects on memory*. Amsterdam: North-Holland.

———. 1977. The structure of prose: Effects on learning and memory and implications for educational practice. In R. C. Anderson, R. J. Spiro, and W. E. Montague (eds.), *Schooling and the acquisition of knowledge*. Hillsdale, N.J.: Lawrence Erlbaum Associates.

Meyer, D. E. 1970. On the representation and retrieval of stored semantic information. *Cognitive Psychology* 1: 242–300.

Meyer, D. E., and Schvaneveldt, R. W. 1971. Facilitation in recognizing pairs of words: Evidence of a dependence between retrieval operations. *Journal of Experimental Psychology* 90: 227–34.

———. 1976. Meaning, memory structure, and mental processes. In C. N. Cofer (ed.), *The structure of human memory*. San Francisco: W. H. Freeman.

Meyer, D. E., Schvaneveldt, R. W., and Ruddy, M. G. 1974. Functions of graphemic and phonemic codes in visual word recognition. *Memory & Cognition* 2: 309–21.

Miller, G. A. 1956. The magical number seven, plus or minus two: Some limits on our capacity for processing information. *Psychological Review* 63: 81–97.

———. 1978. Lexical meaning. In J. F. Kavanagh and W. Strange (eds.), *Speech and language in the laboratory, school and clinic*. Cambridge, Mass.: MIT Press.

Miller, G. A., Heise, G. A., and Lichten, W. 1951. The intelligibility of speech as a function of the context of the test materials. *Journal of Experimental Psychology* 41: 329–35.

Miller, G. A., and Isard, S. 1963. Some perceptual consequences of linguistic rules. *Journal of Verbal Learning and Verbal Behavior* 2: 217–28.

Miller, G. A., and Selfridge, J. A. 1950. Verbal context and the recall of meaningful material. *American Journal of Psychology* 63: 176–85.

Minsky, M. 1975. A framework for representing knowledge. In P. H. Winston (ed.), *The psychology of computer vision*. New York: McGraw-Hill.

Moeser, S. D. 1976. Inferential reasoning in episodic memory. *Journal of Verbal Learning and Verbal Behavior* 15: 193–212.

Moray, N. 1959. Attention in dichotic listening: Affective cues and the influence of instructions. *Quarterly Journal of Experimental Psychology* 11: 56–60.

Morris, C. D., Bransford, J. D., and Franks, J. J. 1977. Levels of processing versus transfer appropriate processing. *Journal of Verbal Learning and Verbal Behavior* 16: 519–33.

Morris, C. D., Stein, B. S., and Bransford, J. D. In press. Prerequisites for the effective utilization of knowledge in text understanding. *Journal of Experimental Psychology: Human Learning and Memory*.

Murdock, B. B., Jr. 1961. The retention of individual items. *Journal of Experimental Psychology* 62: 618–25.

Neisser, U. 1967. *Cognitive psychology*. New York: Appleton-Century-Crofts.

———. 1976. General, academic and artificial intelligence. In L. B. Resnick (ed.), *The nature of intelligence*. Hillsdale, N.J.: Lawrence Erlbaum Associates.

Nelson, K. 1974. Concept, word and sentence: Interrelations in acquisition and development. *Psychological Review* 81: 267–85.

———. 1977. Cognitive development and the acquisition of concepts. In R. C. Anderson, R. J. Spiro, and W. E. Montague (eds.), *Schooling and the acquisition of knowledge*. Hillsdale, N.J.: Lawrence Erlbaum Associates.

Newell, A., and Simon, H. A. 1972. *Human problem solving*. Englewood Cliffs, N.J.: Prentice-Hall.

Nitsch, K. E. 1977. Structuring decontextualized forms of knowledge. Ph.D. dissertation, Vanderbilt University.

Noble, C. E. 1952. An analysis of meaning. *Psychological Review* 59: 421–30.

Noble, C. E., and McNeely, D. A. 1957. The role of meaningfulness (m) in paired-associate verbal learning. *Journal of Experimental Psychology* 53: 16–22.

Norman, D. A. 1969. Memory while shadowing. *Quarterly Journal of Experimental Psychology* 21: 85–93.

———. 1976. *Memory and attention: An introduction to human information processing*. 2nd ed. New York: Wiley.

Norman, D. A., and Bobrow, D. G. 1975. On data-limited and resource-limited processes. *Cognitive Psychology* 7: 44–64.

Norman, D. A., and Rumelhart, D. E. 1975. *Explorations in cognition*. San Francisco: W. H. Freeman.

Novak, J. N. 1977. *A theory of education*. New York: Cornell University Press.

Odom, R. D., Astor, E. C., and Cunningham, J. G. 1975. Effects of perceptual salience on the matrix task performance of four- and six-year-old children. *Child Development* 46: 758–62.

Odom, R. D., and Mumbauer, C. C. 1971. Dimensional salience and identification of the relevant dimension in problem solving. *Developmental Psychology* 4: 135–40.

Olson, D. R. 1974. Towards a theory of instructional means. Invited address presented to the American Educational Research Association, Chicago, April 1974.

————. 1977. The languages of instruction: On the literate bias of schooling. In R. C. Anderson, R. J. Spiro, and W. E. Montague (eds.), *Schooling and the acquisition of knowledge*. Hillsdale, N.J.: Lawrence Erlbaum Associates.

Ortony, A. 1978. Remembering, understanding, and representation. *Cognitive Science* 2: 53–69.

Osgood, C. E. 1971. Where do sentences come from? In D. D. Steinberg and L. A. Jakobovitz (eds.), *Semantics: An interdisciplinary reader in philosophy, linguistics, and psychology*. London: Cambridge University Press.

Owings, R. A., Petersen, G., Bransford, J. D., Morris, C. D., and Stein, B. S. In preparation. Some differences between successful and less successful fifth graders: Detecting and coping with task difficulty.

Paivio, A. 1971. *Imagery and verbal processes*. New York: Holt, Rinehart and Winston.

————. 1974. Language and knowledge of the world. *Educational Researcher* 3: 5–12.

————. 1975. Perceptual comparisons through the mind's eye. *Memory and Cognition* 3: 635–47.

————. 1976. Images, propositions, and knowledge. In J. M. Nicholas (ed.), *Images, perception, and knowledge*. The Western Ontario Series in the Philosophy of Science, vol. 8. Hingham, Mass.: Reidel Publishing Co.

Paivio, A., and Csapo, K. 1973. Picture superiority in free recall: Imagery or dual coding? *Cognitive Psychology* 5: 176–206.

Paivio, A., and Smythe, P. C. 1971. Word imagery, frequency, and meaningfulness in short-term memory. *Psychonomic Science* 22: 333–35.

Paivio, A., Smythe, P. C., and Yuille, J. C. 1968. Imagery versus meaningfulness of nouns in paired-associate learning. *Canadian Journal of Psychology* 22: 427–41.

Paivio, A., Yuille, J. C., and Madigan, S. A. 1968. Concreteness, imagery, and meaningfulness values for 925 nouns. *Journal of Experimental Psychology Monograph Supplement* 76: 1–25.

Palermo, D. S. 1978. *Psychology of language*. Glenview, Ill.: Scott, Foresman.

Pearson, D. P. 1974. The effects of grammatical complexity on children's comprehension, recall, and conception of certain semantic relations. *Reading Research Quarterly* 10: 155–92.

Perfetti, C. A., and Goldman, S. R. 1976. Discourse memory and reading comprehension skill. *Journal of Verbal Learning and Verbal Behavior* 15: 33–42.

Perfetti, C. A., and Lesgold, A. M. 1977. Discourse comprehension and sources of individual differences. In M. Just and P. Carpenter (eds.), *Cognitive processes in comprehension*. Hillsdale, N.J.: Lawrence Erlbaum Associates.

Peterson, L. R., and Peterson, M. J. 1959. Short-term retention of individual verbal items. *Journal of Experimental Psychology* 58: 193–98.

Piaget, J. 1952. *The origins of intelligence in children*. Trans. M. Cook. New York: International Universities Press.

————. 1969a. *The child's conception of time.* London: Routledge & Kegan Paul.

————. 1969b. *The psychology of intelligence.* Paterson, N.J.: Littlefield Adams.

————. 1970. *Science of education and the psychology of the child.* New York: Orion Press.

Piaget, J., and Inhelder, B. 1969. *The psychology of the child.* Trans. H. Weaver. New York: Basic.

Pichert, J. W., and Anderson, R. C. 1977. Taking different perspectives on a story. *Journal of Educational Psychology* 69: 309–15.

Plato. *Meno.* In Plato, *Laches, Protagoras, Meno, Euthydemus.* Trans. W. R. M. Lamb. Cambridge: Harvard University Press, 1967.

Pollchik, A. 1975. The use of embedded questions in the facilitation of productive learning. Ph.D. dissertation, Vanderbilt University.

Polya, G. 1957. *How to solve it.* Garden City, New York: Doubleday Anchor.

————. 1968. *Mathematical discovery.* Volume 2: *On understanding, learning and teaching problem solving.* New York: Wiley.

Posner, M. I. 1973. *Cognition: An introduction.* Glenview, Ill.: Scott, Foresman.

Posner, M. I., and Keele, S. W. 1968. On the genesis of abstract ideas. *Journal of Experimental Psychology* 77: 353–63.

————. 1970. Retention of abstract ideas. *Journal of Experimental Psychology* 83: 304–8.

Posner, M. I., and Konick, A. F. 1966. On the role of interference in short-term retention. *Journal of Experimental Psychology* 72: 221–31.

Postman, L., Adams, P. A., and Bohm, A. M. 1956. Studies in incidental learning: V. Recall for order and associative clustering. *Journal of Experimental Psychology* 51: 334–42.

Postman, L., and Underwood, B. J. 1973. Critical issues in interference theory. *Memory & Cognition* 1: 19–40.

Potts, G. R. 1972. Information processing strategies used in the encoding of linear orderings. *Journal of Verbal Learning and Verbal Behavior* 11: 727–40.

————. 1974. Storing and retrieving information about ordered relationships. *Journal of Experimental Psychology* 103: 431–39.

Proffitt, D. R. 1976. Demonstrations to investigate the meaning of everyday experience. Doctoral dissertation, Pennsylvania State University.

Pronko, N. H. 1969. On learning to play the violin at the age of four without tears. *Psychology Today* 2: 52.

Pylyshyn, Z. W. 1973: What the mind's eye tells the mind's brain: A critique of mental imagery. *Psychological Bulletin* 80: 1–24.

Reed, S. K. 1972. Pattern recognition and categorization. *Cognitive Psychology* 3: 382–407.

Reif, F., Larkin, J. H., and Brackett, G. C. 1976. Teaching general learning and problem-solving skills. *American Journal of Physics* 44: 212–17.

Reitman, J. S., and Bower, G. H. 1973. Storage and later recognition of examplars of concepts. *Cognitive Psychology* 4: 194–206.

Resnick, L. B., and Glaser, R. 1976. Problem solving and intelligence. In L. B. Resnick (ed.), *The nature of intelligence.* Hillsdale, N.J.: Lawrence Erlbaum Associates.

Restle, F. 1962. The selection of strategies in cue learning. *Psychological Review* 69: 329–43.

Rips, L. J., Shoben, E. J., and Smith, E. E. 1973. Semantic distance and the verification of semantic relations. *Journal of Verbal Learning and Verbal Behavior* 12: 1–20.

Rosch, E. H. 1973. On the internal structure of perceptual and semantic categories. In T. E. Moore (ed.), *Cognitive development and the acquisition of language.* New York: Academic Press.

————. 1975. Cognitive representations of semantic categories. *Journal of Experimental Psychology: General* 104: 192–233.

Rosenberg, S. 1968. Association and phrase structure in sentence recall. *Journal of Verbal Learning and Verbal Behavior* 7: 1077–81.

————. 1969. The recall of verbal material accompanying semantically well-integrated and semantically poorly integrated sentences. *Journal of Verbal Learning and Verbal Behavior* 8: 732–36.

Rosenberg, S., and Jarvella, R. J. 1970. Semantic integration and sentence perception. *Journal of Verbal Learning and Verbal Behavior* 9: 548–53.

Ross, A. O. 1977. *Learning disability: The unrealized potential.* New York: McGraw-Hill.

Ross, J. R. 1974. Three batons for cognitive psychology. In W. Weimer and D. S. Palermo (eds.), *Cognition and the symbolic processes.* Hillsdale, N.J.: Lawrence Erlbaum Associates.

Rothkopf, E. Z. 1966. Learning from written materials: An exploration of the control of inspection behavior by test-like events. *American Educational Research Journal* 3: 241–49.

————. 1970. The concept of mathemagenic activities. *Review of Educational Research* 40: 325–36.

————. 1972. Structural text features and the control of processes in learning from written materials. In J. B. Carroll and R. O. Freedle (eds.), *Language comprehension and the acquisition of knowledge.* Washington, D.C.: V. H. Winston and Sons.

Royer, J. M. 1977. Remembering: Constructive or reconstructive? Comments on Chapter 5 by Spiro. In R. C. Anderson, R. J. Spiro, and W. E. Montague (eds.), *Schooling and the acquisition of knowledge.* Hillsdale, N.J.: Lawrence Erlbaum Associates.

Rumelhart, D. E. 1975. Notes on a schema for stories. In D. G. Bobrow and A. M. Collins (eds.), *Representation and understanding: Studies in cognitive science.* New York: Academic Press.

————. 1977. Understanding and summarizing brief stories. In D. LaBerge and S. J. Samuels (eds.), *Basic processes in reading: Perception and comprehension.* Hillsdale, N.J.: Lawrence Erlbaum Associates.

Rumelhart, D. E., and Ortony, A. 1977. The representation of knowledge in memory. In R. C. Anderson, R. J. Spiro, and W. E. Montague (eds.), *Schooling and the acquisition of knowledge.* Hillsdale, N.J.: Lawrence Erlbaum Associates.

Rundus, D. 1971. Analysis of rehearsal processes in free recall. *Journal of Experimental Psychology* 89: 63–77.

Rundus, D., and Atkinson, R. C. 1970. Rehearsal procedures in free recall: A procedure for direct observation. *Journal of Verbal Learning and Verbal Behavior* 99–105.

Rundus, D., Loftus, G. R., and Atkinson, R. C. 1970. Immediate free-recall and three-week delayed recognition. *Journal of Verbal Learning and Verbal Behavior* 9: 684.

Sachs, J. S. 1967. Recognition memory for syntactic and semantic aspects of connected discourse. *Perception and Psychophysics* 2: 437–42.

Schank, R. C. 1972. Conceptual dependency: A theory of natural language understanding. *Cognitive Psychology* 3: 552–631.

————. 1976. The role of memory in natural language processing. In C. N. Cofer (ed.), *The structure of human memory.* San Francisco: W. H. Freeman.

Schank, R. C., and Abelson, R. P. 1975. Scripts, plans and knowledge. In *Advance Papers of the Fourth International Joint Conference on Artificial Intelligence.* Tbilisi, Georgia, USSR.

————. 1977. *Scripts, plans, goals, and understanding: An inquiry into human knowledge structures.* Hillsdale, N.J.: Lawrence Erlbaum Associates.

Scribner, S., and Cole, M. 1973. Cognitive consequences of formal and informal education. *Science* 182: 553–59.

Seamon, J. G., and Murray, P. 1976. Depth of processing in recall and recognition memory: Differential effects of stimulus meaningfulness and serial position. *Journal of Experimental Psychology: Human Learning and Memory* 2: 680–87.

Searle, J. 1969. *Speech acts: An essay in the philosophy of language.* London: Cambridge University Press.

Shaw, R. E., and Bransford, J. D. 1977. Psychological approaches to the problem of knowledge. In R. E. Shaw and J. D. Bransford (eds.), *Perceiving, acting and knowing: Toward an ecological psychology.* Hillsdale, N.J.: Lawrence Erlbaum Associates.

Shepard, R. N. 1967. Recognition memory for words, sentences and pictures. *Journal of Verbal Learning and Verbal Behavior* 6: 156–63.

Shepard, R. N., and Metzler, J. 1971. Mental rotation of three-dimensional objects. *Science* 171: 701–3.

Siegler, R. S. 1976. Three aspects of cognitive development. *Cognitive Psychology* 8: 481–520.

Simon, C. W., and Emmons, W. H. 1956. Responses to material presented during various stages of sleep. *Journal of Experimental Psychology* 51: 89–97.

Simon, H. A. 1969. *The sciences of the artificial*. Cambridge, Mass.: MIT Press.

Simon, H. A., and Gilmartin, K. 1973. A simulation of memory for chess positions. *Cognitive Psychology* 5: 29–46.

Smith, E. E., Shoben, E. J., and Rips, L. J. 1974. Structure and processes in semantic memory: A featural model for semantic decisions. *Psychological Review* 81: 214–41.

Snyder, M., and Uranowitz, S. W. Reconstructing the past: Some cognitive consequences of person perception. *Journal of Personality and Social Psychology*, in press.

Solomon, R. L., and Postman, L. 1952. Frequency of usage as a determinant of recognition thresholds for words. *Journal of Experimental Psychology* 43: 195–201.

Soraci, S. In preparation. Facilitating the detection of meaningfully related sentences as a function of framework type (working title). Vanderbilt University.

Sperber, R. D., Ragain, R. D., and McCauley, C. 1976. Reassessment of category knowledge in retarded individuals. *American Journal of Mental Deficiency* 81: 227–34.

Sperling, G. 1960. The information available in brief visual presentations. *Psychological Monographs* 74: 1–29.

Spiro, R. J. 1977. Remembering information from text: The "state of schema" approach. In R. C. Anderson, R. J. Spiro, and W. E. Montague (eds.) *Schooling and the acquisition of knowledge*. Hillsdale, N.J.: Lawrence Erlbaum Associates.

Standing, L. 1973. Learning 10,000 pictures. *Quarterly Journal of Experimental Psychology* 25: 207–22.

Standing, L., Conezio, J., and Haber, R. N. 1970. Perception and memory for pictures: Single-trial learning of 2500 visual stimuli. *Psychonomic Science* 19: 73–74.

Stein, B. S. 1977. The effects of cue-target uniqueness on cued recall performance. *Memory and Cognition* 5: 319–22.

———. 1978. Depth of processing re-examined: The effects of precision of encoding and test appropriateness. *Journal of Verbal Learning and Verbal Behavior* 17: 165–74.

Stein, B. S., Morris, C. D., and Bransford, J. D. In press. Some constraints on effective elaboration. *Journal of Verbal Learning and Verbal Behavior*.

Stein, B. S., and Bransford, J. D. In preparation. Quality of self-generated elaborations and subsequent retention.

Stein, N. L., and Glenn, C. G. In press. An analysis of story comprehension in elementary school children. In J. R. Freedle (ed.), *Discourse processing: Multidisciplinary perspectives*. Hillsdale, N.J.: Ablex, Inc.

Strupp, H. H., and Bloxom, A. L. 1973. Preparing lower-class patients for group psychotherapy: Development and evaluation of a role induction film. *Journal of Consulting and Clinical Psychology* 41: 373–84.

Tarpy, R. M., and Mayer, R. E. 1978. *Foundations of learning and memory.* Glenview, Ill.: Scott, Foresman.

Templin, M. C. 1957. *Certain language skills in children: Their development and interrelationships.* Minneapolis: University of Minnesota Press.

Thorndike, E. L. 1931. *The psychology of learning.* New York: Teachers College.

Thorndike, E. L., and Lorge, I. 1944. *The teachers' word book of thirty thousand words.* New York: Columbia University Press.

Till, R. E. 1977. Sentence memory prompted with inferential recall cues. *Journal of Experimental Psychology: Human Learning and Memory* 3: 129–41.

Till, R. E., and Jenkins, J. J. 1973. The effects of cued orienting tasks on the free recall of words. *Journal of Verbal Learning and Verbal Behavior* 12: 489–98.

Tolman, E. C. 1932. *Purposive behavior in animals and men.* New York: D. Appleton-Century.

Toulmin, S. 1972. *Human understanding.* Vol. 1: *The collective use and evolution of concepts.* Princeton, N.J.: Princeton University Press.

Trabasso, T. R. 1963. Stimulus emphasis and all-or-none learning in concept identification. *Journal of Experimental Psychology* 65: 398–406.

Trabasso, T. R., and Bower, G. H. 1964. Presolution reversal and dimensional shifts in concept identification. *Journal of Experimental Psychology* 67: 398–99.

———. 1968. *Attention in learning.* New York: Wiley.

Treisman, A. M. 1964. Verbal cues, language and meaning in selective attention. *American Journal of Psychology* 77: 206–19.

Tulving, E. 1962. Subjective organization in free recall of "unrelated" words. *Psychological Review* 69: 344–54.

———. 1972. Episodic and semantic memory. In E. Tulving and W. Donaldson (eds.), *Organization of memory.* New York: Academic Press.

———. 1978. Relation between encoding specificity and levels of processing. In L. S. Cermak and F. I. M. Craik (eds.), *Levels of processing and human memory.* Hillsdale, N.J.: Lawrence Erlbaum Associates.

Tulving, E., and Osler, S. 1968. Effectiveness of retrieval cues in memory for words. *Journal of Experimental Psychology* 77: 593–601.

Tulving, E., and Pearlstone, Z. 1966. Availability versus accessibility of information in memory for words. *Journal of Verbal Learning and Verbal Behavior* 5: 381–91.

Tulving, E., and Psotka, J. 1971. Retroactive inhibition in free recall: Inaccessibility of information available in the memory store. *Journal of Experimental Psychology* 87: 1–8.

Tulving, E., and Thomson, D. M. 1973. Encoding specificity and retrieval processes in episodic memory. *Psychological Review* 80: 352–73.

Tulving, E., and Watkins, M. J. 1975. Structure of memory traces. *Psychological Review* 84: 261–75.

Tulving, E., and Wiseman, S. 1975. Relation between recognition and recognition failure of recallable words. *Bulletin of the Psychonomic Society* 6: 78–82.

Turvey, M. T. 1977. Preliminaries to a theory of action with reference to vision. In R. E. Shaw and J. D. Bransford (eds.), *Perceiving, acting and knowing: Toward an ecological psychology*. Hillsdale, N.J.: Lawrence Erlbaum Associates.

Tversky, B. 1973. Encoding processes in recognition and recall. *Cognitive Psychology* 5: 275–87.

Underwood, B. J. 1948a. Retroactive and proactive inhibition after five and forty-eight hours. *Journal of Experimental Psychology* 38: 29–38.

–––––––. 1948b. "Spontaneous recovery" of verbal associations. *Journal of Experimental Psychology* 38: 429–39.

–––––––. 1949. Proactive inhibition as a function of time and degree of prior learning. *Journal of Experimental Psychology* 39: 24–34.

–––––––. 1957. Interference and forgetting. *Psychological Review* 64: 49–60.

–––––––. 1964. Forgetting. *Scientific American,* reprint 482.

Underwood, B. J., and Richardson, J. 1956. Some verbal materials for the study of concept formation. *Psychological Bulletin* 53: 84–95.

Underwood, B. J., and Schultz, R. W. 1960. *Meaningfulness and verbal learning.* Philadelphia: Lippincott.

Verbrugge, R. R. 1977. Resemblances in language and perception. In R. E. Shaw and J. D. Bransford (eds.), *Perceiving, acting and knowing: Toward an ecological psychology*. Hillsdale, N.J.: Lawrence Erlbaum Associates.

Walsh, D. A., and Jenkins, J. J. 1973. Effects of orienting tasks on free recall in incidental learning: "Difficulty," "effort," and "process" explanations. *Journal of Verbal Learning and Verbal Behavior* 12: 481–88.

Wanner, E. 1974. *On remembering, forgetting, and understanding sentences.* The Hague: Mouton.

Watkins, M. J., Watkins, O. C., Craik, F. I. M., and Mazuryk, G. 1973. Effect of nonverbal distraction on short-term storage. *Journal of Experimental Psychology* 101: 296–300.

Waugh, N. C., and Norman, D. A. 1965. Primary memory. *Psychological Review* 72: 89–104.

Weimer, W. B. 1973. Psycholinguistics and Plato's paradoxes of the *Meno. American Psychologist* 28: 15–33.

–––––––. In press. *Notes on the methodology of scientific research.* Hillsdale, N.J.: Lawrence Erlbaum Associates.

Whimbey, A. 1976. *Intelligence can be taught.* New York: Bantam.

Wickelgren, W. A. 1966. Phonemic similarity and interference in short-term memory for single letters. *Journal of Experimental Psychology* 71: 396–404.

———. 1974. *How to solve problems: Elements of a theory of problems and problem solving.* San Francisco: W. H. Freeman.

Wickens, D. D. 1970. Encoding categories of words: An empirical approach to meaning. *Psychological Review* 77: 1–15.

———. 1972. Characteristics of word encoding. In A. W. Melton and E. Martin (eds.), *Coding processes in human memory.* New York: V. H. Winston and Sons.

Wickens, D. D., Born, D. G., and Allen, C. K. 1963. Proactive inhibition and item similarity in short-term memory. *Journal of Verbal Learning and Verbal Behavior* 2: 440–45.

Winograd, T. 1972. Understanding natural language. *Cognitive Psychology* 3: 1–191.

Wittgenstein, L. 1968. *Philosophical investigations.* Trans. G. E. Anscombe. Oxford: Blackwell.

Wittrock, M. C. 1974. Learning as a generative process. *Educational Psychologist* 11: 87–95.

———. In press. The cognitive movement in education. *Educational Psychologist.*

Wittrock, M. C., Marks, C. B., and Doctorow, M. J. 1975. Reading as a generative process. *Journal of Educational Psychology* 67: 484–89.

Woodward, A. E., Bjork, R. A., and Jongeward, R. H. 1973. Recall and recognition as a function of primary rehearsal. *Journal of Verbal Learning and Verbal Behavior* 12: 608–17.

Wundt, W. 1905. *Grundzuge der physiologischen Psychologie.* 2nd ed. Leipzig: Englemann.

Topic Index

Author Index